CONCISE ENCYCLOPEDIA OF

modern art

RAYMOND CHARMET

Edited by ROGER BRUNYATE

FOLLETT PUBLISHING COMPANY

Chicago

About this book: *The original French text was written by Raymond Charmet (agrégé des lettres), and revised and edited by Roger Brunyate (B.A.). The text was translated by William Hardie, Keeper of Art, Museums and Galleries Dept., Dundee.*

ISBN: 0-695-80469-3

Library of Congress Catalog Card Number: 73-91736

First Printing

Companion volume to
Concise Encyclopedia of Ballet

editor's preface

The chronicler of any aspect of the contemporary world must face the fact that the world changes faster than he can write about it; furthermore each new development shows past events in a different perspective, and the process of distinguishing what is important in our immediate heritage can thus never be completed. The problem is particularly acute in writing about the visual arts, for I believe that the past decade has witnessed a succession of new artistic ideas in a profusion comparable only to the situation in the first decade of the century. Since no one observer has the full picture of the current state of art internationally, the importance he gives to different aspects will inevitably depend partly on his national viewpoint.

The original Larousse *dictionnaire de l'art contemporain*, published in 1965, was an extraordinarily compendious guide to 20th century art which might most readily be seen in the galleries of Paris and provincial France. In preparing this English-language edition I have tried to pay attention to the corresponding needs of the gallery-goer in Britain and in America. This has involved introducing considerable new material, not only on contemporary artists, but also on those who played an essential part in the development of art in the English-speaking countries. I have also tried to quote examples, wherever possible, to be seen on public display in Britain or America, and in some cases have allocated more space or written new entries for foreign artists who are also widely represented in our galleries. A large number of the new entries, however, deal with artists who have only recently come to the fore; I have also tried to update the record of established artists.

Space has necessitated that the scope of the book be confined. It deals only with painting and sculpture—architecture, print-making and the applied arts have been excluded. In principle, only artists are included who were producing significant work after 1900. However, the development of 20th century art owes so much to certain artists such as Seurat and van Gogh, who died young before the turn of the century, that they too have been included. There are also articles on a number of 'precursors' from the earlier part of the 19th century, such as Delacroix and Manet, for the convenience of being able to refer to them within a single book; the entries on these artists concentrate solely on aspects of their art which were most valued by later generations, and may give a distorted view of their contemporary importance. No claim is made for the comprehensiveness in the choice of 'precursors', although I have retained from the French edition the entry **Influences**, which casts its net rather more widely.

The selection of the most recent artists may also appear unbalanced. At the risk of having my tentative conclusions proved false by subsequent events, I have tried to take into account, wherever possible, the latest exhibitions of an artist's work at the time of writing. One resulting accident is that most of the younger artists mentioned have recently been the subject of exhibitions and articles, while many of their contemporaries and seniors may be producing more interesting work in their studios which has not yet received public attention. The perspective of a decade, at the very least, is necessary to achieve proportion, but I felt that to exclude the art of 1960s would unduly impoverish the book.

One purpose of this book is to help the visitor to a gallery of modern art to place a particular work of an artist in an individual and an international context. For this reason, the number of general articles on styles and movements has been greatly increased. The history of 20th century art has been liberally sprinkled with '-isms' and artists have formed and reformed into countless groups and splinter groups. It would have been impossible and confusing to list them all, and I have concentrated instead on tendencies within which several movements may often have been subsumed. Some terms are thus used for cross-reference purposes in a slightly wider sense than may be acceptable to any one group and very often numerous alternatives have been advanced by critics in different countries for what is essentially the same phenomenon. I have chosen the one which makes the most sense to the layman and which makes the clearest distinction between terms used for related and contemporary styles. Cross-references are given in **bold type** whenever another article will give additional information immediately relevant to the topic under discussion. However, most artists and stylistic terms mentioned in the course of an article are also treated as separate entries, whether cross-referenced or not.

Where possible, I have quoted examples of works in public collections in the English-speaking countries. Although I have tried to ensure that all examples cited are characteristic of their period, many of the most important works of modern artists are in private hands; this is more so of the art of the last few years.

Roger Brunyate

galleries, museums

Aarhus: Kunstmuseum. **Aberdeen**: Art Gallery (AG). **Adelaide**: National Gallery of South Australia (NG). **Albi**, France: Musée Toulouse-Lautrec (Museum). **Algiers**: Musée National des Beaux-Arts (MBA). **Amsterdam**: Stedelijk Museum. **Antibes**, France: Musée Grimaldi. **Antwerp**: Musée Royal des Beaux-Arts (MBA); Middelheim Museum. **Auckland**: City Art Gallery (AG).

Baltimore: Museum of Art (MA). **Basle**: Kunstmuseum. **Batley**, Yorks.: Bagshaw Art Gallery (AG). **Beauvais**, France: Musée des Beaux-Arts (MBA). **Berlin, West**: Galerie des 20 Jahrhunderts (20th C Gallery); Akademie der Künste; Nationalgalerie (NG). **Bern**: Berner Kunstmuseum. **Biot**, France: Musée Fernand Léger. **Birmingham**: Museum and Art Gallery (City AG). **Bloomfield Hills**, Mich.: Cranbrook Academy of Art Galleries. **Bordeaux**: Musée des Beaux-Arts (MBA). **Boston**: Museum of Fine Arts (MFA); Isabella Stewart Gardner Museum. **Bradford**: City Art Gallery (AG). **Bremen**: Kunsthalle. **Bristol**: City Art Gallery (AG). **Brussels**: Musée des Beaux-Arts (MBA). **Budapest**: Magyar Nemzeti Galéria (NG); Szépmüvészeti Múzeum. **Buenos Aires**: Museo de Arte Moderno. **Buffalo**: Albright-Knox Art Gallery (AG).

Cambridge: Fitzwilliam Museum. **Cardiff**: National Museum of Wales. **Chapel Hill**: University of North Carolina. **Charleroi**, Belgium: Musée Communal (Museum). **Cherbourg**: Musée des Beaux-Arts (MBA). **Chicago**: Art Institute. **Cincinnati**: Art Museum (AM); Hebrew Union College Museum. **Claremont**, Calif.: Pomona College Gallery. **Cleveland**: Museum of Art (MA). **Colmar**, France: Musée Bartholdi. **Cologne**: Wallraff-Richartz-Museum. **Columbus**, Ohio: Gallery of Fine Arts (AG). **Copenhagen**: Ny Carlsberg Glyptotek; Statens Museum for Kunst. **Coventry**: Herbert Art Gallery (AG).

Dallas: Museum of Fine Arts (MFA). **Darmstadt**, Germany: Hessisches Landesmuseum. **Denver**: Art Museum (AM). **Detroit**: Institute of Arts (Art Inst.). **Dijon**: Musée François-Pompon. **Dresden**: Schloss Pillnitz. **Duisburg**: Wilhelm Lehmbruck Museum. **Durban**, South Africa: Museum and Art Gallery (AG). **Dusseldorf**: Kunstmuseum; Schloss Jägerhof.

Edinburgh: National Gallery of Scotland (NG); Scottish National Gallery of Modern Art. **Eindhoven**, Neth.: Stedelijk van Abbemuseum. **Elat**,

Israel: Museum of Modern Art in Memory of Deported Artists (MMA). **Epinal**, France: Musée Departmental des Vosages (Museum). **Essen**: Museum Folkwang.

Farmington, Conn.: Hill-Stead Museum. **Frankfurt**: Städelsches Kunstinstitut. **Fredericton**, New Brunswick: Beaverbrook Art Gallery.

Geneva: Musée d'Art et d'Histoire. **Ghent**: Museum of Fine Art. **Glasgow**: Art Gallery and Museum (Kelvingrove); Hunterian Museum (Glasgow University). **Gothenburg**, Sweden: Göteborgs Konstmuseum. **Grenoble**: Musée de Peinture et de Sculpture (Museum of Art).

Hague, The: Haags Gemeentemuseum. **Hamburg**: Ernst Barlach Mans; Hamburger Kunsthalle. **Hanover**: Niedersächsisches Landesgalerie. **Hartford**, Conn.: Wadsworth Atheneum. **Harvard**, Cambridge, Mass.: Busch-Reisinger Museum of Germanic Culture; Fogg Art Museum. **Helsinki**: Kansalhismuseo (NG). **Honolulu**: Academy of Arts. **Houston**: Museum of Fine Arts (MFA).

Indianapolis: Herron Museum of Art.

Jabbeke, Belgium: Provincial Museum Constant Permeke. **Jena**, Germany: University of Jena.

Kansas City, Missouri: William Rockhill Nelson Gallery of Art. **Kiel**: Kunsthalle. **Krefeld**, Germany: Kaiser-Wilhelm Museum.

Lausanne: Musée Cantonal des Beaux-Arts. **Leeds**: City Art Gallery (AG). **Leicester**: Museum and Art Gallery (AG). **Leningrad**: Hermitage Museum. **Liège**: Musée des Beaux-Arts (MBA). **Lincoln**: Sheldon Memorial Art Gallery, University of Nebraska (Sheldon AG). **Linz**, Austria: Alfred Kubin Museum; Neue Galerie der Stadt. **Liverpool**: Walker Art Gallery (AG). **London**: Courtauld Institute Galleries; Institute of Contemporary Arts; Imperial War Museum; National Gallery (NG); National Portrait Gallery; Tate Gallery; Victoria and Albert Museum. **Los Angeles**: County Museum of Art. **Lucerne**: Kunstmuseum. **Lyons**: Musée des Beaux-Arts (MBA).

Madrid: Museo Nacional de Arte Moderna. **Manchester**: City Art Gallery (AG). **Mannheim**: Städtische Kunsthalle. **Marseilles**: Musée des Beaux-Arts (MBA). **Melbourne**: National Gallery of Victoria (NG). **Merion**, Penn.: Barnes Foundation. **Miami**: Museum of Modern Art (MMA). **Milan**: Galeria d'Arte Moderna (GAM). **Milwaukee**: Art Center. **Minneapolis**: Institute of Arts (Art Inst.); Walker Art Center. **Montpellier**, France: Musée Fabre. **Montreal**: Museum of Fine

Arts (MFA); Museum of Contemporary Arts. **Moscow**: Museum of Modern Western Art; Pushkin Museum; Tretchiakov Gallery. **Munich**: Bayerische Staatsgemäldesammlungen (NG); Städtische Galerie (Civic Gallery).

New Haven, Conn.: Yale University Art Gallery (AG). **New York**: Brooklyn Museum; Gallery of Modern Art—Huntingdon Hartford Collection; Solomon R. Guggenheim Museum; Jewish Museum; Metropolitan Museum of Art; Museum of Modern Art (MMA); Whitney Museum of American Art. **Nice**: Musée des Beaux-Arts—Jules Chéret (MBA). **Nîmes**: Musée des Beaux-Arts (MBA). **Northampton**, Mass.: Smith College Museum of Art. **Nuremburg**: Städtische Kunstsammlungen.

Oberlin, Ohio: Allen Memorial Art Museum. **Orléans**: Musée des Beaux-Arts (MBA). **Oslo**: Edvard Munch Museum; Nasjonalgalleriet (NG). **Ottawa**: National Gallery of Canada (NG). **Otterloo**, Neth.: Rijksmuseum Kröller-Müller (RKM). **Oxford**: Ashmolean Museum of Art and Archaeology.

Paris: Musée d'Art Moderne de la Ville de Paris (MAMVP); Musée Antoine Bourdelle; Musée Carnavalet; Musée National d'Art Moderne (MNAM); Musée Marmoltan; Musée National du Louvre—Musée du Jeu de Paume and Salles de l'Orangerie; Musée National Gustave Moreau; Musée National Rodin; Musée du Petit Palais; Palais de Chaillot; Palais de l'Iéna. **Pasadena**: Art Museum (AM). **Pau**, France: Musée des Beaux-Arts (MBA). **Périgueux**, France: Musée du Périgord (Museum). **Philadelphia**: Pennsylvania Academy of Fine Arts; Museum of Art (MA); Rodin Museum. **Phoenix**: Art Museum (AM). **Pittsburgh**: Museum of Arts, Carnegie Institute. **Pittsfield**, Mass.: Berkshire Atheneum. **Prague**: Národni Galerie (NG). **Princeton**, New Jersey: Princeton University Art Museum. **Providence**: Rhode Island School of Design.

Racine, Wisconsin: Jonson Foundation. **Randers**, Denmark: Kunstmuseum. **Richmond**: Virginia Museum. **Rochester**, New York: Museum of Arts and Sciences (MA). **Rome**: Galleria Nazionale d'Arte Moderna (GAM). **Rotterdam**: Museum Boymans-van Beuningen. **Rouen**: Musée des Beaux-Arts (MBA).

Saarbrücken: Saarlandmuseum (Museum). **St. Denis**: Musée d'Art et d'Histoire (Museum). **St. Louis**: City Art Museum (AM); Washington University Gallery of Art. **St. Paul-de-Vence**: Maeght Foundation. **St. Tropez**: Musée de l'Annonciade (Museum). **San Francisco**: Museum of Art (MA). **São Paulo**: Museu de Arte Moderna (Modern Art Museum). **Seebüll**, Germany: Nolde Museum. **Southampton**: Art Gallery (AG). **Stockholm**: Millesgarden, Lidingö; Moderna Museet; Nationalmuseum. **Stuttgart**: Galerie der Stadt (Civic Gallery); Staatsgalerie (NG). **Sydney**: Art Gallery of New South Wales (AG). **Syracuse**: Everson Museum of Art.

Tel-Aviv: Museum. **Toledo**, Ohio: Museum of Art (MA). **Toronto**: Art Gallery (AG). **Trieste**: Civico Museo Revoltella—Galleria d'Arte Moderna (GAM). **Tucson**: University of Arizona Art Gallery. **Turin**: Galleria Civica d'Arte Moderna (GAM).

Urbana: University of Illinois, Krannert Art Museum. **Utica**, New York: Munson-Williams-Proctor Institute (Art Inst.).

Valence, France: Musée des Beaux-Arts (MBA). **Valenciennes**: Musée Classé des Beaux-Arts (MBA). **Venice**: Galleria Internazionale d'Arte Moderna di Ca'Pesaro (GAM); Peggy Guggenheim Collection. **Vevey**, Switz.: Musée Jenisch. **Vienna**: Kunsthistorisches Museum; Osterreichische Galerie; Museum des 20 Jahrhunderts (20th C); Osterreichisches Museum of Applied Art.

Washington: Freer Gallery of Art; National Collection of Fine Arts; National Gallery of Art (NG); Phillips Collection; Washington Gallery of Modern Art. **Westbury**, New York: Art Gallery (AG). **West Palm Beach**: Norton Gallery of Art. **Wiesbaden**: Städtisches Museum. **Winterthur**, Switz.: Kunstmuseum. **Worcester**, Mass.: Art Museum (AM). **Wuppertal**: Von der Heydt-Museum der Stadt (Museum).

York: City Art Gallery (City AG).

Zurich: Kunsthaus.

A

ABSTRACT ART, an expression, synonomous with the term 'non-figurative art', denoting a form of art which rejects representation of the exterior world. It conceives of painting and sculpture as an arrangement of pure forms and colours, capable of evoking aesthetic emotion. Abstract art has been a strictly 20th century phenomenon; it should be distinguished from non-representational art, a more general term which can include works that, however distorted, start from an external visual reality. Although much 20th century work has inhabited this halfway house, abstraction proper represents the culmination of the revolution against 19th century realism, and it has aroused furious debate.

The formative influences on abstract art were Fauvism and Cubism, movements which, though still basically figurative, showed how colour and form could be arranged according to purely formal rules. The first manifestations of abstract art occurred in Germany and Russia. In 1910, **Kandinsky** painted his first deliberately abstract watercolour, and wrote his significant work *On the Spiritual in Art*. He said that the sight of one of his paintings placed by chance on its side gave him a shock, and astonished him by its beauty. This separation of art from nature claimed precedents in music, and the Czech painter Kupka executed (1912) compositions with musical titles, *eg Fugue in Two Colours.*

Prior to 1914, abstract art in Russia had advanced systematically, with the Constructivism of Tatlin, the Rayonism of Larionov and Gontcharova and above all the Suprematism of **Malevich.** Paris witnessed several sallies of the ingenious and versatile Picabia; but the principal abstract movement to arise out of Cubism was **Robert Delaunay**'s Orphism. Two American artists from Delaunay's circle, Russell and Macdonald-Wright, founded the breakaway movement, Synchromism, which was

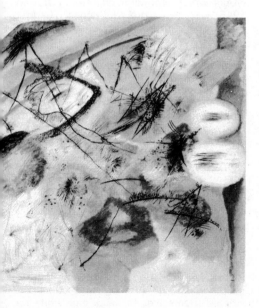

Wassily Kandinsky: Black Lines *(1913, New York Guggenheim).*

Piet Mondrian: Composition with Red, Yellow and Blue *(1929, New York Guggenheim).*

of great influence on American art. Wyndham Lewis introduced abstract art to England as early as 1913, creating the short-lived Vorticism, which had many followers. The most profound experimenter was **Mondrian,** whose intellectual and rigorously geometrical approach was formulated in the review *De Stijl* in 1917. This movement, Neo-Plasticism, proclaimed the universality of mathematics, restricted the palette to three primary colours, and reduced form to rectangular shapes. Pursuing a parallel course, the Italian Magnelli (*c* 1915) painted strictly abstract canvases. Dada introduced irrational forms which had no bearing on reality (*eg* Miró, Arp).

After World War I, abstract art was eclipsed in France; but in Germany, Moholy-Nagy, Schwitters and Baumeister adopted a geometric style. Klee pushed formal invention beyond the boundaries of abstraction.

The first international exhibition of abstract art was held (1930) in Paris; it was followed in 1932 by the founding of the **Abstraction-Création** group. Since World War II many artists, such as Ben Nicholson and Pasmore in England, Herbin in France, and Fontana in Italy, have continued to develop abstraction from Constructivism. A new lyrical abstraction has arisen in France in the work of Bissière, Bazaine, Manessier and de Staël.

However, the most original movements in abstract art since World War II have taken place in the United States, encouraged partly by the start (1937) of the Solomon Guggenheim Foundation for Non-Objective Art and similar bodies, and partly by the influence of the many European artists who went to the U.S. before the War. The most important movement has been **Abstract Expressionism,** which developed in the late 1940s following the lead of Pollock and Tobey; its principal practitioners have included Gorky, Rothko, Kline and de Kooning. The invention of **Action Painting** by Pollock and Hofmann parallelled and influenced the European style of Tachism. **Post-Painterly Abstraction,** the name given collectively to movements reacting against Abstract Expressionism, is also an American phenomenon. **Kinetic Art, Op Art** and **Minimal Art** also attempt a totally dispassionate abstraction. A similar trend in sculpture has followed the examples of Calder, David Smith and Caro.

Van Doesburg and Max Bill, among others, have suggested 'concrete art' as an alternative to the term 'abstract art'. The opposition between abstract and figurative art is denied more and more frequently, but the abstract experience, by its rebuttal of academic realism, expresses the desire to return to a pure form of art.

ABSTRACT EXPRESSIONISM, term used specifically to describe much of American (and related) painting in the fifteen years after World War II. The term had also been used of the art of Kandinsky after 1912, and in the general sense of a non-figurative art that aims to express or arouse emotion it could be applied to a broad spectrum of 20th century painting.

American Abstract Expressionism arose as a result of the presence of many Surrealists during World War II, and especially that of **Arshile Gorky.** On the one hand the Surrealist vocabulary of amoeboid forms provided a new vocabulary for the Americans, while on the other they were also influenced by the various Surrealist techniques of Automatic Writing and free association. The very painterly works which Hofmann was doing around 1945 were also a great influence. The first practitioners of Abstract Expressionism in America were **Jackson Pollock** and **Robert Motherwell,** both of whom started by painting quite specifically Surrealist forms, **Willem de Kooning** who developed the style around a continuing figurative imagery, and **William Baziotes** who remains closest to the European Surrealism exemplified by Miró. It is generally admitted, however, that it was Pollock's development of **Action Painting** that broke the ice for most of the later developments.

By 1950, two trends could be distinguished. On the one hand there was a continuation of the **Gesture Painting** approach exemplified by Pollock: other artists of this tendency included Kline, Brooks, Guston, Tomlin, and Tworkov. They were not much interested in colour for its own sake and indeed Pollock, Motherwell, de Kooning and Kline restricted themselves to black and white for some time around 1950. There was also a group of painters which was primarily interested in colour, generally presented in large fields with formal articulation minimized: **Newman, Rothko** and **Gottlieb** were the leaders of this group, which also included Still and Reinhardt. Both tendencies had in common an avoidance of the usual rules of composition in depth, replacing it by an 'all-over' field in which all the interest is on or in front of the canvas and in which no point is more important than another; this had already been prefigured by **Mark Tobey.** Most of these pictures are also very large in scale. During the 1950s numerous other artists began to paint in an Abstract Expressionist style, among them Frankenthaler, Hartigan, Francis and Leslie, while Nakian and Ferber explored similar effects in sculpture. The movement came to an end as a vital force around 1960 with the reaction towards **Post-Painterly Abstraction;** since this, however, was based on the example of certain of the 'Chromatic' Abstract Expressionists, particularly Frankenthaler, Rothko and Newman, the development of this side of the movement can be said to be continuous. Also the early deaths of Pollock and Kline removed two of the leading Gesture painters.

The scale and freedom of American Abstract Expressionism has influenced the parallel movement in Europe, known as **Tachism.** Within this, Wols and Fautrier invented personal styles which were close to Action painting in their effect, as was the work of the Cobra group. Michaux, Hartung and Mathieu developed free calligraphic styles. The group around Manessier and Bazaine painted in a lyrical abstract style directly after the War. Although the European movement would have developed an expressionist abstraction independently of the American artists, there is no doubt that the subsequent cross-fertilization has particularily stimulated the Europeans. The British Abstract Expressionists, Davie, Heron, Hilton, Lanyon, Scott and Wynter have all been influenced more or less directly by the American example. On the other hand the art of Burri, Crippa, Santomaso and Vedova in Italy, Baumeister and Sonderborg in Germany, and Millares, Saura and Tapies in Spain, while related to American work, also owed much to Tachism.

ABSTRACTION-CREATION, a loosely-composed group of abstract artists formed in Paris by **Gabo, Pevsner,** Vantongerloo and Herbin in 1931. Its members included Kandinsky, Mondrian, Arp and, later, Barbara Hepworth and Ben Nicholson. Many of its members exhibited at the 'Cercle et Carré' exhibition of 1930. The group issued a journal (1932–6).

ACADEMIES. The word 'academy' is derived from the name of Plato's villa near Athens where students and scholars could join in philosophical argument, and use of the term, at least until the 20th century, has always denoted some Classical *parti pris.* The training of the medieval and early Renaissance artist was similar to that of a craftsman, that is to say a long apprenticeship to a practising artist to learn the rudiments of the trade. The rise of Classicism, in the 17th century was accompanied by a need to differentiate between the 'fine' and the 'applied' arts, and to train artists in the historical and philosophical disciplines underlying the Classic ideal. The Paris Academy was founded in 1648, and the French Academy in Rome in 1668. (The Royal Academy in London was founded by Sir Joshua Reynolds in 1768.)

It was against this authoritarian background that the radical artistic movements of the late 19th century rebelled. Besides the official Academy in Paris, now called the Ecole des Beaux-Arts, there arose numerous private academies, of which the Académie Julian, famous for its association with the **Nabis,** and subsequently with Matisse and Derain, was probably the most important.

Perhaps the most radical academy of this century was the **Bauhaus,** founded in 1919 at Weimar by Walter Gropius. This school re-established the principle, lost since the Renaissance, that the artist should be trained in both the 'fine' and 'applied' arts, thus helping modern art to come to terms with the methods and materials of the machine age. In London, the Central School of Arts and Crafts (founded as an offshoot of the William Morris movement) and the Royal College of Art have, by similarly combining the 'fine' and 'applied' arts, produced outstanding creators in all fields.

ACTION PAINTING, term used for the type of **Gesture Painting** first introduced as the entire content of a work of art by **Jackson Pollock.** From about 1947 Pollock laid vast canvases on the floor and covered them with paint dripped from tins pierced with holes, afterwards selecting portions of the canvas for framing. Pollock probably learned the technique from Hans Hofmann and Max Ernst had done something similar during World War II, but Pollock was the first to employ it on a large scale. Other American Abstract Expressionists notably **de Kooning** and **Kline,** continued the development.

The impact of Pollock's art in Europe after the War affected Wols, Hartung and Soulages, each of whom has practised various forms of **Automatic Writing.** The work of the German K. R. H. Sonderborg the Spaniard Antonio Saura, the Italian Emilio Vedova, the Scot Alan Davie, and the Danish and Dutch Cobra groups, all reflect Action Painting. In France, Action Painting is often known as Tachism.

ADAM, Henri Georges (1904–), French sculptor. He created the decor for Sartre's play, *Les Mouches* (1943), then devoted himself to sculpture, as in *Lighthouse of the Dead* (1957–8), a monument commemorating Auschwitz. His broad abstract planes, sometimes animated by delicate carvings, have an expressive grandeur. Adam also works in tapestry design and engraving, the latter reflecting his apprenticeship as a goldsmith.

ADAMS, Robert (1917–), English sculptor. He enrolled at the Northampton School of Art in 1933, but was employed in an engineering works until 1944. His first one-man show (1947) was of figurative sculpture influenced by Moore, but he later became interested in the abstract metal sculpture of Brancusi and González. His abstract works since 1955 have been mostly in bronzed steel and large in scale. Adams works from one or two dominant planes of sheet steel, perforated and emphasized by smaller elements set at slight angles and welded on, *eg Large Screen Form No 2* (1962, London Tate). He exhibited at the Venice Biennale (1962).

ADLER, Jankel (1895–1949), Polish painter. After training as a goldsmith and engraver, Adler moved to Germany and taught at the Academy in Dusseldorf from 1922. He fled from Germany in 1933, eventually settling (1939) in Scotland. His early work was fantastic and highly coloured, rather in the manner of **Chagall,** but during his Dusseldorf period the forms became simplified under the influence of Cubism and 'Pittura Metafisica', though his drawing retained a realistic cutting-edge, *eg Cleron the Catbreeder* (1925, Munich NG). In Britain his work became freer in colour and handling, *eg The Mutilated* (1942–3, London Tate).

AESCHBACHER, Hans (1906–), Swiss sculptor. Self-taught, he began work in sculpture in 1936. His early works are heads and nudes based on primitive classical influences. Since 1945, he has made a conscious effort to preserve a balance between the original stone, which he searches for in the mountains, and the finished product, which he carves only slightly. The stones, representing abstract objets trouvés, are carved only to suggest their inherent images, as in *Face-Abstraction* (1945, Zurich Kunsthaus).

AFRO, originally Afro Basaldella (1912–), Italian painter. He began working in decorative painting, his father's trade, but soon turned to easel painting and, about 1944, to abstraction. His mature works are dominated by broad patches of paint (freely-handled abstract **Cubism** style) and, except for his use of brighter colour within a limited palette for any one work, are similar to those of Soulages. Afro's works often contain elements of **Action Painting,** which can be seen particularly in his drawings: *Volo di Notte* (1957, New York Guggenheim); *Villa Fleurent* (1958, Montreal MFA). His other works include the large mural at UNESCO headquarters in Paris, *Il Giardino della Speranza.* He won the Italian prize at the Venice Biennale of 1956, as well as prizes at São Paulo.

AGAM, Yaacov (1928–), Israeli painter, real name Yaacov Gipstein. Coming to Paris in 1951 he began his 'polymorphic' **Op Art** paintings in which complementary abstract designs are painted on either side of the ridges of a corrugated surface, being seen independently, or combining with each other, depending upon the position of the observer.

ALBERS, Josef (1888–   ), American painter, born in Germany. After achieving a reputation based on works which are among the classics of the 20th century, he was forced to leave Germany, at the age of 45. Unlike most other exiles, however, he continued to develop a type of painting which has influenced both **Abstract Expressionism** and the **Post-Painterly Abstractionists** and which matches the work of avant-garde artists, less than half his age. He has exerted immense influence as a teacher throughout his career.

Albers was born of an artisan family. Visits to Munich and Berlin awakened his interest in art and he began part-time study, producing his first abstract work in 1913. In 1920 he enrolled at the Weimar Bauhaus, first as a pupil and then as a 'journeyman' in charge of the glass workshop. He taught at the **Bauhaus**, concentrating on the famous preliminary course, until the school was closed down in 1933. He was then invited to teach at Black Mountain College, North Carolina, where he remained until 1949, becoming an American citizen in 1939. Since 1950 he has taught at American universities (notably Yale) and has exhibited widely. Apart from a few early drawings and paintings all of Albers' work is abstract. It is based on clear-cut rectangular shapes emphasizing the horizontal and vertical of the canvas, similar to the work of Mondrian. His earlier works at the Bauhaus were painted on glass, or made of glass fragments. The finest of these, eg *Fugue* (1925, Basle Kunstmuseum), involve interlocking bands of strongly differentiated colour. At the same time Albers produced paintings and prints using more complicated shapes, but all had in common an essentially intellectual approach.

In his early years in the U.S., Albers adopted brighter colours with less defined shapes and more painterly handling (a clear forerunner of Abstract Expressionism) eg *Gate* (1936, Yale University AG). The earlier preoccupation with regular shapes returned in a series of *Graphic Tectonics* (1940–8), black and white prints consisting of numerous horizontal and vertical lines forming a labyrinthine pattern which gives rise to endless variations in the way one reads it. These works strikingly anticipated **Op Art**. Since 1950 Albers has been exclusively concerned with the series *Homage to the Square*. All the paintings and lithographs have been built up of three or four nearly-concentric superimposed squares, in one of four basic patterns. Albers has used this simple matrix to explore inter-relationships of colours, a subject which has gradually occupied his teaching and is fully treated in his *Interaction of Color* (1963). But for all their intellectual basis these works (located in numerous museums) have a purely subjective effect and an astounding variety; the colours of some seem to break out of the boundaries of their frames in an incandescent light, whereas others, with only subtle differences, generate the deepest calm.

ALECHINSKY, Pierre (1927–   ), Belgian painter. In 1949 he associated with the **Cobra** group, settling in Paris in 1951. His painting of that period was marked by a dense network of free brushmarks and quasi-calligraphic signs, as in *La Fourmilière* (1954, New York Guggenheim). Since then his colour has become brighter, while figurative suggestions have appeared, eg in *Etrangers de Métier* (1960, St Louis AM), in *Malone Dies* (1962, Eindhoven van Abbemuseum). Recent works place the picture within a black and white border of surrealistic cartoon sketches.

AMIET, Cuno (1868–1961), Swiss painter. He studied at the Académie Julian, Paris (1888–91) before working at Pont-Aven with Gauguin's associates. He returned with their ideas to Switzerland, where he painted *The Yellow Girls* (1905, Bern Kunstmuseum). In 1904, he exhibited with Die Brücke and at the Vienna Secession. By 1910 his style was characterized by vivid colouring, similar to that of Fauvism, but retaining an acute sense of natural light, as in *The Blue Landscape* (1935, Zurich Kunsthaus). His perceptive, often dramatic, portraits are notable for their colour.

ANDRE, Albert (1869–1954), French painter. His work was noted by Renoir after his first contribution to the Salon des Indépendants in 1894. He was to remain a friend of Renoir until the latter's death. André's works are primarily Impressionist landscapes, painted with fresh, striking colour and flowing lines.

ANDRE, Carl (1935–), American sculptor. After studying at the Phillips Academy he moved to New York and began to make sculptures in wood, working for a while as a railway guard; he had his first show in 1964. Andre's definition of sculpture, 'Form = Structure = Place', has become famous as one of the key precepts of **Minimal Art.** The principle is illustrated by Andre's own work. The early sculptures consisted of blocks of wood cut into simple shapes, and this was quickly followed by pieces made of wooden blocks or bricks piled up in simple arrangements, their form being the direct result of the system used in building them up: *Untitled* (1965, Brandeis University). Andre's early exhibitions took the form of arrangements of bricks and other objects on the floor, *eg Lever* (1966, Ottawa NG), thus creating **Environments** rather than sculptural objects. While some of these arrangements are very beautiful in themselves, *eg 144 Lead Plates* (1969, New York MMA), the tendency of Andre's recent work has been away from the creation of objects and towards a **Conceptual Art** in which he uses an astonishing variety of temporary arrangements on the ground to give an identity to the place in which they are arranged.

ANDREOU, Constantin (1917–), Greek sculptor, born in São Paulo, Brazil. After studying in Greece, he moved to Paris in 1945. By 1948 a hammered and brazed sheet of brass had become his favourite working material. He developed a broad and angular, though elegant, manner suitable for interpretations of the animal world. His more recent works are abstract and make use of rougher openwork textures.

ANNESLEY, David (1936–), English artist. He studied in the sculpture department at St. Martin's School of Art from 1958 to 1961, under Caro, who influenced his use of painted steel. Annesley's sculptures tend to be planar and limited in depth, the earlier pieces make frequent use of boxlike shapes, *eg Swing Low* (1964, London Tate), but the later sculptures are based on the curve: *Untitled* (1968–69, London Tate). The increasing subtlety in colour may result from the influence of **Noland,** whom Annesley visited for a

month in 1966. Since 1969 he has devoted himself to painting.

ANQUETIN, Louis (1861–1932), French painter. Initially influenced by Manet and Degas, as in *Girl Reading a Newspaper* (1890, London Tate), he became a disciple of Gauguin, whose technique he systematized in the style he invented with Bernard called **Cloisonnism.** Later, he returned to a classical style in the manner of Rubens, *eg The Finish of a Horse Race* (1900, London Tate).

ANTRAL, Louis Robert (1895–1939), French painter. He entered Cormon's studio at the Ecole des Beaux-Arts and by 1920 he was exhibiting in all the principal salons. His early style was slightly influenced by Cubism, but about 1930, became more flowing, luminous and complex, while losing none of its rigorous construction. Antral concentrated on marine subjects and harbour views, and on Parisian scenes, which are his most remarkable works. They deal with the humidity of the atmosphere, evoked in rich and subtle harmonies.

ANUSKIEWICZ, Richard (1930–), American painter. See **Op Art.**

APOLLINAIRE, Guillaume (1880–1918), French poet and critic, originally Wilhelm Apollinaris de Kostrowitzky. He was an influential art critic, espousing the cause of the artistic avant-garde. One of the first eulogists of Henri Rousseau (le Douanier), by 1904 he had come into contact with Vlaminck, Derain and Matisse; in 1908 his preface to the Modern Art Circle's exhibition at Le Havre extolled purity, truth and unity in the works of Derain, Dufy and Braque. He first praised Picasso in 1905 and began his defence of Cubism in 1908, championing this 'revolution which is renewing the plastic arts' in his book *The Cubist Painters* (1913). In 1913 he directed an avant-garde review 'Soirées de Paris', which brought together painters and poets. Apollinaire invented the term **Orphism** and promoted De Chirico. His posthumously-published works include *Modern Painting* (1939).

APPEL, Karel (1921–), Dutch painter. After studying in Amsterdam, he helped found (1948) the **Cobra** group in Paris and settled there in 1950. He was commissioned to execute murals for the Stedelijk Museum, Amsterdam in 1956, and for the restaurant of the UNESCO building in Paris in 1958 *(Encounter with Spring)*. In 1960 he won the Guggenheim International Award for *Woman and Ostrich* (1957, Amsterdam Stedelijk M). Although it contains figurative elements, childlike human or animal figures treated with great brutality of form and colour, Appel is one of the most enthusiastic exponents of **Gesture Painting**. He works on an enormous scale, using pure pigment which he scoops up on huge palette knives, throws at the canvas and splashes with his hands, or which he squirts directly from the tube. The paintings, *eg Amorous Dance* (1955, London Tate) and *Dance in Space* (1961, Edinburgh Gallery of Modern Art), demonstrate his creative energy yet retain a satisfactory formal balance. Appel has written: 'My paint tube is like a rocket which describes its own space. What is happening I cannot foresee: it is a surprise. Painting, like passion, is an emotion full of truth and sings a living sound like the roar coming from the lion's breast.'

ARCHIPENKO, Aleksandr (1887–1964), American sculptor, born in Russia. After studying at the Art School in Kiev and exhibiting in Moscow, he settled (1908) in Paris, where he enrolled at the Ecole des Beaux-Arts. In 1910 he opened a school in Paris, where he taught and developed a style of sculpture influenced by **Cubism,** which exploited the possibilities of concave surfaces and composition in space: *Woman Combing Her Hair* (1915, London Tate). He took his school to Berlin (1921–3), and then settled in the United States (naturalized 1928). His teaching posts included one at the New Bauhaus founded in New York by Moholy-Nagy in 1938. Archipenko's stylistic range was astonishingly varied, though the quality remained consistent; he used many materials including mother of pearl, turquoise, bakelite and glass. He produced paintings and a larger number of 'sculpto-paintings', *eg In the Boudoir* (1915, Philadelphia MA). Many of his sculptures use colour in an inventive way, *eg Medrano II* (1914, New York Guggenheim), a form of Synthetic Cubism. After 1920 he renounced Cubism, but continued to develop his interest in concave surfaces. Many of his works show classical idealized naturalism; but the lines of the body are highly polished and sinuous, as in *Silver Torso* (1931, Hanover Landesgalerie) and *Walking Woman* (1937, Bloomfield Hills, Cranbrook Academy). There are a number of completely realistic portraits of great perception and power, *eg Wilhelm Furtwängler* (1927, Darmstadt Landesmuseum).

ARMITAGE, Kenneth (1916–   ), English sculptor. A pupil of Leeds College of Art and the Slade School, he was in charge of sculpture (1946–56) at the Bath Academy. He took part in the Biennales at Venice in 1952 and 1958 and at São Paulo in 1957; he won the international competition in 1956 for the monument commemorating the dead of Krefeld. Working chiefly in bronze, he specializes in figure sculpture. His figures have large bulbous, rather square bodies, small heads, and twiglike arms and legs. The mass of the body gives a quality of eternity to the sculpture while the limbs set it in motion and indicate balance or mood, as in *Sibyl III* (1961, London Tate). Many of his figures consist of bodies fused into one so that the whole group assumes a corporate existence, *eg People in a Wind* (1950, London Tate), *Family Going for a Walk* (1951, New York MMA) and the powerful *Sentinels* (1955–6, New York, Brooklyn Museum).

ARMORY SHOW, an exhibition in New York (17 February, 1913) intended to introduce modern art to America. Sponsored by the newly-formed 'Association of American Painters and Sculptors', it was organized by **Walt Kuhn** and **Arthur Davies** and called the 'International Exhibition of Modern Art'. That first showing, at the 69th Regiment Armory on Lexington Avenue, decisively influenced American art. Although American works predominated (most of them highly conservative) the European selection had the more lasting impact. There was a survey of French art from **Ingres** and **Delacroix** to the **Impressionism;** a very large section was taken up by the Symbolists (particularly **Redon**) and the Post-Impressionists; there was also a large collection of works by

Henri Rousseau. Most of the contemporary art movements such as **Fauvism**, **Cubism** and **Orphism** were represented, but not Futurism. The fiercest discussion centred on the work of **Picabia**, and on **Duchamp**'s *Nude Descending a Staircase* (1912, Philadelphia MA). A high proportion of the pictures were sold, forming the basis of many American collections of modern art.

ARP, Jean or **Hans** (1887–1966), French sculptor and painter. He studied painting at Weimar (1905–7) and went to Paris in 1908 to work at the Académie Julian. In 1909 he first attempted abstract painting and took up sculpture. He exhibited (1912) with Der Blaue Reiter. In 1916 he joined the **Dada** movement which aroused his interest in random arrangements in art, and, with Sophie Täuber, whom he married in 1921, he executed several **Collages.** He later contributed (*c* 1926) to the Dutch review *De Stijl*, and at the same time was involved in **Surrealism** in Paris. In 1931 he joined the **Abstraction-Création** group and thereafter he sculpted increasingly in the round.

Arp once declared: 'I love nature, but not its substitutes; naturalistic, illusionistic art is a substitute.' All his work is non-representational, but it makes repeated use of rounded, amoeba-like forms associated with basic natural shapes: human breasts and navel, hips and thighs, bulbs, buds and petals, rounded pebbles and clouds. Arp's output can be divided into three categories: two-dimensional works, flat reliefs, and sculpture in the round. Painting represents a small part of his output, but it shows his ideas in a simple form, *eg Mountain Table Anchors Navel* (1926, New York MMA) and often reflects a preoccupation with the 'figure-ground' relationship (an optical illusion caused by, for example, a black disk painted on a white ground appearing ambiguously either as a black disk or as a white rectangle with a hole cut from it) as in *Configuration* (1927, Basle Kunstmuseum). The collages often arise from randon arrangement: shapes are thrown down and glued into place where they fall. This principle has also been applied to many of the reliefs, which are collages of shapes cut like jigsaw pieces out of wood an inch or more thick, *eg Constellation According to the Laws of Chance* (*c* 1930, London Tate). His sculptures in the round, however, are usually completely rounded, one form merging into another without a break, as in *Hybrid Fruit Called Pagoda* (1934, London Tate) and *Concrétion humaine* (1935, New York MMA). Arp's genius is probably reflected best in those works in which the rounded forms are offset by hard lines and edges such as the *Orphic Dream* (1959), or the large-scale sculptures cut out from free-standing slabs of stone.

ART NOUVEAU (also called 'Jugendstil' and 'the Modern Style'), the principal stylistic tendency in the applied arts at the turn of the century. Distinguished by its approach to decoration, the style transformed the arts of glass-making, typography, textile design, jewellery and metal work; it was applied to architecture, both in detail and overall form. Its influence on the 'fine arts' of painting and sculpture was considerable. The aim of the movement, propagated by means of countless magazines, among them *The Hobby Horse, The Dial, Evergreen, L'Art Moderne, La Revue Blanche, Jugend* and *Ver Sacrum*, was to free art from academic rules and reliance on traditional forms, and search for new shapes and new principles of construction which would grow out of nature itself.

The origins of Art Nouveau were various. Probably the most important root was the 'Arts and Crafts Movement' in Britain. This was formed around the firm which William

Jean Arp: Concrétion humaine *(1935, New York MMA), ph. Larousse.*

Morris (1834–96) founded (1860) to return to traditional standards of craftsmanship in the applied arts. Morris himself drew on the traditions of William Blake (1757–1827) and the **Pre-Raphaelites**. The taste for Japanese prints, and the style of the first Symbolists also contributed to Art Nouveau.

Art Nouveau took its name from the shop founded in Paris by Samuel Bing in 1895, which marked the start of the finest period of the style. In Paris the leaders were Hector Guinard (1867–1942), some of whose Métro Stations still survive, and René Lalique (1860–1945); a school in Nancy formed around the glassmaker Emile Gallé (1846–1904). Another glassmaker, Louis Tiffany (1848–1933), developed a characteristic style in New York. In Belgium the leaders were the architects Victor Horta (1861–1947) and **Henri van de Velde**. In Barcelona Antonio Gaudí (1852–1926) designed buildings which, with their undulating walls and plant-like details, were probably the most original architectural contributions to the movement. Among the leaders of the German 'Jugendstil', were Hermann Obrist (1863–1927) and August Endell (1871–1925). In Austria the style was closely associated with the Vienna **Secession** and the most influential designers were Adolf Loos (1870–1939) and Josef Hoffman (1870–1955). Finally, in Glasgow a school grew up round the architect and designer Charles Rennie Mackintosh (1868–1928), the architect Herbert McNair (1870–1965) and their wives, the sisters Margaret (1865–1933) and Frances (1874–1921) McDonald; the Glasgow school reflected the highest degree of classical refinement and restraint possible within the style.

Many painters and sculptors at the turn of the century showed a similar predilection for curvilinear design. It was an important feature of **Gauguin**'s style from the late 1880s, and was developed in turn by the Pont-Aven School and the Nabis. The paintings of van de Velde and **Toorop** were in this style, as was poster painting (*eg* Chéret). Art Nouveau influence can be seen in much of the work of **Munch** and even in early German Expressionism. All the painters of the Vienna Secession shared aspects of this style, notably **Klimt** and **Hodler**. Finally, in recent years there has been a noted revival of interest in Art Nouveau and designers in all fields are recapturing some of its essential principles.

ASH CAN SCHOOL, popular name for the group of American painters calling themselves 'The Eight' who exhibited in New York in 1908. Their leader was **Robert Henri**. The others were Glackens, Luks, Shinn and Sloan, who had met Henri while working as artist-reporters in Philadelphia, and the New York artists **Davies**, Lawson and Prendergast. All except Sloan had also studied in Europe. Their aim as a group was to found an American art based on a realistic portrayal of the contemporary scene. Henri and the Philadelphians, with their newspaper backgrounds, adhered most closely to this, painting in a style influenced by **Manet** and Velázquez, but not following European 20th century developments. The New York artists, however, were less realist, being influenced by **Impressionism**, **Symbolism** and, in the case of Prendergast, by several Post-Impressionist movements.

ASSEMBLAGE, a more general term for **Collage**, applicable to sculpture as well as painting, and to multi-media works such as the 'combine paintings' of **Rauschenberg**. The technique was much favoured by the **Dada** artists, by the **Surrealists** and by many in **Pop Art**; it is generally involved in the creation of **Environments**. It could also be applied to the sculpture of César, Nevelson, Paolozzzi and Tinguely, among others.

ATLAN, Jean Michel (1913–60), French painter, born in Algeria. He began painting in 1941 after studying for a philosophy degree. In 1945 he abandoned figurative for non-figurative painting, and in 1948 joined the **Cobra** group. He forged an original style employing enormous black, undulating signs reminiscent of primitive idols, *eg Baal Guerrier* (1953, London Tate). In his more recent work, all quasi-figurative elements disappear and the black lines become boundaries between areas of strong colour, as in *Kahena* (1958, Paris MNAM).

AUBERJONOIS, René (1872–1957), Swiss painter. He studied at the Ecole des Beaux-Arts in Paris, where he lived until 1914. Most of his works portray the human figure with expressive but somewhat melancholy realism. His style was slightly influenced by Cubism. *Homage to Mme. Pitoeff* (1920) and *Caravan at the Lakeside* (1925) are in the Basle Kunstmuseum.

AURICOSTE, Emmanuel (1908–), French sculptor. A pupil of Bourdelle and Despiau, he began his career with figures and busts in bronze. After his first one-man exhibition, held in 1935, he turned towards monumental sculpture, as in the bas-reliefs for the Palais de Ghaillot, Paris (1936) and a bronze door for the League of Nations in Geneva. Most of his recent work has been in beaten lead and iron primarily inspired by rustic and popular themes.

AUTOMATIC WRITING, a technique of drawing or painting which dissociates conscious associations from the performance of the pen or brush—in fact, doodling. One of the principal techniques employed by **Surrealism**, Automatic Writing attempted to express the inner world of the mind, not the visible world. **Max Ernst, Baumeister** and **Arp** independently made several experiments in Automatism under the influence of **Klee**, many of whose drawings had a similar basis. **Wols** and **Jackson Pollock** (*c* 1945) also practised this technique thus associating it with **Action Painting**. Current experiments in painting under the influence of hallucinogenic drugs are probably motivated by similar aims.

AVERY, Milton (1893–1965), American painter. He studied art in Hartford, Connecticut. His style did not emerge until 1925, when he moved to New York. He was greatly influenced by contemporary French art though more by **Fauvism** than by Cubism, especially by **Matisse**. His earlier oils tend to be rather heavy, though the caricature-like drawing is always perceptive, *eg Harbor at Night* (1932, Washington Phillips Collection), *Dessert* (1939, New York MMA). After early success with watercolours he began to use oil colour in translucent washes, often omitting all detail so that the pictures would appear like a collage of subtly harmonizing coloured areas, *eg Poetry Reading* (1957, Utica Art Inst.), *Yellow Sky* (1958, London Tate). His refined Matisse-like use of

colour and his sense of abstract design were a considerable influence on **Hofmann** and **Rothko**.

AYRTON, Michael (1921–), English painter and sculptor. His main training was in 1936, copying Old Master drawings in the Vienna Albertina Museum. His work is entirely figurative though he has been influenced by **Sutherland** and **Moore**, particularly in the way his drawing assumes strong bone-like lines, *eg Nino* (1949, Hartford Wadsworth Atheneum), *Snow-bird* (1954, Philadelphia MA). Even his most naturalistic figures are painted in ghostly sculpture-like chiaroscuro, as in *The Shepherds* (1951, Manchester City AG). After a visit (1958) to Greece to make a film on Classical sculpture, Ayrton turned to the medium himself, sometimes even incorporating bones into the original model for casting in bronze. He has explored several themes in series, 'Figures in Balance' (1956) and the 'Daedalus and Icarus' series (1960–1), especially *Icarus Transformed* (1961, London Tate).

B

BACON, Francis (1909–), British painter, born in Dublin. An isolated figure, outside the main streams of modern art, Bacon has established himself among other artists as possibly the greatest living British painter. He had no conventional art training, spending his early years in Germany and France before settling in London around 1930. He did occasional work as a decorator in a style much influenced by the **Bauhaus**, and later began to paint in the style of **Cubism** with Surrealistic elements. Most of these paintings, and a high proportion of his subsequent work, were destroyed.

Bacon's extant oeuvre dates from late 1944, the first being *Three Studies for Figures at the Base of a Crucifixion* (London Tate). The work of this period already contains many of the elements of his style; *Figure Study II* (1945, Batley AG), incorrectly known as 'The Magdalene', shows his curiously disturbing use of recognizable props (the tweed coat, the umbrella, the palm tree) with a human figure in a non-realistic composition to create an atmosphere of nameless horror. *Painting* (1946, New York MMA) introduces the dark figure with teeth bared, the sides of beef, the hanging tassels, the Turkey rug and the setting composed of a rotunda with drawn blinds fenced off by rails in the foreground, all of which occur frequently in his later work. From 1945 until about 1957, Bacon painted on unprimed canvas, frequently giving the background a thin stain of colour in broad vertical strokes creating an effect like a hanging curtain. His figures are usually placed in space either by a perspective grid of white lines often resembling a glass cage, as in *Study for Crouching Nude* (1952, Detroit Art Inst.), or else by the use of a pattern on the floor shown in strong perspective, as in *Dog* (1952, London Tate). His subjects are drawn almost exclusively from photographs, especially newspaper cuttings and film stills. Certain images recur obsessively, *eg* Velázquez' *Pope Innocent X*, the screaming nurse from Eisenstein's *Battleship Potemkin* film which are combined in *Pope II* (1951, Mannheim, Kunsthalle), a snap of an American diplomat and some action studies by the Victorian photographer Eadweard Muybridge.

Since 1957 he has replaced these anonymous settings with modern interiors with characterless furniture; the backgrounds are painted more conventionally, but in modish decorative colours. He has introduced greater distortions in his treatment of the human figure, painted in a heavy, dragged pigment, as in *Study for Portrait on Folding Bed* (1963, London Tate). Bacon's principal achievement is to make one come to terms with the loneliness, frustration, brutality and degradation which are, unfortunately, part of the modern world: his art has thus a therapeutic value.

BAENNINGER, Otto Charles (1897–), Swiss sculptor. A pupil of Bourdelle, in 1941 he received the sculpture prize at the Venice Biennale. His style has been influenced by Maillol, but it has a naturalistic flavour of its own, as in *Old Man Seated* (1939, Winterthur Kunstmuseum).

BAJ, Enrico (1924–), Italian painter. After studying simultaneously at the Brera Academy and the Faculty of Law in Milan, Baj practised as a lawyer, painting in his spare time. In 1950 he met the painter Sergio Dangelo (1932–) and with him began a series of paintings, exhibited (1951) under the name of 'Nuclear Art'. The Nuclear Art movement growing out of this was joined (1952) by the sculptor Joe Colombo (1930–) and later by **Crippa** and **Fontana** in Italy, and the **Cobra** group. Baj's style at this time was a type of **Tachism**, using a technique called 'flottage' (a marbling effect achieved with fluid blobs of enamel paints). As early as 1952 he began to experiment with collage using wallpapers, fabric, broken mirror, Meccano and a variety of other materials. These have usually been combined with paint to produce curious composite figures. The satirical 'Military Personages' consist of a display of real medals and uniform accoutrements on a shapeless blob of impasto.

BAKST, Lev Nikolayevich (1868–1924), Russian painter and designer, known as Léon Bakst. A student at the Academies of Moscow and Paris, Bakst was a cofounder (1890) of the *Mir Iskusstva* ('World of Art') group and co-editor of the magazine of the same name. He translated the style of this group to a series of brilliant designs for Diaghilev's Ballets Russes (see **Ballet**), beginning with *Carnaval* and *Schéhérazade* in 1910. His style, related to Klimt and to Fauvism but most closely drawn from Russian folk art, made striking use of exotic motifs. However, he avoided over ornateness by the use of bold simplifications and striking effects of scale. He also made daring use of colour, though his muted effects were often as successful as his brighter ones. His easel paintings are more conventional, but strongly characterized, *eg Ida Rubinstein* (Washington, Chester Dale Collection). There are large collections of Bakst's designs in the Victoria and Albert Museum, London, the Musée des Arts Décoratifs, Paris, and in the Wadsworth Atheneum, Hartford, Connecticut.

BALLA, Giacomo (1871–1958), Italian painter. Initially an academic painter, he was converted to **Futurism** by Marinetti. His painting, *Dog on a Leash* (New York MMA) is a pertinent example of simultaneous analysis of movement though trivial, comparable to Duchamp or Boccioni. From 1913 to 1916 he painted pictures such as *Abstract speed—wake of a speeding car* (1913, London Tate, Estorick Loan) which pushed Futurism to the limits of abstraction. His subsequent work returned to a near-realist style.

BALLET. The influence of ballet on 20th century art has been considerable, primarily by bringing a new synthesis of choreography, music, and painting. This renaissance of ballet is largely the result of the remarkable success enjoyed by Les Ballets Russes under their magnetic impresario, Serge Diaghilev (1872–1929). The first performance (18th May, 1909) at the Théâtre du Chatelet of the 'Polovetsian Dances' from *Prince Igor* aroused great enthusiasm, revealing for the first time to the Western public all the brilliant colour and energy of a new kind of art. The decor for this was by **Leon Bakst**. Other Russian artists designing for Diaghilev were **Gontcharova** (*Le Coq d'Or*, 1914) and Larionov (*Chout*, 1921). After 1918, Diaghilev engaged some of the greatest painters of the **School of Paris**, including Braque, Rouault, Matisse and Derain; he began with the proto-Surrealist *Parade* (1917) designed by Picasso.

The principal function of ballet in 20th century art has been to popularize contemporary trends by giving artists commissions in a medium which enables them to work in a non-realistic style, yet attracts the attention of a wide public. A few notable attempts have been made to give design more than a merely decorative role in ballet, notably the experiments of **Schlemmer** at the Bauhaus, and of **Gabo** and **Pevsner** in the Constructivist ballet *La Chatte* (1927). However, it is only in recent American ballet that avant-garde design can be said to hold its place in the work of a permanent company, *vide* the designs by **Noguchi** for Martha Graham and those by **Rauschenberg** for Merce Cunningham.

BALTHUS, originally Balthasar Klossowsky de Rolla (1908–   ), French painter. As a young painter without formal training, he met Bonnard, Roussel and Derain through his family (his father was an art critic, his mother a painter). In Switzerland he met the poet Rainer Maria Rilke, who had his first drawings published and wrote an introduction to them. In 1933, he attracted the attention of the Surrealists, and became a close associate of Antonin Artaud and Giacometti. His first exhibition was held in 1934, and his portraits, *Derain* and *Miró* (1936–38), were acquired by the Museum of Modern Art, New York. Balthus lived alone in the country until his appointment (1961) as Director of the Villa Medici in Rome. His pictures contain human figures going about their business at a street corner, or in sober indoor surroundings; the mysterious lighting, the prison-like atmosphere, the transfixed attitudes and disquieting expressions of the figures and frequent deadpan sexuality, are astonishing, *eg Sleeping Girl* (1943, London Tate). The drawings are clear and realistic, the surfaces highly finished and the colours restrained. Balthus has created a world at once strange and familiar, which grips the viewer immediately by means of an almost Surrealist style which, nevertheless, does not employ the usual artifices associated with that movement.

BARBIZON, School of, see **Daubigny** and **Millet**.

BARLACH, Ernst (1870–1938), German sculptor. A pupil at the School of Arts and Crafts, Hamburg, and at the Academy, Dresden, he did drawings for the reviews 'Jugend' and 'Simplizissimus' from 1898 to 1908. He turned to sculpture from about 1907. After World War I, he was elected Member of the Berlin Academy of the Fine Arts, but the Nazis proscribed him, and destroyed or expelled his works. Among them was the war memorial in the cathedral of his home town, Güstrow (1927, now in the Antonite Church Cologne; version of head, New York MMA). His sculpture, principally in wood with some in bronze, is primarily Expressionist. His subjects are usually peasants, and most of the works are elegiac or pathetic in nature, although there are some radiantly happy pieces, *eg The Ecstatic One* (1916, Zurich Kunsthaus), *Singing Man* (1928, New York MMA). The striking quality of Barlach's work is the condensation of the emotion of a figure into a single expressive form, often using devices such as an all-enveloping cloak, *eg Freezing Girl* (Hamburg Barlach

Haus) and *Shivering Old Woman* (Tucson, University of Arizona). His principal inspiration for this was medieval sculpture and a substantial part of his work is designed to fit Gothic niches, *eg The Crippled Beggar* (1930, Harvard Busch-Reisinger Museum). In 1934 he completed a frieze of such figures entitled *Frieze with Listeners*, consisting of nine figures in bas-relief, intended as a monument to Beethoven. Barlach was also a writer and engraver, who illustrated his own writings. His art has a compact, violent strength which places him high, together with Wilhelm Lehmbruck, among modern German sculptors.

BARRAUD, Maurice (1889–1954), Swiss painter. His easel works are realistic and were done in a style influenced by **Matisse**, as in *Girl in a Sailor Shirt* (1939, Glarus Museum). Barraud also painted large murals, such as the hall of Lucerne's railway station (1928), a room in the League of Nations Building, *Nicholas de Fluë* in the Archives de Schwitz (1941), and a room at the Museum of Art and History, Geneva.

BASKIN, Leonard (1922–   ), American printmaker, sculptor and teacher. Probably best known for his graphic work, he studied at the Yale School of Art, the New School in New York City, and in Paris and Florence. In his graphic work, Baskin prefers the intaglio print. His etchings are generally figurative and their vivacity derives from his exaggerated imagery. The line he creates in his prints is controlled, but not static.

BATEAU-LAVOIR, name given to a group of buildings situated on the heights of Montmartre on a piece of ground which is now called Place Emile-Goudeau. About 1900 **van Dongen**, followed by **Picasso**, took up residence in the building. Gradually the poets and painters Mac Orlan, André Salmon, Max Jacob, **Juan Gris**, Gargallo and Mando joined them. The rent was very low (Picasso's was 15 francs a month). Among those who frequented the place were the authors Apollinaire, Jarry, Cocteau, Coquiot, Warnod, Radiguet; the painters Matisse, Braque, Derain, Marie Laurencin, Modigliani; the sculptors

Laurens and Lipchitz; the actors Dullin and Harry Baur; and the dealers Vollard, Kahnweiler and Berthe Weill. They shared the characteristics of being young and virtually unknown. Discussions there led to the creation of **Cubism**. Picasso finished his *Demoiselles d'Avignon* (1907) there. This artistic and intellectual ferment ended at the outset of World War I. Most of the artists and writers who were beginning to gain recognition dispersed, emigrating chiefly to Montparnasse.

BAUCHANT, André (1873–1958), French painter. One of the principal **Naive** artists in France, he was championed by Le Corbusier, Ozenfant and Lipchitz. Jeanne Bucher organized regular exhibitions of his work until 1941. His first canvases were mainly large compositions of a mythological, Biblical or historical nature. Their pale fresh colouring displays considerable imagination. They are peopled by strange draped beings making eloquent gestures in a landscape of monuments and fantastic rocks, as in *Greek Dance in a Landscape* (1937, London Tate) and *Cleopatra's Barge*

André Bauchant: Fleurs *(1930, private collection); ph. Giraudon.*

(1939, New York MMA). Later, he painted landscapes and familiar flowers in more vivid colours.

BAUHAUS, an art school founded in Weimar in 1919, by the architect Walter Gropius. It was at once a school of art and crafts, and a centre of artistic culture inspired by a determinedly modern spirit. The aim of the institute, as expressed in its first manifesto, was to unite in harmony architecture, sculpture and painting. The name 'Bauhaus' ('Bau' is German for 'building') is used to refer to the concept that a work of art, like a building, is produced from many different practical skills, as expressed in the first words of the manifesto: 'Our final aim, however distant it may be, is the complete work of art— "der grosse Bau"—in which there will no longer be any distinction between monumental and decorative art.' Gropius recruited artists of great ability, who taught in the school with unflagging zeal. **Paul Klee** taught theory, tapestry design, and painting on glass. **Kandinsky,** apart from giving instruction in general theory, taught monumental painting and abstract composition. **Moholy-Nagy,** Oskar Schlemmer and Lyonel Feininger also taught there. **Johannes Itten,** in charge of the preliminary course, devised a revolutionary training programme designed to teach awareness of the basic components of art (colour, form, volume, texture, sound, scent) and the inherent characteristics of different materials and tools. The Bauhaus thus comprised the first group of artists to come to terms with the machine age and with modern materials, producing designs in plastic and tubular steel (*eg* the stacking chair) that are still in production today. The diversity of the programme was manifested in the range of subjects taught, including ballet and theatre, typography, advertising, and photography. All these activities were inspired by the ideals of **Constructivism.** In 1929 the Bauhaus was obliged to move to Dessau, where it carried on its activities until 1933. Most of the school's teachers were expelled by the Nazis and fled to the United States, where in 1937 Moholy-Nagy, Gropius and Feininger founded the New Bauhaus in Chicago.

BAUMEISTER, Willi (1889–1955), German painter. He produced (*c* 1919) a series of abstract panels influenced by Cubism and Constructivism, which he called *Mauerbilder* ('Wallpictures'), a reference to his practice of mixing of sand, *etc,* with the paint to achieve a stone-like texture, as in *Two figures with Blue and Red* (1920, Berlin 20th C Gallery). In the early 1920s he met Ozenfant and Léger and began introducing machine-like forms into his compositions, *eg Composition* (1922, New York MMA). He then turned to a series of pictures based on sporting subjects, in which the figures gradually became abstract elements in the composition, *eg Gymnast* (1928, Stuttgart NG). He ceased exhibiting during the Nazi regime, but continued to develop a free style of painting using calligraphic styles inspired by **Automatic Writing.** He produced results not unlike the abstract Surrealism of Miró, as in *Eidos V* (1939, Munich NG) and *Happy Days* (1950, Bloomfield Hills, Cranbrook Academy). His post-war work was confined almost entirely to creating series, each based on a large sign or group of signs, like prehistoric inscriptions, but treated in a way which brought Baumeister close to the forefront of **Abstract Expressionism,** *eg Montaru 2a* (1953, Milwaukee Art Center); *Aru 6* (1955, New York MMA).

BAZAINE, Jean (1904–), French painter. He attended the Ecole des Beaux-Arts, studying sculpture, and after 1924 he turned entirely to painting, attending the Académie Julian. At his first one-man exhibition (1932), he met Bonnard, who was to encourage him. In 1938 he received the Blumenthal Prize. He designed windows for a private chapel (*Instruments of the Passion,* 1937); he executed (1944–6) two of the stained-glass windows for the Church of Our Lady at Assy and produced (1948–51) a large tiled mural for the façade of the Audincourt church. In 1958 he was commissioned to carry out a large mosaic for the UNESCO Building, Paris. He founded (1941) the group 'Peintres de Tradition Française' with Bissière, Manessier and Singier. Their style was derived from **Orphism** and was influenced by Klee. As Bazaine said in his book, *Notes on Modern Painting,* his aim was 'to embody the profound kinship between man and his world'. In his drawings one can see his interpretation of the patterns of the bark on a tree with the graceful rhythms of a dancer, and together with a stylization of a group of dancers into a natural pattern resembling tree bark. His paintings reduce the elements of landscape to a completely abstract pattern on the canvas surface with areas of rich, evocative colours separated by dark lines, *eg Dawn* (1952, Pittsburgh Carnegie Institute). In the late 1950s his drawing became softer and the patterns more ambiguous.

BAZIOTES, William (1912–63), American painter. Moving to New York in 1933, he studied at the National Academy of Design before working (1936–41) on the **WPA Art Project**. He became friends with most of the New York Abstract Expressionist painters and in 1948 founded an art school with Motherwell, Newman and Rothko. Unlike them, however, Baziotes always included quasi-figurative, or at least biomorphic elements in his work, reminiscent of Arp and Miró, with amoeboid forms reaching out with tentacles across the canvas. There is thus a Surrealist aspect to his work, as in *Dwarf* (1947, New York MMA), *Primaeval Landscape* (1953, Philadelphia MA). His delicate but powerful canvases are characterized by the merging of the images in fields of glowing colour.

BEARDSLEY, Aubrey Vincent (1872–98), English painter and illustrator. Although he died tragically just before the end of the 19th century, he practised daring stylizations which have been a recurrent influence on later artists. He worked originally in an architect's office, but left because of ill-health. He met (1891) William Morris, and during the next few years also Burne-Jones and **Whistler**. Their influence is evident in the book illustrations which comprise the bulk of his work; his style is also related to **Art Nouveau**. Nonetheless, the economy of drawing with which he created form out of large areas of white paper, without the use of shading or half-tone and his novel conception of space (both of which can be seen in his illustrations to Oscar Wilde's *Salomé* of 1894) were completely original. They rival in their own medium the parallel innovations of **Toulouse-Lautrec**.

BEAUDIN, André (1895–), French painter. A pupil at the Ecole des Arts Décoratifs (1911–13), he travelled in Italy in 1921. However, the decisive event in his life was his meeting in 1921 with Juan Gris. His works of the 1920s are developments of the Cubism of **Gris** and are principally figure-studies involving multiple outlines of great softness and fluidity, deriving ultimately from Gauguin. In the 1930s he began to paint landscapes more frequently and the graphic elements in his style became more vague and disjointed, *eg The White Birds* (1933, Paris MNAM). In 1938 he suddenly began painting within a network of straight lines emanating from the subject (though stylized, they were more realistic than before) and sectioning the surrounding space. This style is related to that of Villon. *The Faun* (1939, Baltimore MA) is an early example, but works such as *The Horses of the Sun* (1953, Stockholm, Moderna Museet) reveal considerable powers of architectural construction.

BEAUX-ARTS, Académie des, one of the five departments of the Institut de France. It controls the Académie de France in Rome, and wields great influence on such matters as state commissions, the role of the museums and the distribution of honours. This influence has been exercised in a narrowly traditional direction which has often run counter to the interests of modern art. Rodin, Renoir, Degas, Bonnard, Matisse and Rouault were never elected members, although a tepid liberalism prevailed when Maurice Denis and Vuillard were received in 1936 and 1938 respectively.

BECKMANN, Hannes (1909–), American painter, born in Germany. See **Op Art**.

BECKMANN, Max (1884–1950), German painter. Originally influenced by Cubism, he adopted a style after World War I mainly comprising Expressionist elements. His drawings and prints of this time were similar to Grosz' depiction of city life with satirical realism. Beckmann's paintings show figures in a claustrophobic atmosphere achieved by an illogical interplay of the bulky forms. This is an essential feature of his conception, as in *The Family* (1920, New York MMA) and *Pierrette and*

Clown (1925, Mannheim Kunsthalle). His landscapes and portraits, aided by a growing use of rich colours, became the most artistic of his works, *eg Naila* (1934, Stuttgart Kunstkabinett). In the late 1930s he began to paint large mythological and allegorical compositions, *eg Departure* (1937, New York MMA), *Blind Man's Buff* (1945, Minneapolis Art Inst.). Ultimately, his works became lighter in tone and showed the influence of Matisse: *Young Men by the Sea* (1943, St. Louis AM). He moved (1947) to the U.S., where he lived until his death.

BELLOWS, George Wesley (1882–1925), American painter and lithographer. Essentially a traditionalist, he is important for having popularized realist American subjects as material for art. Together with his own teacher **Robert Henri** he initiated the realist movement which has been among the strongest forces in American art of this century. Bellows elected to study art with Henri in New York (1904). In 1909 he was elected an Associate, and in 1919 a full member, of the National Academy of Design. Bellows never went abroad and was virtually unaffected by contemporary European developments, on view in the **Armory Show** and elsewhere (except in that they led him to tighten his design in his later work). His models were Rembrandt (particularly in his lithographs), Delacroix, Degas and Renoir, *eg Emma and her Children* (1923, Boston MFA). For Degas' theatre and race-course subjects, he substituted the circus, the billiard-hall and above all the prize-fight. His most famous picture, closer however to Daumier in its raw technique, is *Stag at Sharkey's* (1909, Cleveland MA). Bellows also executed a number of landscapes in an Impressionist style, *eg Up the Hudson* (1908, New York Metropolitan). He was famous before his early death.

BENTON, Thomas Hart (1889–), American painter. Although he had studied in Paris for three years and up to 1920 had painted Cubist abstractions influenced by **Macdonald-Wright**, Benton became the chief of the 'American Regionalists' (see **Realism**). His mature painting is entirely realistic and almost exclusively devoted to subjects from the country life of the Midwest. His style uses bold contrasts of light and shade, and incorporates figures painted in a broadly classical modelling. Some works (*c* 1930) have an almost van Gogh-like sense of movement, *eg Wyoming Corral* (1929, New York, Brooklyn Museum). Although the later works are generally far more solid and detailed, this sense of movement still shows in a slight exaggeration in the poses of the figures (rather similar to those of **Stanley Spencer**). Benton also painted a number of mural compositions, for example in the Whitney Museum, New York (1932), the University of Indiana (1933) and the Jefferson State Capitol (1936). His most successful pictures, however, are those in which a necessary simplicity of subject dictates a tautening of the form, as in *Portrait of Carl Ruggles* (1934, Kansas City Nelson Gallery).

BEOTHY, Etienne (1897–), Hungarian sculptor. Having studied architecture in Budapest, he settled in Paris in 1925. His first works were fundamentally Constructivist, but he soon abandoned this style for a fluid, elongated portrayal of the human figure. This differentiated between concave and convex with rhythmic outlines and contrasts in the manner of Archipenko, as in *The Man* (1927, Honolulu Academy). In 1931 he adopted an abstract style of carving, treating the sharp edges of a bar of wood so that the finished product would resemble a fluttering ribbon. He sometimes intertwined the undulations in order to create contrasting rhythms of beauty and some complexity, *eg Rythmes Entrecroisés* (1937, Paris MNAM). The proportions of these are carefully calculated according to the system published in his book *La Série d'Or* (1939).

BERGHE, Fritz van den (1883–1939), Belgian painter. A student at the Art School in Ghent, he formed (1905), with Permeke and the de Smet brothers, the second School of **Laethem-Saint-Martin**. He settled permanently in Ghent in 1925. He was a highly self-conscious artist whose Expressionism had moral and symbolic overtones. His very rich palette was deployed to give strange, often nightmarish lighting effects. The influence of folk art was also prominent in his work, although the stylization of forms may have been the result of Cubism, *eg Bather*

(1922–3, Grenoble Museum of Art), *La Vie* (1924, Antwerp MBA). After 1927, he executed a number of near Surrealist works with strangely terrifying, sneering figures, as in *Généalogie* (1929, Basle Kunstmuseum).

BERMAN, Eugene (1889–1972), American painter, born Russia. He was generally associated with the French Neo-Romantic movement. Vuillard was one of his teachers at the Académie Ranson in Paris. Berman went to the United States in 1935. His work was frequently an exploration of the subconscious, and the tone is often oppressive: *The Jug on the Window* (1934, London Tate). Noted for his achievements in the theatre, Berman became actively involved in designing for ballet and opera during the late 1930s.

BERNARD, Emile (1868–1941), French painter and sculptor. At sixteen, he entered the Cormon studio at the Ecole des Beaux-Arts, where he met Toulouse-Lautrec, but he was expelled for insubordination. In 1886 he struck up a friendship with van Gogh and Gauguin, and went to work at **Pont-Aven** where he became the leading member of the group around Gauguin. With his friend Anquentin, he formulated **Cloisonnism**, a style characterized by the direct juxtaposition of large areas of strong colour, which are separated only by heavy black or blue lines, as in *Haymaking* (1888, Paris MNAM). On the back of his painting, *Stone Pots and Apples* (1887, Paris MNAM), he wrote: 'First attempt at synthesism and simplification', a summary of the stylistic intentions of the Pont-Aven group. By 1890 he was publishing documented studies of Cézanne, Redon and van Gogh. In 1894 he left for Italy, and then spent ten years in Egypt, working out a new style which came closer to that of the Italian masters he admired. Later, he renounced modern art for a strict classical style.

BERNARD, Joseph (1866–1931), French sculptor. The son of a stone mason, his first studies were at the Art School, Lyons, and then at the Ecole des Beaux-Arts, Paris, in Cavelier's studio. For five years he worked on the *Monument to Michel Servet*, erected at Vienne (Isère) in 1910. His classical style was founded on the principles of Greek sculpture and of Donatello, whose ability to capture adolescent grace is reflected in Bernard's *Girl Singing* (Grenoble Museum of Art) and *Young Girl with the Jug* (Paris MNAM).

BERSIER, Jean Eugène (1895–), French painter and engraver. A pupil of Maurice Denis and J. P. Laurens at the Académie Julian, he received (1937) the Cottet Prize and the Gold Medal at the International Exhibition, Paris. A figurative painter, with a realistic but Expressionist style, he has painted landscapes and still life, *eg Still Life with Brioches* (1935, Paris MNAM). He is also an engraver and illustrator.

BERTHOLLE, Jean (1909–), French painter. A pupil of the Ecole des Beaux-Arts at Lyons, he came to Paris in 1930 to study under Bissière at the Académie Ranson, where he met Manessier. His style is not unlike theirs, employing a stained-glass-like mosaic effect created by colours on a dark background. He has, in fact, executed several commissions for glass. Figurative elements occur in the earlier work, *eg Hero* (1949, Paris MNAM), but more recent paintings are abstract.

BEUYS, Joseph (1921–), German sculptor. After a distinguished service in World War II as a fighter pilot, he studied sculpture in Dusseldorf. He then withdrew to live alone until being appointed Professor of Sculpture at Dusseldorf in 1961. Apart from a few fairly conventional early works, Beuys works entirely in the field of Conceptual Art, involving **Happenings** (which very often take the form of political action) and **Assemblage** (including the use of decaying material and of his favourite symbol, the dead hare). His recurrent theme is the nature of death. Since around 1964 he has attained enormous notoriety and has exhibited all over Europe, but his art demands personal contact with its creator to be appreciated.

BEVERLOO, Cornelis van, see **Corneille**.

BEZOMBES, Roger (1913–), French painter. A pupil at the Ecole des Beaux-Arts, he was encouraged by Maurice Denis. His first showing was at the Salon

Max Bill: Endless Ribbon *(1961).*

d'Automne in 1937. His early canvases were inspired by oriental themes, *eg Moroccan Woman* (1938, Paris MNAM). He is also the creator of several tapestry designs for the Gobelins and Aubusson tapestry workshops. His painting, with its bright and contrasting colours, has developed increasingly towards a nervous and lyrical stylization.

BILL, Max (1908–), Swiss painter, sculptor and architect. He studied at the Dessau **Bauhaus** from 1927 to 1929, and his work exemplified that ideal. Stylistically, he owes much to the De Stijl movement, as do many of the other artists of the **Abstraction-Création** group, of which he was a leading member. Most of his life has been spent teaching in Zurich, specializing in the field of design. However, he was Director (1951–5) of the Art School of Ulm, which he ran on Bauhaus lines. In 1953 he visited Argentina. Bill's paintings mainly continue the De Stijl exploration of the inter-relationships of colour in simple rectangular forms, in a manner similar to that of Albers. He has also explored the ways in which a plain surface can be activated by the simplest of means, *eg Energies of the White Surface* (1948–9, Zurich Kunsthaus). Among his most interesting sculptures are those which study endless surfaces, the mathematical phenomenon known as a 'Möbius Band'.

BIROLLI, Renato (1906–59), Italian painter. He studied at the Verona Academy before moving to Milan in 1928. His early works were deceptively simple, almost naive, but with a delicate line and subtle pale colouring, *eg S. Zeno* (1931, Milan GAM). Later, his colouring became richer and his treatment more naturalistic and painterly. In the 1950s he adopted a Cubist-inspired schematization in his pictures (rather similar to the work of Sutherland). He retained the rich tonality, generally based on green, which he had developed, as in *Scythe, Seat and Boat* (1952, São Paulo MAM). In his last works the representational elements were reduced without changing the overall impression that the pictures were closely related to the natural world.

BISSIER, Julius (1893–), German painter. In 1934, a fire at Freiburg University, where Bissier was a teacher, destroyed all his work. He abandoned representational painting and executed a series of monochrome 'ink paintings'. Although influenced by his friend **Baumeister**, and by Klee, these paintings struck in a new calligraphic direction. Remarkably simple, they are based on two or three forms, part abstract, part symbolic. After World War II, Bissier began to use colour and his works became freer and more varied. They involved a variety of symbolic forms as well as letters of the alphabet and written inscriptions, on a background of subtly handled washes of colour. His frequent use of gold and little rectangles of bright colour are often reminiscent of **Klimt**. However, his contemporary affinities are with the Abstract Expressionists of his own generation, in particular his close friend **Mark Tobey**.

BISSIERE, Roger (1888–1964), French painter. A member of the 'Esprit Nouveau' group, he only began to exhibit in 1920, practising a moderate, decorative form of Cubism. He exercised considerable influence, particularly on Manessier, while teaching at the Académie Ranson. During World War II, he contracted a serious eye disease, and gave up painting to concentrate on mural decorations executed on cloth, *eg Tenture Murale* (Paris MNAM). In 1947, having recovered his sight, he exhibited a group of new paintings (his first for ten years), which gained him immediate recognition. He joined the 'Peintres de Tradition Française' group, led by **Manessier** and **Bazaine**, whose ideas had derived, in part, from his own. Though sharing with them the same basic style of a mosaic of orchestrated colours, Bissière differed from most of the group in being more refined, perhaps as a result of his experience with tapestry. His works incorporated graphic signs suggesting figurative elements, leaving the actual interpretation of them to the imagination, as in *Composition Blanc et Jaune* (1950, Paris MNAM).

BJØKLUND, Poul (1909–), Danish painter. A self-taught artist, he began to paint in 1932. His realistically and sometimes brutally vigorous painting is characterized by its sculptural relief, vivid, contrasting colours and violent effects of light, as in *Self-portrait* (1953, Randers Kunstmuseum).

BLADEN, Ronald (1918–), Canadian sculptor. See **Minimal Art**.

BLAKE, Peter (1932–), English painter. After studying at Gravesend Art School and serving in the Air Force, he attended (1953–6) the Royal College of Art, sharing a studio there with **Richard Smith**. He has always been interested in popular art and in 1956 was awarded a travel scholarship to study the subject. This interest can be seen in his Diploma Composition, *On the Balcony* (1955–7, London Tate), a portrait of working-class children covered with lapel badges, postcards, magazine covers, car pennants, printed wrappers and the like. Although this work appears to be collage (he has used collage in later works), it is in fact all paint. It is characteristic of Blake that he does not reject traditional means. All his work is distinguished by fine painting, somewhat in the manner of **Stanley Spencer**. One of the pioneers of British Pop Art, many of his subjects are popular heroes (boxers, jazz musicians, singers, and more recently, pin-up girls), treated with inventiveness and respect. In 1964 he executed three huge murals for the Shakespeare Exhibition at Stratford-on-Avon.

BLANCHARD, Maria (1881–1932), French painter, born in Spain. She first studied at Madrid, and then went to Paris in 1910. After working with van Dongen, she joined the Cubists. Her works, however, are more realistic in style, although they contain elements of Cubism. From 1920 to her death she produced a series of figure studies, of peasants and children, eg *Boy with Ice Cream* (Paris MNAM), one of a large collection in that museum. Her work was also influenced by popular art, and by primitives such as Rousseau, particularly in the outlines, the unexpected viewpoints, and by the way in which the figures stand out from the background.

BLANCHE, Jacques Emile (1861–1942), French painter. He is best remembered as a portrait painter of high society and of literary and artistic celebrities, eg *Aubrey Beardsley* (1895, London, National Portrait Gallery), *Thomas Hardy* (1906, London Tate), *Igor Stravinsky* (1915, Paris MNAM). His works are primarily of documentary interest, but the best of them do show an original sense of composition and of line, as in *The Savile Clark Sisters* (c 1908, Leeds AG). He also painted scenes from public life and street scenes, in a vaguely Impressionist style, eg *Coronation of King George V* (1909, Manchester City AG), *Lunch on the River* (1907, Rouen MBA, where there is a large collection of Blanche's works). He exhibited at the Royal Academy in his lifetime.

BLAUE REITER, Der, initially the title of an almanack of contemporary art started in 1911 by **Kandinsky**, aided by Marc and Macke. The name (meaning 'the blue rider') was arbitrarily chosen. In fact only one issue was published (1912), but two exhibitions were organized in Munich (1911 and 1912) which launched Der Blaue Reiter as an artistic movement. Kandinsky's idea was to provide a united front for avant-garde practitioners of all the arts. Arnold Schoenberg encouraged the project from the start, contributing a musical work 'Herzgewachse' to the almanack, and paintings to the exhibitions. Much of the original impetus came from Berlin through the influence of **Die Brücke** group. Most of the painters associated with Der Blaue Reiter (Kandinsky himself, Marc, Macke, Münter, Jawlensky, Klee and Campendonk) were working in an Expressionist style at the time of its inception. However, French avant-garde work was also exhibited. The group was further influenced by the Cubism of Picasso and Braque, and particularly by the Orphism of **Delaunay**, whom Marc, Macke and Klee visited in Paris in 1912. The impact of **Futurism** (late 1912) established the style thereafter associated with Der Blaue Reiter. The influence of Cubism had been towards more regular forms and disciplined colours. Orphism and Futurism enunciated the principles of presentation, involving the creation of a simultaneous and unified whole, the composition (background as well as subject) being inter-related in a network of faceted colour planes. The style can be seen most clearly in the work of Marc. This sense of unity was essential to the Blaue Reiter artists, which makes their work, on the whole, more serious than the more decorative Orphism. World War I curtailed the development of the movement as such, but the Blaue Reiter style inspired Kandinsky's subsequent completely abstract paintings.

BLOC, André (1896–   ), French sculptor, born in Algeria. He took up sculpture during World War II, progressing towards an abstract style, which he adopted for his monumental *Signal* (1947, Paris, Palais de l'Iéna). His later sculptures depict space through hollowed out areas of the body. The various surfaces intertwine as though made of some more pliable material than stone. In 1951, he founded the 'Espace' (Space) group.

BLONDEL, Emile (1893–   ), French

painter. A self-taught Naive artist, he did not begin painting full-time until 1935. In his work, Blondel has shown a predilection for compositions containing innumerable tiny figures set in an enormous landscape and for vivid, fresh colours. His canvases portray his early life at sea, Normandy, and his wanderings in Paris. They express the wonder of life, and a primitive and simple joy.

BLOW, Sandra (1925–), English painter. After studying at St. Martin's School of Art, the Royal Academy Schools and in Rome, she travelled in Spain and France. She returned to London in 1950 and had her first exhibition in the following year. She exhibited at the 1958 Venice Biennale. Her paintings, seemingly influenced by Burri and by Tapiès, are abstract, bold in design but restricted to near monochrome colours. She has used sand, ash and sacking to obtain effects of texture, *eg Space and Matter* (1959, London Tate).

BOCCIONI, Umberto (1882–1916), Italian painter and sculptor. His early work, influenced by Severini and Balla, shows a considerable interest in Impressionism, as in *Landscape* (1910 Rome GAM), and in the rhythms of Art Nouveau. After 1910 he devoted himself to **Futurism**, publishing his theories in *Futurist Painting and Sculpture* (1914). His first great work of this period was *The City Rises* (1910, New York MMA), in which the sensation of movement is conveyed by a predominence of flowing Art Nouveau lines and by the blurring of one event into another by use of the Neo-Impressionist technique, **Divisionism**. He did this despite his abhorrence for traditional and decorative art (the essence of Art Nouveau). The first version of his famous triptych, *States of Mind* (1911, Milan GAM), is a study of the feelings aroused by the departure of a railway train. In the same year, he went to Paris and painted a second version in which the forms, instead of being blurred, are fragmented and re-assembled in a **Cubism** style. He then tried to follow up his preoccupation with movement within a Cubist framework, one effect being reduction in colour, as in *Dynamism of the Human Body* (1913, Milan GAM).

Although Boccioni was the greatest

Umberto Boccioni: Unique Forms of Continuity in Space *(1913, New York MMA); ph. Giraudon.*

painter of the Futurist movement, his work as a sculptor is even more significant, though few pieces have survived. In the destroyed *Head and House and Light* (1911), he expressed the idea that figures, their surroundings, and the attendant light and sound should be considered as forming an entity (a bold conception since sculpture allows for none of the blurred effects that are possible in painting). In *Development of a Bottle in Space* (1912, New York MMA) he allowed a simple still-life motif to disintegrate, thereby involving it with the space around it. In *Unique Forms of Continuity in Space* (1913, New York MMA) and *Walking Man* (Milan GAM), he expressed movement in the bold stylization of a human figure in rag-like trailing forms that have since become something of a cliché, but which Boccioni employed with considerable monumental grandeur.

BOLDINI, Giovanni (1845–1931), Italian painter. After painting in Ferrara and then in London, he settled (1871) in Paris, where he became a friend of Degas. He painted urban landscapes in a fussy style, slightly influenced by Impressionism, but he was best known as a portrait painter of fashionable society. His portraits are interesting for their artificial style. They flatter the subject, giving it a mannerism of pose and colouring as bold, in its own way, as the unconventional portraits of Degas himself, *eg Comte Robert de Montesquiou* (1897, Paris MNAM).

BOLUS, Michael (1934–), South African sculptor. Coming to England in 1957, he studied at St. Martin's School of Art until 1962. Like other pupils of Caro he works with coloured sheet materials and although he uses these to enclose volumes as in traditional sculpture, he always ensures that the hollowness of the forms and the thinness of the sheet is apparent: *7th Sculpture 1965* (London Tate). Many of his recent works use simple elements in series: *1st Sculpture 1970* (London Tate).

BOMBERG, David (1890–1957), English painter. The son of a Polish Jewish leather worker, Bomberg studied with Sargent and Sickert, and later at the Slade School, London. In 1913 he visited Paris with Epstein, where he met the leading avant-garde artists, including Picasso and Modigliani. Even before this visit, however, Bomberg had been experimenting with abstraction, based on what he could discover of Cubism. He had begun *The Mudbath* (1912–13, London Tate), a picture which in the vigour of its angular shapes, strong red, blue and black colour scheme, and complete independence from figurative considerations went far beyond Cubism at the time. His *In the Hold* (1913–14, London Tate) went even further, but had a brilliance of colour and proliferation of multi-faceted forms showing the influence of **Orphism**. At the time, he, as the most progressive English painter, was inevitably associated with Vorticism, though he declined to join the movement. He served in France during the War and in 1919 finished his *Canadian War Memorial* (Ottawa, NG) in which a trench composed of shapes like those of *The Mud Bath* is peopled with realistic figures. From then on his painting remained figurative, although it became more and more painterly, showing the influence both of Soutine and of Matisse, *eg Castle Ruins, St. Hilarion* (1948, Liverpool, Walker AG). Bomberg had considerable influence as a teacher at the Borough Polytechnic, London, but was consistently ignored by the critics.

BOMBOIS, Camille (1883–), French painter. His earliest works were drawings of rural scenes, based on his life as a farm labourer. He later became a wrestler in a travelling circus and circus life became one of his favourite themes. After World War I he began to show his paintings in the street, where he was noticed by Wilhelm Uhde (see **Naive Art**), who encouraged him to devote himself to painting the scenes and events of his former life, *eg Before Entering the Ring* (1930–5, New York MMA). The main lines of his compositions are simple, while the details are minute. His figures, particularly his nudes, have roundness which is close in style to some later Cubists, *eg Athlete* (*c* 1930, Paris MNAM).

BONNARD, Pierre (1867–1947), French painter. Raised in a middle-class family, he enrolled in 1888 in the drawing class at the Ecole des Beaux-Arts. Then at the Académie Julian he was first taught by Sérusier and began to associate with the **Nabis**, many of whose members became his friends. A colour lithograph, *France-Champagne*, composed for a Rheims vintner, was his entry for the 1889 Concours de Rome. It failed to win a prize, but did attract the attention of Toulouse-Lautrec and launched Bonnard's career as a poster painter and applied artist. In 1891 he exhibited at the Salon des Indépendants. He often spent the winter in southern France, and the autumn in the Dauphiné. His work reveals his intimacy with both metropolitan and provincial scenes. He turned repeatedly to his environment and his friends for inspiration. His style was the product of a natural spontaneity, and also of an interest in **Japanese print** techniques which earned him the name of 'the Nipponizing Nabi'.

His first one-man exhibition was organized by Durand-Ruel in 1896. His second one-man exhibition took place in

Pierre Bonnard: Portrait of Reine Natanson and Marthe Bonnard *(1928, Paris MNAM); ph. Giraudon.*

1906, at the Bernheim-Jeune Gallery. He took part in the first Salon d'Automne (1903) and in the founding (1906) of the Académie Ranson, where he taught. He was a tireless traveller, visiting Belgium and Holland in 1907, Spain, Tunisia and Algeria in 1910, Britain, Germany and Italy in 1922. In 1926 he went to Pittsburgh, U.S., where he became a member of the jury of the Carnegie Foundation, whose first and second prizes he received in 1923 and 1936 respectively. In 1939 he settled finally in his little house at Le Cannet.

In his early years (1886–8), he remained faithful to nature, depicting it in exact, clear forms. Around 1890, his painting, comprising figure subjects and genre scenes, tended towards a decorative flatness influenced by Art Nouveau, eg Le Peignoir (1890, Paris MNAM). He painted Parisian street scenes, especially of Montmartre, in quiet and often sombre tones, but with wit and finesse and a remarkable sense of movement, eg Rue Thologé (1897, Washington Phillips Collection). His originality can be seen in the unexpected presentation of the figures and in the tender and direct sentiment with which he approaches his human subjects.

Around 1900 he began to produce studies of home life and family relationships, making use of original viewpoints, as in Les Leçons (c 1903, Southampton AG). He studied the effect of artificial light, as in La Soirée sous la Lampe (c 1903, Merion, Pa., Barnes Foundation). Like his friend Vuillard, he was interested in the trappings of the bourgeois milieu (the furniture, wallpaper, set dining-table, the children and pets), but his works have more grace than Vuillard's. One of the finest paintings of this period, L'Indolente (1899, Paris MNAM), shows many of the recurring features of his style. It is among the earliest of many studies of the female nude, seen from a fresh (but plastically coherent) angle. The figure of the girl splayed out on the bed serves both as a three dimensional concept and as an interesting surface pattern.

After discovering the clear southern light of Provence, he turned to the use of deep blues and strong contrasts of light and shade, with flaming reds and oranges. In this period, even his shadows are composed of rich, saturated colours, eg Les

Deux Soeurs (1909, Washington Phillips Collection), En Barque (1912, Paris MNAM), Salle à Manger à la Campagne (1913, Minneapolis Art Inst.). His palette lightened and became softer as he began to prefer garden and bathing scenes, transformed by the effect of light, eg Pont de la Concorde (1913, London Tate), Ruelle à Vernouet (1914, Edinburgh, NG of Scotland). Although he still painted simple interior genre scenes, the viewpoints became more daring and the pattern of colours on the canvas more striking, eg Le Café (1915, London Tate).

After World War I, he underwent a spiritual crisis: 'I have become a student again . . . I have been allowing colour to carry me away. But the truth is that form also exists, and that it cannot be arbitrarily diminished or transposed'; he returned to drawing and composition. He declared: 'Compose well, and the picture is half finished.' His last works show extraordinary freedom. His curious remark, 'I can no longer draw', comes from this period. Characterized by complete abandon· and recalling the Water-Lily series of his life-long friend, Monet, Bonnard's late works, epitomized by Méditerranée (Paris MNAM), brought him great prestige among post-World War II painters and placed him in competition with Picasso as an influential artist. His last large composition was a St. Francis of Sales, his only religious work, which he did for the Church of Our Lady at Assy.

Bonnard's work was influenced most by **Degas**, with whom he shared an interest in Japanese art, leading to compositions with the frame cutting across the subject unexpectedly. Many of his colour schemes develop those of Degas. Both artists explored unusual lighting effects, especially the contre-jour lighting which dissolves form. Most of his subjects had also been used by Degas: street scenes, theatre scenes, intimate genre scenes and above all, nudes.

It is for his nudes that Bonnard will probably be best remembered. Although he was not an avant-garde artist he showed, in his countless figure paintings, a single-minded search for perfection in recording the most complex of sensations, painting variation after variation with the slightest changes of colour and light. Apart from contre-jour lighting, eg L'Eau de Cologne

(1908, Brussels MBA), he experimented with the effect of reflection in a mirror, *eg La Glace* (1908, Paris MNAM) and with lamplight, *eg Nu, Eclairage de Lampe* (1911, New York MMA). Bonnard also combined the figure in a single colour harmony with a glowing background, as in *Standing Nude* (1913, St. Tropez Museum). In the important series of late pictures of his wife in the bath, from the *Baignoire* of 1925 (London Tate) to the *Nu dans le Bain* of 1935 (Paris, Petit Palais) and especially in his very last works, Bonnard's subject is light. Streaming through the window, reflected off the water and caressing the flesh beneath and refracted by the tiles, it makes a symphony sometimes of iris blues and gold, sometimes of sunset colours. In these works Bonnard proved himself the heir of Impressionism.

BORES, Francisco (1898–   ), Spanish painter, member of the School of Paris. Borès joined (1922) the avant-garde Ultraist group in Madrid, before going to Paris, where in 1927 he exhibited works reflecting the influence of Cubism, but with a feeling of movement. Around 1930 he returned to more realistic themes such as landscapes, still life and particularly genre scenes in the tradition of **Degas**, but retaining the Cubist fragmentation of all but the essential elements. Many of these, *eg The Fitting* (1934, New York MMA), include elements of fantasy and show startling effects of light and simplifications of figures rather in the manner of Picasso. After World War II, he began using richer colours and softer lines. His subjects are painted in a manner reinterpreting **Bonnard** through Cubist eyes *eg Table with Black Background* (1948, Amsterdam Stedelijk), *People at Table* (1955, Paris MNAM).

BOSHIER, Derek (1937–   ), English painter. One of the group of ex-students of the Royal College of Art to exhibit at the 'Young Contemporaries' show in 1961 (see Kitaj), Boshier has always combined **Pop Art** imagery with passages of free painting. In the later 1960s his style moved closer to the 'abstract Pop' of **Richard Smith**, and specific popular references (*eg* to brand names) diminished, although his work still contains figurative elements, *eg The Identikit Man* (1971, London Tate).

BOUCHE, Georges (1874–1941), French painter. He studied architecture at the Art School, Lyons (1893) and then worked with Blondel in Paris. The characteristic feature of his painting is its extraordinarily heavy impasto. He overlaid his canvas with paint to an unprecedented degree. His palette was restrained (pale greens, pinks and ochres), but subtly expressive in treatment of simple subjects (a violin, a bunch of flowers). An allusive shadowy light reinforced the impression of mystery and nostalgia in his work.

BOURDELLE, Antoine (1861–1929), French sculptor. He learned cabinet-making from his father, for whom he carved ornaments. He was sent to the Art School, Toulouse, and then, on scholarship, to the Ecole des Beaux-Arts, Paris, where he received instruction from Falguière and Dalou. He was employed (1893) as a pupil of **Rodin**, staying with him until 1908. From 1888 he had been engaged on a statue of *Beethoven*, for the Salon au Rose-Croix, on which he worked with his friend **Emile Bernard**. He was to carve twenty-one other portraits of the composer, *eg Beethoven* (1902, New York MMA), *Tragic Mask* (1901, Cologne, Wallraff-Richartz-Museum), *Beethoven* (1905, Zurich, Kunsthaus), finishing only in 1929. In 1893, he was commissioned to carry out the *Monument to the Dead of Montauban*; he spent six years working on it, using a dramatic, naturalistic style. There is a *Nude Warrior* (Rochester, N.Y. MA) related to it. He learned the basis of his craft from Rodin, but he was drawn by his own temperament towards the restraint and inner concentration, evident in his *Head of Apollo* (1900, Paris, Musée Bourdelle), which he called 'the first work in which I discovered my own laws', and in all his subsequent works. These laws involved a search for permanence and universality, and they drew him towards monumental sculpture. His main works in this domain were: *Hercules the Archer* (1909, casts in Stockholm Moderna Museet, Brussels MBA, Rome GAM and Los Angeles County Museum); the high reliefs of the Théâtre des Champs-Elysées (1912), inspired by the dancing of Isadora Duncan and Nijinsky; *Dying Centaur* (1914, Princeton Univ.) and the Mickiewicz Monument, Paris (1928). Bourdelle also left numerous busts, broadly and expressively handled with a stylized accuracy, *eg Sir James Frazer* (1922, London Tate, casts Oxford Ashmolean, Cambridge Fitzwilliam and Glasgow Kelvingrove), and several allegorical or intimate works of a majestic fullness combined with a robust sensuality. The art of Bourdelle, avowedly influenced by ancient Greek and Roman sculpture, allowed French sculpture to escape from the over-powering, and sometimes crushing, naturalism of Rodin and achieve a greater directness of expression.

BOUSSINGAULT, Jean-Louis (1883–1943), French painter. He studied at the Académie Julian, where he worked with **Dunoyer de Segonzac** and Luc Albert Moreau. With André Mare, the three took part in the reaction against the abuse of colour. Boussingault's paintings gradually became lighter and are distinguished by their original composition, their expressively naturalistic drawing and their soft and harmonious colour. His landscapes are composed of dense patterns rather like, although less flamboyant than, those of the Nabis.

BOYD, Arthur (1920–   ), Australian painter. At first a student (1934) at night classes in Melbourne, he began by painting in his spare time. His early works were landscapes, but in 1943, while running a pottery business in order to support himself, he produced a number of biblical paintings. In these he took a primitive, rather terrible view of the Christian story. Some were strongly influenced by Bosch and Bruegel, *eg The Mockers* (1945, Sydney AG), others were placed in an Australian genre setting. The most powerful of them concentrated on two or three figures in oppressive forest surroundings. In about 1950 he made a large number of pictures in tempera of the bleak Wimmera area, influenced by **Drysdale**, *eg Irrigation Lake, Wimmera* (1950, Melbourne NG). In the mid-1950s Boyd began the 'Half-Caste Bride' series: a number of paintings involving recurrent ghostly figures of a bride, lovers, or a nude, set once more in the dark aboriginal forest, *eg Persecuted Lovers* (1957–8, Adelaide NG). These works have strong Surrealist overtones; much of their imagery was derived from **Chagall**. Boyd went to London in 1959

and has lived there since. Among his more recent works are a polyptych illustrating *Romeo and Juliet* (1964, Melbourne NG), a series of pastels on the life of St. Francis (1964–5) and a group of very bleak, but richly painterly canvases on the theme of *Nebuchadnezzar   in   the   Wilderness* (1968–9).

BRANCUSI, Constantin (1876–1957), Romanian sculptor. A vagabond from the age of eleven, he eventually became an apprentice cabinet-maker at Craiova before enrolling (1898) at the Art School, Bucharest. In 1902 he left Romania on foot to make his way to Paris, where he arrived in 1904 after passing through Munich, Zurich and Basle. At the Ecole des Beaux-Arts, Paris, he was the pupil of Antonin Mercier, but he was influenced primarily by **Rodin**'s work. His first showings were at the Société Nationale des Beaux-Arts (1906, 1907). His exhibits brought him to Rodin's notice and he was invited to work with him but Brancusi refused the offer. He became friendly with **Modigliani**, whom he persuaded to take up sculpture for a while. Modigliani's elongated heads and simplified features reflect Brancusi's style at this time. He was then exhibiting at the Salon des Indépendants and at the Salon d'Automne. In 1913 he sent five pieces of sculpture to the **Armory Show** in New York, the first of his many successes in America. His first one-man exhibition was organized by A. Stieglitz for his Gallery 291 in New York. From 1914 he concentrated on using wood, especially oak, producing bronzes of each subject once the conception was fully formed. He produced several Cubist works at this time, *eg The Prodigal Son* (1915, Philadelphia MA), but did not continue in this direction. The abstraction of his work in wood increased with *Eve* (1921) and culminated in *Endless Column* (1918–37, Targu-Jiu, Romania), composed of identical elements joined together to reach a height of thirty metres and made of gilded steel. His phallic *Princess X* (1916, Lincoln, Neb., Sheldon AG) created a scandal in the Salon des Indépendants in 1920. It was removed by the police, only to be brought back in triumph by Blaise Cendrars and Fernand Léger. Thereafter he stopped exhibiting in France. In Paris he took lodgings in the

Impasse Roncin, the studio of which was completely reconstructed after his death in the Musée de l'Art Moderne. He went to India in 1937 in order to supervise the construction of a Temple of Deliverance, which was never finished.

Brancusi returned again and again to a few subjects, always bringing the conception nearer to some primordial form, usually that of the egg. *The Kiss* (1910, Paris, Montparnasse Cemetery; 1911 version, Philadelphia MA) demonstrates the degree to which his art had separated itself from that of Rodin, whose treatment of the same theme is well known; Brancusi's figures are almost reduced to two adjacent cubes of stone. His several versions of *Portrait of Mlle. Pogany* (1912, Philadelphia MA; 1913, London Tate) moved towards a conception of the head as a smooth egg with a few simplified features. In *Torso of a Young Man* (1917, Cleveland MA) this theme, which was originally treated naturalistically, was reduced to a vertical cylinder of polished bronze, resting on two disks representing the tops of the thighs. The egg-shape is realized in a number of abstract sculptures entitled *The New-born* (1915, Philadelphia MA; 1915, New York MMA; 1920, Paris MNAM). The Paris reconstruction of his studio also contains several egg-shapes designed for the blind, to be appreciated by touch.

His transformation of the bird motif is particularly interesting. As early as 1910 he had produced a fairly naturalistic sculpture of a standing bird with vertically outstretched neck, based on Mayan sculpture, *Pasarea Maiastra* (1910, New York MMA). In numerous subsequent versions, the form became more elongated, smoother and more abstract until, in a work such as *Bird in Space* (1928, New York MMA), the bird shape became a metaphor of flight. This soaring curve epitomizes Brancusi's own aspiration towards perfection.

BRANGWYN, Frank (1867–1956), English painter. Although Brangwyn worked (1882) under William Morris, he was essentially self-taught. His easel paintings won him a great reputation. They were painted in a 19th century style, with rich colour, preference for dappled lighting effects, and a fondness for exotic detail. There are large collections in the Brangwyn

Museums in Bruges and in Walthamstow, London. His decorative work is more interesting. It consists of large tapestry-like panels on historical themes which involve considerable powers of organization. The finest examples are at the Skinners' Hall, London (1904–9), the Civic Centre at Swansea, originally executed for the House of Lords (1926–30), and the Rockefeller Center, New York (1932). Brangwyn was knighted in 1941.

BRAQUE, Georges (1882–1963), French painter. The son of a house painter, he learned his father's trade as a youth in Le Havre where he also attended Art school. He went (1902) to Paris and befriended Friesz, making excursions with him to Anvers (1906) and La Ciotat (1907). He adopted Fauvist techniques, but used colour and separated brush strokes with a certain restraint, *eg Antwerp Harbour* (1906, Basle Kunstmuseum). In 1907 he met Apollinaire, who introduced him to **Picasso** who influenced Braque's landscapes at L'Estaque (1908). These already contained, in essence, Cubist stylization and flattening of space, as in *Road near L'Estaque* (1908, New York MMA). In 1908, rejected by the jury of the Salon d'Automne, he held an exhibition at Kahnweiler's Gallery. Matisse and Vauxcelles commented on the little cubes that appeared on his canvases (the origin of the expression **Cubism**). He worked with Picasso in the south of France in the summers of 1911–13. This was the period known as Analytic Cubism, in which Braque's work was very similar to Picasso's. Both were characterized by an intense intellectual quality, a very restricted palette, and a certain decorative tendency, as in *Man with a Guitar* (1911, New York MMA). The printed letter was incorporated in many of Braque's paintings, *eg The Portuguese* (1911, Basle, Kunstmuseum), and he was the first to use the **Collage** technique. Synthetic Cubism began in 1912 but was interrupted by World War I.

From 1920 nudes and landscapes took their place with still-lifes in his repertoire. At the same time, his treatment of form became more realistic, and his delicate, subtle palette became very rich, *eg Still Life* (1925, London Tate), *The Table* (1928, New York MMA). He acquired an exuberant, decorative style,

Georges Braque: Still Life with Black Fishes *(1942, Paris MNAM).*

retaining elements of reality only to give weight in his pictures, some of which are among the finest of all his works, *eg Still Life* (1926, Glasgow Kelvingrove), *Still Life with Black Fishes* (1942, Paris MNAM). He painted on a larger scale, in sharply contrasting colours (*eg* lemon yellows and pinks), flattening the figures: the result was a form of mannerism containing elements of fantasy, as in *Le Duo* (1937, Paris MNAM). In 1931 he temporarily adopted a neo-classical style, and executed plaster engravings and illustrations. He achieved success in the United States winning the Carnegie Prize in 1937. His post-War works, often depicting his studio, were lighter and more fragmented in drawing style, the subject broken up into a mosaic of colour rather like that of Bissière and Bazaine, without upsetting the basic realism of the portrayal, *eg Le Philodendron* (1951, Washington, Phillips Gallery); *Red Still Life* (1955, Stuttgart). Commissioned to decorate a large ceiling in the Louvre, he painted a controversial flock of great black birds. He designed pieces of jewellery, also presented to the Louvre. Braque was an absolute master of colour and his permanent concern was the depiction of beauty. He continually attempted to produce an art that conceals 'art' in order to create profoundly meditated works.

BRATBY, John (1928–), English painter. After studying at the Kingston School of Art and at the Royal College of Art (1950–4), he embarked upon a series of interiors, still-lifes, and portraits. These featured the bric-à-brac of everyday life *eg Still Life with Chip Fryer* (1954, London Tate) in chaotic profusion, deliberately assaulting traditional taste with pictures of dustbins, *Dustbins* (1954, London RCA), and even lavatories. He is one of the most successful of English realists. He has acknowledged some affinity with **Stanley Spencer**. His strong colour and drawing in heavy lines of impasto are derived from van Gogh. His more complex pictures, however, while remaining realistic in detail, contain multiple viewpoints: portraits of his wife and reflected self-portraits, and sometimes even the image of his own hands painting the picture all lock into a composition of large format that is a kind of painter's autobiography, *eg Window, Self-Portrait, Jean and Hands* (1957, London Tate).

BRAUNER, Victor (1903–66), Romanian painter of the School of Paris. His early work in Romania was controversial. He went to Paris in 1930, where he met his compatriot Brancusi. A contribution of his to the Salon des Surindépendants gained the attention of the Surrealists, and he became friendly with Tanguy. He took part in all the activities of the Surrealists until 1949, both in Europe and America. His painting of fantastic themes, technically very accomplished, incorporates figures in part inspired by primitive art, treated in flat areas of bright colour, and standing out against well-unified backgrounds. After World War II, he practised wax modelling to great effect. His art is derived from the images of psychoanalysis, the central tenet of Surrealist art, and its effect is strange and often decorative. His *Endotête* is in the Musée d'Art Moderne, Paris.

BRAYER, Yves (1907–), French painter. A pupil of Lucien Simon, his *Riding School* (1927) brought him the Chanavard Prize and a travelling scholarship. This enabled him to visit Spain, where brilliant lights and hard shadows helped him to simplify his drawing. He won the Prix de Rome in 1930 and spent some time in Italy, producing a large number of compositions in which he vividly captured the Italian scene and people. In 1942 he designed for the ballet, eg *El Amor Brujo*, and painted portraits of dancers. Provence provided him with the inspiration for a large number of paintings, airy, vibrant landscapes including horses, eg *Chevaux de Camargue* (1954, Paris MAMVP). He is essentially an illustrator and decorator, but his ability to extract the essential details from a scene and to place them in a firm composition make him more than a mere popularizer.

BREITNER, Georges Hendrick (1857–1923), Dutch painter. A realistic artist, his career parallels aspects of contemporary French art. He produced freely executed genre studies in the manner of Manet, eg *Girls Playing* (Amsterdam Stedelijk M) and was also briefly influenced by Japanese art, eg *Reclining Girl in a Red Kimono* (Amsterdam Stedelijk M). His views of Amsterdam, although influenced by Impressionism, are darker, more detailed, and closer to the tradition of the Dutch 17th century masters.

BRETON, André (1896–1966), French author. In 1919, he helped found *Littérature*, the organ of the **Dada** movement, which advocated the destruction of traditional values in logic, morality and art. The cult of the irrational led him to **Surrealism** which he helped to found, gaining the name 'the Pope of Surrealism'. His *Surrealist Manifesto* (1924) was based on psychological automatism and the rejection of all conventions. His *Second Surrealist Manifesto* (1930) rejected political motives; five years later Breton left the Communist Party. He fled to the U.S. in 1941 but returned to Paris after the War and in 1947 organized an international Surrealist exhibition.

Breton's concept of art as a supernatural agency to be cultivated in its purest form led to his inflexible attitude towards the deviations of his friends. He attacked De Chirico for his repudiation of the movement, Max Ernst and Miró for their collaboration with the Ballets Russes and Salvador Dali on whom he inflicted the cruel and celebrated anagram 'Avida Dollars'. In *Surrealism and Painting* (1928) and *Genesis and Perspectives of Surrealism* (1941), he attempted to discover the lyrical unity between the perceptions of the subconscious mind and a fabled, superior form of reality. His ultimate aim was to renounce the principle of identity.

BRIANCHON, Maurice (1899–), French painter. He taught at the Ecole des Arts Décoratifs in 1937, and from 1949 at the Ecole des Beaux-Arts. He has had considerable success as a theatrical designer, and theatre scenes make up a large proportion of his easel painting. They are very much in the tradition of **Degas**, but with a bold simplification of form, and rather deep colours (slightly similar to those of Braque). Since 1940 his range has increased and includes landscapes, still life, race-course scenes, and scenes of contemporary life, eg *Coronation of Queen Elizabeth II* (1953). His palette has become lighter and more vivid, with the colours deployed in geometrical areas on the background. His modelling is delicate, and he is a lover of subtle atmospheric effects.

BRODSKY, Isaac (1884–1939), Russian painter. A typical representative of Socialist

Realism, his most important work is *Lenin at the Smolny Institute* (Moscow Tretchiakov Museum).

BROOKS, James (1906–   ), American painter. He went to New York in 1926 and he found work as a lettering artist, attending art classes and painting in his spare time. He worked on the **WPA Art Project** (1938–42) as a mural painter, and, in his enormous *Flight* (New York, La Guardia Airport, obliterated), developed a monumental Cubist realism. After World War II he became a close friend of **Pollock** and **Tomlin** and, following their lead, developed an Abstract Expressionist style with broad Gestures. The earlier works in this style were the more fluid, using calligraphic swirls and drips of paint, *eg Number 27* (1950, New York, Whitney Museum). More recently the colour-patches have become larger, tending to conflict more with each other, as in *Boon* (1957, London Tate).

BRUCE, Patrick Henry (1881–1937), American painter. After studying with Robert Henri in New York he moved to Paris where he passed the remainder of his life. He studied with Matisse and from 1912 to 1914 worked with **Delaunay**. In the 1920s he isolated himself from other artists to develop a classically austere form of **Cubism**, using simple shapes and the interplay of plane surfaces painted in flat colours.

BRUCKE, Die (the Bridge), group founded (1905) in Dresden, Germany, by the four painters **Heckel**, Bleyl, **Kirchner**, and **Schmidt-Rottluff**. These artists worked in the studios of Kirchner and Heckel, whose walls they covered with paintings. They also practised engraving and sculpture. In 1906 Pechstein, Nolde and Amiet joined the group. Their first exhibition was held in a factory, and then in the Dresden Art Gallery. They organized a travelling exhibition, and when their works were rejected by the Berlin Secession in 1910, they founded the 'New Secession' with Pechstein as president. The group's headquarters moved to Berlin and Müller joined the group. In 1913, after a last exhibition in Munich, the group disbanded because of differences between Kirchner and the other members.

Although not the only manifestation of German Expressionism, Die Brucke can be said to define the style and, with Der Blaue Reiter, it was the most important movement in Germany before World War I. The early style, represented by Heckel's *Nude on Sofa* (1909, Munich NG) is closely allied to **Fauvism**, although Kirchner had already developed a related style independently of any contact with France. Similarily, in works such as Kirchner's *Staberhof Farm* (1911, Hamburg, Kunsthalle), members of the group had also been experimenting with unconventional treatments of space, before the full impact of Cubism had reached them. Eventually this produced the final style of the movement, which combined Cubist fragmentation with Fauve colour and Expressionist intensity, *eg* Schmidt-Rottluff's *Villa with Tower* (1912, Mannheim, Kunsthalle).

BRUSSELMANS, Jean (1884–1953), Belgian painter. He began as a lithographer, worked with the landscapist Verheyden and finally embarked on painting in an Impressionist style. He spent most of his life at Dilbeek, near Brussels, and painted mainly landscapes of Brabant and the North Sea coast. His style evolved towards **Expressionism**, although he was never exclusively an Expressionist, and never belonged to the Laethem-Saint-Martin group. He applied the paint thickly, in little dabs creating a patchwork in which the drawing is simplified and the colour violent. His snow-clad winter scenes are particularly successful, *eg Winter Landscape* (1942, Brussels MBA).

BRUTALIST ART, see **Dubuffet**.

BUFFET, Bernard (1928–   ), French painter. Brought up in Paris, he was admitted to the Ecole des Beaux-Arts in 1944, and soon attracted attention. He disliked the teaching there and preferred going to the Louvre to study the works of David, Gros, Rembrandt, and above all those of **Courbet**. Meanwhile, he became interested in the work of Permeke, Ensor, and of Gruber, the initiator of Miserabilism. In 1946 he exhibited a *Self-Portrait*, which had a striking, personal accent. At the age of nineteen he was admitted to the Salon des Indépendants, and to the Salon d'Automne. His canvases were already

Bernard Buffet: Still Life with Back-gammon Board *(1955, private collection); ph. Marc Vaux.*

distinguished by their inexorable linear rigidity, their austere, cold tonality, and by a feeling of space. After receiving the Prix de la Jeune Peinture in 1948, he was supported by several collectors. In 1949 he exhibited his still lifes, notably the *Raies* in which sumptuous subject-matter was allied to elegance and an economy of expression. He also painted landscapes of an intensely tragic character, *eg The Burial* (1949). In 1950 his reputation was confirmed by an exhibition in New York, and he left Paris to live in Provence. There, he painted a *Passion*, a gigantic triptych containing modern figures and permeated by a feeling of intense drama. From that time, he exhibited regularly every year in Paris, each time treating one sole theme ('Horror of War', 'Circus', 'Paris', 'Joan of Arc', 'New York', 'Birds', *etc*). Gradually, losing none of that stiff and monumental simplicity with which he summarizes forms, Buffet began to employ bright and occasionally garish colours, and a rich impasto.

His interpretations of religious themes and his great urban landscapes (Paris, New York, London, Venice) present a new and desolate view of the modern city and convey a deep sense of man dwarfed by his own civilization.

BURCHFIELD, Charles (1893–1967), American watercolourist. Although he studied for four years at the Cleveland School of Art, most of his early work was done in his spare time while working as a clerk, and later as a designer in a wallpaper firm. Highly original, it consisted largely of close-up studies of nature, drawings of individual plants and motifs in a style that was both observant and symbolic of the larger universe, similar to the late drawings of van Gogh, but quite independent, *eg Insects at Twilight* (1917, New York MMA). Out of these motifs, and from studies of human expressions, Burchfield distilled a number of symbols, which he called 'Conventions of Abstract Thoughts'. These were incorporated in, for example, drawings of houses to produce Expressionist pictures of great power, *eg Church Bells Ringing, Rainy Winter Night* (1917, Cleveland MA). Again, Burchfield's development seems to have been independent of Europe, though he was influenced by 19th century books of fairy-tales, the illustrations of which show similar anthropomorphic distortions. In 1929 he gave up his job to paint full time. His work of this second period (*c* 1930–43) was entirely realistic, though still with emotional overtones, taking the dirty rainy cities and industrial landscapes as subjects, as in *Rainy Night* (1930, San Diego, Fine Arts Gallery), *Freight Cars in March* (1933, London Tate). In some ways it paralleled the work of **Hopper**. After 1943 Burchfield returned to lyrical nature subjects.

BURRA, Edward (1905–), English watercolourist. Encouraged to paint by his parents after severe illness, he preferred to use watercolour, which can be worked while sitting down. He studied at the Royal College of Art. His work, large in scale and scope, is figurative, but he uses hard forms and colours, rather like **Léger**. Most of his subjects are comments on contemporary life and he often uses subtle caricaturing, a development from Grosz, *eg Harlem* (1936, London Tate). Burra was also associated with the Surrealist movement and many of his works of 1935–45 show the influence of De Chirico and especially of **Dali**, *eg Soldiers* (1941, London Tate). After World War II, he painted a higher proportion of more naturalistic pictures, showing a purity of design less apparent in his earlier work.

BURRI, Alberto (1915–), Italian painter. He was trained as a doctor and did not paint until his internment in Texas during World War II. His experiences as an army doctor gave him an obsession with the image of blood soaking through torn bandages. When he returned to live in Rome (1946) he began to paint a series of large abstract compositions on this theme, combining pieces of torn sacking with paint. The stitches in the material barely hold, but what seeps through is paint, not blood, and it often has a triumphant quality which belies the origin of the image, as in *Sacco e Rosso* (1954, London Tate), *S.C.5* (1954, Harvard, Fogg Museum). Since then he has used other materials, exploring the possibilities of each in a series of works before moving on: burnt cloth, burnt wood as in *Legno e Bianco I* (1956, New York Guggenheim) and rusted iron as in *Ferro Grande* (1958, Houston MFA). Burri's art is related to Abstract Expressionism, but he works quite independently. He is a natural painter whose feeling for his materials and power of monumental statement places him at the forefront of post-War art.

BURY, Pol (1922–), Belgian painter and sculptor. A student at the Académie des Beaux-Arts at Mons, at first he painted in a figurative Surrealist style, exhibiting in the International Surrealist Exhibition in Brussels (1945). He later became associated (1949–53) with the **Cobra** group, painting in an abstract style. In 1953 he gave up painting and turned to constructions of flat planes which slid over and under one another, at first moved by hand, later by motor. In 1959 he started to use 'érectiles' (fine wires projecting from the surface like stems or antennae and moved very slowly from behind), *eg 3069 Dots on an Oval Ground* (1966, London Tate). He has also adapted this technique to arrangements of sculptural elements, as in *Trente et Un Batons* (1964, New York

MMA), *16 Balls, 16 Cubes on 7 Shelves* (1966, London Tate). More recently, he has used objects with polished surfaces to create a constantly changing series of reflections. Bury's works are among the most remarkable products of **Kinetic Art**. They never look as if they are going to move, the separate elements moving so slowly and unexpectedly that one wonders if one is seeing things. Consequently, the movement has something primeval about it, like a stirring deep in the earth accompanied by a subdued rustling noise. Sometimes the nuzzling, stroking movements in his works have strong erotic overtones.

BUTLER, Reg (1913–), British sculptor. He trained as an architect, and practised until 1950. In 1941, however, he had begun working as a blacksmith and took up sculpture, becoming an assistant to Henry Moore in 1947. He was represented at the Venice Biennales (1952, 1954) and won the 'Unknown Political Prisoner' competition in London with *Three Heads of Watchers* (1951–2, London Tate). Butler's bronzes are all of the human figure. First they were Surrealist in style, but they soon became more naturalistic, emphasizing the roundness of the torso and exaggerating by contrast the thinness of the arms and legs. Nonetheless his works can be very expressive in a direct human sense, not unlike the sculpture of Degas, *eg Girl* (1953–4, London Tate; New York MMA; and elsewhere). In his more recent works, Butler has been more concerned with the plastic and spatial qualities of his figures, making them less realistic portrayals.

C

CADELL, Francis (1883–1937), Scottish painter. After going to school in Edinburgh and attending classes at the Royal Scottish Academy, Cadell was sent (1899) by his father to Paris and Munich. There he was influenced by Post-Impressionism but, following his return to Edinburgh in 1909, he gradually developed his own style, that of a naturalistic composition in pale colours set in motion by touches of brilliant hues. Eventually, his paintings became less

Alexander Calder: Stabile *(1963, St. Paul-de-Vence, Maeght Foundation); ph. Gaspari.*

painterly and almost geometrical in composition. His pictures were cooler in feeling than those of his contemporaries, Hunter and Peploe, though in his striking use of colour he was completely original.

CAILLARD, Christian (1899–   ), French painter. His art is basically realistic in the Fauve tradition, although it makes full use of rich impasto and brilliant colours not invented earlier in the century. Caillard's colour accents, however, often tended to be trivial, and set up a colour pattern which is at odds with the structure of the subject. The strongest influence on his work was his experience of North Africa, and African scenes recur frequently in his work, as in *Petite Arabe* (1937, Algiers MBA). His pictures of figures, despite his preference for children *eg La Petite Gitane* (1936, Paris MNAM), are neither picturesque nor sentimental.

CALDER, Alexander (1898–   ), American sculptor. Although standing somewhat aloof from the main fashions of 20th century art, Calder cannot be neglected, both for his creative mind and for his invention of the mobile, a type of **Kinetic** sculpture which has greatly enlarged the possibilities of modern art. He went to Paris in 1926, where he began to make small wire models, some of which he exhibited at the Salon des Humoristes in 1927. The models resemble highly economical line drawings executed in wire and are lighthearted in intent. However, Calder soon began to make the wire outlines defining quite complex spaces, *eg Romulus and Remus* (1928, New York Guggenheim). At the same time, for his own amusement, he made a group of models representing acts from a *Circus*, many of which could be set into motion in shows he gave for his friends. At one of these he met Miró, with whom he was to find much in common. In 1931 he had his first exhibition of abstract sculpture, using metal painted in black, white and the primary colours of Mondrian's painting, but using rounded shapes which were basically organic. In 1932 his interest in motion led him to make his first mobiles, operated both by electric motors, as in *Dancing Torpedo Shape* (1932, Pittsfield, Mass., Berkshire Atheneum) and in the Neo-Constructivist *White Frame* (1934, Stock-

holm Moderna Museet). Others were freely suspended structures which swung about in light draughts of air. Early examples from 1934, 1935 and 1936 are in the Guggenheim Museum, New York.

Since, Calder's work has been divided between mobiles and non-moving sculpture (named 'stabiles' by Arp). These are usually made of flat pieces of metal forged together and occupy simple shapes which seem to be based on natural forms, as in *Whale* (1937, New York MMA). The secret of Calder's best mobiles, *eg Lobster Trap and Fish Tail* (1939, New York MMA); *Antennae with Red and Blue Dots* (1960, London Tate) lies, at least partly, in the limitation in their range of movement. Although there is an infinite number of positions any one sculpture can take up, the structure of the joints is such that they all fall into a meaningful pattern. Frequently the pattern is one in which the solid elements of different sizes act as a series of reflections or echoes of each other. Some of Calder's finest work has been done since the War, in commissioned pieces of very large scale. These include a huge mobile for Kennedy Airport, New York (1957), an outdoor motorized mobile, *The Four Elements*, for the Moderna Museet, Stockholm (1962), gigantic stabiles (*The Spiral*, 1958, Paris, UNESCO HQ; *Teodelaio*, 1962, Spoleto), and a fountain at the Los Angeles County Museum, *Hello Girls!* (1965), in which the mobile elements are ingeniously powered by the jets of water. See illus. p. 39.

CALLIGRAPHIC PAINTING. There is a tendency in modern art to consider the act of painting, like writing, as the setting down of signs meaningful in themselves. European art in the 20th century has been influenced by the use, in China and Japan, of highly stylized pictures in ordinary writing. Calligraphic signs have increased the repertoire of forms available to the modern artist; their use has provided a release for his inspiration by incorporating the spontaneity of the art of writing into the artistic process without undue interference from the intellect. Some Calligraphic Painting thus comes under the heading of **Automatic Writing**. Klee, Wols and Pollock, however, indulged in more conscious use of sign-writing in their work, *eg* Klee's *Pastoral* (1926, New

York MMA). The most consistent exponents of Calligraphic Painting are **Mark Tobey** and **Mathieu**. Hans Hartung's inspiration is also calligraphic, although in many of his works, he uses single strokes rather than whole signs. Other artists who owe something to Calligraphic Painting are Birolli, Bissière, Bissier and Vieira da Silva. A different aspect of modern art is the use of letters, numbers and words, not for their meaning, but rather as a source of familiar shapes without emotional connotations. The forms, unlike those of Calligraphic Painting, are the expressively neutral ones of a stencil or of printer's type. Exponents include Herbin and Johns.

CAMARGO, Sergio de (1930–), Brazilian sculptor. He went to Paris in 1948 to study philosophy, but took up sculpture, influenced by Brancusi and Picasso. After a period of making free plaster casts of sand and cloth he began his series of white reliefs in 1963. These consist of cylinders of wood, cut across a diagonal, fastened at various angles on to a board and the whole painted white. The formal language obviously owes much to Cubism, yet since the effect of these reliefs is to break up light in different ways depending on the position of the observer, their greatest association is with **Op**, or even **Kinetic Art**, *eg Large Split White Relief No 34/74* (1965, London Tate).

CAMDEN TOWN GROUP, a group of English artists formed (1911) from a circle of painters who used to gather in Walter Sickert's studio in Camden Town, London. They included Spencer Gore (president), Duncan Grant, Augustus John, Wyndham Lewis and Lucien Pissarro. Like the French Impressionists, they used everyday scenes from London life with a similar free handling. The colour, however, was generally sombre, in keeping with the unsalubrious subject-matter. They exhibited as a group several times between 1911 and 1913, when they merged into a larger and less coherent entity, the London Group. The Camden Town Group was one of the first cells of progressive artists in England. As a result of their experience in the group, many members became rapidly aware of more radical influences from France, exemplified by the Neo-Impressionists, the Post-Impressionists and the Fauves.

CAMOIN, Charles (1879–1965), French painter. A pupil of Gustave Moreau at the Ecole des Beaux-Arts, he was one of the Fauves, although his style retained an element of balanced realism, *eg Place de Clichy* (1907, Glasgow, Kelvingrove). During his military service in Provence he became friendly with Cézanne. Later, he was closely associated with Renoir, and was influenced by him. His work includes portraits, still lifes, nudes, interior scenes, and many landscapes of the Côte d'Azur. His art is spontaneous, with simple forms and rich colours.

CAMPENDONK, Heinrich (1889–1957), German painter. After studying in his native Krefeld and Munich, Campendonk became (1911) a member of Blaue Reiter. He taught at the Düsseldorf Academy from 1926 until he was dismissed by the Nazis (1933). His earlier style, influenced by Marc, was deliberately naive, *eg Female Nude with Cow* (1920, Wuppertal Museum). Gradually Cubist influence grew stronger, as in *The Sculptor (Zadkine)* (1924, Yale University AG), and by 1930 he had adopted a hard drawing style, with glowing colours and stippled and irridescent textures. Although influenced by Klee at this period, his work was entirely figurative, *eg Woman with Basket of Fish* (1930, Cologne, Wallraff-Richartz-Museum). Campendonk also executed many stained-glass windows.

CAMPIGLI, Massimo (1895–1971), Italian painter. While in Paris in 1919 as an Italian newspaper correspondent, he taught himself to paint. He was influenced at first by **Cubism**, as in *La Carricola* (1928, Amsterdam Stedelijk M). In 1928 he was impressed by frescoes in the Museum of Etruscan Art in Rome. His style, which remained basically unchanged, employed the same pastel colours, the same flattening of space, the same archaic simplification of the body. Another influence was that of Fra Angelico and early Renaissance frescoes.

Almost all his works consist of a number of figures, presented frontally on a plain background (often textured like a wall), sometimes illustrating legendary themes, *eg The Shipwreck* (1937, Hartford, Wadsworth Atheneum), sometimes modern scenes, *eg The Grand Concert* (1935,

Richmond, Virginia Museum). Very often the picture surface is arbitrarily divided into areas which frame the figures. In his more recent work he permitted himself a greater abstraction within the basic structure, *eg White Woman and Houses* (1960, Paris MNAM). He also executed frescoes for the League of Nations, Geneva (1941) and for Padua University (1940).

CAPOGROSSI, Giuseppe (1900–   ), Italian painter. He lived in Paris (1927–32), began to produce abstract work in 1949, and in 1950 founded the Gruppo Romano. His art, which was originally influenced by Magnelli, is concerned exclusively with the picture surface. This is articulated by clusters of large black pseudo-Calligraphic signs (shapes like the letters E, H and A predominate) sometimes with touches of other colours.

CARDENAS, Augustin (1927–   ), Cuban sculptor. He was a member of the Cuban avant-garde Eleven group (1953–6) and later of the School of Paris (1955). His abstract carvings in wood are lyrical and distinguished by open-work passages with thin filaments of wood which are set off against the main masses. A number of his works have a vertical, totem-like form.

CARLES, Arthur (1882–1952), American painter. While studying in Paris, where he exhibited at the Salon d'Automne, he was given his first American show by Stieglitz in 1910. His works at that time were very firm in structure and influenced by Matisse in their bright colour and brilliant handling, *eg L'Eglise* (1910, New York Metropolitan Museum). After the **Armory Show**, at which he exhibited, he became influenced by **Cubism**, though he gradually allowed his profuse colour and free brushwork to break free of the Cubist grid in a manner anticipating Abstract Expressionism.

CARO, Anthony (1924–   ), English sculptor. He studied engineering at Cambridge, then sculpture at the Royal Academy Schools, and became assistant to Henry Moore (1951–3). His early bronzes of the human figure are chunky, *eg Woman Waking Up* (1955, London Tate). In 1959 he went to the U.S. on a Ford Foundation grant and adopted a non-figurative style. He has since returned to America several times as a guest teacher. His present style, unlike his earlier work, is not only totally abstract, but makes no concessions to human scale or taste. It is executed in steel sheets and girders, painted in strong colours and arranged with total disregard for the normal criteria of sculpture as an object. His works rest directly on the floor, often apparently precariously: girders and rods project at all angles, claiming the surrounding space. Obviously influenced by **David Smith**, Caro arrives with difficulty at statements which are often highly compelling, as in *Yellow Swing* (1965, London Tate). Caro won the sculpture prize at the 1959 Paris Biennale and a prize at the 1966 Venice Biennale. He is one of the strongest influences on young British sculptors, partly through his work as a teacher at St. Martin's School of Art, London, where his pupils included Annesley, Bolus, King, Scott, Tucker and Witkin.

CARRA, Carlo (1881–1966), Italian painter. Originally an interior decorator, he took up easel painting in Milan. At the 1900 Universal Exhibition in Paris, he was impressed by French painting and returned to the Art School at Milan. After participating (1909–11) in **Futurism**, *eg Leaving the Theatre* (1910, London Tate), *Burial of the Anarchist Galli* (1911, New York MMA), he returned to Paris, meeting Apollinaire, Picasso and the Cubists. He introduced the printed word into large **Collages**, in which, unlike Cubist collage, the meanings as well as the shapes of the words were significant. In 1916 he met **De Chirico** at Ferrara, and enthusiastically took up **Metaphysical Painting**, using very sharp drawing, clear light and a restricted range of subject elements. He said: 'I do not see why tailor's dummies, brass fish and geographical maps should be less worthy of study than Cézanne's apples, bottles and pipes.'

Carrà later returned to a more naturalistic style, based on the hieratic art of Giotto (about whom he wrote an important book) and Masaccio, and became the founder of the Novecento group. He painted seascapes such as *Summer* (1930, Milan GAM), in which a curious sense of space is brought into play. Carrà's art with its pale tonality and precise and rigorous formal imaginativeness is a synthesis of primitive painting and modern art.

CARTON, Jean (1912–), French sculptor. A pupil of the Ecole des Arts Appliqués, and of the Ecole des Beaux-Arts, he was exhibiting works by the time he was twenty-three. In London (1937), his works were placed beside those of his friends, Despiau, Malfray and Maillol. His first one-man exhibition was in 1938. In 1946 he was awarded the Prix Blumenthal, and in 1948 the Prix de la Villa Abd-el-Tif, where he lived for three years. His sculpture includes bronze nudes and busts. Strongly classical in manner, they reveal profound psychological insight, and a constant search for complete expression. Carton's work thus attains a balanced, lucid character which is exceptional in modern art.

CARZOU, Jean (1907–), French painter. A self-taught artist, he began by drawing for newspapers and journals. He experimented with abstract art, and made collages (1931–4), then painted compositions with schematic human figures bathed in fluorescent light. He spent World War II in the south of France, and became interested in drawing farm implements, which became a recurring theme. They litter the desert landscape of the work with which he won the Hallmark Prize in 1949: *Shepherd and the Magi* (Kansas City, Nelson Gallery).

In 1953, his exhibition on the theme of Venice established his condensed graphic style with bright, intense colours. In 1957, his *Apocalypse* series presented a desolate view of barren forests of pylons, rail junctions and guided missiles ready to fire. Carzou's canvases, influenced by **Surrealism** and by Metaphysical Painting usually evoke fantastic landscapes with ruins and abandoned objects, seen across immense nostalgic vistas and bathed in an inexplicable light, *eg Le Port Abandonné* (1951, Adelaide NG). Sometimes they include nudes, who haunt these ruins as in the pictures of **Delvaux**, *eg La Baie des Songes* (1949, Paris MNAM).

CASORATI, Felice (1886–1963), Italian painter. His earlier works were influenced by Art Nouveau, *eg Old Woman* (1907, Turin GAM); but *c* 1919 he began to paint in a style akin to the Valori Plastici movement. The cold clear light and statuesque figures and objects showed early Renaissance influence, *eg Woman with Basin*

(1919, Turin GAM); *Noon* (1922, Trieste GAM). In the 1930s his compositions became more varied, his colour richer and his drawing style more summary, *eg The Citizens* (1932, Boston MFA). After World War II his works became more abstract, *eg Woman* (1956, Venice GAM).

CASSATT, Mary (1845–1927), American painter. She studied at Art School in Philadelphia, and in 1870 travelled in Europe before settling in Paris. She was accepted at the Salon of 1872 but refused in 1875 and 1877, she began to move towards Impressionism under the influence of **Degas** who admired her work. In 1878 she took part in the fourth Impressionist exhibition. Her drawing remained very precise and solid, but her interest in light and her familiar feeling for contemporary life relate her style to Impressionism. This is evident in the paintings on her favourite theme, namely, motherhood, *eg Mother and Child* (1892, Chicago Art Inst.; *c* 1902, Cincinnati AM); *Lady at the Tea Table* (1885, New York Metropolitan). She was also influenced by Japanese prints, especially those of Utamaro, whose style she adapted ingeniously in her own prints. She was instrumental in introducing modern French painting to the United States.

CAULFIELD, Patrick (1936–), English painter. After studying at the Royal College of Art he had his first one-man show in 1965, and exhibited at the São Paulo Bienal in 1967. He paints traditional subjects (often free versions of works by Old Masters) in a rather mass-produced style, with simplified forms, unvarying black outlines and flat unmodelled colour, as in a cheap reproduction; there are clear parallels with **Lichtenstein**. Caulfield's earlier works are Pop Art only in the negative sense that they seem to criticize the popular taste, and in many recent paintings he uses a similar principle of design as a vehicle for a colour composition not so different from **Matisse**, *eg Pottery* (1969, London Tate).

CAVAILLES, Jules (1901–), French painter. His painting belongs to what has been called the poetic realist style developed from Impressionism and Fauvism. In his landscapes, *eg Fenêtre à Honfleur* (Paris MNAM), his interiors, and his still-

Paul Cézanne: La Montagne Sainte-Victoire *(1904, Philadelphia MA); ph. Giraudon.*

lifes, *eg Blue Ewer* (1945, Paris MNAM), he employs bright, limpid colours and light, undulating forms. These are some- times outlined against the blue back- ground of the canvas, producing a fresh and poetic effect.

His first sculpture in iron and plaster dates from 1947. He began with repoussé work in thin sheets of lead, and later used very thin wire, which he beat, twisted and soldered. In 1954, he exhibited his first sculpture, *Le Poisson* (Paris MNAM). Then, using many different materials (scrap iron, springs, belts, tin cans) he composed his 'amalgams' in the form of insects, winged men, and fantastic beasts, all possessing curious expressive power, *eg Torso* (1956, New York MMA); *The Man of St. Denis* (1958, London Tate). Around 1955 he used large sheets of iron and created more solid structures with controlled rhythm. One of them, a car crushed by a pile-driver, brought him a good deal of publicity. In 1970 he changed direction completely, exhibiting *Plastiques*, soft shiny undulating sculptures in coloured Polyurean. He exhibited at the 1956 Venice Biennale and won the Carnegie Prize in 1959. César's art is primarily in the stream of **Expressionism**, although the use of **Assemblage** relates it to Surrealism and to the work of Eduardo Paolozzi and John Chamberlain.

CEZANNE, Paul (1839–1906), French painter. After a short period in his father's bank, he turned to painting and lived in Paris and Provence until 1872. His difficult temperament was a deterrent to friendship and conventional success. In 1866 his first painting for the Salon was rejected, as indeed were all those (with one exception) which he submitted during his life. His early style was close to that of Courbet, though he concentrated more on compositional structure using heavy impasto in sombre colours. These works had a massive solidity, *eg L'Homme au Bonnet de Coton* (1865–7, New York Metropolitan), *Portrait of his Father* (London NG), *L'Eglise du Village* (*c* 1868, Cambridge, Fitzwilliam Museum). He also painted flamboyant Romantic figure compositions influenced by Veronese and Delacroix, *eg The Rape, The Orgy*. He was refused admission to the Ecole des Beaux-Arts on the grounds that he had 'a colourist's temperament' and painted 'with excess'.

From 1872–83 his style had affinities with **Impressionism**. For two years he lived and worked with his friends Pissarro and Guillaumin, learning the use of light colour, as in *La Maison du Pendu* (1873,

CESAR Baldaccini (1921–   ), French sculptor. A pupil at the Ecole des Beaux-Arts, Marseilles, from the age of fourteen he learned carving in stone and wood. Later he studied at the Ecole des Beaux-Arts, Paris.

Paris Louvre) and *View of Anvers* (1873–5, Chicago, Art Inst.). He took part in the Impressionist exhibitions of 1874 and 1877, when, in spite of the sarcasm of some critics, he found people willing to buy his paintings; among them was Victor Choquet who was to become an enthusiastic admirer. His style grew more expansive and developed the classical qualities of balanced line and radiant colour, *eg The Bay of Marseilles* (1883–5, New York Metropolitan). While retaining a very subtle tonality, he no longer used small brush strokes but painted boldly in large masses.

Becoming extremely morose, Cézanne was less and less approachable. Guillemet succeeded in having one of his canvases hung in the Salon of 1882, but it attracted little attention. He spent most of the period from 1883–95 living in obscurity in Provence. He severed his friendship with Emile Zola, who had used Cézanne as the model for his failed artist Claud Lantier in *L'Oeuvre*. In 1888, which he spent in Paris, he frequently met van Gogh, Emile Bernard and Gauguin but never got on very well with them. In 1894 he met Clemenceau and Rodin in Monet's house, and threw himself at Rodin's feet in homage. His painting, at this time, had achieved an extraordinary degree of maturity and perfection, *eg La Montagne Sainte-Victoire* (1887, London Courtauld Galleries), *Bathers in Front of a Tent* (1885, New York Metropolitan), *Portrait of Mme. Cézanne in Red* (1890, São Paulo MAM). These works clearly show both the similarities and differences between Cézanne and the Impressionists. Like them, he was exclusively concerned with the subject before him and with the business of converting visual sensation into a picture, but his process of setting down the visual world was unique. The Impressionists were concerned with the immediate qualities of the scene (light, colour, atmosphere, space, *etc*); Cézanne was more interested in the structure of the picture, which had to have its own logic while remaining true to the motif. Cézanne painstakingly studied objects to grasp the relationship between them. Unlike the Impressionists, he admired the Old Masters for their composition; he stated that his ambition was to 're-do Poussin from Nature'. His finest works show a classical balance of form and a sense of space similar to Poussin's. He emphasized and subtly alternated shapes to express more truly their relationship to nearby forms, *eg* the player's arms in *Joueurs de Cartes* (1885–9, London, Courtauld Galleries).

Another important aspect of Cézanne's style was his use of colour to indicate space. He almost entirely abandoned conventional modelling and used little touches of colour juxtaposed to create the effect of curvature, either to distinguish one form from another or to make the picture recede in a perspective that was independent of the drawing. Thus, the picture surface is a mosaic of colour touches which are used (even in the sky) to relate one object to another and to build up an independent structural net.

Recognition began to come very slowly after 1895. In his gallery in the Rue Lafitte, Vollard exhibited a hundred and fifty of Cézanne's paintings. The press and the public reaction was scornful. However, Cézanne's reputation grew, especially in Germany and Switzerland. Several young painters, including Emile Bernard and Camoin, visited him in Aix. In 1900 **Maurice Denis** exhibited his famous *Homage to Cézanne* (Paris MNAM) showing the painter working at a still life surrounded by his admirers, Odilon Redon, Roussel, Sérusier, Vuillard and Maurice Denis. Cézanne took part in the Centennial Universal Exhibition of 1900 although his contribution went almost unnoticed. His canvases began to command fairly high prices at sales; in 1904 a room at the Salon d'Automne was devoted to his work and in 1905 he showed the *Grandes Baigneuses* (Philadelphia MA; version of 1900–6, London NG) on which he had been working for seven years. In 1906, during a storm, he caught a chill and several days later he died. The style of his last years is represented by works such as *Le Lac d'Annecy* (1896, London Courtauld Galleries), *La Montagne Sainte-Victoire* (1898, Baltimore MA), *Sous-bois Provençal* (c 1900, New York MMA), *Le Cabanon de Jourdan* (1906, Basle Kunstmuseum). In these the structural qualities are intensified, in particular the use of a second structure of colour patches. Even 'non-significant' areas such as the sky, are given as much detail as foliage or buildings and are an active part in the composition. A characteristic feature of his late works is the growing freedom in the treatment of form which tends increasingly to be reduced to geometrical volumes, sometimes isolated on the canvas. He believed that nature should be regarded as curved forms, cones, cylinders and spheres, the famous maxim so often quoted by the Cubists. His stylistic exercises were, however, based on direct observation of nature.

After his death, large exhibitions of his work were held with increasing frequency in France and elsewhere. In particular Roger Fry's two Post-Impressionist exhibitions in London in 1910 and 1912, and the Armory Show in New York in 1913 contributed to Cézanne's influence.

Although Cézanne's oeuvre and career belong mainly to the 19th century, his influence on modern art, which is greater than that of any other forerunner, dates from the first decades of the 20th century. His theories were a basis for **Cubism**, which revolutionized 20th century art. Also his works have been the example for many other artists seeking to balance fidelity to nature and pictorial design.

CHABAUD, Auguste (1882–1955), French painter. He exhibited at the Salon des Indépendants and at the Salon d'Automne (1902–12), painting in a Cubist style with violent colour contrasts and simplified forms. His café-concerts, balls, circuses, views of Paris and night scenes, are highly modelled and curiously composed in relation to the surface of the canvas. From 1921, he lived a solitary life in Provence, where he painted landscapes and rustic scenes in a sober, almost monochrome style.

CHADWICK, Lynn (1914–), English sculptor. He trained as an architectural draughtsman. He began making **Mobiles**, however, which he exhibited in London (1950). These, eg *Dragonfly* (1951, London Tate), are more complex than **Calder's** and are more biomorphic. From these he turned to stabile sculpture, welding iron in a manner rather like that by César. Success came quickly. He won a prize in the *Unknown Political Prisoner* competition of 1953 and took the International Sculpture Prize at the 1956 Venice Biennale. His works are to be seen in New York (MMA), Buffalo, Chicago, Ottawa and Pittsburgh. He sculpts figures with bulky faceted bodies with spiky legs and birdlike heads. They are often joined either in a sexual encounter, or in a dance, or both, eg *Winged Figures* (1955, Brussels MBA; version in London Tate). Although more angular, his style has much in common with that of Reg Butler.

CHAGALL, Marc (1887–), French painter, born in Russia. He spent his childhood in a Jewish community which had a great influence on him. In his autobiography, the painter has described the liveliness and kindliness of the people. He learned to draw at Vitebsk, and his first works depicted Jewish life. He failed the entrance examination for the School of Art in St. Petersburg in 1907, but was admitted to Bakst's studio. With the help of the lawyer Winaver, he went to Paris (1910), where he met Apollinaire, Soutine, Modigliani, Léger and La Fresnaye. He was influenced by **Fauvism**, which inspired his characteristic use of intense colour, by **Cubism**, eg *The Poet* (1911, Philadelphia MA), and particularly by the **Orphism** of Delaunay, cf *View of Paris through a Window* (1913, New York, Guggenheim). This last showed him how to create a powerful nostalgic vision, juxtaposing naive and realistic elements, using subjects from his childhood and from Jewish folklore, eg *I and the Village* (1911, New York MMA). His style, however, remains exclusively his own. A study of one of his simpler works, such as *The Poet Reclining* (1915, London Tate) shows how Chagall was able to dispense with current fashion and use a primitive vision, as pure as that of Rousseau.

His first one-man exhibition held in Berlin (1914), in the Der Sturm Gallery, caused a sensation. On his return to Russia in 1914, he was mobilized as a camouflage painter in St. Petersburg. In 1915 he married Bella, whom he painted in a number of happy works, eg *Double Portrait with Wineglass* (1917, Paris MNAM). During the Russian Revolution he was in charge of Fine Arts in the region of Vitebsk, where he founded local museums, and an academy to which he invited as teachers avant-garde painters such as Malevich, Pougny and Lissitzky. He executed decors, costumes and murals for the Jewish theatre. He left Russia in 1922, and returned to France. Ambroise

Vollard commissioned him to illustrate Gogol's *Dead Souls* (96 engravings, first published in 1949), the *Fables* of La Fontaine (1926, published in 1952), and the Bible. During this time Chagall discovered the beauty of the flowers and vegetation in the Midi, and composed a series of landscapes and still lifes in more flowing style, *eg Landscape at Ile Adam* (1925. St. Louis AM). He also continued his fantasy works, with the frequent recurrence of images of flying lovers and bouquets of flowers, themes which brought him close to **Redon**, *eg Bouquet with Flying Lovers* (1934–47, London Tate).

Chagall's painting style remains basically ,naturalistic, as can be seen in such 'straight' works as *Bella in Green* (1934, Amsterdam Stedelijk M). In 1931 he went to Palestine to open the Tel-Aviv Museum; his art gained from this contact with the Orient and from his reading of the Old Testament. After 1935, much of his work was inspired by social and religious themes (*eg* intolerance) dramatically presented. He painted numerous Crucifixions, *eg White Crucifixion* (1938, Chicago Art Inst.). In 1939, after being awarded the Carnegie Prize, he left with his wife Bella and his daughter Ida for the United States, where he had a triumphant reception. After World War II, he returned to Paris and became a French citizen. He painted several ballet decors, including ones for Stravinsky's *Firebird* (1945) and for *Daphnis and Chloe* (1958). From this time onwards his fame was international. He received the Grand Prix of the Venice Biennale for engraving in 1948. His painting became progressively more luminous, with vibrant colours and undulating forms, and like many other artists (*cf* **Miró**) possibly in response to the rise of **Abstract Expressionism**, he simplified his colour schemes, producing canvases with a dominant hue, *eg Blue Circus* (1950, London Tate). His interest in ceramics and stained glass emerged at this time. He composed a series of twelve windows symbolizing the Twelve Tribes for the synagogue of the Hadassah Medical Centre in Jerusalem. They were installed in 1962 after being exhibited in New York and Paris. At André Malraux's request he painted the ceiling of the Opéra in Paris; this work was unveiled in September 1964. Chagall's art cannot be said to belong to any one school. There are obvious analogies with Surrealism (as André Breton pointed out in 1940), Cubism and German Fauvism, his inspiration in Jewish and Russian folklore and the influence of the Paris School are equally apparent, but all these stylistic elements have been subordinated to the personality of the artist. His lyrical art, with its imaginative grace, is profoundly nostalgic and humanitarian.

CHAMBERLAIN, John (1927–), American sculptor. Born in Rochester, Indiana, he studied at the Art Inst. of Chicago, and Black Mountain College. He pioneered the use of automobile metal. The pieces of steel are often painted, then welded together to form abstract sculpture. His work has been compared with the artist César, who uses crushed and compressed cars for his sculpture. Chamberlain belongs to the New York School, and exhibited at the 'New York Painting and Sculpture: 1940–70' show at the New York Metropolitan.

CHANCE IN ART. Artists of very different tendencies have been interested in chance procedures in art. Leonardo da Vinci recommended study of rough patches on stones and walls as a means of discovering new forms of composition. Analogous is the use of *objets trouvés* as starting points for works. The **Dada** movement, the very name of which was chosen by a chance procedure, made use of accident as a way of attacking the traditional attitude to the craftsman-artist. Duchamp systematically investigated chance procedures in the construction of his *Bride Stripped Bare . . . .* (1915–23). In 1915 Arp made collages by dropping scraps of paper at random and gluing them where they fell.

Chance procedures have been adopted both by artists in the Surrealist/Expressionist orbit, and by those with a Constructivist approach. In the one case, chance offers a release from inherited traditions of subject and form, and frees the artist's subconscious; in the other, chance forms the necessary variable element for works which are otherwise developed according to strict rules. **Automatic Writing** is an example of the former technique, as is the large role played by accident in **Action Painting**. On the other hand, even an artist as disciplined as Kelly has drawn numbers from a box to determine the arrangement of shapes in some works of the early 1950s. Attempts to teach computers to 'create' art usually follow the same pattern. In much **Kinetic Art** similarly, the artist makes the rules, but the actual appearance of the work at any one moment is unpredictable. This applies especially to the work of Calder, Bury. Medalla and von Graevenitz.

Finally, chance procedures are sometimes used for realistic ends; rather than be bound by his prejudices and sense of composition, the artist resolves to reproduce what he sees exactly as it happens to be arranged. The table-tops of Daniel Spoerri (see **Pop Art**) are a case in point.

CHAPELAIN-MIDY, Roger (1904–), French painter. He won the 1938 Carnegie Prize and the 1955 Grand Prix des Beaux-Arts. His early works include some interiors, reworking themes favoured by Dutch masters. These are remarkable for their sense of light and composition, *eg Le Raisin* (1934, Paris MAMVP); *La Symphonie d'Eté* (1937, Paris MNAM). He has also painted landscapes somewhat in the style of Marquet, but with more obtrusive detail. Since World War II, besides theatre decors, he has concentrated on figure studies, *eg La Liseuse* (1953, Birmingham City AG) and still lifes, the more recent of which introduce brilliant colour often at odds with the subject.

CHARCHOUNE, Serge (1888–), Russian painter of the School of Paris. After his arrival (1921) in Paris, his work was influenced by Cubism; he also participated in the Dada movement. Since World War II, he has painted in an abstract style, concentrating on themes suggested by music. The paintings are characterized by frequent use of monochromatic colour schemes; at times reduced to an almost pure white, in which form is created by the brush-strokes in heavy impasto.

CHASTEL, Roger (1897–), French painter. He exhibited his first work in 1930, took part in the Salon de Mai, won the Grand Prix for painting in 1932, and prizes at the Biennale of Menton and São Paulo in 1951. His style is a simplified form of Cubism which uses forms on the borderline of abstraction, painted with a very rich palette, *eg Le Lys Blanc* (1945, Paris MNAM).

CHAVIGNIER, Louis (1922–), French sculptor. He studied at the Ecole des Beaux-Arts and has worked as a restorer of antiquities at the Louvre. His early work was figurative, but his style has become more abstract with allusions to plant and animal forms. His recent work, in plaster and metal, consists of monumental forms often resembling stripped tree-bark or splintered bone.

CHERET, Jules (1836–1932), French painter. The son of a typographer, he worked initially in a printing shop while taking art lessons from Lecoq de Boisbaudran. He soon began to do poster work, the field in which he became famous, *eg La Saxoleine* (1894), *Loie Fuller aux Folies-Bergères, Bal au Moulin Rouge*. His works also include some paintings and pastels. He is regarded as one of the best exponents of **Art Nouveau** and as the creator of the modern poster. However, Chéret's idealized Neo-Rococo eroticism prevents his work from achieving the distinction of **Toulouse-Lautrec** in this field. There is a Chéret Museum at Nice containing 200 of his works.

CHILLIDA, Eduardo (1924–), Spanish sculptor. All his works are characterized by a remarkable sense of rhythm and consistency of style. His mature works, which date from about 1950 when he settled in France, all give meaning to a central space which is enclosed in a network of forged iron. In the first of these, *eg Silent Music* (1955, Bern Kunsthalle), this network is like a group of spikes invading the inner space; *From Within* (1953, New York Guggenheim) has a number of metal 'hands' which define the space within. In his later works, the iron bars become thicker and their relation to the space (which they seem to be crushing as between jaws) appears to be more forceful and dynamic, as in *Modulation d'Espace No. 1* (1963, London Tate). He says of his own work: 'It is the three-dimensionality of space which gives the form its structure, it arises naturally from the requirements of space which constructs its own outer cover in the way an animal grows its shell.'

CHIRICO, Giorgio De (1888–), Italian painter, born in Greece. The son of a Sicilian railway engineer, he studied at the Polytechnic College in Athens, and then in Munich (1906), where he was impressed by the intense realism coupled with a dramatic foreboding (as though all action had been suspended) in the work of Böcklin. This influence can be seen in the first of De Chirico's works which seem characteristic of his style, *The Enigma of the Oracle* (1909, private collection). He went to Paris (1911), exhibiting his *Sabaudian Enigmas* and a group of paintings inspired by Montparnasse Station: *The Soothsayer's Recompense* (1913, Philadelphia MA); *The Anguish of Departure* (1914, Buffalo AG). He met Picasso, Max Jacob and Apollinaire, who declared that he was the most astonishing painter of his time. On his return to Italy in 1915, he met Carlo Carrà in Ferrara, with whom he invented **Metaphysical Painting**. In some of his most original compositions, the architectural setting was inspired by the arcades of Ferrara, bathed in a mysterious light, with vaulted shadows. The perspective and meticulous realism only heighten the irrational elements. The colours are rich and deep, and these paintings are of a concentrated and sculptural plasticity. The magical power of these canvases, and their chromatic beauty make them at once the precursors and supreme examples of **Surrealism**.

Gradually, his compositions became more complicated and disquieting, evoking mystery by means of the unexpected association of the most surprising objects, in an idealized setting. He included tailor's dummies, statues, vegetables, and even dry biscuits in his compositions, transforming them into objects almost belonging to another world, *eg The Painter's Family* (1926, London Tate). In 1919 he became one of the animators of the **Valori Plastici** group, experimenting with distemper techniques, and copying the masters of the Renaissance. On his return to Paris in 1925, he exhibited with the Surrealists at their first exhibition, and designed decors for the Ballets Russes and the Ballets Suédois. But his style had evolved considerably, and he adopted new themes, taking horses and gladiators as his subjects, and treating them in pale colours in a style combining Classical and Baroque.

His dream-like novel, *Hebdomeros*, developed these obsessive fantasies still further. In 1930 he repudiated all his past work, categorically condemned all Post-Impressionist art, and reverted to a strictly traditional style of painting, using purely Classical techniques. In 1938, having broken off all his former friendships, he settled in Rome.

CHRISTO, see **Javacheff**.

CHROMATIC ABSTRACTION, term sometimes applied to the work of those artists within **Abstract Expressionism** who rejected Gesture Painting in favour of a style exploring the expressive power of colour. The work of **Newman, Rothko, Gottlieb** and **Reinhardt** can be described in these terms, as can that of **Albers, Frankenthaler, Francis** and **Youngerman** who were outside the Abstract Expressionist movement proper. Since it was the art of such painters which had the most influence on the succeeding generation of painters, much so-called **Post-Painterly Abstraction** is also a continuation of Chromatic Abstraction, notably the art of Loms, Noland, Olitski and Jenkins. Several British artists working in the 1960s among them Denny, Hoyland, Plumb and Turnbull, were following a similar approach. The most important influences on Chromatic Abstraction include the late works of Monet, Bonnard and Matisse, and Orphism and Synchromism.

CIRY, Michel (1919–), French painter. He studied in Paris at the Ecole des Arts Appliqués and worked first as an engraver. He specializes in realistic portraits and figure subjects, particularly of a religious nature. His fine drawing and subtle colour give a searching inward quality which reveal his deep human sympathy, as in *La Meilleure Part* (1965, Westbury, N.Y., AG). In his technique, Christian faith and compassion, he resembles Dürer.

CLAVE, Antoni (1913–), Spanish painter of the School of Paris. In his early years in Barcelona he contributed illustrations to weekly magazines and experimented with **Collage**, using unusual materials such as egg whisks, parts of an old telephone, *etc* (*cf* Duchamp). He settled in Paris in 1939 and his painting, influenced at first by Bonnard and Vuillard, changed as a result of his experiments with collage and through the influence of Cubism. He does not organize the whole canvas according to Cubist principles, however, but uses a similar technique to break down individual forms as in a mosaic, producing an effect of rich, jewel-like colour glowing from a dark background, *eg Roi et Reine* (1957, Paris MNAM); *Child with a Water-Melon* (London Tate). He has also made a number of sculptures, in a technique closely related to collage, in which pieces of clay are treated with the imprint of various objects.

CLOISONNISM, a word sometimes used to describe the style of painting adopted by **Gauguin** around 1899 in Pont-Aven, and taken up by his followers, the **Nabis**. The term is used metaphorically by analogy with *cloisonné* enamel, in which the pigments are kept in separate compartments by raised partitions of metal. In this style of painting, areas of pure colour are separated from one another by clear lines.

COBRA GROUP, the name of a group derived from the initial letters (*Co; Br; A*) of the home towns of the artists who founded it in Paris in 1948: **Asger Jorn** from Copenhagen, **Corneille** and **Alechinsky** from Brussels and **Karel Appel** from Amsterdam. The style of the group is an intense form of Gesture Painting; a non-intellectual painting giving free rein to the expression of emotion through uncontrolled handling and colour (also see **Action Painting**). Cobra paintings are rarely completely abstract. They are usually based on, or contain, strange animals, figures and masks often similar to children's drawings, but with an individual evocative power.

COCTEAU, Jean (1889–1963), French writer. A poet, novelist and playwright, he took an interest in all aspects of artistic activity, and played an important role as leader and inspirer of avant-garde movements for fifty years. Before World War I he was the friend of the musicians Erik Satie, Darius Milhaud and Stravinsky, and of painters such as Picasso and Derain. He played an active part in the development of Cubism, Dadaism and Surrealism. He was the author of several avant-garde

ballets, notably *Parade* (1919, designed by Picasso, music by Satie) and *Le Boeuf sur le Toit* (1920, designed by Dufy, music by Milhaud). He himself executed numerous drawings and pastels, of which he published several albums, and he also illustrated some of his own books, *eg Opium* (1929). These works are characterized by a continuous, strangely labyrinthine line. His human figures, bearing a curious resemblance to statues, seem ambiguously pure and asexual, mixing myth and legend with a modern approach.

COHEN, Bernard (1933–), English painter. He studied with his brother Harold at the Slade School and afterwards spent two years in France. His first one-man show was held in 1958, and he took part in the 'Situation' shows of 1960–62 (see **Post-Painterly Abstraction**). The works of this period are geometrical and very large in scale. The rectilinear forms are put into a dynamic relationship with one another by the interaction of muted colours and by occasional passages of freer painting, *eg Early Mutation Green No. 11* (1960, London Tate). In 1962, however, he became interested in intertwined ribbon motifs and created paintings using a dense mass of brilliant writhing, worm-like lines, both destroying the conventional form and surface of the picture and yet holding it together in a novel way, as in *Untitled* (1964, Minneapolis, Walker Art Center), *In That Moment* (1965, London Tate).

COHEN, Harold (1928–), English painter. A student at the Slade School, he now teaches there. His earlier painting was related to **Abstract Expressionism**. On a visit to the United States on a Harkness Fellowship (1959–61), he was able to come to terms with the American influence and strike off in the direction of **Post-Painterly Abstraction**. The immediate result was a series of pictures based on horizontal stripe shapes, built up slowly by splicing new pieces into the canvas as the work progressed, as in *Benedictus* (1961, London Tate). In 1962 he initiated a series of experiments which were both more painterly and more mathematical in nature. They included studies in perspective *eg Alcide* (1962, Rugby AG), studies of abstract three-dimensional forms, and pictures like maps, indicating rather than representing the third dimension. At first sight these canvases lack formal coherence, but the forms are interrelated intellectually. Cohen's works were shown at the Venice Biennale of 1966 with those of his brother, Bernard.

COLDSTREAM, William (1908–), English painter. After studying at the Slade School, Coldstream exhibited with the New English Art Club and the London Group. From 1934 to 1937 he worked in the Post Office Film Unit, but took up full-time painting again in 1938 when he opened the Euston Road Art School with **Victor Pasmore**. As Slade Professor of Art at London University after 1949, he is an important figure in official art circles. Coldstream's style has changed little during his career; his painting is disciplined and highly intelligent. He is primarily a portrait painter, though a few meticulously constructed landscapes exist, *eg Bolton* (1938, Ottawa, NG), *Casualty Reception Centre* (1942, London Tate). His draughtsmanship has the expressiveness of Degas, and he adopts rather similar poses, as in *Sleeping Cat* (1938, Oxford, Ashmolean Museum), *The Rt. Rev. G. K. H. Bell* (1954, London Tate). Most remarkable of all are his nudes, conceived almost architecturally. They also show a unique development of Cézanne's method of indicating depth. Coldstream scatters little cross-shaped marks over the picture, each defining the direction of the plane beneath, while at the same time emphasizing the surface, *eg Reclining Nude* (1953, London, Arts Council). He was knighted in 1956.

COLLAGE, strictly a term for the sticking together of scraps of paper or other material to form a design. No technical innovation has had such an effect upon the course of 20th century art as the introduction of collage to the realms of serious art; the range of technical procedures open to the contemporary artist has been widened, and the concepts of the purpose and function of art have been revolutionized. A wider, more useful definition of 'collage' must include **Assemblage**. *ie* works of art created by assembling and fastening together materials retaining their original identity. These include paper, wood, metal, rubbish or even discarded motor cars. This contrasts with the colouring, carving or moulding of some neutral material (*eg* a piece of canvas) to disguise its origin and turn it into something else. Also included should be works built up by an assembly process in which the original objects do not actually appear, but leave their traces on the final material, such as the frottages of Max Ernst, the photomontages of Man Ray, the silk-screen techniques of Rauschenberg or the plaster casts of Paolozzi. Such a wide definition obviously leaves a disputable borderline between collage and conventional art. The development of collage has had the inevitable effect of breaking down classifications. Another category that must be considered, though not strictly within the definition, is the use of conventional illusionist techniques of painting or sculpture to create works that look like collages. This device has precedents in still-life painting from the 16th century onwards, and it is realized in the work of Jasper Johns and Oldenburg.

Modern collage originated *c* 1912 when Braque and Picasso were simultaneously making *papiers collés*, and the evolution of **Cubism** stimulated their experiments. Braque seems to have initiated the trend with his *Nature Morte au Compotier* (1912, private collection). Earlier he had painted imitation wood and marble and in 1911 he introduced printed letters into his compositions. From this it was a logical step to include real objects in his paintings, or to paste newspaper, wrapping paper and wallpaper on the surface of the canvas, on which he would then draw or paint, as in *The Courier* (1913, Philadelphia MA). Picasso used a similar procedure in *Guitar, Glass and Bottle* (London Tate) and *Violin and Fruit* (1912, Philadelphia MA). Later, other materials were added: fragments of wood, cloth or sand, and even matchboxes and playing cards. But the aims of these artists were different: Braque was looking for a form of poetic plasticity, and he soon gave up collage; Picasso, however, was enamoured of the surprising effects of the method and repeated the experiment at different stages in his career, notably with his huge *papier collé, Femmes à leur Toilette* (1938). Other Cubist painters have used the same technique, *eg* Gris, Laurens and Kupka.

Futurism, the paintings of which were in effect a montage of events, also turned to collage: Carrà in particular, with his collages consisting entirely of words, went a stage further than the Cubists. The meanings of the words were as important as the shapes built up by them. In this, he was in effect approaching Concrete Poetry from the painter's point of view, as Apollinaire approached it from the poet's.

From these early beginnings two main aspects of collage are distinguishable: the use of it as a convenient way of creating new formal effects (as in Cubism) and the use of it to introduce a wider range of meaning into the work of art, by retaining the original associations of the incorporated material (as in Carrà's work). Both tendencies are to be found within **Surrealism**: Magritte, Miró and Dali used collage as an alternative to their illusionistic painting. Arp used collage techniques to enable him to practise a totally irrational art governed only by chance, *eg Squares arranged according to the Laws of Chance* (1916–17, New York MMA). Whether by accident or not, his works initiated a concept of collage as a way of exploring the formal tensions inherent in an abstract work of art. Arp himself, Mondrian, Pasmore, de Staël, Motherwell and Gwyther Irwin (among others) developed the technique as a conscious process. This view of collage is closely allied to **Constructivism** and many of the works of Gabo, Pevsner and Archipenko can be looked upon in this light.

Collage techniques have enabled artists to make use of new materials notably

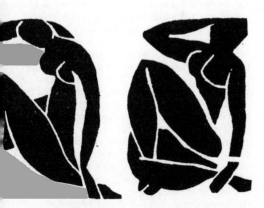

Henri Matisse: Blue Nudes *(cut-outs).*

Burri's use of sacking, wood and iron in his paintings, and Yves Klein's experiments, *eg Mural of Sponges* (1959, Gelsenkirchen Opera). The finest extended use of collage as an alternative to painting is found in the late work of Matisse. He executed a number of huge compositions by cutting or tearing coloured papers when he was too ill to work at his easel, *eg L'Escargot* (1953, London Tate). These contained large surfaces of pure colour and are arguably the artist's best works. They have influenced many other artists, for example Gischia, Vasarely, Frankenthaler and Hoyland.

The most significant effect of collage has been the 'juxtaposition of meaning'. **Dada** was the first to make extensive use of this, introducing incongruities intended to shock: Duchamp's moustache on the *Mona Lisa*, Picabia's pictures made of matchsticks, the spikes soldered on to the smoothing-iron to make Man Ray's *Gift*. Of prime importance are Duchamp's 'ready-mades', such as the urinal he exhibited as *Fountain* in 1917. These brought into play a new respect for the object as a thing of value in itself, irrespective of its function; Schwitters' *Merzbilder* related to Dada in their use of the detritus of commerce ('Merz' is the second syllable of 'Kommerz'), bus tickets and so forth. They did not seek to shock, but attempted to build up interesting formal patterns to make the viewer aware of a new beauty even as he recognized its source. The sculptures of César and Chamberlain, which make use of car bodies and mechanical bits and pieces, or the vast temples built by Louise Nevelson out of junk wood do much the same thing. Max Ernst used a large range of techniques to incorporate alien objects into his works, ranging from juxtapositions of 19th century technical engravings, *eg The Horse, He's Sick* (1920, New York, MMA), through frottage and grattage (the use of scrapings taken from foreign material) to photomontage, a technique also practised by Moholy-Nagy and Man Ray. Most of Ernst's collages were Surrealist in intent, as were those of Masson.

Since World War II the greatest development has been in the direction of **Pop Art**. All its exponents attempt to establish a new relationship between contemporary art and the contemporary world. On one level, it is little more than a form of nostalgic realism, as in Peter Blake's recording of popular ephemera such as advertisements and children's badges. Dine and Rauschenberg combine objects or the image of them with passages of painting, using the everyday associations of their material to create new forces within the work of art. George Segal, by placing plaster casts of human figures in a real environment, evokes a keen awareness of pathos and sympathy for the human condition. Finally Jasper Johns, with his handmade, but utterly realistic, replicas of light bulbs or beer cans, attempts to bridge the gap between the aesthetic and the material world. Although 'pure' painting is also at its height today, there is every reason to believe that collage explorations of the everyday world will continue to inspire creativity.

COLLINS, Jess (1923–), American painter. A precursor of Pop Art, he is associated with the San Francisco poets. He produced seven comic-strip **Collages**, called *Tricky Cad* (1959, Los Angeles Museum). Collins cut and pasted images from the original Dick Tracy series, producing a surrealistic new set of images. Recently, he has moved away from Pop Art and has worked on Picabia-like images.

COLOMBO, Gianni (1937–), Italian sculptor. He started abstract sculpture in 1954, and in 1960 produced his first mechanically operated sculptures (see **Kinetic Art**). He then began to study the effects of moving lights and vibrating mirrors and to create **Environments**. He won a prize at the 1968 Venice Biennale.

COMMERE, Jean (1920–), French painter. A student at the Ecole des Beaux-Arts until 1942, he won the Othon-Friesz Prize in 1952. He works principally in watercolour using sharp animated drawing and vivid colours, as in *Le Vél d'Hiv* (1957, Paris MAMVP). His beach scenes, with their airy quality, are particularly effective.

CONCEPTUAL ART, term for an art in which the idea for a particular work is more important than the finished work, if any. The first international survey of Conceptual Art was an exhibition held at Bern in 1969, entitled 'When Attitudes become Form'. The title aptly illustrates the contention that art is merely an attitude to life. To permit other people to observe this attitude it must be recorded in some way, but the record may not be a tangible object, and will certainly not be an art work in the conventional sense. Since this approach by its very nature opens up a vast field of activities, it is impossible to make meaningful subclassifications within Conceptual Art; nevertheless it may be useful to mention some of the forms in which the artist's attitudes are expressed.

One important branch of Conceptual Art is the **Happening** which, being an event occurring in time, has no permanent reality except as recorded in words or on film. However, the Surrealist happenings associated with the Pop movement have given way on the whole to simpler activities such as making a journey in a car (Kienholz and Tinguely), walking across a moor, or just sitting in a room (Beuys). Several artists merely supplied autobiographical notes as their entry to the exhibition. It is interesting that as long ago as 1960, **Robert Morris**, who must be regarded as one of the founders of the movement, made a piece recording all his actions for a while on a card index. In this case the index cards record the artist's activity; other artists have recorded personal happenings by collecting a number of newspapers bought in various towns, or a series of earth samples taken from different points.

Another aspect of Conceptual Art is an extension of **Environments**. When Sol Le Witt inscribes the dimensions of a room on the walls of the room he creates an art work by the nature of his reaction to the environment, but it is not an art work that can be bought and sold. Similarly the fluorescent-tube arrangements of Flavin and the floor-pieces of Carl Andre (especially those created by random scattering of objects) become ordinary electric lights and simple piles of junk once they are removed from the exhibition, but they make considerable sense in their specific environment. Environmental pieces may also be made out of doors such as Andre's line of hay bales linking an open area to a wooded area, or the large scale earthworks of Morris.

The *Objet Trouvé* also has a place in

Conceptual Art (and this is the closest link of the movement with **Dada**), since the artist's attitude is revealed in the objects he selects, whether they be stones, samples of material or even pieces of blank paper. The art of Christo, who appropriates objects, buildings or parts of the landscape by wrapping them up, is a special case of this. Finally there are conceptual works which are comprised of artifacts created by the artist, and here the category overlaps with **Minimal Art**.

Futurism, Dada and Pop also tried to widen the artist's horizons. Surrealism and Abstract Expressionism demoted the status of the picture to a mere record of the artist's feelings, as Constructivism made it the logical outcome of his ideas. Conceptual Art owes something to all these, and yet if differs from them in that the personality of the artist is largely excluded and by the fact that, with the partial exception of Dada, it is the only movement in which the artist's ideas are expressed other than in the traditional media of painting and sculpture.

CONCRETE ART, a term originally synonymous with the broadest sense of the word Constructivism. Used particularly from about 1930 onwards to describe the geometrical aspect of abstract art, it was exemplified by *De Stijl* and continued in the Abstraction-Création group, the art work being a distillation of the balance of forces in nature. In 1948, the 'Movimento Arte Concreta' was founded in Italy: its members included **Magnelli**, **Capogrossi**, Osvaldo Licini (1894–1958) and Atanasio Soldati (1896–1953): the group around Fontana pursued a parallel course.

CONCRETE POETRY, term for poetry in which poets have tried to add greater meaning to their words by forming them into a particular shape on the printed page. The earliest known example (about 300 BC) is a poem in the shape of an egg by the Greek poet Simmias. In English poetry George Herbert (1593–1633) tried some interesting experiments, notably poems in the shape of a chalice and of doves' wings, and Lewis Carroll (1832–98) used pictorial typography in *Alice in Wonderland*. In the early 20th century, several artists experimented with the relationship between words and visual form, notably the

advocates of **Futurism** and Apollinaire. Apollinaire's poems have complex shapes which delay the process of piecing together the words so that the appearance of the poem gives rise to expectations which are deepened and developed by the actual reading. The members of the **Dada** movement also made use of experimental typographic effects to superimpose a visual rhythm on their posters. Man Ray's *Lautgedicht* (1924) consists of a wordless 'poem' with the words represented by horizontal black lines as if scored out. In recent years there has been considerable interest in exploring the common ground between poetry and painting.

CONSAGRA, Pietro (1920–), Italian sculptor. In 1947 he founded the 'Forma' group of non-figurative sculptors. He worked exclusively in metal at first, composing tight, slightly anthropomorphic figures, of chisel-shaped bars, *eg Unknown Political Prisoner* (1952, London Tate). Since 1953 his work has been primarily two-dimensional, composed of perforated sheets of metal set parallel to one another as in *Colloquio Pubblico* (1955, Chicago Art Inst.). Gradually the sculptures have become thicker, and show reverse relief rather than perforation, using other materials, such as wood, *eg Coro* (1958, Minneapolis Art Inst.). In 1960 he won the Sculpture Prize at the Venice Biennale.

CONSTRUCTIVISM, a term referring specifically to certain manifestations of Russian art between 1913 and 1922. The term was proposed (1914) by **Tatlin** to describe art, such as his own, constructed from solid elements rather than painted or sculpted. The term was later extended to cover any art (even in two dimensions) which was composed of simple geometrical units. The doctrine was propounded by the brothers **Gabo** and **Pevsner** in their *Realist Manifesto* (1920). Larionov had already led the way towards pure abstraction with his **Rayonism** of 1912 onwards; but the decisive step was that of Malevich who launched **Suprematism** in 1913 with pictures using the simplest of all elements, a black square on a white ground. He influenced Rodchenko, Lissitzky, Moholy-Nagy and, briefly, Kandinsky. The **De Stijl** movement, founded (1917) in Holland by van Doesburg and Mondrian independently of the Russian group, concerned itself with very similar principles. The basic tenets of **Bauhaus** were also Constructivist, the result of Moholy-Nagy's and Lissitzky's presence and of the influence of the De Stijl artists.

The painters and sculptors following Constructivist principles were united (1930) by the founding of the 'Cercle et Carré' group in Paris, and they formed a large part of the far more influential **Abstraction-Création** group, founded in 1932. This acted as an international rallying point, confirming the determination of abstract artists. Arp, Bill, Calder, Herbin, Moore, Ben Nicholson and Pasmore were among the most prominent members, apart from the 'first-generation' Constructivists.

The term 'Constructivism' is often given an extended meaning to encompass the Apollonian tendency in abstract art, *ie* any non-figurative analytical art operating through the balance and interaction of pure formal elements (simple shapes, pure colours, clear spatial relationships). It thus forms an antonym to **Expressionism**, which reflects the spontaneous Dionysiac element, 'heart rather than mind'. Much of the art produced in the spirit of **Post-Painterly Abstraction** can be gathered under this heading, including hard-edge abstraction, Op Art, Kinetic Art (since movement is another basic element to be explored) and Minimal Art.

CORBUSIER, Le, see **Jeanneret, Edouard**.

CORINTH, Lovis (1858–1925), German painter. Despite frequent sojourns in Paris, he produced typically German work. He was a pupil of Bouguereau and Bastien-Lepage at the Académie Julian; his *Body of Christ* received an honourable mention at the Salon in 1890. He worked in Munich for ten years, and then settled in Berlin around 1900. He was one of the principal exhibitors of the **Secession**. At this period he produced rather academic figure studies, *eg The Temptation of St. Anthony* (1908, London Tate) transfigured by a fine sense of light. Sometimes he achieved a powerful Expressionism, though with 19th century means as in *Die Totenklage* (1908, Hanover Landesgalerie). His name has been bracketed with that of Liebermann as a leader of the German

Impressionist movement, because of his naturalism and vivacious brush-work, but this only became true after an attack of apoplexy in 1911 when his painting became vibrant and nervous. He executed vast mythological and religious compositions, *eg Ecce Homo* (1925, Basle Kunstmuseum) and dramatic, pantheistic landscapes, painted with convulsive, frenetic strokes, *eg Walchensee* (1924, Hanover Landesgalerie). These anticipate Kokoschka's outbursts in colour. His portraits, such as *Last Self-Portrait* (1925, Zurich Kunsthaus) reveal a violent pathos and passionate energy in which form is dissolved in light.

CORNEILLE, originally Cornelis van Beverloo (1922–), Dutch painter. A self-taught artist, he was one of the founders, in 1948, of the Cobra group, and he is now a member of the **School of Paris**. Like the other members of the group he is an Expressionist, using intense colour. However, he relies scarcely at all on figurative elements and his paintings show a greater degree of linear design, *eg La Grande Terre Apre* (1957, Eindhoven, van Abbemuseum).

CORNELL, Joseph (1903–72), American sculptor. He specialized in **Assemblage**, making small shallow boxes filled with diverse objects and often with their surfaces decorated in **Collage**; many of these constructions show an intriguing use of empty space, *eg Hotel du Nord* (1953, New York, Whitney Museum). Cornell who had his first one-man show in 1939, was indebted to Duchamp and to Schwitters, except that many of the objects included were curious and beautiful in their own right.

COROT, Camille (1796–1875), French painter. Although he had a strong influence on the artists in **Impressionism**, and hence on the course of modern art, Corot's significance as a precursor is not as great as is sometimes thought. Many of his now most popular works are landscape sketches of French and Italian scenes showing a broadness of touch, simplicity of construction and freshness of colour (though within a restricted palette), unusual for their time. These, however, were never exhibited in Corot's lifetime but were used as studies for large closely-worked Salon pictures, based on mythological subjects in which the landscapes were idealized in the manner of Claude Lorrain. The numerous silver-grey landscapes executed towards the end of his life with their romantic blurring of detail are totally different from the superficially similar Impressionist landscapes, both richer in colour and blurred with realistic intent rather than sentimental.

Nevertheless, all the Impressionists admired him and those who, like Pissarro, actually studied with him would no doubt have been able to see the revolutionary sketches we now know. Furthermore the figure compositions Corot executed during his last years, *eg Woman with a Book* (1865–70, Chicago Art Inst.), combining Classical solidity and human tenderness, had a growing influence when exhibited after his death (most notably in the 1909 Salon d'Automne), especially on Degas and on the Neo-Classical style of Picasso.

COTTET, Charles (1863–1925), French painter. A pupil of Puvis de Chavannes and Roll, he made his debut at the Salon in 1889. With Lucien Simon, Ménard, Prinet and Dauchez, he formed the 'Bande Noire', so-called because of their taste for dark colours. A figure painter and landscapist, he was inspired chiefly by the scenery of Brittany, *eg The Circus* (1913, Paris MNAM).

COURBET, Gustave (1819–77), French painter. Courbet's influence on late 19th and early 20th century painting is significant. The most important aspect of his art was its realist, even socialist, intentions whereby the peasants in pictures such as *The Stone Breakers* (1849, Dresden Schloss Pillnitz) or the *Funeral at Ornans* (1849, Paris Louvre) are seen from their own point of view as human beings engaged in an exhausting and limited life, which also has a ritual quality. He thus made a clear break with the idealizing traditions inherited from the previous century. Courbet was a particular influence on **Manet**, and also on **Impressionism**, the art of which, though less doctrinaire, was also exclusively concerned with modern life. Courbet's technique in his later landscapes (particularly in the remarkable seascapes of about 1870) was influential in its use of patches of strong colour applied with a palette knife, with no conventional modelling.

COUTAUD, Lucien (1904–   ), French painter. A pupil of the art school in Nîmes, and of the Ecole des Beaux-Arts, Paris, he began as a stage designer in 1926. His characteristic style in painting emerged in the 1930s as a decorative, non-realistic form of **Surrealism** as in *Souvenir de Mozart* (1937, Worcester, Mass., AM). After World War II he began to paint bleak landscapes containing tall figures, influenced by Cubism, with parts of the body split off from the rest and joined together with passages of drapery, spikes and plant forms into fantastic figures, *eg La Jupe Verte* (1945, Paris MNAM). Since then he has gradually built a complete world of the imagination in which certain elements repeat themselves obsessively: the female pelvis used to build up the shapes of bulls, horses or fish, mannequin figures with tight striped bodices, a deserted beach with figures buried up to the thighs, a horse of brick, motifs from the bullfight, *etc*, *eg Paysage Taurin* (1956, Paris MAMVP). Although influenced by Dali and by Tanguy, Coutaud's work commands respect for its personal vision and consistency.

COUTURIER, Robert (1905–   ), French sculptor. He worked in Maillol's studio from 1928 for many years. In 1937 he executed bas-reliefs in stone for the International Exhibition, Paris. He changed his classically realistic style (*eg Monument to Etienne Dolet*, commissioned by the city of Paris) by changing to plaster and elongating his forms to develop the art of sculpture in space, forming a more personal, dynamic style. His works, *eg Femme à la Cruche* (1964), present figures in original rhythmic configurations, often holding objects which dictate the pose.

CRIPPA, Roberto (1921–   ), Italian painter and sculptor. A student at the Brera Academy, Milan, his first one-man show was in 1947. He became friends with **Fontana** and signed the Manifesto of 'Spazialismo' in 1950. His paintings at this time combined **Gesture Painting** with pure **Action Painting**; dominating slabs of colour are seen through a maze of lines of poured-on paint, *eg Aurora Borealis* (1952, London Tate). About 1956 he changed to a more formal style in a firmly-constructed series of collages of paper, cork, wood and other materials, somewhat similar to the work of Burri, and owing much to **Schwitters**. The large shapes usually have disturbing representational overtones, as in *Head* (1959, Amsterdam, Stedelijk).

CROSS, see **Delacroix, Henri Edmond**.

CROTTI, Jean (1878–1958), French painter of Swiss origin. A pupil of the School of Art in Munich, he went to Paris (1901), and exhibited paintings from 1907. At first influenced by Cubism, *eg* in *La Tasse de Thé* (1914, Paris Petit Palais), he took part in the Dadaist movement, *eg Portrait of Marcel Duchamp* (wire construction, 1915, Philadelphia MA). He married Susanne Duchamp, the sister of Jacques Villon whose style he approached in his works between the Wars, *eg Composition* (1925, Yale University AG). He created what he called 'Gemmaux', translucent works composed of pieces of coloured glass superimposed upon one another as in *Femme au Chien* (1943, Columbus, Ohio, AG).

CRUZ-DIAZ, Carlos (1923–   ), Venezuelan painter. See **Op Art**.

CSONTVARY, Theodore (1853–1919), Hungarian painter. He began to paint at the age of fourteen. A visionary and a mystic, he executed large compositions in a slightly naive, highly coloured style, revealing a fantastic imagination and oriental bias.

CUBISM, the term used to describe the aesthetic revolution which took place in painting and sculpture between 1907 and 1914. The movement as a whole has had a greater impact than any other in the history of modern art. It has provided a formal language, pointing the way for other 20th century artists to express themselves and its introduction of collage initiated an approach to art which influenced many other movements with quite different aims. The Cubist movement grew up around **Braque** and **Picasso**. The term 'Cubism' is derived from Matisse's reference to 'little cubes', which he made on seeing a painting by Braque in the 1908 Salon d'Automne. Later that year, the critic Louis Vauxcelles used it in his review of Braque's first exhibition at the Kahnweiler Gallery. As with Impressionism and Fauvism, the artists accepted the term although it made their work seem both more radical and more limited than they intended.

The rapidity of the development of Cubism has tended to obscure its natural continuity with the past, while its great influence on other, abstract, art movements leads one to forget that the aim of the Cubists was essentially representational. They did attempt, however, to represent more aspects of the motif and to employ a more complex organization of pictorial space than their predecessors. The movement started as a reaction against **Impressionism** and **Fauvism** although it accepted the violent distortions of space in some Fauve pictures. The artist most revered was **Cézanne** who, in a letter to Emile Bernard (published in 1907), said that nature can be reduced to the cylinder, the sphere and the cone.

Cubism, however, was not merely a matter of regularizing natural shapes in a coherent space in this way (that was to be a feature of Purism): Cubist pictures deliberately set out to dislocate space and eliminate perspective. Of far greater importance was Cézanne's ideal of relating all the elements of the picture to patterns both on its surface and in depth, and the Cubists simplified form, as he had done, in order to make this process of cross-reference easier. In addition, they split forms up so as to be able to isolate individual elements and relate each one to the overall pattern in new ways. Instead of presenting the subject from one viewpoint they would try to include aspects of several viewpoints, both to give a 'truer' representation and to bring new elements into the pattern. This can be seen as early as 1907 in Picasso's *Demoiselles d'Avignon* (New York MMA) which also shows the impact of Negro and Iberian sculpture, other important influences on the movement.

These processes proved immensely difficult and ultimately impossible. The history of Cubism shows how, in order to concentrate on these elements, the artists were forced to restrict themselves in the use of colour, shape and subject matter, and how they were eventually forced to introduce new techniques to enable their

Pablo Picasso: Man with a Pipe *(1911, private collection); ph. Giraudon.*

Juan Gris: Still Life on a Chair *(1917, Paris MNAM); ph. Giraudon.*

works to be recognized as being figurative at all. From the start, therefore, Cubism proper carried the seeds of its own destruction and ended up as little more than a style of decoration. Three phases of this development are usually distinguished: the Cézannesque period (1907–9), Analytical Cubism (1910–12) and Synthetic Cubism (1913 onwards).

The first phase is best represented by the landscapes painted by Picasso at Horta de San Juan in 1908, by Braque at L'Estaque in the same year, and by both at La Roche-Guyon in 1909, *eg* Braque's *View from La Roche-Guyon* (1909, Eindhoven van Abbemuseum). The subject and colours are still reminiscent of Cézanne, but the forms are more simplified and the viewpoint closer, so that the various large masses fill the picture and begin to cancel each other out.

The development in the next phase can be seen by comparing two figure paintings such as Picasso's *Portrait of Vollard* (1909, Moscow Pushkin Museum) and his *Ma Jolie* (1912, New York MMA). The first is still recognizable as an individual al-

though the figure is broken into more facets than the earlier landscapes. In the second, one can hardly make out the human figure; the number of facets have been further increased and the colour reduced to a near-monochrome. Such a painting can no longer be called representational and the artists recognized this difficulty. To help solve it they reduced their subject matter to a few familiar things (the human figures, glasses, bottles, musical instruments, *etc*), they scattered graphic 'clues' around their paintings (in *Ma Jolie* the guitar strings and the four fingers of the player, for instance), and they introduced letters and signs which could easily be read and which would provide the eye with a point from which to start. This led, in 1912, to the introduction of **Collage**.

From this point the artists gave up the struggle to analyze a given subject, however restricted, and concentrated on making patterns on the picture surface. With this third, Synthetic, phase of Cubism, *eg* Picasso's *Card Player* (1913–14, New York MMA) colour returned, the compositional elements of the picture became fewer and simpler and the range of references began to widen. This eventually led to compositions such as Picasso's *Three Musicians* (1921, New York MMA) which enable us to imagine the naturalistic arrangement once more, although they are stylized.

Braque and•Picasso were undoubtedly the most important members of the Cubist movement but many other artists joined it: Léger and Delaunay in 1908; Gleizes, Metzinger and Archipenko in 1909; La Fresnaye, Villon, Duchamp-Villon and Marcoussis in 1910, and Gris in 1911. Cubist theory was set before the public by Gleizes and Metzinger in their *Du Cubisme* (1912), and in Apollinaire's *Les Peintres Cubistes* (1913). Of these other artists, **Juan Gris** was the most important; as a Cubist painter as such he was probably the most polished of all of them and his works generally avoid the unfinished look of those by Picasso and Braque, *eg Still Life with Bottles* (1912, Otterloo RKM).

The others all took the ideas of Cubism and developed them in their way. Duchamp-Villon and Archipenko developed Cubist sculpture. Delaunay and Villon took Cubist fragmentation and united it to a new study of colour in **Orphism**. Léger went his own way with **Purism**. Many other movements were also influenced by Cubism. **Futurism** found in it a means of linking disparate events in the one work, as an alternative to their previous impressionistic blurring. It was the influence of Cubism which provided the decisive push which made the **Blaue Reiter** painters develop their distinctive style out of German Expressionism. It set Mondrian on the long exploration which was to culminate in the doctrine of **Neo-Plasticism** and in the purity of his late works. Even such an individual artist as Chagall found in Cubism the clue to the presentation of his personal vision. It is safe to say that no 20th century movement concerned with form has remained entirely free from Cubist influence.

CUBO-REALISM, a term coined by American critics to describe the work of **Sheeler**, **Demuth** and many of their followers after World War I. It means the realistic portrayal of motifs such as industrial architecture and machinery, chosen for their similarity to the abstract forms in **Cubism**. Both artists were influenced by **Duchamp** in seeing the possibility of machinery as a subject. Their interpretation of these subjects, particularly in the case of Demuth, was also influenced by the Futurist technique of using 'lines of force' to section the various elements in the picture and reduce them to a uniform pattern. It differed from Cubism, however, in that the lines, so far from breaking up the original forms, were used to make their structure more clear, and both artists were gradually able to assimilate more and more realistic detail into their designs. Several other artists were affected by this style, among them Spencer and Joseph Stella; a similar approach can be seen in the work of Wadsworth and Hillier in England.

The importance of the movement, which is also known as 'Precisionism', lay in the fact that it was the first attempt since that of the **Ash Can School** to create an art which would come to terms with the contemporary American scene. Unlike the earlier painters, however, the Cubo-Realists were not content merely with recording their environment in an outworn style, but developed a new mode of expression to assimilate and enoble it, as in Demuth's *My Egypt* (1927, New York, Whitney Museum), a picture of grain silos.

D

DADA, an international literary and artistic movement which took place between 1915 and 1922; its essential spirit has regained importance in recent years. Although not primarily a pictorial movement, it was an extension of the techniques of **Collage** borrowed from Cubism, and it led directly to **Surrealism**. The name (a children's word for 'rocking-horse') was chosen (February 1916) from a dictionary at random. It was founded at the 'Cabaret Voltaire', Zurich, by **Arp**, the poet Tzara and the German writers, Hugo Ball and Richard Hülsenbeck. On March 30th they presented the first of a series of performances calculated to provoke the public: music was made by tapping with keys on boxes, while other incongruous events and grotesque dances took place to the accompaniment of the growling of bears. Once the public had overcome its astonishment, it protested in a violent manner. The whole spirit of mystification and anarchy behind Dadaism was symptomatic of the spiritual disorder of the World War I period, and of the need to destroy a seemingly bankrupt social and moral order. The movement's aim was to destroy all existing art forms by a systematic appeal to the arbitrary and the absurd.

At the same time an analogous movement was formed in New York around **Duchamp**, **Man Ray** and **Picabia**. The two groups were united (1918) in Lausanne, and Tzara founded the review *Dada*, in which the Dadaist Manifesto was printed in the same year. The Manifesto revealed the tremendous destructive energy of the movement. Tzara was enthusiastically welcomed in Paris by the group responsible for the review *Littérature*. including Breton and Aragon. Several exhibitions were held in Paris. Dadaism was an even more important force in Germany, where the most active and outspoken group of all had been formed in Cologne. The group formed in Berlin by Hülsenbeck had existed since 1917. **Max Ernst** and Arp created collages outspoken enough to be banned by the authorities, notably the *Fatagaga* series (*Fatagaga:* abbreviations of 'fabrication de tableux garantis gazométriques'). Another Dadaist movement, in Hanover, inaugurated by the painter and poet, **Kurt Schwitters**, produced collages called 'Merz', made of rubbish. But when Max Ernst moved (1922) to Paris, Dada had begun to break up as a movement and its main supporters were interesting themselves in Surrealism.

Although the basic impulse of the movement was nihilistic, *eg* Duchamp's *L.H.O.O.Q.* ('Elle a chaud au Cul', a reproduction of the *Mona Lisa* adorned with a moustache), it was not unconstructive in its effect. At the lowest level it provided a valuable purge of traditional notions of the place of art; in particular, by shocking the public, it attacked the idea of the artist as a servant of the bourgeois community. More positively, it extended the boundaries of art forcing people to consider a wider range of phenomena. Marcel Duchamp's *Fountain* (1917), a urinal set on end and signed, was an attempt to reveal mundane things as having a life of their own and being worthy of respect.

This approach has been continued, often with great seriousness, by a number of contemporary artists. The **Pop Art** movement is the best-known manifestation; its aim, too, has been to make the viewer come to terms with the ephemera of the post-War culture. Dada elements can also be seen in other types of contemporary art: the auto-destructive machines of Tinguely or the burnt books of John Latham are Dada in spirit; the **Happenings** organized by Oldenburg, Warhol and others are modern equivalents of Dada demonstrations; and the attitudes of the Dadaists have influenced **Conceptual Art**. Much modern music, particularly that of John Cage and Karlheinz Stockhausen, emphasizes the Dadaist principle of chance.

DALI, Salvador (1904–), Spanish painter. He studied at the Madrid School of Fine Arts before coming into contact (1928) with **Surrealism** of which he was to become the most famous practitioner. His style is based on the realistic technique of Vermeer which gives an extraordinary power even to his most *outré* inventions. His work is underlaid by the assumption that if the individual components and the settings look real then what they portray must reflect reality. His devices include enormously distorted heads or other parts of the body, as in *The Great Paranoiac* (1936, London Tate, James Loan); there are ambiguities with one form hidden in the outlines of others, time is indicated by watches and other hard objects becoming soft and melting *eg Persistence of Memory* (1931, New York MMA) or by ossified and decaying forms *eg Metamorphosis of Narcissus* (1938, London Tate, James Loan). His visions are usually set in wide landscapes, often beach scenes of Cadaqués or Port Lligat, his home, or hot bleak deserts. They are often peopled with tiny figures, insects and long-legged, flying animals derived from the works of Bosch. They evoke dreams and are considered to be pictorial equivalents of some aspects of Freudian psychoanalysis.

In 1937, Dali broke with the Surrealist movement as such, and remained in the United States during the War years. Since then he has devoted himself to religious paintings and historical works *eg The Discovery of America by Columbus* (1959,

New York MMA). Generally, he uses monumental forms based on Renaissance prototypes intertwined with wide Catalan coastscapes, as in *Christ and St. John of the Cross* (1951, Glasgow Kelvingrove). Many of these works have reclaimed a large public for religious themes. They contain mystical quasi-mathematical ideas *eg Crucifixion (Corpus Hypercubus)* (1954, New York MMA); *The Sacrament of the Last Supper* (1955, Washington NG). Dali has capitalized persistently on personal publicity and has surrounded his exotic life and works with the spirit of **Dada**, *eg Venus de Milo with Drawers 1936*, a model of the statue with pull-out drawers in the body. He collaborated with film director Buñuel on two works of critical importance in the history of the cinema, *Un Chien Andalou* (1928) and *L'Age d'Or* (1932).

DALWOOD, Hubert (1924–   ), English sculptor. He began to study sculpture with **Kenneth Armitage** (1946) after an apprenticeship in the Navy and later, in 1950–51, he worked in Milan with **Mario Marini**. Both these artists have influenced Dalwood's style, in particular his use of drapery to reduce the human figure to a single monumental form as in *Standing Draped Figure* (1954, London Tate). His forms gradually became even more compact and also more enigmatic, especially the non-figurative works such as the egg-like *Large Object* (1959, London Tate). Since 1969 he has been concerned with groups of columns and other regular forms in metal, exploring architectonic ideas on a small scale. Dalwood won a prize at the 1962 Venice Biennale.

DARDEL, Nils (1888–1943), Swedish painter. He visited (1911–14) Paris, where he was influenced by Cubism, Matisse and Henri Rousseau. He then travelled extensively. His best works consist of folk scenes or exotic landscapes, artificially arranged on the canvas, *eg Midsummer* (1924, Hamburg Kunsthalle).

DAUBIGNY, Charles-François (1817–78), French painter. He was one of the leading painters of the Barbizon School (see **Millet**). Settling at Barbizon in the Forest of Fontainebleau, they attempted to create a French school of landscape painting in opposition to the Academic classically-inspired one. In fact, Barbizon landscape was closely based on Dutch 17th century models and quickly developed its own clichés, but Daubigny was the painter most able to develop his own style. His best paintings, *eg The Banks of the Oise* (1872, Paris Louvre), are river scenes painted in nearly pure colours, though with a rather sombre harmony, and are especially sensitive in their treatment of reflections on the water. In 1857 he built a house-boat studio from which to study his subject better, thus anticipating Monet by some 15 years.

DAUMIER, Honoré (1808–79), French painter and lithographer. From 1830 Daumier devoted himself to political and social satire, and he helped to create the first French magazines with regular caricatures. He turned to painting in about 1840 and produced a large number of compositions, mostly concerned with contemporary life. His themes included satirical treatments of the law courts and the art world. Although the paintings were never as pointed as his drawings and the anecdotal element was usually compressed into a concise visual image, they had great subtlety.

Manet and **Toulouse-Lautrec** were among the many artists influenced not only in subject but also in simplification of design, bold compression of space, and the way in which muted colour was used in large plain areas, one balanced with another. Daumier's drawing style, characterized by curvilinear outlines, probably also influenced van Gogh. Before he began to go blind in 1870 he also produced a number of objective representations of scenes from everyday life, without idealism and, unlike his contemporary Courbet, without overt social comment, *eg The Third Class Carriage* (New York Metropolitan Museum). These, although quite different in technique, were very similar in approach to the later works of the Impressionists. **Degas** in particular owed much to Daumier, especially to the influence of his theatre scenes, with their use of artificial lighting and contrast between performers and audience.

DAVIE, Alan (1920–   ), Scottish painter. He was influenced by his teacher at the Edinburgh College of Art, **John Maxwell**, who no doubt confirmed his characteristically Scottish taste for rich colour and bold handling. During the War and shortly afterwards he was involved in poetry and jazz (he was for a time a professional saxophonist) rather than painting, although he was assimilating the work of Picasso, Klee and especially **Jackson Pollock**. About 1950 his painting had the dense texture of calligraphic works and cabalistic signs associated with Pollock, *eg Interior Exterior* (1950, Wakefield City AG) and *Spook Case* (1950, Providence, Rhode Island, School of Design). Towards 1955 he became interested in Zen Buddhism and his painting became richer in colour, although he continued to use a deliberately crude unpretentious handling, and to allow free dripping and running of the paint. His style came closer to **Gorky** than to Pollock: *Magic Box* (1955, New York MMA); *Sacrifice* (1956, London Tate). His work became increasingly simplified in the 1960s, although his uncompromising boldness, the power of his brilliant colour, and the tantalizing effects of his abstract shapes with their elusive figurative connotations (all his titles are retrospective) are undiminished: *Entrance for a Red Temple* (1960, London Tate); *Bird Food* (1962, Hartford, Wadsworth Atheneum); *In the Face of the Witch* (1965, Leeds City AG).

DAVIES, Arthur B. (1862–1928), American painter. Although he exhibited with the **Ash Can School**, Davies had not worked as a newspaper artist and avoided realism, painting instead idyllic dream-landscapes which are influenced by the Symbolism of Puvis de Chavannes and of Böcklin, *eg Unicorns* (1906, New York Metropolitan). After the **Armory Show** he was briefly influenced by Cubism.

DAVIS, Gene (1920–), American painter. After studying at Maryland University he settled in Washington and began to paint in a variety of styles deriving from **Abstract Expressionism**. Influenced by reproductions of Newman and Johns, he started painting in even vertical stripes, and has continued in this style since. Davis' stripe paintings usually employ a large number of colours recurring in quasi-musical rhythms, and they differ from Op Art works in that the chords and progressions of colour, almost romantic in effect, are more important than the flicker of the regular pattern: *Quiet Firecracker* (1968, London Tate). Although now associated with the 'Washington School' of **Post-Painterly Abstraction**, Davis developed his style independently of Kenneth Noland.

DAVIS, Stuart (1894–1964), American painter. An art student at **Robert Henri**'s school in New York, he was encouraged to reject academicism and to take his subjects from the urban landscape, which was to be a formative influence on his style. Davis always handled his subject matter with a rigid discipline, making form more important than content. He exhibited at the **Armory Show** in 1913, and came into contact with French avant-garde art. He was greatly influenced by **Matisse** in his use of strong non-local colours, by **Cubism** which showed him how to fragment his pictures to achieve a tauter and more complex unity, and by Léger.

Davis did not immediately synthesize these influences but for a time alternated imitations of Cubist collages, *eg Lucky Strike* (1921, New York MMA), with more representational landscapes in a Fauvist style, as in *New Mexican Landscape* (1923, New York, Whitney Museum). In 1927, he began a series of near-abstract pictures based, like those of **Cubo-Realism**, on everyday motifs, especially machinery: many of these are called *Eggbeater* (*eg* New York, Whitney Museum). On a long visit to Paris in 1928, however, he reverted to a highly simplified representational style, *eg Place des Voges, No. 1* (1928, Newark Museum). In his paintings of the 1930s, representational elements still occurred, though they were arranged in a purely pictorial composition by means of colour. Many of these works were divided in half vertically, like a stereoscope picture, one side being a gloss on the other, *eg Swing Landscape* (1938, Indiana Univ.). By 1940 the representational elements had completely disappeared (except for Davis' frequent use of lettered inscriptions during all periods of his work), and the flat collage-like shapes in pure colour had been extended to cover the whole surface of the picture, without any apparent representational intentions *eg Something on the Eight Ball* (1954, Philadelphia MA).

DEBRE, Olivier (1920–), French painter. A pupil of the Ecole des Beaux-Arts from 1938, Debré turned to abstract painting in 1943. His works of the 1950s use blocks of paint applied with a knife, sometimes with slight figurative implications, as in *Signe-Personnage 'Cliffs'* (1956, Washington Phillips Collection). They are somewhat in the manner of de Staël, though the colours are less pure. More recently, his canvases have been dominated by one basic colour applied much more thinly.

DECHELETTE, Louis Auguste (1894–), French painter. A self-taught artist, he held his first exhibition in 1943. A contemporary practitioner of Primitive Art, Déchelette's compositions are full of little human figures and reveal a freshness of vision and a refined use of restrained colours, as in *Un Mariage à l'Eglise St. Etienne-du-Mont* (1949, Paris MNAM).

DEGAS, Edgar (1834–1917), French painter, christened Hilaire Germain Edgar de Gas. The son of a wealthy banker, he first studied law but had family approval to paint and draw. He was influenced by Ingres, who said at their first meeting: 'Draw lines and yet more lines, whether by memory or from nature, it does not matter'; this advice lay at the core of Degas' work. He spent a short time at the Ecole des Beaux-Arts and made many copies from *quattrocento* paintings in the Louvre. He went to Italy in 1856, and 1857–9, where he studied the 15th century masters and drew the local inhabitants. Returning to Paris, he completed several historical paintings in a Classical style, *eg Young Spartan Girls Provoking the Boys to a Fight* (1860, London NG). At this time he also painted a number of psychological portraits, the most important being the large *Bellelli Family* (1860, Paris Jeu de Paume), which reflects the influence of **Japanese Prints** which was to be one of the most striking elements in Degas' style. They showed him how to reduce depth of space, and to place the main subject off-centre or nearly outside the frame, *eg L'Absinthe* (1876, Paris Jeu de Paume). He learned to treat the setting as a series of rectangular shapes parallel to the edge creating striking divisions, as in *Women at a Café* (1877, Paris Jeu de Paume).

He met **Manet**'s friends at the Café Guerbois and, like them, took an interest in contemporary life, in racecourse scenes, *eg The Start* (1862, Harvard Fogg Museum); then in the theatre, *eg The Orchestra of the Opéra* (1868, Paris Louvre) and *Mlle. Fiocre dans la Source* (shown at the Salon of 1868 and now in the Brooklyn Museum, New York); and in family scenes, *eg Pouting* (1873, New York Metropolitan), all subjects to which he returned throughout his life. His extremely precise style at this stage sought the effects of relief, and a realism similar to that of Holbein, whom Degas greatly admired. His interest in evoking decor, as well as the psychological portrayal of his subjects, anticipated the **Nabis**.

In 1872, he went to the United States, where he painted *The Cotton Market at New Orleans* (Pau MBA). He began to treat increasingly naturalistic subjects, *eg The Rape* (1874, Philadelphia MA); *At the Bourse* (c 1878, Paris Jeu de Paume); and *Laundresses* (1884, Paris Jeu de Paume). Their execution reveals Degas' adoption of the ideals of **Impressionism**. He took part in the 1874, 1876, 1877 and 1879 Impressionist exhibitions. His colours became increasingly bright, especially in his racecourse scenes, *eg Jockeys* (1881–5, Yale Univ. AG), but he never allowed light to obliterate the areas of local colour in his work.

He became increasingly morose and solitary (his last thirty years were spent as a recluse in Paris). From about 1875, he often painted scenes from the circus, *eg Miss Lola au Cirque Fernando* (1879, London NG), the cabaret and the ballet. In cabaret scenes, such as *The Song of the Dog* (c 1875–7, New York Metropolitan) and *Chanteuse au Gant* (1878, Chicago Art Inst.), his interest in the effects of artificial lighting, particularly lighting from below, reversed the normal technique on which modelling of the features was based; in *A Ballet Seen from an Opera Box* (1885, Philadelphia MA) this lighting, seen over the shoulder of a viewer in the box, creates a psychological perspective between two different worlds.

His main interest in these topics was not the spectacle which the audience saw, but the view from the wings, behind the scenes, as in *The Rehearsal* (c 1877, Glasgow Kelvingrove, Burrell Collection).

Edgar Degas: Dancers Adjusting their Slippers *(1893—8, Cleveland MA); ph. Giraudon.*

Those casual pictures of dancers stretching, dressing and resting, depict the inherent beauty of the human body, which Degas revealed as more interesting than the artificial poses on the stage, *eg The Dancing Class* (1880, Denver AM). In these works, Degas may have initiated a new objective approach to the human figure in modern art. The more conventional theatre pictures, however, quickly brought him wealth and fame.

Degas's sight began to fail in 1885, and, towards 1892, he abandoned oil painting, though he continued with pastels. He began a series of studies of female nudes at their toilet, analyzing their forms and attitudes and using colours of even richer tones. These works were a decisive influence on **Bonnard**. Degas was aware that his models were far from being conventionally lovely, saying that he was obliged to paint women in their bath-tubs instead of Venuses, *eg The Tub* (1886, Paris Jeu de Paume); *The Tub* (1886, Farmington, Conn., Hill-Stead Museum). His last works, of trembling draughtman-

ship and a near-geometrical structure, were dappled with patches of dazzling light: *Scène de Ballet* (1896—8, Edinburgh NG of Scotland); *Woman Drying Herself* (1903, Chicago Art Inst.).

Degas was also a prolific sculptor, and created many statues of horses in motion, and of dancers. The most important of these is *Petite Danseuse de Quatorze Ans* (Paris Jeu de Paume; London Tate; New York Metropolitan), exhibited in 1881; Renoir affirmed: 'Degas is the first of sculptors'. Degas used this medium increasingly as his sight failed, achieving some excellent results in a finished, expressive style, although he himself regarded this work as purely experimental.

DEINEKA, Aleksandr (1899–), Russian painter. His early work was somewhat similar to the Expressionist drawings of Grosz, although his monumental compositions, such as *The Defence of Petrograd* (1928, Moscow Tretchiakov Gallery), show a fine and original sense of form. His later paintings have been overlaid with a gentle luminosity, influenced by the Fauves. His work suffers less than that of most official Soviet artists from propaganda content.

DELACROIX, Eugène (1798–1863), French painter. One of the most frequently quoted influences on late 19th and early 20th century art (*cf* Signac's book *D'Eugène Delacroix au Néo-Impressionisme*, 1899), Delacroix's influence was the result of his style more than his subjects. His work is distinguished by vigour of composition and by directness of handling. This technique influenced **van Gogh**, **Fauvism**, **Expressionism** and indirectly, Action Painting. Delacroix was not only a bright and adventurous colourist, but made extensive use of the discoveries of Chevreul (published as *La Loi du Contraste simultané*, 1839). He gradually banished grey and earth colours from his palette, adopted colour schemes making careful use of complementary colours and he increasingly superimposed broken touches of pure hues on another colour to enliven it or to relate one area to another, the various strokes blending when viewed from a distance. This was a direct precursor of the techniques of **Impressionism** and a very powerful influence on **Neo-Impressionism**.

DELACROIX, Henri Edmond, known as Cross (1856–1910), French painter. One of the most important of the Neo-Impressionists, he painted in the Divisionist manner invented by **Seurat**. He worked in Provence at the beginning of the century in the company of Matisse and Signac. Although lacking Seurat's clarity of design, he had a similar ability to portray an atmosphere permeated by light. Figures play a large part in his work, *eg Bal Villageois dans le Var* (1896, Toledo, Ohio, MA), but these are not the most suitable subjects for his style as can be seen from *L'Après-Midi au Jardin* (1904, Frankfurt, Kunstinstitut) in which the realism of the figures forms hard knots in the Impressionist texture of the foliage. His landscapes were undoubtedly his most successful works, not only those such as *Amandiers en Fleurs* (1902, Copenhagen, Ny Carlsberg Glyptotek), in which he merely repeats Impressionist successes, but in remarkable works such

as *Les Iles d'Or* (1891–2, Paris MNAM), simple seascapes barred with rows of coloured dots in which he comes near to abstraction.

DELAUNAY, Robert (1885–1941), French painter. He was initially influenced by **Divisionism** techniques of the Neo-Impressionists, and by **Cézanne**. His first significant works are a series of paintings of the interior of *St. Severin Church* (1909, Philadelphia AM; Stockholm Moderna Museet; New York Guggenheim Museum) in which the architecture is pushed outwards by a dominant free play of colours. He allied himself with **Cubism** and exhibited in the Salon des Indépendants (1911, 1912) when he showed his large, partly allegorical composition *The City of Paris* (Paris MNAM). This was the culmination of a number of views of the Eiffel Tower and cityscapes, *eg Window overlooking the City No. 4* (1910–11, New York Guggenheim). In 1912, with a series of paintings of *Windows* (Paris MNAM; Dusseldorf Kunstmuseum), he produced near-abstract works in contrasting colours, which reacted against the austerity of analytical Cubism and initiated the movement Apollinaire called **Orphism**. In the years 1912–13 he created the first abstract works in France: *Formes Circulaires, Soleil, Lune* (Amsterdam Stedelijk M). These target-shaped forms in prismatic colours made a powerful and decorative impact with no objective or symbolical meaning. His later works tend to adhere to the target motif, but the forms are arranged with increasing discipline: *Endless Rhythm* (1935, London Tate).

DELVAUX, Paul (1898–), Belgian painter. He was a pupil of the Académie des Beaux Arts, Brussels, and began by painting nudes and landscapes in an Impressionist style. In 1932 he visited the 'Musee Spitzner' (a booth at the Brussels Fair), where he was fascinated by the conjunction of two neighbouring exhibits, a sleeping Venus and a skeleton. He painted several versions of them, replacing the clothed Venus by a nude; this version of the proximity of love and death was to recur in many of his greatest works, *eg Venus Asleep* (1944, London Tate). He came into contact (1934) with **Surrealism**, a movement obviously related to his approach. In the same year he became acquainted with the work of **De Chirico** which inspired his own works combining nude and clothed figures in a static architectural setting, all transfixed by an unreal light as in *The Red Bows* (1937, Antwerp MBA). His later works were variations on these and a few other themes, *eg* the bespectacled professor taken from an illustration to Jules Verne, first seen in *The Phases of the Moon* (1939, New York MMA), or the deserted railway station, *The Staircase* (1948, Cleveland MA). In the early 1950s he painted a number of impressive religious subjects, conceived in terms of skeletons and figures in helmets from World War II, *eg Crucifixion* (1952, Brussels MBA).

DE MAISTRE, Roy (1894–   ), Australian painter. Educated at home, he went to Sydney in 1913 to study music and painting. He became interested in the implications of **Post-Impressionism**, and during World War I made valuable experiments with colour in decorating the rooms of shell-shocked patients. His own paintings in the Post-Impressionist manner sold well, *eg White Roses* (1922, Sydney AG), and in 1923 he got a scholarship to visit Paris and London. He settled in Europe in 1926, dividing his time between London and southern France. De Maistre was strongly influenced by **Cubism**, and his work oscillates between stylization and near abstraction. This is particularly powerful in his religious subjects, *eg Crucifixion* (1942–4, Leicester AG), *Pieta* (1950, London Tate); *Stations of the Cross* (1940–56, London, Westminster Cathedral).

DEMUTH, Charles (1883–1935), American painter. He was a student at the Pennsylvania Academy of Fine Arts and later in Paris (1907–8, 1912–14, 1921), although he did not at first succumb to the influence of Cubism. His early painting (up to 1915) consisted of flower-pieces influenced by **Redon**, and landscapes influenced by Fauvism and John Marin. On his return (1914) to New York, he began painting vaudeville subjects which showed an increasing amount of stylization: the figures, in graceful poses, were isolated in curvilinear patterns *eg Vaudeville Musicians* (1917, New York MMA). In 1917 he went with **Hartley** on a

holiday to Bermuda. His influence, and a growing awareness of **Cubism** which had come from contact with Duchamp from 1915 on, led him to develop a personal style, first in landscape and then in urban views and pictures of machinery. He used lines extending from the objects in the picture to section the surrounding space in a rectilinear mesh, a technique derived from **Futurism**, *eg Sails* (1919, Santa Barbara MA). These shapes were at first largely abstract, but from about 1920 they gradually acquired more detail, in the manner of **Sheeler**'s Cubo-Realism, as in *Paquebot 'Paris'* (1921, Columbus AG). Many of these industrial views have ironic titles revealing the influence of Duchamp, *eg . . . and the Home of the Brave* (1931, Chicago Art Inst.), *After All . . .* (1933).

The most remarkable of Demuth's works, though also prefigured by Hartley, are his 'Poster Portraits': abstract tempera paintings using letters and other forms in symbolic reference to one of his friends, *eg 'I Saw the Figure 5 in Gold'* (1928, New York Metropolitan Museum), a 'portrait' of William Carlos Williams. These have had a considerable influence on **Pop Art**.

DENIS, Maurice (1870–1943), French painter. After studying at the Académie Julian, where he met Paul Sérusier, he joined the **Nabis**, and became their spiritual leader. In 1896 he discovered the art of the Nazarenes in Germany, and of the Florentine *quattrocento*. His style was influenced by **Cézanne**, in whose honour he had painted the famous *Homage to Cézanne* (1900, Paris MNAM). His work used bright colours, with the third dimension only hinted at. He took an interest in religious art, (*eg Paradise*, 1912, Paris MNAM), and founded the Ateliers d'Art Sacré with Desvallières in 1919. His most important decorative work was the ceiling of the Théâtre des Champs-Elysées (1912). His easel painting includes work which, with its sinuous lines, recalls **Art Nouveau** (*eg The Muses*, Paris MNAM), fresh and natural family scenes (*eg On a Balcony in Venice*, 1907, Paris MNAM), and Italian landscapes in pure, vivid colours. Speaking of painting he said, 'Remember that a picture, before being a horse, a nude or some kind of anecdote, is essentially a flat surface covered with colours assembled in a certain order.'

DENNY, Robyn (1930–), English painter. He studied at the St. Martin's School of Art and the Royal College of Art. His work, dating from late 1950s, is a form of **Post-Painterly Abstraction**, though its muted, subtle colours soften outlines and create sensations of depth. Most of his more recent works are Classical in conception. They are 6 or 7 foot high symmetrical paintings in which horizontal and vertical bands frame shapes like overlapping doorways—a metaphor inviting one to 'step in' and explore the space created by the interplay of colours: *Into Light* (1967, Leeds City AG). The doorway motif is not always explicit, however, as in *Garden* (1967, London Tate). Denny represented Britain at the Venice Biennale of 1966.

DERAIN, André (1880–1954), French painter. He decided to devote himself to painting in 1897. After meeting Vlaminck by chance in a train, he shared a makeshift studio with him at Chatou, while painting on the banks of the Seine and copying the Old Masters in the Louvre. In 1904, Vlaminck introduced him to Negro art, and he enrolled as a student at the Académie Julian. In 1905 he was bound under contract to Ambroise Vollard, and took part in the famous Salon d'Automne, exhibiting with the **Fauvism** group. One of its most brilliant members, his style at that time was characterized by pure colours of extraordinary intensity, and by fragmented drawing in an almost **Pointillism** style, *eg Portrait of Matisse* (1905, Philadelphia MA); *Collioure* (1905, Paris MNAM). He went to London in 1906 and painted extraordinarily richly coloured river-scapes, including *The Pool of London* (1906, London Tate), *Barges on the Thames* (1906, Leeds AG), *Shipping on the Thames* (1906, Glasgow Kelvingrove). In these works Derain went as far as any of his contemporaries in his efforts to record the maximum *éclat* of light and colour, but his Fauve period was short. In 1908 he turned to a darker style, more limited in colour and with more solid painting influenced by **Cézanne**, *eg Trees by the Lake* (1909, London Courtauld Inst.). He pursued this development partially in the direction of **Cubism**, *eg Still Life* (1911, Paris MAMVP), *The Table* (1911, New York Metropolitan Museum).

At this time he destroyed much of his early work and developed a Neo-Classical style of antique art. This kind of retrenchment after the first heroic years of the century is to be found in a number of artists, but Derain changed his style completely and did not try to prolong the life of one whose possibilities he had exhausted. In his ballet designs, however, (*eg La Boutique Fantasque*, 1919, for Diaghilev; *Mam'zelle Angot*, 1947, for Sadler's Wells Ballet, London) he retained the freshness which had characterized his Fauve period.

DE RIVERA, José (1904–), American sculptor. His recent sculpture marks the same sort of reaction to the rough, open forms of the art of the 1950s as is found in **Post-Painterly Abstraction**. His sculptures are all meticulously made and polished, usually by a commercial firm, and are very simple in content consisting often of a single twisted loop of metal forming a Möbius band, *eg Construction #127* (1970, New York Whitney Museum).

DESNOYER, François (1894–), French painter. He studied at the Ecole des Arts Décoratifs, Paris, from 1913 and later travelled widely. The dominant feature of Desnoyer's art is his robust and vigorous style based on strong tonal contrasts and on modelling with boldly defined planes, similar to **Cézanne**. From a restrained realism, *eg Recumbent Nude* (1936, Paris MNAM), he moved on to a **Cubism**-inspired style, realistic in detail but composed as if of abstract elements with structural considerations paramount. At the same time, his colours became brighter and warmer, as in *Grande Kermesse* (1941, Paris MNAM). He often combines landscape and figure study in expressing joyfulness and optimism.

DESPIAU, Charles (1874–1946), French sculptor. In 1907 he entered Rodin's studio, where he worked for several years. His work developed gradually and logically. It consists entirely of figure sculptures, which show a naturalism related to Classical models. His busts reveal a very personal art. Their extreme linear precision (Despiau made thousands of drawings, and he was a very sound draughtsman) results in a concentrated simplicity, with a calm and yet vibrant expression *eg Miss Schulte* (1934, London Tate).

DESPIERRE, Jacques (1912–), French painter. The son of the painter Céria, his almost monumental style combines vigorous and rhythmical drawing, bright clear colours, well-integrated and adventurous compositions and frequently bold perspectives. He has painted numerous landscapes of the Loire district, in harmonies of blue and white, and interior scenes in which the figures blend with their backgrounds in a very carefully determined manner. The Musée National d'Art Moderne, Paris contains his *Beach at Cassis* (1938) and *The Hunters* (1946).

DESVALLIERES, George (1861–1950), French painter. He was taught by Gustave Moreau at the Ecole des Beaux-Arts; his first exhibition was in 1883, and he later became the President of the Salon d'Automne. He is best known for his devotion to religious art, after the death of his son during World War I. From 1919 he directed the Ateliers d'Art Sacré, with Maurice Denis, and undertook many decorative projects in churches in France (*eg* Verneuil-sur-Avre, Saint-Privas and the Eglise du Saint-Esprit, Paris) and America. His art is bitterly realistic; he tried to convince non-believers of the ugliness of society, as in *Christ at the Column* (1910) and *L'Ascension du Poilu* (1922), both in Paris MNAM.

DILLER, Burgoyne (1906–65), American painter. Diller, who studied in New York at the Art Students' League, was the first American disciple of **Mondrian**. He made an exhaustive study of the possibility of developing a simply stated **Constructivism** 'theme', via logical extensions approximating Mondrian's style of the 1930s (*Second Theme*, 1938–40, New York Metropolitan Museum) and to the more complex style of his last works: *Third Theme* (1946–8, New York Whitney Museum). The various stages were executed contemporaneously, although Diller produced most of the more complex works later in his life. In the 1960s he also executed several monumental three-dimensional constructions in wood covered with formica. Diller was in charge of the W.P.A. Mural Project (1935–40).

DINE, Jim (1935–), American painter and sculptor. Dine studied at the University of Cincinnati and moved to New York in 1959. Since 1967 he has lived in London. There are two main features in his art. One is his concern with everyday objects as things of interest in their own right, a tradition stemming from Duchamp and paralleled in **Pop Art**. The other is a continuation of the **Abstract Expressionism** interest in freely painted surfaces. Like Jasper Johns, he frequently combines both approaches in a single work as if to study the relationship between painting and alternative means of specification. His paintings of paint-boxes, palettes and colour charts are particularly close to Johns', but his style is more economical with the passages of painting often reduced to a few strokes. Clothing and simple household objects form his main subjects. In the early paintings they were merely painted in the centre of an otherwise blank canvas and combined with a written description. After 1961 Dine began to incorporate part of the article itself with passages of painting, as in *Toaster* (1962, New York Whitney Museum). Some of these works are quite large with objects standing against painted walls, *eg Black Bathroom No. 2* (1962, Toronto AG). In 1965, Dine produced works contrasting the imagined world of the daydream and hard fact: *All in one Lycra plus Attachments* (1965, Eindhoven, van Abbemuseum). *Walking Dream with a Four Foot Clamp* (1965, London Tate) is a picture of shapely female legs with the whole canvas gripped in a woodworker's clamp, thus contrasting the intangible world of the imagination with the measurable one, and emphasizing the fact of the painting as a man-made object, not as a window into another world. His most recent works have been darker in tone, more self-contained, using the object in a more creative way. Dine has also been active as an organizer of **Happenings**.

DI SUVERO, Mark (1933–), American sculptor. Born in Shanghai, China, he went to the United States in 1941. His bold abstract sculpture uses materials from construction sites or an old railway yard *eg* 'I beams', pieces of wood, and railway sleepers, often held together by guy wires.

DIVISIONISM, a technique of painting, the principal characteristic of the **Neo-Impressionism** group which, in about 1886, formed itself around **Seurat** and **Signac**. Signac's book *D'Eugène Delacroix au Néo-Impressionisme* (1899) sets out the basis of the Divisionist technique. There are four principles:

1. All colours are to be achieved through an optical mixture of pure colours, as found in the spectrum; 2. A distinction is to be made between local colour, colour due to lighting and colour due to reflection; 3. The elements of the picture are to be balanced taking the effects of mutual colour contrast into account; 4. The paint is to be applied in touches proportionate to the size of the canvas.

Divisionist technique develops the ideas published by Chevreul in his *La Loi du Contraste Simultané* (1839), and found, in less systematic form, in the later works of Delacroix and the Impressionists. Divisionism refined the more general Pointillist practice of using small touches of colour. The aim, as with Impressionism, was to preserve freshness and only pure colours were used. But whereas the Impressionists varied their handling according to the subject and allowed colours to be mixed on the palette, the Neo-Impressionists used dots small enough, and colours pure enough, to mix in the eye. They made use of the fact that complementary colours (*eg* red and green) enhance each other if juxtaposed, whereas other combinations produce the effect of shadow. In recent years doubt has been cast on the adequacy of Signac's explanations of the true effect of these pictures. When looking at a work such as Seurat's *Un Après-midi à la Grande Jatte* (1886, Chicago Art Inst.) one can never forget the individual touches and allow them to merge into apparent mixed colours. Instead, the peculiar fascination of these pictures seems to come from the eye's awareness of their broken quality, and the resulting effort required to interpret them gives rise to a series of readings, each of which contributes to the overall sensation.

DIX, Otto (1891–), German painter. Although one of the most important German painters working in the **Expressionism** tradition, Dix is linked in style with the painters of the German Re-

naissance, Dürer, Grünewald and Altdorfer especially. His first *Self-portrait with Carnation* (1912, Detroit Art Inst.) is in imitation of Dürer and works such as *The Schrammsteine in the Clouds* (1938, Berlin NG) might almost be mistaken for the work of Altdorfer. These influences give strength to Dix's interpretations of the contemporary scene, rather than the opposite, and it is the meticulous naturalism which underlies even his most apocalyptic scenes which give them their horror. He was briefly influenced by Futurism, *eg War* (1914, Dusseldorf Kunstmuseum). After World War I, he painted studies of horribly deformed cripples and beggars; *eg Matchseller I* (1920, Stuttgart NG); *Matchseller II* (1927, Mannheim Kunsthalle), often contrasting them with the frivolity of post-War society, *The 'Great City' Triptych* (1927, Stuttgart Civic Gallery). In these works he is close to the world of Brecht, and also to the style of George Grosz. There were a few large-scale apocalyptic works in which war is evoked with a concentration of gruesome detail worthy of Bosch: these include *The Trench* (1920–3, destroyed) and *War Triptych* (1929–32, Dresden, Schloss Pillnitz). He also painted portraits, both compassionately detailed studies such as *My Parents* (1924, Hanover Landesgalerie) and pictures of doctors and other professional people in which the apparatus of their work is given as much attention as the sitter himself, often appearing to hold him in a sort of gruesome bondage, *eg Portrait of the Urologist Dr. Hans Koch* (1921, Cologne, Wallraff-Richartz Museum). Since World War II, Dix has been painting in a more cheerful, broader style.

DOBELL, William (1899–1970), Australian painter. After attending the Julian Ashton Art School in Sydney, he won (1929) the Society of Artists' Travelling Scholarship and enrolled at the Slade. Acute social satire, humour and character perception are first seen in paintings from 1936–8: *Mrs. South Kensington, The Sleeping Greek* and *The Irish Youth*. He returned to Australia in 1938, afterwards developing an elongated style, *eg The Cypriot* (1940). He first won the Archibald Prize in 1943 with his portrait of *Joshua Smith* (the subject of a court case, the prosecution claiming the prize had been wrongfully awarded for a caricature) and in 1948 was awarded Wynne Prize for the landscape, *Storm Approaching, Wangi.* His principal portraits of later period were of the aging *Dame Mary Gilmore* (1955) and beautician *Helena Rubenstein* (1957). Dobell represented Australia at the 1954 Venice Biennale with Drysdale and Nolan. He was knighted in 1966.

DOBSON, Frank (1888–1963), English sculptor. Although starting as a painter, he devoted himself largely to sculpture after 1920 when he met **Wyndham Lewis**, with whom he had much in common. His earlier work in stone and bronze, both allegorical pieces and portrait busts, was stylized under the influence of Cubism, *eg The Man Child* (1921, London Tate). Later he was influenced by **Maillol**.

DOESBURG, Theo van (1883–1931), Dutch painter. The founder (1917), with **Mondrian** of the *De Stijl* review, he propagated the aesthetics of Neo-Plasticism in Germany and France. In 1926 he broke away and founded the **Elementarism** movement. Though lacking that refusal to compromise aesthetic theory which made Mondrian a great painter, van Doesburg was nevertheless important as a theoretician.

DOMELA NIEUWENHUIS, Cesar (1900–), Dutch painter. Domela was brought up in Paris where with no formal training he began painting formalized landscapes in 1922. Almost immediately, however, he turned to abstract painting, influenced by Kandinsky, *eg Composition* (1923, Amsterdam, Stedelijk M). In 1924 he joined the **De Stijl** group and since then all his works have been Constructivist. In 1926 he followed van Doesburg into the more liberal style of **Elementarism**, as in *Neo-Plastic Composition* (1927, Hague Gemeentemuseum), and in 1929 abandoned Neo-Plasticism completely. His later works have been constructions using a wide variety of materials and involving curved shapes which seem to grow out of the materials themselves. Each work makes exquisite use of the contrasted colour, texture and character of the materials; their delicate relief activates but does not disrupt the basically two-dimensional composition, *eg Relief* (1962, Paris MNAM).

Domela returned to Paris in 1933 and became involved with the Abstraction-Création group.

DONGEN, Kees van (1877–1968), Dutch painter. As a youth he worked in his father's malt-house during the day and took evening courses in drawing. At the age of twenty, he went to live in Paris. He lodged in the Bateau-Lavoir in Montmartre, where he met Picasso and his circle. An enthusiastic advocate of **Fauvism**, he was attracted by the heady violence of colour and the uninhibited play given to formal and compositional values characteristic of the movement. He said that a picture should be something which excites and exalts life, because life is dark and dreary. He painted music-hall scenes and nudes of an overwhelming sensuality, *eg The Old Clown* (1906, Amsterdam, Stedelijk M); *The Singer Modjesko* (1908, New York MMA). In 1909, a painting of his in the Salon d'Automne was judged indecent and was taken down by the police. This scandal brought him great success, and he became the portrait painter of Parisian society. Some of his portraits have an admirable honesty, *eg* the scruffy *Charles Rappoport* (1913, Rotterdam, Museum Boymans-van Beuningen), but the majority of them pandered to the tastes of his clients, not least through titillating them with the shock of dramatic but superficial modernity as in *Mme. Jasmy Alvin* (1925, Paris MNAM).

DOVE, Arthur Garfield (1880–1946), American painter. At first a successful illustrator and cartoonist, he turned to painting in 1907 and exhibited at the Paris Salon d'Automne the following year, where he was struck by **Fauvism**. He was encouraged by Alfred Stieglitz and exhibited at the Gallery 291 in 1910 (see **Galleries**). All the works of this period, and many of his later output, are abstract in appearance, *eg Nature Symbolized, No. 2* (1911, Chicago Art Inst.), yet their particular strength is that they are never far from Nature, represented sometimes by rich harmonies of colour, as in *Summer* (1935, Leominster, Mass., Lane Foundation), sometimes by the inclusion of natural forms into an otherwise two-dimensional composition, as in *Goat* (1935, New York Metropolitan Museum). In the finest works, *eg Cows in Pasture* (1935, Washington, Phillips Collection), the abstract and the natural are perfectly balanced. The early influences on his style were Orphism and Synchromism. Later he was also influenced by **Kandinsky**, by **Schwitters** as in the collage *Portrait of Ralph Dusenberry* (1924, New York MMA), and by **Klee**, *eg High Noon* (1944, Wichita AM). Some of Dove's most remarkable paintings, such as *Sunrise III* (1937, Yale Univ. AG), and *Flour Mill II* (1938, Washington Phillips Collection), have influenced **Abstract Expressionism** by their acceptance of accidental effects, and by their combination of colours in undefined patches for emotive purposes.

DOWNING, Thomas (1928–), American painter. See **Post-Painterly Abstraction**.

DRACHKOVITCH, Albert (1928–), Yugoslav painter. He went to Paris in 1939, where he painted in complete solitude, becoming known to connoisseurs only after 1955. His panoramic landscape, influenced at first by Bruegel, is remarkable for its minute approach, and for the artist's extraordinary feeling for perspective and luminous effects of light.

DRIES, Jean (1905–), French painter, born Jean Driesbach. He has executed mural decorations for the Cité Universitaire, Paris, and for the Caen Chamber of Commerce. He paints landscapes and figure studies with robust, sculptural forms, and vivid contrasting colours, *eg Le Port de Saint-Tropez* (1952, Paris MNAM). His recent style is harder, in the manner of **Buffet**.

DRYSDALE, Russell (1912–), Australian painter, born in England. Originally a farmer, he gave this up in 1935 to study art, first in Melbourne and later in London and Paris. His first paintings show the strong influence of **Matisse**. Having settled in Sydney in 1940, he began to develop his characteristic paintings of the bleak Australian desert and small towns, and the loneliness and isolation of people in this alien environment, *eg Man Reading a Newspaper* (1941, Sydney Univ.); *The War Memorial* (1949, London Tate); *Man with a Fish Spear* (1958, Aberdeen AG).

His later pictures are richer in colour; in them the figures often have blurred, anonymous faces—although his portraits are closely and economically observed. His personal view of Australia has been a considerable influence on **Sydney Nolan**. He was knighted in 1969.

DUBUFFET, Jean (1901–), French painter. His first exhibition was in 1944, and in 1949 he founded the Société de L'Art Brut. His early paintings had figures drawn in a deliberately naive, child-like style. They illustrate Dubuffet's search for escape from conventional artistic forms and return to primitive roots, by way of child-like drawings, graffiti, accidental marks on walls, and even the bare earth itself. In 1946 his one-man exhibition, which he called *Mirobolus, Macadam et Cie, hautes pates*, was held at the Galérie Drouin where it caused a sensation. As an alternative to conventional painting he prepared the canvas with a thick monochrome impasto, encasing sand, cinders and bits of string, on which he scratched simple outline drawings. His later works continue these experiments, with increasing colour and widening range of subjects, each usually explored in a group of paintings at a time, *eg The Busy Life* (1963, London Tate). Sometimes he merely explored the texture or appearance of a single surface, *eg Work Table with Letter* (1952, New York MMA); or created pictures with metal foil and papier-mâché which work entirely on texture, as in *Le Cadastre* (1960, Eindhoven van Abbemuseum). In 1953 and again in 1955 he made a number of **Collages** of butterfly wings, *eg The Garden of Bibi Trompette* (1955, Claremont, Calif., Pomona College). These led him on to a series of **Assemblages** which are in effect collages of pieces of numerous paintings and textures, often with natural materials added, *eg Door with Couch Grass* (1957, New York Guggenheim). In all these works, Dubuffet has given a new meaning to representative painting often by making the physical composition of the painting as representative as the pictorial content.

In 1961 Dubuffet produced a number of complex cartoon-like graffiti of street scenes peopled with figures in little cars and on foot, *eg Vire Volte* (1961, London Tate). This led in 1963 to his great series

L'Hourloupe in which similar subjects are treated with an entirely new language. Red, blue, white and black are the only colours used, and these are rarely in solid areas. Instead the paintings are made up of a large number of interlocking curvilinear cells, like pieces in a jigsaw, either left plain or hatched with one of the colours in diagonal lines. The forms are recognizable as caricature heads, houses, cars and so forth, but there is often an intentional ambiguity between what is image and what is background, eg L'Escampette (1964, Amsterdam Stedelijk M). In his series of **Environments** entitled Edifices and Monuments (1969–71), similar forms are drawn on the white undulating walls of claustrophobic cells and grottoes, presenting the conflict between real and fictive space with terrifying power. This style owes a little to Cubism and Purism, but its use in Dubuffet's hands is utterly different and illustrates the artist's ability to do something completely new in the history of art.

DUCHAMP, Marcel (1887–1968), French artist. Although he produced comparatively few works, the extraordinary range and fertility of Duchamp's ideas place him among the most influential painters of our time. His art at different periods relates closely to Fauvism, Cubism, Futurism and Surrealism; he was one of the leaders of the **Dada** movement; he was the first to make a systematic investigation of the rôle of **Chance in Art**; his invention of 'Ready-mades' and development of Kinetic sculpture have both proved crucial (though at a remove of some 30 years) to developments since World War II. The work of Duchamp is not easily seen outside Philadelphia, and it may often surprise one by its lack of conventional beauty, but he was an intense and serious artist, exploring the nature of art itself. His frequent changes of direction and complete lack of self-plagiarism (despite his use of earlier works as material for new developments) show the depth of his enquiry in that he would leave a subject or technique once all its implications were clear to him without feeling it necessary to make them explicit.

Duchamp's early work consists of conventional representational paintings, first in **Impressionism**, as Church at Blainville

(1902, Philadelphia MA), and then Fauvist, eg Chess Game (1910, Philadelphia). He came comparatively late to Cubism, eg Portrait (1911, Philadelphia), and almost immediately struck off in his own direction. The Portrait already shows an interest in simultaneous views of a moving figure as does Coffee-mill (1911, private collection) done for Jacques Villon, in which he included plan, elevation and sectional views of the machine and shows several positions of the handle. This led on in two directions, to the Nude descending a Staircase (1911, second version 1912; both Philadelphia) in which the superimposed successive views of a Cubist figure caused a sensation at the **Armory Show** in 1913; and to a whole series of more or less abstract works derived from Cubism which treat apparently 'human' frames in terms of pieces of machinery, eg Le Passage de la Vièrge à la Mariée (1912, New York MMA).

These themes were brought together in his most famous work, the so-called 'Large Glass', La Mariée mise à nue par les célibataires, même (1915–23, broken 1926, repaired version in Philadelphia MA). This work is made from paint and wire varnished on to glass, and also reflects his interest in chance. In 1913 he had dropped three threads, one metre long, on to canvas from a height of one metre; these were then mounted with varnish on the canvas exactly as they had fallen, and boxwood rulers made from the resulting curves, eg Trois Stoppages Etalon (Philadelphia). Some of the lines in the 'Large Glass' are drawn with these rulers; other points are placed in a pattern determined by firing from a toy cannon a matchstick tipped with paint. The whole picture was then left for some weeks to accumulate a random coating of dust, which was preserved in several areas. At this time Duchamp began his series of 'Readymades', objects mounted in an exhibition with little or no alteration: the Bicycle-Wheel (a wheel on a wooden stool) of 1913 was followed by the Bottle Rack of 1914 and the notorious Fountain (a porcelain urinal) of 1917. His L.H.O.O.Q. ('Elle a chaud au cul'—an obscene pun), a reproduction of the Mona Lisa with a moustache. was the sensation of the first Dada exhibition in Paris in 1920. Many of these works are signed with the pseudonyms R. Mutt or Rrose Selavy (a pun on 'c'est la vie'). Many of the subsequent works of this genre are more complex 'Assisted Ready-mades', and often highly evocative, *eg Why not sneeze Rrose Selavy?* (1921, Philadelphia), a small bird cage filled with marble cubes imitating sugar lumps, containing a thermometer and with a cuttlefish bone stuck through the bars. In 1920 Duchamp produced the first of a small number of Kinetic works, *Rotary Glass Disks* (Yale Univ. AG). After that he produced comparatively little, but the importance of his ideas is only now being fully recognized. In 1966, Richard Hamilton presented the retrospective exhibition 'The Almost Complete Works of Marcel Duchamp' at the London Tate Gallery.

DUCHAMP-VILLON, Raymond (1876–1918), French sculptor, born Raymond Duchamp. The brother of the painters Jacques Villon and Marcel and Suzanne Duchamp, he studied medicine and took up sculpture during periods of ill health. He was very interested in **Cubism** and exhibited with the Section d'Or movement in 1912. In the same year, with André Mare, he presented, at the Salon d'Automne, the *Cubist House* of which he had constructed the façade. In 1913 he showed *Lovers* at the Salon d'Automne and, in 1914, animal figures, including a cat, a dog, a pigeon and a parrot. The following year he completed some of his most famous compositions, *eg Horse* and *Seated Woman* (both Paris MNAM).

The sculpture of Duchamp-Villon, initially influenced by Rodin, gradually began to show an increasing interest in the interplay of simple surfaces and large masses. His forms became progressively more synthetic, even in his portraits in which he strove to show the inner character of the subject. His 1914 version of the *Horse* (a favourite subject) presents a strange synthesis of mechanical elements which, very schematically, suggest a horse jumping. This tendency corresponds to the Cubists' (*eg* Léger) interest in machines. A number of his works are in Yale University AG.

DUFRESNE, Charles (1876–1938), French painter. He was an admirer of Delacroix, some of whose favourite subjects (exotic landscapes, jungle and hunting scenes) he executed in a style influenced by Cézanne, *eg Le Spahi* (1919, London Tate).

DUFY, Raoul (1877–1953), French painter. After studying painting at night school in Le Havre, he won a scholarship to the Ecole des Beaux-Arts, Paris in 1900. He was influenced by **Impressionism** (1901–4), and also drew studies of high life in the style of Toulouse-Lautrec. In 1903 he exhibited at the Salon des Indépendants, where he saw for the first time **Matisse**'s *Luxe, Calme et Volupté*. This was a revelation to him: he called it 'the contemplation of the miracle of the imagination expressed in terms of design and colour'. From then he adopted a Fauve palette, painting gaily-bedecked streets and country festivals. He had become friendly with Marquet, and worked with him at Trouville in 1906. His work at this time included *Les Affiches à Trouville* (1906, Paris MNAM). In 1908, after spending some time in Estaque in the company of Braque, he began to use a more rigorous construction, in the spirit of **Cézanne**. He then met the couturier Paul Poiret, who induced him to try his hand in the field of textile design, and he worked for the Bianchinni textile firm at Lyons. His colours became even brighter, and his draughtsmanship increasingly supple; from this period dates the separation of drawing and colour into two separate elements: the blocks of colour provide a frame for the freer draughtsmanship which is a characteristic of Dufy's style. In 1920 he went to Vence, where he painted many landscapes in a Rococo style, full of curly details irrelevant to the main structure, *eg The Three Bathers* (1919, Paris MNAM). He was introduced to the Turf, and this theme inspired some of his wittiest and most lively paintings, *eg The Paddock at Deauville* (1930, Paris MNAM). He lived on the Côte d'Azur (1925–40) where he painted several series of canvases and watercolours in a style even more luminous than before, *eg Olive Trees by Golfe Juan* (1927, London Tate). In 1937 he was commissioned to decorate the Electricity Pavilion at the Paris Exhibition, for which he produced the gigantic composition, *La Fée Electricité* (Paris MAMVP). In 1940 his health began to deteriorate, but his fame continued to spread, and he developed a variety of

Raoul Dufy: Orchestra with Singer *(1942, private collection); ph. Galerie Louis-Carré.*

themes, orchestras, threshing, regattas, official receptions *etc*. The predominant feature of Raoul Dufy's art is its complete technical freedom, and brilliantly fresh colours. Although bordering at times on triviality, the delicacy of his talent and his poetic grace are in many ways typically French.

DUNOYER DE SEGONZAC, André (1884–   ), French painter. He entered the Ecole des Beaux-Arts in Paris in 1902. In 1908, he made the first of many journeys to Saint-Tropez and sent his first painting to the Salon d'Automne. In 1910,

one of his major works, *Buveurs* (Paris, MNAM), was exhibited at the Salon d'Automne. This realistic composition owes much to Cézanne, with its broad surfaces, restrained colouring and profound expressiveness. The influence of the Cubists was also important at this time, as in *Still Life with a Cabbage* (1919, London Tate). His impasto became increasingly rich and was built up with patiently superimposed layers. His landscapes are restrained and realistic, using ochres and greens to express the calm profundity of nature. Mobilized in 1914, he made numerous drawings of life in the trenches, many of which are now in the Musée de l'Ile de France at Sceaux, where there is a large Segonzac collection. After World War I, he began to use bright reds, blues and dazzling greens. He painted a series of lyrical landscapes in which he suppressed detail to suggest the panoramic sweep of the scene before him. He also undertook a series of nude studies, *eg Nude with Newspaper* (1922, London Tate) and large figure compositions of which *Les Canotiers sur le Morin* (1921) is perhaps the most important. This work, brilliant and sensual, attempts and almost accomplishes the task Cézanne had set himself in painting his *Grandes Baigneuses*; this was to depict the splendour of the human body and of nature in one harmonious picture, without compromising reality. Segonzac was elected to the Royal Academy, London in 1947 and, in 1948, to the Royal Academy of Belgium. He has said 'One must be absolutely sincere; interpretation belongs to the realm of the Unconscious. You are lost if you find yourself interpreting what you do.' The Musée National d'Art Moderne in Paris contains a fine collection of his works.

DURAND-RUEL, Paul (1831–1922), French gallery director and art dealer best known for his defence of the Impressionists. In Paris, in 1869, he founded the *Revue de l'Art et de la Curiosité* for which he contributed articles on Renoir and Pissarro. In 1872, he bought 23 of Manet's paintings and became the champion of the Impressionists who, at that time, were poor and regarded with contempt by the public. In 1886 he achieved the important step of interesting the United States in the new school of painting.

E

EARDLEY, Joan (1921–63), Scottish painter. She grew up in London, but moved to Glasgow in 1939 and studied at the School of Art. Her paintings may be divided into three main groups: landscapes, studies of children in the Glasgow slums where she had a studio, and seascapes. All her paintings use oil paint as a plastic medium, but inelegantly, with a deliberate disregard for the rules of fine painting.

The landscapes typically emphasize the foreground where little flowers shine out in blobs of brilliant impasto against a rough surface of dragged and scraped paint. The Glasgow pictures feature remarkably tender, yet unsentimental pictures of children often against a background of chalked-on walls, *eg Glasgow Kids* (Glasgow Kelvingrove). Most remarkable of all are the seascapes which Joan Eardley painted in her last years in her tiny windswept cottage at Catterline on the east coast of Scotland, *eg A Stormy Sea* (1960, Glasgow Kelvingrove). These huge panoramas are almost abstract, and translate the surge of the sea directly in terms of tormented paint, making these works a remarkable link between the Scottish painterly tradition (compare her contemporary **Philipson**) and **Abstract Expressionism**.

ELEMENTARISM, an offshoot of Neo-Plasticism founded in 1926 by **van Doesburg**. This movement decreed that the strictly rectilinear horizontals and verticals of **Mondrian** be replaced by a mode of expression involving inclined planes. Mondrian, however, believed that the horizontal and vertical lines of his paintings were not arbitrary creations of the painter but a symbol of the underlying structure of the universe: he could and did rotate the angle of the frame, or the 'window' through which he looked at the world, but what was to be seen remained constant. Van Doesburg's variation involved tilting the universe and revealed a fundamental misunderstanding of Mondrian's ideas. This departure had another advocate in the Dutch painter **Domela**.

ELMER, Edwin Romango (1850–1923), American painter. This Naive painter supported himself by inventing agricultural machinery and painting portraits from photographs. He took a course at the New York Academy of Design in 1895. Despite his considerable technical skills, his style remained essentially naive in the trancelike clarity and literalness of his vision. His works include *Memorial Portrait* (c 1889, Northampton, Mass., Smith College).

ENSOR, James (1860–1949), Belgian painter. Considered to be the greatest of modern Belgian painters, he studied at the Art School in Brussels and, in 1879, painted *Woman with a Turned-up Nose* (Antwerp MBA). For twenty years after his return to Ostend he worked with great intensity. His canvases, painted initially with a sombre palette, evoke middle-class domestic life; they resemble those of the **Nabis** but have a terrifying dramatic violence. After this period his painting became more highly coloured and the forms became abrupt and tumultuous. He introduced masks, skeletons and ghosts to depict everyday life, *eg Skeletons fighting over a Herring* (1891, Antwerp MBA). The resultant works are disquieting in their virulent symbolism. The largest of these, *Entry of Christ into Brussels* (1888, Antwerp MBA), is a tract on contemporary society. The impasto and colour of *The Skate* (1892, Brussels MBA) are technically most impressive Comparisons between Ensor's work and that of Bosch have been prompted by the melancholy in his art which sometimes borders on the manic depressive. But Ensor's style is more romantic and more truculent. He is regarded as one of the main sources of **Expressionism** and **Surrealism**. After 1900, his output gradually diminished; this period was characterized by the use of pale colours and wan lighting, his work consisting chiefly of subtle, dreamlike landscapes, *eg Effect of Light* (1935, London Tate).

ENVIRONMENTS, a term which has recently come to refer to a work which operates by creating a three-dimensional space of human scale. On the one hand there are works, such as the groups of **George Segal**, in which the artist uses various props to build up an environment for his own artifacts; on the other hand there are the environments which demand the penetration of the spectator. The first of these is little different in concept from those Renaissance commissions involving the collaboration of architect, painter and sculptor, although in Segal's work the fact that the environment is composed of everyday objects means that the spectator can react to it mentally and emotionally even though he may be observing from the outside. The second kind of environment is merely an extension of the way in which an architect controls space. Many sculptures are intended to set up a spatial relationship between the beholder and

themselves, and **Giacometti**, for instance, desired his figures to create space for each other in an open grouping. **Schwitters** created environments in his *Merzbaue*. **Louise Nevelson**'s exhibit at the 1962 Venice Biennale was arranged in three rooms, containing works all painted black, gold and white respectively, and each room appropriately lit so that the effect of each group of works was greater than the sum of the individual parts. **Fontana** has also arranged entire exhibitions to create a spatial ambience.

In the last decade, the concept of the environment has been developed in two opposite directions, towards greater complexity and towards extreme simplicity. The complex environments are generally associated with Pop Art in the work of **Rauschenberg**, **Dine**, Oldenburg and Wesselmann among others. (Richard Hamilton and **Eduardo Paolozzi** created one in 1956 in the 'This is Tomorrow' exhibition which launched Pop). These generally include real furniture and other objects, and may bring into play cinematography, and the senses of sound, smell and even taste as well: Edward Kienholz' *Portable War Memorial* (1968, private collection) includes a working Coca Cola machine. The term would also apply to Rosenquist's huge paintings which may occupy all the walls of one room. **Happenings** are really environments, further extended in complexity. The *Edifices* and *Monuments* of **Dubuffet**, although complex, use environments to explore the purely plastic concerns of real and fictive space.

The other development, towards **Minimal Art**, involves the use of a very few very simple elements to create an effect on the beholder. This is the case with some of the displays of Andy Warhol and with nearly all the work of **Robert Morris**. A high proportion of **Conceptual Art** also involves either modifying the natural environment, or controlling the way we react to it.

EPSTEIN, Jacob (1880–1959), British sculptor, born in New York. He studied in his native city and Paris, and became a British subject after moving to London in 1905. The first of several scandals which accompanied him throughout his life was provoked by the realism of his eighteen statues for the British Medical Association in London. In 1911, he executed the tomb of Oscar Wilde in Père Lachaise cemetery, Paris, met Picasso and his friends and encountered Negro art for the first time. On his return to Britain, he moved among the Vorticists; in their style he completed his *Rock Drill* (1913, London Tate). Some of his subsequent works, in a brutally Expressionist vein, *eg The Visitation* (1926, London Tate), *Ecce Homo* (1935) and *Lazarus* (1948, Oxford, New College), shocked the public, but his reputation grew steadily. He received honorary doctorates from the universities of Aberdeen and Oxford, and was knighted in 1954.

The power and the delicacy of his monumental sculptures is exceptional, as in *Virgin and Child* (1952) in Cavendish Square, London, the *Christ in Majesty* (1955) at Llandaff Cathedral, the *Saint Michael* (1960) at Coventry Cathedral, and the impressive busts of some of the most prominent people of the day, *eg Sir Winston Churchill* (New York MMA) and Jacob Kramer (1921, London Tate). The vigorous realism, boldness and dignity of Epstein's style wrested British sculpture from the restrictions of academic conventionalism and contributed much to its present vigour.

ERNI, Hans (1909–   ), Swiss painter. He was a pupil at the Académie Julian, Paris, in 1928, and became a member of the **Abstraction-Création** group. His drawings and paintings are often done with gouache on hardboard, and combine highly realistic images with geometrical tracings in compositions which are full of symbolic and Surrealist overtones, *eg Ikarus Lilienthal II* (1941, Lucerne Kunstmuseum). He has also had several important mural commissions, *eg The Victory of Mankind over Disease* (1958, Geneva WHO).

ERNST, Max (1891–   ), German painter. A self-taught artist and a co-founder of the **Dada** movement in 1919, he established himself in Paris in 1922 and became one of the promoters of the Surrealist movement. He lived in the United States during World War II. In 1954 he was awarded the Grand Prix at the Venice Biennale. There is no great distinction between his original and varied work within the Dada move-

ment and as a Surrealist. From the beginning Ernst avoided the simple aesthetic reversals and pointed jokes of many of his Dada colleagues: his works are effective in their startling conjunction of complex ideas, *eg The Little Tear Gland that Says Tic Tac* (1920, New York MMA). Even in the heyday of the Surrealist movement, Ernst avoided the highly illusionistic painting of Dali, Tanguy and others, though many of his works have the same clean colour and intense, empty atmosphere, as in *Les Hommes n'en Sauront Rien* (1923, London Tate). Instead, he achieved links with reality by the frequent use of **Collage**, in particular taking 19th century engravings as his material. In his two great 'collage novels', *La Femme 100 Têtes* (1929) and *Une Semaine de Bonté* (1932), the pictures are obviously stylized, but they so resemble the painstaking novelette illustrations from which they are derived, that the reader is prepared to accept them as a whole and so be struck the harder by the contradictions they contain. He also used illustrations from old scientific textbooks, making curious fusions of the machine with the human figure, exploring further the line started by Marcel Duchamp. In addition to straight collage, Ernst has used a variety of techniques of which **Frottage**, a process analogous to brass-rubbing, is the most frequent. His collages also included solid pieces combined with painting, as in *Two Children as Threatened by a Nightingale* (1924, New York MMA) which contains solid wooden elements, including a hinged gate overlapping the frame of the painting. The mystery of this picture, testifying in some indefinable way to the frightening power of nature, is a frequent theme.

In the late 1930s and early 1940s he began producing paintings full of disturbing detail of unidentifiable scale, seemingly representing lush foliage, moss, patina or jewelled textures, as in *Europe after the Rain II* (1940–2, Hartford, Wadsworth Atheneum). Some of these look remarkably like the forest series of Henri Rousseau, and may well derive from him. Since the War Ernst's painting has been more cheerful, using bright colours in large areas, each work being dominated by one hue or group of hues, *eg The Pink Bird* (1956, Berlin 20th C Gallery). Although the figurative elements have remained, these works are close in spirit to **Abstract Expressionism**. He has also produced a number of sculptures, showing strong influence of Primitive art, *eg Lunar Asparagus* (1935, New York MMA).

ESTEVE, Maurice (1904–), French painter. He designed furniture and directed the design studio of a textile factory in Barcelona in 1923. He worked at the Académie Colarossi in Paris until 1927. In 1937 he collaborated with Delaunay in the design of the Air and Railway Pavilions at the Universal Exhibition in Paris. His work around 1930 is a clear-cut, strongly coloured, near-abstract style derived from **Cubism** and similar to that of Léger, *eg Red Stockings* (1935, Paris MAMVP). Around 1940, his work became more realistic and he adopted a glowing colour similar to late Bonnard. This has remained even in his recent works which have progressively reverted to abstraction, *eg July Interior* (1950, Paris MNAM), *Composition 166* (1957, London Tate).

ETIENNE-MARTIN (1913–), French sculptor whose original name was Martin Etienne. In 1933 he went to Paris and studied under Malfray at the Académie Ranson. Influenced by **Marcel Duchamp**, he used wood and string to execute avant-garde sculptures on the theme of night. In 1948, he was awarded the Blumenthal

Maurice Estève: Landaise *(1954); ph. Marc Vaux.*

Prize and, in 1949, the Prix de la Jeune Sculpture. Since World War II, his work has been characterized by convulsive, visceral forms violently intertwined as in *Large Dragon* (1947). It has subsequently evolved towards labyrinthine forms with startling complexities which he calls 'dwellings'.

EVENEPOEL, Henri Jacques Edouard (1872–99), Belgian painter. Although he died very young, Evenepoel had a considerable influence on Belgian Expressionism. Born in Nice, he was trained in Brussels before going to Paris, where he studied under Moreau. The principal influence on his art, however, was **Impressionism**, and particularly the work of Manet, *eg Le Café d'Harcourt* (1897, Frankfurt, Kunstinstitut). He also painted a few scenes in which there is an almost audible horror, rather as in the work of Munch, *eg The Drowned Man at the Pont des Arts* (1895, private collection), and some remarkable landscapes in which the detail is subsumed in very heavy impasto and vital brushwork.

EXPRESSIONISM, term describing general tendency in several countries in Europe, dating especially from 1890 to 1930. The word was invented by the Germans and given wide currency by Herwarth Walden, the publisher of the review *Der Sturm*; he used the term for all revolutionary movements in art between 1910 and 1920. Expressionism can be considered as a type of art, most frequently found in the northern countries, which emphasizes spontaneity and vitality, it also stresses painterly qualities, stylistic distortion, and finally the individualism of the artist, which may be pushed towards the limits of madness.

The first Expressionist wave in modern art came at the end of the 19th century. Its main representatives were **van Gogh**, **Toulouse-Lautrec**, **Ensor**, **Munch** and **Hodler**. Some stylistic similarities revealed aims common even to such independent artists: form was distorted for expressive purposes, and their themes tended to be naturalistic and dramatic. Their art was the final manifestation of romanticism in its attempt to express revolt and anguish.

The second Expressionist wave was represented above all in Germany by the

Die Brücke movement. The Blaue Reiter movement also developed out of Expressionism, and in the work of Kandinsky and Klee in particular gave rise to an abstract art which nevertheless revealed inner feelings or ideas. The work of Kokoschka and Schiele in Austria, deriving from the style of Klimt, has been another important tendency of Expressionism, characterized by emphasis on realistic elements. In Germany, Austria and the Scandinavian countries, the terrifying and passionate work of Munch exercised a profound influence. The work of Nolde and Grosz in Germany sometimes went so far as to be a caricature of Expressionism.

At the same time, in France, the work of Rouault, Picasso in his blue period (the Spanish Civil War inspired his *Guernica*, a key work of Expressionism) and certain Fauves, especially Matisse and Derain, all contributed to the predominantly frenzied tone of art in this period. Certain Jewish artists in Paris created the most typically expressionistic works of this period in France: Modigliani, Soutine, Chagall and Pascin are undoubtedly the real Expressionists of the School of Paris. After 1925, the most noteworthy French Expressionists were Gromaire, and some of his followers, such as Georg and Gruber. The latter was the main precursor of the so-called Miserabilist group.

In Belgium, after Ensor, whose inspiration was above all symbolic and fantastic, an important group of painters, the school of Laethem-St-Martin, practised a frankly expressionistic art which was derived its inspiration from the Flemish past. The painter and sculptor Permeke was perhaps the most typical representative of this school. Expressionism in the United States has also had its forceful exponents: Weber, Shahn and Peter Blum represented a form of Expressionist realism, and the Abstract Expressionism impulse initiated after the War by Pollock has been one of the most influential modern movements. The art of the Mexican painters Orozco, Rivera and Tamayo is also Expressionist in intention. Bacon is the chief exponent of British Expressionist art at present.

Certain other painters are connected with this type of art by virtue of their vitality of expression and their search for strange effects. The Surrealists may be included among their number, and also Balthus, Lorjou and Fautrier. Expressionism has been one of the most vigorous and constant currents of 20th century painting and has provided a complement to the Constructivist research into basic artistic principles.

F

FAUTRIER, Jean (1898–1964), French painter. He was admitted to the Royal Academy in London at the age of fourteen, but his career was interrupted by World War I. In the 1920s he began to paint semi-realistic works in a sombre, diffuse style, which gradually became bolder and more stylized, eg *Crucifixion* (1927, Paris MNAM). In 1943 he adopted a new non-representational style in a series entitled *Hostages*. This style, which he retained in its essentials to the end of his life, usually involves an area of heavy impasto in the centre of the canvas, built up with plaster, sprinkled with coloured powders and worked with the knife and it anticipated the Tachist style of Dubuffet. In 1950 he issued the first of several 'Multiple originals'; in a technique in which a basic drawing is printed on anything up to 300 canvases, which the artist then works up by hand.

FAUVISM, name given to the artistic movement in the first decade of the 20th century, principally characterized by the liberation of colour; more specifically, it refers to the work of the group of artists around Matisse. The term was invented by the art critic Louis Vauxcelles at the Salon d'Automne, 1905, while standing in front of a statue in the Classical style by the sculptor Albert Marque, surrounded by the violently coloured paintings of Matisse and his friends, he remarked: 'Donatello parmi les fauves!' ('Donatello among the wild beasts'); and, like the derogatory remark which launched the Impressionist movement, the name was taken up by the artists in triumph. Several different groups participated in the Fauvist movement, including that from the studio of Gustave Moreau and the Académie Carrière (Marquet, Manguin, Matisse, Camoin, Puy), that from Chatou (Derain, Vlaminck), and the Le Havre group (Friesz, Dufy, Braque). These were joined by several independent figures such as the Dutch **van Dongen** and the Provençal painters Chabaud and Seyssaud.

Initially, **Moreau** was the law-giver of the movement. He said: 'I do not believe in what I can see and touch, but only in my innermost feelings, which seem eternal and unquestionably real.' The movement can also be seen as a late development of Impressionism, although the Fauvist aims were not primarily realistic. But the power latent in the juxtapositions of pure colours introduced by the Impressionists was seized by the Fauves and used for its own sake. Fauve technique, too, was derived from that of Impressionism, and **Post-Impressionism**. The broken stroke and dabs of colour of most Fauve works was developed from Monet via **van Gogh**, while the appearance of Pointillism in Matisse's work of about 1905 can be traced to the influence of Seurat and Signac on him. After Moreau's death (1898), Matisse, working in the south of France and in Paris, painted landscapes, figures and still-lifes in areas of pure colour. Meanwhile at Chatou, Derain and Vlaminck, who had been much moved by the van Gogh retrospective exhibition of 1901, painted canvases in which the colours exploded like cartridges filled with dynamite. The Berthe Weill Gallery exhibited (1902–4) their works, with those of Manguin, Camoin, Friesz and Dufy. A group was formed at the Salon des Indépendants in 1903. Matisse showed 13 paintings at the Salon d'Automne of 1904, and his famous canvas *Luxe, Calme et Volupté* was shown in 1905. The sight of this painting overwhelmed Dufy as the 'contemplation of the miracle of the imagination introduced into drawing and colour'. In 1905 the group increased to include Puy, Valtat and Rouault; in 1906 Braque and van Dongen joined.

Matisse, who was the leader of the group, declared: 'Composition is the art of arranging in decorative manner the various elements which the painter can make use of in the expression of his feelings.' Colour was the element with which members of the group took the greatest liberties, often being completely transposed, so that trees became violet, the earth pink, houses

André Derain: The Bridge at Le Pecq *(detail, 1904, Paris, R. Gros Collection); ph. Giraudon.*

Maurice de Vlaminck: La Danseuse du 'Rat Mort' *(1906, Paris, private collection); ph. Giraudon.*

green. Very often, too, the colour of a single object such as a tree-trunk would be altered in different parts to give the maximum contrast with the background behind it at each point. Derain, in his gleaming views of that normally grey city, London, eg The Pool of London (1906, London Tate), Vlaminck in his explosive scenes of the life of the people, eg Gardens at Chatou (1904, Chicago Art Inst.) and van Dongen in his sensuous female nudes, expressed their individual lyricism at an extreme pitch. It should be noted that the painters of the Die Brücke movement in Germany were exhibiting similar tendencies, but their savage, symbolic works were less harmonious and more critical than those of the Fauves.

Fauvism had a short but euphoric life: the influence of Cézanne was to bring painters to consider anew problems of form and to react against this outburst of pure sensation in painting which had been, as Derain put it, a 'baptism of fire' for the artists concerned. Fauvism was the first manifestation in this century of the Dionysiac element in painting, and as such it helped to make possible most of the modern Expressionism.

FAVORY, André (1889–1937), French painter. A pupil of Marcel Baschet at the Académie Julian, he exhibited at the Salon des Indépendants and, after 1919, at the Salon des Tuileries. He was influenced initially by Fauvism, and then by Cubism; but, as a result of his discovery of Rubens during a journey to Flanders in 1922, he reverted to a lyrical, realistic style. He began to paint nude studies, eg Female nue étendue (Paris MNAM), and other compositions remarkable for their precise outline, rich colouring, and generous lyrical sensuality.

FEININGER, Lyonel (1871–1956), American painter, the son of a German violinist. At the age of 17 he went to Berlin where he studied art. For several years he was a successful cartoonist both in Germany and in the United States. In 1906 he went to live in Paris and began to paint in a flat, graphic style but with colour strongly influenced by Fauvism. In 1911 he exhibited at the Salon des Indépendants alongside his friend Delaunay: it was at this exhibition that he first came into contact with Cubism which vitally influenced his work. His interest in colour remained and his development resembles the Orphism of Delaunay or Villon, rather than the pure Cubism of Picasso. His Bathers on the Beach (1912, Harvard Busch-Reisinger Museum) is one of the earliest works to show these new influences. Feininger's subjects are mainly landscapes and seascapes, in which the works of man, houses, bridges, churches, steeples, ships, tower aloft, linking land and sky, cutting the landscape into sections which are further developed in the multicoloured facets of the painter's style. Early works of this period show a considerable sense of movement as in Bridge, (1913, St Louis, Washington Univ.), but very soon perspective begins to assert itself more strongly and the compositions become more rectilinear and stable, eg Behind the Church (1916, Leicester AG).

In 1912 he returned to Germany and met the artists of Die Brücke, later exhibiting with the Blaue Reiter group. In 1919 he became a signatory of the Bauhaus Manifesto and taught at the Bauhaus in Weimar and Dessau until 1932. In 1937 he left Germany for good and settled in New York once more. After about 1933 his style became less austere and he painted sometimes in a rather Expressionist manner, eg Spook I (1940, Washington Phillips Collection). More frequently he used a delicate graphic style over a shimmering background of great subtlety, eg Cathedral (Cammin) (1942, Cleveland MA). Feininger's work was a crucial influence on all the pupils of the Bauhaus, and, more recently, his manner of combining close observation of the real world with an overall formal discipline has influenced many American artists, notably Mark Tobey.

FENOSA, Apelles (1899–   ), Spanish sculptor and member of the School of Paris. He executed many busts of authors and artists of the day, eg Cocteau, Poulenc (both Paris, MNAM) and Eluard (1942, Sydney AG). He has also sculpted nudes and compositions with several figures, eg Métamorphoses des Soeurs de Phaéton (1951). Fenosa's style is based on modelling rather than carving and very often approaches the limits of representationalism in its search for undulating compositions of supple, elongated forms.

FERBER, Herbert (1906–), American sculptor. From 1930 until about 1945 he produced figurative sculpture and then turned to abstract but bonelike forms in the manner of Henry Moore. His work of about 1950 was also influenced by **Surrealism** particularily in the conjunction of quirkily suggestive shapes in open lattices which seem to change as the observer moves. His more recent work has much in common with **Abstract Expressionism**, and particularily in reproducing Calligraphic forms in three dimensions: *Full Circle* (1966, Boston, Kennedy Building). All his work is in welded metal.

FERGUSSON, John Duncan (1874–1961), Scottish painter. He studied medicine at Edinburgh University, but soon devoted himself to art. Fergusson visited Paris regularly and stayed there from 1907 to 1914 and again between the Wars. He knew most of the contemporary French painters and included their work in his periodical *Rhythm* (1911–13). In 1939 he settled finally in Scotland and held an influential position in Scottish life and letters. Fergusson's early pictures are delicate little oils influenced by **Whistler** and by **Impressionism**, capturing everyday scenes in clear colours, freely applied, *eg Café Concert des Ambassadeurs* (1907, London Tate). He soon became influenced by the Fauves, however, and particularly by **Cézanne**, combining these styles in a number of almost architectonic figure paintings with bold drawing and striking colour-schemes: *The Blue Beads* (1910, London Tate); *Torse de Femme* (1911, Glasgow Kelvingrove). His later work, however, was rather repetitious and sterile.

FIGARI, Pedro (1861–1938), Uruguayan painter. He had a successful career as a lawyer, an inspector of arts and crafts, a member of Parliament, and then, at the age of fifty, turned to literature and painting. He worked in Buenos Aires (1921–5) and lived in Paris (1926–35) where he became a friend of **Bonnard**. He was a self-taught artist, but his work shows the influence of the **Nabis**. He painted popular festivals and native dances, *eg Creole Dance* (New York MMA) but also quieter, more intimate scenes which convey a deep insight into South American life. In technique Figari was bold and almost primitive, using vivid

colours and an interplay of curved forms on the surface of the canvas, but the feeling of his work and its recurrent pathos give it a subtle quality.

FLANDRIN, Jules (1871–1947), French painter. A pupil of Gustave Moreau, he achieved some popular success with his landscapes of France, Italy and Greece. These contain figures, and are treated broadly, with fresh effects of vivid light.

FLANNAGAN, John (1895–1942), American sculptor. He worked at first in wood, carving flattened forms with curved outlines reminiscent of primitive sculpture, and reminiscent of the semi-abstract shapes in the painting of Dove and Hartley *eg Jonah and the Whale* (1937, Minneapolis Art Inst.). He was influenced by **Brancusi** in his later works, which are mainly in stone.

FLAVIN, Dan (1933–), American artist. Since graduating from Columbia University in 1959 he has become one of the leaders of the **Minimal Art** movement. He works entirely with ordinary fluorescent tubes, sometimes white and sometimes coloured. He uses these straight, in conventional holders so fixed onto the walls, floor or ceiling of the gallery that they articulate the space both as a hard line of light, and by washing the surrounding surfaces by graduated colour *eg The Nominal Three* (1963, Ottawa NG). He is therefore concerned with making **Environments** and, since his work has no independent existence outside the display situation, he is a foremost exponent of **Conceptual Art**.

FONTANA, Lucio (1899–1968), Italian painter and sculptor, born in Argentina. He began his career in Italy in 1930 as a sculptor, working in a very free, though figurative, style somewhat influenced by Cubism. He joined the **Abstraction-Création** group in 1934. In 1947 he founded in Milan the Spatialist Movement, whose doctrines were propounded in a series of manifestoes from the 'White Manifesto' of 1946 to the 'Manifesto Tecnico dello Spazialismo' of 1951. In these Fontana calls for an art which will recognize the new scientific discoveries which are creating new dimensions for man to live in. The traditional limitations prescribing each art form and dividing one from another must be cast aside: not only should the artist use new materials, such as neon lights, but the techniques of the sculptor must be made available to the painter and vice versa. Fontana's work includes many abstract paintings which make use of a spatial element. He created this by perforating the canvases (1948–59) or by slashing them in long parallel razor cuts (1959–65), by using glass collage (1953–68), by incorporating neon tubes (1952), and by mounting two or more cut-out planes behind one another (1965). He has also created whole rooms, arranging the lighting and the progression of the spectator from place to place in order to create spatial **Environment** around him.

FOUGERON, André (1913–   ), French painter. Influenced at first by Picasso, he adopted the style of Socialist Realism after 1948, as in the series of paintings commissioned by the miners of the north of France in 1951. His work is always powerful, especially the drawings, which often recall early van Gogh. Latterly he has returned to a freer, more colourful style.

FOUJITA, Tsuguharu (1886–1968), French painter, born in Japan. He studied at Art School in Tokyo before going to Paris in 1913. He had acquired fame by 1923, travelled round the world in 1929 and remained in Tokyo during World War II. He returned to Paris and became a Catholic in 1959. His style unites Japanese finesse, minuteness and precision of draughtsmanship, with the broad, objective realism of Western art. He began by painting views of Paris in a linear, almost primitive style, concentrating on practically deserted streets, squares and railway yards in which the few figures serve only to increase a feeling of bleakness. He then painted the nude studies which brought him fame, in which still life and the human figure are cleverly integrated. The *Self-Portrait of the Artist* (1928, Paris MNAM), in which he is crouched over his painter's table with his cat on his back, is particularly expressive and natural. *Mon Intérieur à Paris* (1921) pushes the minute description of objects to a point where it acquires a spiritual significance. His later works are more mannered and use strong colours.

FRANCIS, Sam (1923–   ), American painter. One of the second generation of Abstract Expressionists, he has achieved, like **Frankenthaler**, a synthesis between Gesture Painting and Chromatic Abstraction of **Abstract Expressionism**. After taking a degree in Art History at the University of California, he studied in Paris (1950–7). Since then he has made several round-the-world trips, living and working in Tokyo and Basle, as well as in the United States. His paintings tend to be large, and are completely abstract, featuring large agglomerations of blots and dabs of brilliant colour on a white ground. The earlier works are in oil or gouache, but since 1959 he has used acrylic dye which permits richer colour. Whether the predominant tone of the works is light, as in *Around the Blues* (1957, London Tate), or dark, as in *Red and Black* (1954, New York Guggenheim), there is always an optimistic, affirmatory quality. Francis said in one of his poems 'Heaven and hell is also a place to live / Alive even if you cry / Alive even if you laugh.' There are large murals by him in the Basle Kunstmuseum (1958) and in the Chase Manhattan Bank, New York (1959).

FRANKENTHALER, Helen (1928–   ), American painter. One of the chief figures in the development of **Post-Painterly Abstraction**, she found her personal style in about 1952, only shortly after she had completed her degree at Bennington College, Vermont. Starting off from the accidental blots of black and white paint used by Jackson Pollock, she developed a language of her own. She pours colour-dye directly on to the unstretched, un-primed canvas so that instead of being applied to the surface, the paint becomes the picture surface, giving an exceptionally rich effect both of colour and of form. She taught this 'poured stain' technique to Noland and Louis who were impressed by her *Mountains and Sea* (1952, artist's collection). Louis said later that she 'was a bridge between Pollock and what was possible'. Over the next ten years her colours became richer and she achieved greater control over the forms so that the accidental shapes of the blots (rather like the later works of Miró in form) give way to large areas of colour with clear boundaries between them, *eg The Bay* (1963,

Detroit Art Inst.). From 1964 onwards she has used hard-edged forms more frequently, giving effects similar to the late *papiers coupés* of Matisse. She was selected for the Venice Biennale of 1966. In 1958 she married Robert Motherwell.

FRASCONI, Antonio (1919–), Uruguayan-American printmaker. He studied at the Circulo de Bellas Artes, in Montevideo, Uruguay, the Art Students League, and the New School for Social Research. With Leonard Baskin, he has been responsible for reviving the woodcut in American art.

FREUD, Lucian (1922–), English painter born in Germany. A grandson of Sigmund Freud, he came to England in 1932 and took British nationality in 1939. He studied at the Central School of Art and at Goldsmith's College. His work, mainly portraits and figure subjects, is remarkable for its painstakingly detailed observation and freshness of vision— qualities which link him to **Stanley Spencer**: *Girl with a White Dog* (1950–1, London Tate). In his portraits Freud achieves a penetrating analysis of the sitter, expressed in slight distortions and rearrangements, and by stripping away the mask of decorum behind which sitters conventionally pose, *eg Francis Bacon* (1952, London Tate). Freud was included in the 1954 Venice Biennale.

FREUNDLICH, Otto (1878–1943), German sculptor. After studying in Berlin and Florence, he went, in 1908, to live in Paris where, for a time, he was the neighbour of Picasso in the Bateau Lavoir. The influence of **Cubism** lasted throughout his life and can be seen in the rectangular facets of his pictures and the numerous globules or cells of material in his sculptures. His colour is bright but subtly modulated, as in the work of Klee, *eg Composition* (1932, Basle Kunstmuseum). The paintings are mostly abstract, though in his stained glass, mosaics and sculpture he did attempt figurative schemes. All the works have a supple dynamic quality despite their Cubist fragmentation and a sense of movement more organic and gentle than that of, say, Delaunay, whose reaction to Cubism is somewhat similar. This quality characterizes sculptures such

as *Ascension* (1929), which seem to thrust themselves out into space like growing organisms.

FRIESZ, Othon (1879–1949), French painter. He studied art at the Ecole des Beaux-Arts in Paris and began to paint in an Impressionist style, *eg The Seine at Paris* (1901, Glasgow Kelvingrove). His palette soon became brighter and his drawing bolder, using sweeping dark outlines. He was one of the original **Fauvism** group, *eg Fair at Rouen* (1905, Montpellier Musée Fabre). Most of his works are landscapes, but a few include nude figures in Arcadian settings and these show the influence of Cézanne, *eg Landscape with Figures* (1909, New York MMA). After a visit to Portugal in 1911 he became preoccupied with attempts to reduce the depth of his pictures as in *Jeune Femme à la Fenêtre* (1919, London Tate) and produced some more ambitious figure pieces such as the powerful Michelangelesque *Les Horreurs de la Guerre* (1915, Grenoble Museum of Art). His later style is more realistic and sober.

FRINK, Elisabeth (1930–), English sculptor. She studied at the Chelsea School of Art under **Bernard Meadows** and first exhibited in 1952. Her sculptures of birds, animals and figures are characterized by a strong sense of movement and by a very free treatment of the bronze, almost Expressionist, as though the figures were portents of terrible things: *eg Harbinger Bird IV* (1960, London Tate). There are monumental works by her at Harlow, at Bethnal Green and in Coventry Cathedral.

FROST, Terry (1915–), English painter. Although he had studied art at evening classes, he did not begin to paint until he became a prisoner of war in 1943. On his return to England he studied in St. Ives and then with Pasmore and Coldstream at the Camberwell School of Art. He was a Gregory Fellow at Leeds University 1954–6, and then taught at Leeds College of Art until 1959. His mature paintings are all abstract, and are generally divided into a number of regularly shaped areas. Many of these are further divided by a bold texture effect within a restricted colour range, *eg Khaki and Lemon* (1956, London Tate); *Brown Verticals* (1959, Leeds City AG).

FROTTAGE, a technique consisting of placing a sheet of paper on a rough surface and rubbing over it with a soft pencil or crayon, thus producing an impression of the surface on the paper. It was used extensively by **Ernst** from 1925 onwards, pre-eminently in his series of drawings entitled *Natural History*. Ernst used wood, leaves, fabrics and other materials. He often elaborated the images thus formed, using the technique to evoke suggestions and associations made in **Surrealism**.

FRY, Roger Eliot (1866–1934), English painter and critic. After taking a first class degree in Natural Science at Cambridge, Fry studied painting in London and in Paris, and travelled extensively. However, he first made his reputation as a critic and historian, with essays (reprinted as 'Vision and Design') extolling the powers of design of the then less popular early Renaissance masters. In 1910 he organized, at the Grafton Galleries, London, the exhibition 'Manet and the Post-Impressionists'; it had a tremendous impact on British artists (the **Armory Show** is the U.S. parallel), for it was the first large-scale representation in Britain of Cézanne, van Gogh and Gauguin, and the very first appearance of Symbolism and Fauvism. A second exhibition followed in 1912. In 1913 Fry founded the 'Omega Workshops' to produce works of applied art designed by young artists. Among those who worked there before its closing in 1919 were Duncan Grant, Wyndham Lewis and Gaudier-Brzeska. Fry also produced a considerable body of painting in a Cézannesque style, *eg Still Life* (1913, London Tate), *The Bridge House* (1928, Leeds City AG).

FUTURISM, an Italian movement which was the first and arguably the most radical of the revolutionary artistic movements of the 20th century. Embracing all the arts, it was launched by the poet Filippo Tommaso Marinetti who published the initial Manifesto in *Figaro* (February 20, 1909). This document was a hymn of youth, a hymn to the age of the machine, of movement, of power, noise and speed: 'We shall sing of the great crowds in the excitement of labour, pleasure and rebellion; of the multi-coloured and polyphonic surf of revolutions in modern capital cities . . . of the greedy stations swallowing smoking snakes; of factories suspended from the clouds by their strings of smoke; of bridges leaping like gymnasts over the diabolical cutlery of sunbathed rivers; of adventurous liners scenting the horizon; of broad-chested locomotives prancing on the rails, like huge steel horses bridled with long tubes . . . .' Marinetti glorified war and danger, and denounced romanticism and feminism. He proclaimed a break with the art of the past in his desire to burn the museums. Just over a year later, in Turin, a group of painters gave a public reading of the 'Technical Manifesto of Futurist Painting' which applied Marinetti's points specifically to the visual arts. They fulminated against bituminous colours, Classical technique, the use of the nude and the superficial modernism of the **Secession**. More positively, they insisted 'that universal dynamism must be rendered in painting as a dynamic sensation' and 'movement and light destroy the materiality of bodies'. The signatories to this second Manifesto were **Boccioni**, (undoubtedly the most important), Carrà, Russolo, Balla and Severini.

The Futurists' love of machinery was in fact little more than another form of Romanticism, and they failed to develop a real aesthetic for the machine age in the way that the artists at the Bauhaus did. The real contribution of Futurism was its concept of simultaneity: a work of art is not static but records a whole existence, a jumble of events in time, sound and movement. Works such as Balla's *Rhythm of the Violinist* (1912, London Tate, Estorick Loan) by superimposing a number of positions of a violinist's hand and bow make the point clearly, though they are comparatively trivial. Boccioni's *The Noise of the Street Penetrates the House* (1911, Hanover Landesgalerie), a more valid example, shows a view from a window into a square shattered into jarring visual fragments, not in obedience to some visual aesthetic as in Cubism, but as a response to the jarring and inescapable noise of the builders at work in the square. Nonetheless, Futurist paintings were influenced by Cubism in appearance, if not in intention. The technique applied to early Futurist works, *eg* Boccioni's *The City Rises* (1910–11, New York MMA), was a version of Impressionist Pointillist technique, enabling the forms to blur into one another. After

Boccioni's visits to Paris (1911, 1912 exhibitions at the Bernheim-Jeune Gallery), he painted the triptych *States of Mind* (New York, Nelson Rockefeller Coll.) showing scenes at the departure of a railway train in which the new Cubist influence enabled him to substitute clearer, more mechanical forms for the earlier fuzziness.

Futurism also extended to music and architecture. The 'Intonarumori' or sound-machines of Russolo, were a minor manifestation, but the work of Antonio Sant'Elia, the architect, was not. None of Sant'Elia's Futurist schemes were built, but his visions of cities in which skyscraper blocks built around huge lifts were penetrated by railways and road tunnels, and topped by landing spaces for aircraft, were strangely prophetic of advanced city-design of today. When Italy declared war in 1915, Marinetti, Russolo, Boccioni and Sant'Elia enlisted in a motor-cycle battalion; Boccioni and Sant'Elia were killed in the following year. World War I brought about a disillusionment with the brutal mechanized ideal world of the Futurists, and the movement rapidly disintegrated.

G

GABO, Naum (1890–   ), Russian sculptor. In Paris, in the years 1913–14 he executed his first works in the Cubist style. In 1917 he returned to Russia with his brother Pevsner in order to spread the doctrines of **Constructivism**. *The Head of a Woman* (1917, New York MMA), in which the human head is composed of interlocking sheets of celluloid and metal, adheres to this doctrine. He was obliged to leave Russia in 1921 and went to live in Berlin where he made contact with the Bauhaus and with the Neo-Plasticism movement. *The Column* (1923, Yale Univ. AG) is a work of this period and shows how almost all Gabo's works can be viewed as models for larger, architectural constructions. So far, however, only one of his works has been made on such a scale, the spirelike sculpture for the Bijenkorf building in Amsterdam (1954–7). In 1932 Gabo moved to Paris, in 1935 to England and in 1946 to the U.S. Most of his work from the English period onwards is concerned with expressing movement in sculpture by means of curved planes of perspex, metal or even stone. The various works entitled *Linear Construction* (1942, London Tate; 1943, Washington Phillips Collection; 1952, Amsterdam Stedelijk M; *etc*) in which the planes are connected by a mesh of plastic threads, are perhaps the most beautiful examples. Gabo is also a pioneer of **Kinetic Art**; as early as 1920 he made a sculpture consisting only of a verticle rod so weighted as to form an apparent series of volumes when set vibrating, and several of his pictures were intended to be viewed on a turntable.

GALLERIES. As the investment value of modern works has gone up and the international art trade increased, the number of dealers' galleries in every large city has risen proportionately. The galleries have largely taken over the function of art patronage from the private individual, and many have played an essential part in the development of new movements, through their encouragement and even subsidizing of artists at times when their own financial returns were very small. The dealer Paul Durand-Ruel (1831–1922) was the first champion of Impressionism and his enthusiastic activity in America is reflected in the excellent collections in the U.S. today. The Galérie Bernheim-Jeune in Paris was responsible for organizing important exhibitions of van Gogh (1901) and of Cézanne (1907 and 1910), and went on to champion the Nabis, the Futurists and Matisse, among others. K. H. Kahnweiler took up the Fauves, and then became both the theoretician and leading dealer for the Cubists. In 1910, Herwath Walden founded the magazine *Der Sturm*, and two years later a gallery of the same name, which was responsible for propagating the works of, not only the German Expressionists of **Die Brücke** and **Der Blaue Reiter**, but also the Fauves, Orphists and Futurists.

The most important figure in the U.S. was Alfred Stieglitz who opened in 1905 the 'Photo-Secession Gallery' at 291 Fifth Avenue, New York. It was originally intended to champion modern photography, but Stieglitz also encouraged many of the more original American painters of the time, among them, Dove, Hartley, Marin, Maurer, Weber and Georgia O'Keefe, whom he married. Peggy Guggenheim, who opened her 'Art of ihis Century Gallery' in New York in 1942 emphasized the Surrealists, and in the years immediately following the War, introduced most of the older Abstract Expressionists to the public.

GARGALLO, Pablo (1881–1934), Spanish sculptor, of the School of Paris. A pupil of the Art School of Barcelona, he went to Paris in 1906 where he was much influenced by **Picasso** and particularly by Analytic **Cubism**. Gargallo worked principally in metal, using thin sheets, scrolls and even filaments to describe complex volumes with amazing fluency. His subjects are almost all taken from Picasso's range of Neo-Classical figures, harlequins, bullfighters, *etc*, but his treatment always trivializes them. There are, however, some well observed portraits including one of *Greta Garbo* (1930) which, with only one eye, half a mouth, the curve of her nose and cheek, and a few locks of hair, captures the essence of the woman; the manner is oddly prophetic of Pop Art.

GATCH, Lee (1902–), American painter. He studied at the Maryland Institute and at the Académie Moderne in Paris with Andre Lhote. He executed murals for the U.S. post offices of Mulline, South Carolina, and Elizabethtown, Pennsylvania. While his earlier works were realistic, Gatch's paintings have become highly stylized.

GAUDIER-BRZESKA, Henry (1891–1915), French sculptor. He was educated in France but studied in England (1906–9). In 1911 he settled in England with a Polish woman, Sophie Brzeska, whose name he added to his own. He became an influential member of the **Vorticism**. His early work in England consists of beautifully fluid drawings, including many of animals, and sculptures influenced by Rodin and Brancusi. The portraits of his Vorticist days, such as *Horace Brodsky* (1913, London Tate; Bristol AG and Leeds AG), show a new sense of fiery movement, almost of caricature, which threatens to disturb the representational quality. In some of his last sculptures, including the near-abstract *Birds Erect* (1914, New York MMA), the form is split up into rectangular-faced blocks in a Cubist manner. Gaudier-Brzeska differs from most post-Cubist sculptors in retaining a sense of the original unity of the stone block and, paradoxically, a sense of natural movement. The largest collection of his work is in the Tate Gallery, London.

GAUGUIN, Paul (1848–1903), French painter. Although almost the whole of Gauguin's life was in the 19th century, he is one of the major shapers of the art of the 20th and he is one of the greatest exponents of **Post-Impressionism**. He developed the Impressionist style far beyond the point where it was merely representational and he made radical discoveries about composition and the use of colour. His influence extends not only to the groups with which he had personal contact, such as the **Pont-Aven School** and the **Nabis**, but also to **Fauvism** and beyond to **Abstract Expressionism** and to most of the 20th century's serious experimenters with colour. Furthermore he was one of the first artists to explore **Primitivism** which became such a potent force in the 20th century. Indeed Gauguin's whole life could be seen as a search for a means of returning to primitive values and an unsophisticated sensibility: through his study of **Japanese Prints**, in his attempt to give religious painting something of the immediacy of a vision, and in his travels to Brittany, Martinique and ultimately Tahiti.

About 1871, when he was working as a broker on the Paris Stock Exchange, he began to spend his spare time painting and buying paintings, especially the works of the Impressionists. He became friendly with the members of that movement, and exhibited with them in 1881, 1882 and 1889. At this stage his style was realistic, with bold atmospheric effects, *eg Garden in the Snow* (1883, Copenhagen, Ny Carlsberg Glyptotek). In 1883, he left the Stock Exchange to devote himself to painting. In 1886 he lived for a few months with a number of friends in Pont-Aven, in Brittany. In the following year, he went to Panama and Martinique with the painter Laval. Continuing his wanderings, he returned to Brittany, and went to Arles with **van Gogh**. After their tragic quarrel they separated, and Gauguin returned to Brittany for the winter of 1889–90. In Pont-Aven, he was the acknowledged leader of a group of eight painters, who

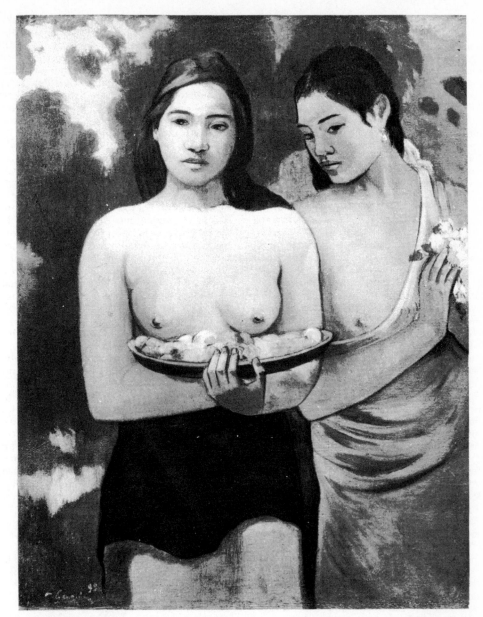

Paul Gauguin: Tahitian Girls with Red Flowers *(1899, New York Metropolitan); ph. Giraudon.*

became known as the Pont-Aven school. His style changed profoundly during this period in Brittany. He formulated the new doctrine of Cloisonnism, although his friend **Emile Bernard** also laid claim to its invention. The forms had become simpler and the colour was applied in flat areas separated from each other as in cloisonné enamel.

At the same time the colour became richer within a controlled colour chord. The whole conception of the canvas changed from being a window on nature to that of a flat surface on which the painter made a pattern of line and colour. This applies even to his relatively straight-forward landscapes *eg Les Alyscamps* (1888, Paris Jeu de Paume), *Old Maids of Arles* (1888, Chicago Art Inst.), *Harvest in Brittany* (1889, London Courtauld Galleries), and also to a number of religious works which introduce Breton elements such as the *Vision after the Sermon* (1888, Edinburgh NG of Scotland), *The Agony in the Garden* (self-portrait) (1889, West Palm Beach Norton Gallery), *The Yellow Christ* (1889, Buffalo AG).

In 1891 he left for Tahiti. There, he led much the same life as the natives. His canvases became progressively more powerful, with flowing lines and more daring colour, although still retaining their realistic element *eg Tahitian Landscape* (1891, Minneapolis Art Inst.), *Nafea Foa Ipoipo?* (1892, Basle Kunstmuseum), *Women of Tahiti* (1891, Paris Jeu de Paume). These paintings exalt the heavy, voluptuous splendour of the women of Tahiti, whom Gauguin sets in a brilliant decor suggesting an earthly paradise. At the same period he sculpted several wood panels in a strangely fin-de-siècle style *eg Soyez amoureuses, vous serez heureuses.* In 1893, penniless and ill, he returned to France, where he found a legacy awaiting him, which he immediately squandered. An exhibition and sale of his work, held on the advice of **Degas**, was a complete failure. Despite his success among the young Nabis group, especially with **Vuillard** and **Bonnard**, he left Paris again for Tahiti in 1895. His health deteriorated, he had some violent disagreements with the local authorities and fled to Pata-Iwa, one of the Marquesas Islands, where he died in 1903.

It was during those last years that he painted his best works: *Nevermore* (1897, London Courtauld Galleries), *D'où venons-nous? Que Sommes-nous? Où alons-nous?* (1899, Boston MFA), *The White Horse* (1898, Paris Jeu de Paume), *Breasts with Red Flowers* (1899, New York Metropolitan), *Riders on the Beach* (1902, Essen Museum). In this final period Gauguin's style became increasingly pure and classical, with a type of draughtsmanship and modelling which recall Ingres. A calm and sumptuous harmony sets in relief the nostalgic and sometimes mysterious expression of the hieratic yet supremely sensual and sensitive figures. Gauguin felt that he had returned to the very sources of art, to its primitive, wild grandeur. He hoped to rejuvenate decadent European art by immersing himself in the life of a primitive people. But he retained his taste for the linear beauty of Classical art. This strange mixture of elements in his work accounts partly for Gauguin's fascination and influence.

GEAR, William (1915–   ), Scottish painter. He trained at Edinburgh College of Art and at Edinburgh University, where his teachers included Gillies and Maxwell. In 1937–8 he studied in Paris with **Léger**. He returned to Paris after World War II, but settled in England in 1950. Gear's work is basically abstract, with strong landscape references. Under the influence of Léger and Cézanne (up to 1950 and 1954–8), he used a strong **Cubism** grid to hold together patches of colour. His pictures also recall Bazaine, *eg Interior* (1949, Toronto AG). He experimented with **Action Painting** in 1948–9 (*Landscape Structure*, 1948, London Tate) and in 1949 shared an exhibition with Jackson Pollock in New York. A general softening, towards a sort of Impressionism, is seen in his work of the 1950s and early 1960s, *eg Feature in a Landscape* (1960, London Tate), although in the mid-1950s he reverted to much harder, jagged forms. His recent work combines a strong pattern of hard-edged vertical flashes (having some affinity with Op Art) with freer dappled painting.

GENERALIC, Ivan (1914–   ), Yugoslav Naive painter. Although his works are hardly known outside Yugoslavia, he is worth noting for the extraordinary atmosphere of his country scenes. His figures recall Bruegel and his use of light the early Dutch and Flemish painters.

GERASSIMOV, Aleksandr Mikhailovich (1881–1963), Russian painter. A pupil of the Moscow School of Painting, Sculpture and Architecture, he painted propaganda placards and made his mark in 1926 with a portrait of Marshal Voroshilov and in 1932 produced an equestrian portrait of the same subject. He became the official painter of the Soviet government and painted *Lenin addressing a Gathering* (1932), and *Stalin at the Seventeenth Congress of the Communist Party* (1933). He was made an Artist of the People of the Soviet Socialist Republics, a member of the Fine Arts Academy of the USSR. and a doctor of arts. He took a part in all the official Soviet art exhibitions abroad. In 1947 he published in *Pravda* an article which is the manifesto of Socialist Realism, and in it he totally condemned all modern Western art.

GESTURE PAINTING, term used in general for painting in which the marks on the canvas are important as records of the artist's gesture in wielding the brush, and specifically for one of the main tendencies within **Abstract Expressionism**. Gesture Painting may be said to epitomize the Dionysiac stream in modern art (just as Constructivism epitomizes the Apollonian). The importance of free handling was one aspect of **Delacroix** admired by 19th century artists. In the work of **van Gogh** the handling of the paint often has a life of its own and, in *Vincent in the flames* (1890, Paris Jeu de Paume), it seems to be evidence of an inner turmoil barely mastered to achieve the objectivity of the portrait itself. Expressive handling also occurs within **Fauvism**, **Expressionism** and **Surrealism**.

It was in fact the Surrealist emphasis on the expression of the subconscious, particularly through **Automatic Writing**, which gave the main impulse to Abstract Expressionism in America after World War II.

Jackson Pollock, in his development of **Action Painting**, made gesture the entire content of a large-scale picture. Although no other artists of stature used Pollock's drip technique as their principal means of painting, **Motherwell**, Kline, Brooks, Guston, Tomlin and Tworkov all used the abstract gestures of charged brushes on their pictures while **de Kooning** applied the technique to figurative objects. Although an earlier and independent development, the **Calligraphic Painting** of Tobey is obviously a related phenomenon.

Many European painters have also been involved in Gesture painting, especially following the American example. These include Davie, Hilton and Lanyon in Britain, Sonderborg in Germany, Soulages,

Alberto Giacometti: The Forest *(detail, 1950, St. Paul-de-Vence, Maeght Foundation); ph. Larousse.*

Hartung and Mathieu in France, Crippa and Vedova in Italy and Saura in Spain. The **Cobra Group**, especially Appel, apply very free gesture to figurative subjects.

GIACOMETTI, Alberto (1901–66), Swiss painter and sculptor, the son of the painter Giovanni Giacometti. He modelled his first portraits at the age of thirteen, and from 1919–20 studied at the School of Arts and Crafts, Geneva. From 1922–5 he worked at the Académie de la Grande-Chaumière, producing painted sculptures which he later destroyed. His early work was considerably influenced by **Cubism**, but he began to develop in two directions, towards flat, smooth self-contained sculptures such as the *Head* or *Spoon Woman* of 1926 to 1928, and towards intricate combinations of thin spiky forms. It is in the latter direction that the main impulse of his later work was to carry him. From 1925–34 he was briefly a member of the Surrealists, whose influence is exemplified by the skeletal, dream-like *Palace at four o'clock in the Morning* (1932–3, New York MMA). At the same time he was experimenting with sculptures with movable parts, thus anticipating **Kinetic Art**. During the period 1940–5 he found that only by making his sculptures an inch high could he get them 'to be like', as he put it. Even when he resumed work on large-scale figures in 1945 he found that he could only get a resemblance when they were very thin, *eg Man Pointing* (1947, London Tate). In 1938 he was immobilized for a long time after injuring his foot. He had to learn again how to stand upright and how to walk again, and he transmuted this experience into art. From then he worked in a strictly figurative vein, although he tended to dematerialize mass, and to use rough surfaces. Above all, he emphasized the space surrounding his works: 'The sculptor carves the object out of space, and in its turn the object creates a space.' He did not like architectural settings for his works, and he would have liked to place his statues in the streets among the passers-by. Most of the later works exist in bronze casts in several museums; the Tate Gallery, London, has a room of his work, arranged to bring out the spatial relationships the artist strove after.

Giacometti's painting, essentially graphic and almost totally monochrome, in light tones of grey and ochre, usually presents solitary figures sitting stretched out, like his statues, only more precisely drawn with lines which seem to relate the forms to a network of interpenetrating planes. They express a curious melancholy and a sense of expectancy in their calm, fixed attitude, *eg Diego* (1950, London Tate). Giacometti's art is removed from the main stream of modern trends; it derives from a highly sensitive personality able to achieve remarkable effects in the disembodiment of the human figure, while remaining in contact with the revitalizing forces of nature.

GIACOMETTI, Augusto (1877–1947), Swiss painter, a cousin of the father of Alberto Giacometti. He went to study in Paris in 1897 where he painted the wings of butterflies in a museum, saying that he must learn about colour from the microcosm before applying it to the macrocosm. He chose his subjects solely for their colour interest and his paintings are a mosaic of coloured patches. They have so little figurative content that they are astonishing forerunners of abstraction and specifically of **Tachism**.

GILI, Marcel (1914–   ), French sculptor. Originally a member of the Abstraction-Création group, in 1935 he destroyed his previous works and renounced abstraction. His favourite material is terra-cotta and his subject almost invariably the human figure, sometimes treated with a lithe Classicism, but more often with a simplification related to primitive art.

GILIOLI, Emile (1911–   ), French sculptor. In 1931 he went to the Ecole des Arts Décoratifs at Nice, and later became a pupil of Jean Boucher at the Ecole des Beaux-Arts, Paris. His first monumental works were commissioned and executed in the Isère, *eg* the *Christ* in the Sacré-Coeur of Grenoble (1941), and memorials at Voreppe (1946), Grenoble (1950) and La Chapelle-en-Vercours (1952). His work, at its best, uses large clear-cut forms with a simple relation of mass to mass which owes something to Cubism. His entry for the Unknown Political Prisoner Memorial competition in 1952, *Prayer and Force*, is in the Tate Gallery, London.

GILL, Eric Rowland (1882–1940), English sculptor, engraver and designer. The religious, moralizing overtones in his work intensified when he was converted to Catholicism in 1913. An ardent socialist, he regarded the artist as a craftsman, and much of his work was devoted to lettering, carving and engraving on commission. His most important influence has probably been on the development of calligraphy in Britain. His engraving style depended on an expressive pure line, but tended to be self-consciously medieval. His sculptures were based on simple, solid forms, somewhat similar to post-Cubist French work. The best examples are the *Stations of the Cross* (1913–18) in Westminster Cathedral, London, and carvings at the Palestine Museum, Jerusalem (1934) and the League of Nations, Geneva (1935–8).

GILLIES, William George (1898–), Scottish painter. He studied at the Edinburgh College of Art and then in Paris with André Lhote. The influence of Matisse, Bonnard and Munch has been filtered through the artist's awareness of his own nationality, and his determined attempt to foster the Scottish tradition of men like **Peploe**. Although he is more controlled and subdued than most of his Scots contemporaries such as **Philipson** and **Maxwell**, his landscapes and still-lifes show a richness of colour and a strong sense of pattern, as in *Esperston* (1950, London Tate); *Dusk* (1959, Aberdeen AG). He was Head of Painting, and later Principal, of the Edinburgh College of Art.

GILMAN, Harold (1876–1919), English painter. As a student at the Slade School, he met Spencer Gore with whom he had much in common. He became friendly with **Sickert** in 1906, and adopted an Impressionist style similar to his, *eg In Sickert's House at Neuville* (1907, Leeds City AG). He was a founder-member of the **Camden Town Group** (1911), and his forceful personality responded the most strongly of all to van Gogh and Gauguin after the **Post-Impressionism** exhibition of 1910. Gilman's personal style crystallized during a visit to Scandinavia (1912–13): *eg Canal Bridge, Flekkefjord* (1913, London Tate). In this work he balanced vigorous handling and exuberant colour (scarlet set off against emerald and lime—as in van Gogh) against firm architectonic construction in a picture which is nonetheless basically representational.

GIMOND, Marcel (1894–1961), French sculptor. He was taught the basic skills of wrought iron work by his father. He was deeply interested in archaic art, and later collected many examples of it. His first exhibition was at the Salon d'Automne of 1922, and for forty years he produced work with two main themes: the female nude, *eg Jeune Fille Debout* (Paris MNAM), and, his main preoccupation, the bust. His works, inspired by Egyptian, Greek and Renaissance models, capture something of their external poise. There is a museum devoted to him in Aubenas, France.

GISCHIA, Léon (1903–), French painter. He is a figurative, but non-realistic artist with a dry, brilliant style. Many of his paintings are geometrically ordered compositions, much influenced by Matisse, *eg La Lanterne Japonaise* (1938, Paris MNAM).

GLACKENS, William (1870–1938), American painter. While an artist-reporter on the 'Philadelphia Record' he met **Henri** and shared a studio with him in 1894. He painted urban and genre scenes in a style very close to that of Manet, *eg Chex Mouquin* (1905, Chicago Art Inst.). After the foundation of the **Ash Can School** in 1908, however, he paradoxically became less realist in style and adopted the polychrome manner of **Renoir**, sometimes incongruously applied to American scenes, *eg Soda Fountain* (1935, Pennsylvania Academy).

GLEIZES, Albert (1881–1953), French painter. He began to paint in 1900, under the influence of Impressionism. In 1908 he met **Metzinger** with whom he developed his own brand of Cubism, *eg Landscape* (1911, Paris MNAM) independently of Picasso, whom he did not meet until late in 1911. In 1912 he wrote, with Metzinger, his famous apologia 'De Cubisme' and joined the **Section d'Or**. In 1918 he experienced a religious conversion and devoted himself to a revival of religious art. Gleizes' work is most obviously in the tradition of **Orphism** although the colour is always very positive, and the

Albert Gleizes: Landscape *(1911, Paris MNAM); ph. Giraudon.*

drawing and composition are pure and clear-cut, as in *Painting* (1921, London Tate).

GOERG, Edouard (1893–   ), French painter. A pupil at the Académie Ranson in 1912, he had his first one-man exhibition in 1925. His paintings all have glowing colours and a heavy, broken impasto. The subject is always the human figure and the pictures frequently include rather mannered nude girls surrounded by flowers. Many of his early works have brothel subjects and display a disturbing erotic quality. Around 1936 Goerg became influenced by **Surrealism** and painted Bruegelesque allegorical works such as *Les Moeurs et Malheurs du Paysan.* Goerg has repeatedly returned to the female nude in his later work, introducing a mysterious light, now soft and sensuous, possibly influenced by Redon. He became President of the French Society of Painters and Engravers.

GOGH, Vincent van (1853–90), Dutch painter. Completely unknown during his own lifetime, van Gogh had a fantastic posthumous success. His influence on modern painters, especially the Fauves and the Expressionists, has been of profound importance.

The son of a Protestant pastor, Vincent was expected to follow his father. But, in 1869, he accepted employment in Goupil's gallery in the Hague, and his young brother Theo entered the Brussels branch of the same firm in 1873. In the same year, Vincent was transferred to the London branch, but his temperament led to dismissal (1876). After this first contact with the world of painting, he prepared to go to university and become a lay preacher. In 1878, he went to the district of Borinage, Belgium, where he became deeply involved in the hardships of the miners. His visionary fervour alarmed his superiors and he was forced to give up his religious mission. In 1880 he realized his artistic talents and moved to the Hague, where a relative, the painter Mauve, gave him lessons. He returned to his parents at Nuenen in 1884, devoted himself to painting and attracted a number of followers. At this time he was using dark heavy impasto and painting in a powerful realistic manner, *eg The Potato Eaters* (1885, Amsterdam Stedelijk M, van Gogh Loan). He then left for Antwerp where he enrolled at the Art School to study drawing. He soon went to Paris, and, working at the Atelier Cormon, he was befriended by **Toulouse-Lautrec** and **Emile Bernard**. By 1887 he was associating with the Impressionists and especially with Signac. Under their influence he completely changed his style and began employing bright colours in divided brushstrokes. However, he used bars rather than dots of colour and, unlike the Divisionists, made no attempt to achieve optical mixtures. The paintings of this period were bright and airy but did not have the compositional strength of his later work, *eg Montmartre* (1886, Chicago Art Inst.), *Gardens at Montmartre* (1887, Amsterdam Stedelijk M), *Père Tanguy* (1888, Paris Musée Rodin). He also bought and copied Japanese prints at this time, such as *The Bridge, after Hiroshige* (1887, Amsterdam Stedelijk M). An exhibition held in a restaurant in the Boulevard du Clichy, in which Bernard, Gauguin, and Toulouse-Lautrec also took part, was a complete failure.

Van Gogh at this time was also interested

in the work of the Provençal painter Monticelli, whose influence is especially apparent in his still-lifes with flowers. In 1888 he went to Arles, where he discovered the dazzling light of the Midi, the 'Japan of France'. Almost all the works by which van Gogh is best known today date from this intensely productive period, the last two years of his life. The tentativeness of the Paris works vanished completely, and although he retained and even exaggerated the characteristic stabbing brushstrokes, they fused rather than conflicted, producing pictures filled with whole areas of brilliant colour. This intensity, even in the landscapes, was far greater than anything produced by the Impressionists, and gave his pictures an independent life as pure design, eg La Crau (1888, Amsterdam Stedelijk M). In the interiors and still lifes he was much freer with his colour, and he invested the simplest things with an idyllic poetry, as in Vincent's Chair (1888, London Tate), Vincent's Bedroom (1889, Amsterdam Stedelijk M). His portraits of the period were also very fine, demonstrating his great understanding and also a fine sense of linear design against a plain or patterned background. He also developed a characteristic colour scheme of two related colours plus the complement of one of them (eg emerald/lime/scarlet or yellow/orange/blue), as in Postman Roulin (1888, Boston MFA), La Berceuse (1889, Otterloo RKM). As he explained in his letters to his brother, he intended to found an artists' colony at Arles. He persuaded **Gauguin** to come to his house in October, 1888. But van Gogh was already mentally upset, the two friends quarrelled, and Vincent mutilated one of his ears as an act of penance. Gauguin departed and van Gogh placed himself under the care of a doctor. After a visit by Signac in mid-1889 Vincent decided to enter the asylum in St.-Rémy-de-Provence, where cases of chronic maladjustment were treated. He read avidly during this period and copied engravings by Rembrandt, **Delacroix**, **Millet** and Daumier. In the paintings of this period, and still more in the drawings, van Gogh developed a completely original use for the individual stroke, which he would elongate and bend into lines as in a fingerprint.

Thus he did not merely delineate forms but showed the tumultuous life inside them and, by implication, inside himself. Sky, corn, olive trees and cypress shared this common rhythm, at times reaching a richness not unlike the psychedelic art of today, but much more powerful, eg Starry Night (1888, New York MMA), Cornfield and Cypresses (1889, London Tate). The critic Aurier published in Mercure de France an article praising van Gogh's work and in February he learned that one of his paintings, La Vigne Rouge, had been sold in Brussels: both events were unique in van Gogh's lifetime. He returned to Paris in May, full of confidence and energy. He went immediately to Auvers, where he met Dr. Gachet, and painted both him and his daughter. For two months he produced a painting a day in an increasingly bright, ethereal and fantastic style. Almost all these works were masterpieces: perhaps the most extraordinary of all being Eglise d'Auvers (1890, Paris Jeu de Paume), The Wheat Field with Crows (1890, Amsterdam Stedelijk M) and the fascinating Self Portrait (1890, Paris Jeu de Paume) with its solid face suggesting all is well, contradicted by the tumultuous monochrome brushstrokes. After secret difficulties with Theo, who was now a husband and father and could no longer continue to subsidize him as before, Vincent shot himself. A mental illness lay at the root of van Gogh's drama, aggravated by the tragic incomprehension which his work met. Even Cézanne told him: 'You paint like a madman.' His brother alone had confidence in his genius, but he was unsuccessful in persuading his clients to buy Vincent's paintings.

Van Gogh attacked the feebleness of the art of his time; he wrote: 'There is a new art on the horizon, and it must be so beautiful, so young.' The example of the Impressionists transformed his palette, but his true masters, Delacroix and Millet, belonged to an earlier generation. His struggle to create a style was therefore all the more laborious, and he was very far from relying on pure instinct as did his self-professed followers, the Fauves. 'One does not reach greatness simply by abandoning oneself to impulse,' he wrote, 'but by patiently filing away the steel wall which separates what one feels from what one is capable of.' See illus. p. 96.

GONTCHAROVA, Natalia (1883–1962), Russian painter. She studied in Moscow

Vincent van Gogh: Starry Night *(1888, New York MMA); ph. Giraudon.*

from 1898 to 1902 where she met Larionov with whom she lived for the rest of her life. With him she worked in a **Rayonism** style from about 1909, *eg Autumn* (1910, London Tate). Some of her works, influenced by Cubism and possibly by

Gontcharova began to work for Diaghilev, notably on *Le Coq d'Or* (1944, set design, New York MMA) and *L'Oiseau de Feu* (1926).

GONZALEZ, Julio (1876–1942), Spanish sculptor. His father and grandfather were goldsmiths: he worked metals in his father's studio, and also studied at the art school. Towards 1900 he began to sculpt, and executed some melancholy figures in repoussé bronze. During World War I, he worked as a welder in the Renault factory and as a result of this experience he turned in 1927 to sculpture in iron. Gonzalez' oeuvre is very varied, and although the influences of **Cubism**, **Brancusi** and **Gargallo** can be detected, it has peaks of tremendous individual power and economy. On the one hand there are abstract works employing the spear, scythe and tooth shapes also found in the painting of Picasso. *Head* (1936, New York MMA) is a particularly harsh example; *Prayer* (1933, Otterloo RKM) a movingly sensitive one. On the other hand there are works with a greater degree of realism, such as the *Woman combing her Hair* (1935, New York MMA) which unites expressive curves with a splendid conception of mass. Works such as the *Torso* (1936, New York MMA) and the screaming head of a peasant woman *Montserrat* (1937, Amsterdam Stedelijk M) are almost completely realistic and are probably the most powerful of his works.

GOODNOUGH, Robert (1917–), American painter. He studied at Syracuse and New York University, and later with **Hans Hofmann**. His paintings reveal the influence of Hofmann; but Goodnough does not belong to the New York School, nor is he an Abstract Expressionist. He deserves a category of his own. He couples an emotional with an intellectual response to achieve an understanding of each part of the canvas as it becomes integrated with the whole. A Goodnough painting often deals with a figure which is being pulled out of the canvas, but which nevertheless is part of the action of the painting. His colour modulates in an intense rhythm.

Futurism, contain words and signs as elements in a painted quasi-collage, *eg The Laundry* (1912, London Tate). The two artists settled in Paris in 1914, where

GORE, Spencer (1878–1914), English painter. After studying at the Slade School, he travelled to France in 1904 and met **Sickert**. His painting at this time was influenced by **Impressionism** similar to that of Sickert but with a lightness and poise, as in his evocations of English gardens, epitomizing the Edwardian era, *eg The Garden, Garth House* (1908, Liverpool Walker AG), *The Cricket Match* (1909, Wakefield City AG). In 1910 he was shaken by Roger Fry's first *Post-Impressionism* Exhibition which made him aware of Gauguin and above all Cézanne. He was co-founder and president of the **Camden Town Group**, and from then on gradually abandoned the vague statements of Impressionism. He produced a series of landscapes where every house and tree contributed to a rhythmically taut structure and contained a patchwork of colours of the greatest vitality, *eg From a Window, Richmond* (1913, London Tate).

GORKY, Arshile (1905–1948), American painter born in Turkish Armenia. Born Vosdanig Manoog Adoain, he went to America in 1920 to join his family in Rhode Island. He worked as a quick-sketch artist in a theatre, but in 1924 he got a job at the Boston School of Design where he had already been a part-time student. In 1925 he moved to New York, enrolled at the Grand Central School of Art and, in 1931, became a member of the faculty there. His career from then on was increasingly successful, but he had two unhappy marriages and, in 1948, committed suicide on the evening his second wife left him. For economic reasons, Gorky had to express himself in drawing rather than painting in the early years, and the strong graphic element never left his style.

His early works were influenced by Cézanne and then by **Picasso** as can be seen in *Painting* (1936–7, New York Whitney Museum). Around 1940 he began to develop a more personal style in which a number of multi-colour curvilinear forms are presented against a uniform background as in *Garden in Sochi* (1941, New York MMA). The textures became more complicated and the contrasts stronger between sharply-drawn and more suggestive passages. In 1944 André Breton hailed his *The Liver Is the Cock's Comb* (1944, Buffalo AG) as a masterpiece of Surrealism. This, though true, is deceptive: Gorky's paintings are completely abstract and his titles purely capricious, although many of the forms do have biomorphic overtones and the sharp claw-like elements which occur in his drawing have a disturbing quality. Furthermore the organization of the picture space has much in common with Surrealist painters such as **Miró**. The vaguer passages which predominate in paintings such as *The Waterfall* (1943, London Tate) or *Water of the Flowery Mill* (1944, New York MMA) provided a starting-point for the **Abstract Expressionism**, in particular de Kooning. They admired his juxtapositions of glowing colour, roughly brushed on to the canvas, and the vitality of the haphazard outlines and drips of paint which he allowed. Gorky's own work became more and more dominated by line. He used colour in small blobs to act as indications of space, within a single overall colour mood. Often, as in the *The Plow and the Song* (1947, Oberlin, Ohio, Allen Museum) he achieves a beautiful lyrical calm.

GOTTLIEB, Adolph (1903–), American painter. He studied at the Art Students League, New York, under Robert Henri, and worked in Paris, Berlin and Munich. He was attracted to Surrealism, but soon abandoned a representational style for what he refers to as 'pictographs'. The canvas is divided into compartments by an arbitrary grid with highly simplified symbols painted in each, some figurative and some not, derived from primitive painting. During this period, and throughout his later career, he was closely associated with **Mark Rothko**, and with him issued an important statement of principle in 1943, the first tenet of which was 'that colour is an adventure into an unknown world'. In about 1951, Gottlieb abandoned the pictograph and started a series of 'Imaginary Landscapes' in which the canvas was divided horizontally into two, with patches of pure colour floating on a plain 'sky' above an 'earth' of more violently worked paint, *eg The Frozen Sounds No. 1* (1951, New York Whitney Museum); *Blue at Night* (1957, Richmond, Virginia Museum). In 1957 with his series of 'Bursts' Gottlieb began to condense the basic dualism of these paintings into a simple statement of polarity, with one glowing orb of colour floating above one frenzied patch of black paint, as in *Blast 1* (1957, New York MMA). These canvases, like most **Abstract Expressionism** paintings, are huge. His paintings, like those of Rothko, have a considerable purity, which is intensified in the later examples in which the lower area is reduced to a simple hiero-glyphic, *eg Dialogue 1* (1960, Buffalo AG). Since the mid-1960s he has also made coloured metal sculptures, reminiscent of Calder and Caro.

GOYA Y LUCIENTES, Francisco José de (1746–1828), Spanish painter. The influence of Goya on 19th and 20th century painters stems from the comparatively small proportion of his works which were most unusual for their time: his private sketch-books, his series of etchings (*Los Caprichos,* 1796–8; *The Disasters of War*, 1808–14, first published in 1863; the *Disparates*, 1813–19), and the murals painted for his own house, the *Quinta del Sordo* (1820–2, now Madrid Prado). In these works, Goya viciously satirized his time, attacking the idealization of war and presenting the darker side of human nature. All this has struck a chord in those modern artists who are also concerned with making serious comment on the less attractive aspects of life. Goya's use of fantasy as a means to a profound exploration of human nature, *eg* in his famous etching *The Sleep of Reason produces Monsters*, has made him a 'Sur-realist' before the term was invented. In technique, the violence of his late works, his use of unexpected colour and certain particularly striking compositions have acted as models for several later artists, notably **Manet**.

GRAEVENITZ, Gerhard von (1934–   ), German artist. He became a major figure in **Kinetic Art** shortly after completing his studies in Munich in 1961. He is a Con-structivist by nature, and his works consist of numerous identical elements (bars, crosses, circles *etc*) distributed over a plain field, and slowly rearranged by a random motor system, *eg Object with White Moving Disk* (1965, Berkely Univ. AM).

GRAHAM, John (1881–1961). American painter of Russian birth. A member of the aristocratic Dabrowsky family, he studied law in Moscow and entered the army, but fled via Paris to New York at the Russian Revolution. His first-hand experience of **Cubism** and his intellectual approach made him a valuable influence on American artists in the 1930s, notably de Kooning, Pollock and Gorky. Few of his works remain in existence.

GRANT, Duncan (1885–   ), British painter and designer. Educated at the West-minster School of Art, he travelled exten-sively in Italy and France. He met Matisse during his stay in Paris (1907–9). He was a close friend of Roger Fry and a member of the so-called 'Bloomsbury Group' of artists and writers; he also belonged to the Camden Town Group. His own art is eclectic, influenced at first by Matisse and by **Divisionism**, *eg The Queen of Sheba* (1912, London Tate), and also by Cézanne. His later work has been generally more con-ventional, *eg Window, South of France* (1928, Manchester City AG). He has also designed furniture, fabrics and stage sets, and, with Vanessa and Quentin Bell, decorated the church of Berwick, Sussex.

GRAVES, Morris (1910–   ). American painter. As a seaman Graves visited the Orient where he became interested in animal painting as a means of studying life in a state of innocence. In 1931 he began drawing in the Los Angeles zoo and when he moved to Seattle in 1934 he became a painter. In 1937 influenced by **Mark Tobey** and inspired by Oriental philosophy, he developed his personal style in which images of animals are crystallized in a maze of fine calligraphic lines, like Tobey's 'white writing', *eg Blind Bird* (1904, New York MMA). He called the series which made his reputation, the 'inner eye'. In recent years his range has developed and the abstract element has increased, *eg Spring with Machine Age Noise* (1957, London Tate).

GRECO, Emilio (1913–   ), Italian sculp-tor. Apart from apprenticeship to a maker of funerary monuments, Greco is self-taught. He has lived in Rome since 1945 and has exhibited since 1933; he won the Venice Prize at the 1956 Venice Biennale. His inspiration comes from Hellenistic and Mannerist (late 16th century) sculpture, and his subjects are the same: 'character' pieces, *eg Wrestler*, (1947–8, Antwerp Middelheim Museum), portrait heads, *eg La Masseuse* (1955, Wakefield City AG) and female nudes. The nudes, which make up the bulk of his oeuvre are shown gener-ally in twisted poses, with the body at times elongated, at times swelling out as if it were of rubber, *eg Seated Figure* (1949, St. Louis City AM); *Seated Figure* (1951,

London Tate); *Kneeling Figure* (1956, Verona GAM). He has recently explored this manner in a series of variations on the *Bather* theme, *eg No. 1* (1956, London Tate; Rome GAM); *No. 3* (1957, Paris MNAM; Otterloo RKM); *No. 4* (1959, Toronto AG). In 1960–1 he executed a series of high reliefs for the Church of San Giovanni Battista in Florence; these show strong Classical inspiration, but reveal a vital dramatic sense.

GRIS, José Gonzalez ('Juan') (1887–1927), Spanish painter. He studied at the school of arts and crafts in Madrid. He made his livelihood for a while from humorous drawings, and in 1906 went to Paris and moved into the Bateau Lavoir, where he came into contact with Picasso's circle. He was converted to **Cubism**, and exhibited at the Salon des Indépendants in 1912. Beginning as an analytical Cubist, he multiplied points of perspective so that the object could be seen from all sides, as in *Glasses and Newspaper* (1914, Oberlin. Ohio, Allen Museum). Then he instigated Synthetic Cubism, the non-representational phase of Cubism in which it is the pattern on the canvas which is dominant, *eg Chessboard* (1917, New York MMA); *Violin and Fruit-dish* (1924, London Tate). His work is allied to the Cubism of Braque and Picasso, but is even more intellectual. He said in 1920, 'I begin by organizing my painting, then I render the objects identifiable.' These objects are mandolins, fruitdishes, and fruit spread on a table, which are superimposed on one another, dissected and sharply outlined. His paintings are highly finished, and effects of colour and light are sought after for their own sakes. Even in the period of high Cubism he was perhaps the most purely decorative of all the Cubists, *eg Le Petit Déjeuner* (1915, Paris MNAM). After 1920 his colours became paler and more subdued, and he introduced human figures, refined into geometrical shapes, which are almost ghostly, *eg Pierrot* (1919, Paris MNAM). The work of Juan Gris remains the most typical expression of Cubism. There is a large collection of his work in the Basle Kunstmuseum.

GRITCHENKO, Alexis (1883–   ), Ukrainian painter of the School of Paris. A student at the Universities of St. Peters-burg and Kiev, he settled in Paris in 1921. His painting was noticed by Paul Guillaume and Dr. Barnes, who bought seventeen of his works for his foundation at Merion near Philadelphia. Later, Gritchenko travelled widely and drew particular inspiration from maritime landscapes. His paintings are rapidly executed in a very lively style. They consist chiefly of panoramic landscapes with unexpected perspectives, in which the activity of the elements, including the state of the wind and the play of light on the surface of the sea, are captured with a vigour which, in his later canvases, attains considerable lyricism.

GROMAIRE, Marcel (1892–1971), French painter. He studied at the Colarossi, Ranson and La Palette Academies, and was encouraged by Matisse. After World War I, exhibitions of his work were held in the Paris Salons, and his work *La Guerre* (1925, Paris Petit Palais) had a tremendous

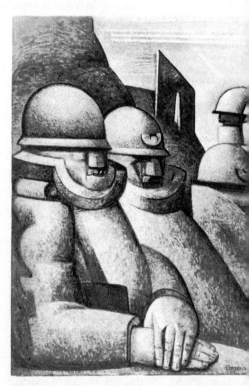

Marcel Gromaire: La Guerre *(1925, Paris, Petit Palais); ph. Larousse.*

success at the Salon des Indépendants. From that time all his canvases were bought by Dr. Girardin, who on his death bequeathed them to the Musée de Petit Palais, Paris. In 1937 he executed a frieze for the Sèvres pavilion at the Exposition Internationale in Paris. As a result he became interested in tapestry design and, with Lurçat, founded the new tapestry school of Aubusson. He was made a member of the jury of the Carnegie Prize in 1950, winning it two years later, and in 1956 he won the Guggenheim Prize. Gromaire's art always employed realistic elements, but with a monumental, Cubist-inspired stylization of form and colour. Gromaire was very often called an Expressionist, but he denied this connection by saying 'I oppose the *deformation* of the object with an *affirmation* of it.' In his early works, his originality consisted in the monumental power of the forms, which he treated in a style having much in common with Léger. All forms emerged as regular geometrical shapes painted in a few colours, *eg Pêche à la ligne* (1927, Paris Petit Palais). Subsequently, after a journey to the U.S., he began to paint urban landscapes, which he depicted in stronger colours and with increased formal schematization which lend his vision of New York and Paris a lyrical aspect and a resemblance to stained glass, *eg Brooklyn Bridge* (1950, Paris Petit Palais).

GROOMS, Red (1937–), American sculptor. After studying at the Peabody Institute, the Art Institute of Chicago, and the Hofmann School, he became prominent in the Pop Art movement. Perhaps the most grandiose of his sculptures is *Chicago*, a lilliputian characterization of the city in painted plywood. Grooms uses painted wood cut-outs quite frequently, but generally on a smaller scale than *Chicago* which fills an entire gallery.

GROSVENOR, Robert (1937–), American sculptor. See **Minimal Art**. He is chiefly concerned with pieces suspended overhead and bearing down on the observer.

GROSZ, George (1893–1959), German draughtsman and painter. As a student at the Art Schools of Berlin and Dresden, he contributed humourous drawings to periodicals. After a stay in Paris, his work began to reflect the influence of Futurism, as in *Homage to Oscar Panizza* (1917–18, Stuttgart Museum); it was also affected by Dada, *eg Republican Automatons* (1920, New York MMA). On his return to Germany, he founded the review *Pfeife* and turned to the Realism of the 'Neue Sachlichkeit' movement. His work, graphic for the most part, was derived from Expressionism, with cruel and even ferocious distortions, *eg Married Couple* (1930, London Tate). Grosz used his art as an instrument of social criticism, mercilessly satirizing social corruption (capitalism, prostitution, the Prussian military caste, the middle class). Several works in this spirit were published by him: *History of Ruling Class* (1919), *Ecce Homo* (1923) and *Spiesser-Spiegel* (1924) which provoked a lawsuit (drawing in London Tate). In 1932 he left for the U.S., where he settled permanently. During the last years of his life, he painted apocalyptic pictures on a large scale, but his drawings became softer and more realistic. Grosz combined a violent **Expressionism** with graphic precision in a spirit that is typical of Germanic art.

GRUBER, Francis (1912–1948), French painter. His earlier work owes something to Surrealism, but his real importance is as a pioneer of **Realism**. He used intense, bitter colours, and his large canvases include studies of thin nudes, of desolate landscapes and symbolic scenes, *eg Job* (1944, London Tate; painted at the time of the Liberation of Paris). He is regarded as the creator of the 'Miserabilist' strain in French art.

GUILLAUMIN, Armand (1841–1927), French painter. He lived in Crozant after 1893, and painted his best works there. They were rich, brilliant **Impressionism** landscapes in orange and violet tones. Their authority and power of execution relate them to Cézanne, but they lack Cézanne's structural mastery. Guillaumin's pastels are also of high quality and the richness of his palette makes him seem a precursor of **Fauvism**.

GUSTON, Philip (1913–), American painter, born in Canada. Guston moved with his parents to Los Angeles in 1919 and attended art school there. After spending a year in Mexico, he arrived in New York in 1935 where he worked on the **WPA Federal Arts Project** which introduced him to the work of his contemporaries. He took up easel painting again in 1940 and painted works, influenced by the Renaissance, in which human figures and symbols are blended into a provoking allegorical composition by means of a remarkably fluid technique: *If this be not I* (1945, St Louis, Washington Univ.). By about 1948, however, he had abandoned representational painting in favour of a thick network of shimmering colour applied in horizontal and vertical strokes, not unlike the 'white writing' of Tobey though showing a sensitive colour sense which betrays their real ancestry in the late works of **Monet**. About 1955, the colour touches began to be more important with elements of solid form floating on the shimmering haze, *eg Dial* (1956, New York Whitney Museum). Gradually these colour patches have assumed a violent life of their own, as in *The Return* (1958, London Tate). In 1964, however, Guston renounced colour and began to produce a number of paintings in which a central black space is surrounded by a network of strong grey brushmarks, expressing the same conflict of tension and equilibrium as he had reached in his colour paintings, but more effective because of their limited range. He is one of the most sensitive of the Abstract Expressionists to have worked within the basic tradition of **Gesture Painting**.

GUTTUSO, Renato (1912–), Italian painter. He began to paint full-time in 1931 in a Neo-Realist style, *eg Eruption of Etna* (1938, Rome GAM). Bitterly opposed to Nazism, he made a series of bitter drawings entitled *Gott mit uns* during World War I!. His post-War work employs brutal simplification to convey a Marxist message, as in *The Mafia* (1948, New York MMA). In his large-scale works of socialist polemic such as *Occupation of the Virgin Land* (1948, Berlin Akademie) there is a high degree of naturalism but garish colour. He is a co-founder of the 'Fronti nuovi delle Arti'. His works, both on canvas and paper, are remarkable for their vigorous dynamic draughtsmanship, *eg Sulphur Miners in Sicily* (1949, London Tate). He has painted a few portraits, *eg*

Noel Annan (1961, King's College Cambridge).

H

HAJDU, Etienne (1907–), French sculptor of Hungarian birth. He went to Paris at the age of twenty, and was taught first by Niclausse and then by Bourdelle. His work became abstract towards 1934. From 1941 to 1945 he worked mainly in marble, deriving inspiration from insect forms. He went on to execute some large bas-reliefs in plaster, and more recently has used lead, copper and aluminium. Most of his sculptures are arrangements of flat forms, very precisely executed and highly polished. Some show a highly simplified figurative element influenced by Cubism, others, especially the reliefs, are more abstract but never far removed from nature. There are examples of his work in the Museum of Modern Art and the Guggenheim Museum in New York.

HALLER, Hermann (1880–1950), Swiss sculptor. He began as a student of painting and architecture, took up sculpture in Rome in 1905, and lived in Paris from 1907–14. In 1934 he obtained a gold medal at the Venice Biennale, and in 1949 won the Grand Prix of Zurich. His strictly Classical art is characterized by the idealization of a certain type of slender woman, *eg Young Girl Standing* (1926, New York MMA).

HAMBOURG, André (1909–), French painter. He studied at the Ecole des Beaux-Arts and his first paintings were shown in 1928. He won the Abd-el-Tif Prize in 1933, and spent ten years in North Africa. His landscapes which show Impressionist influence interpret the beaches of Normandy and scenes of Venice with the same iridescent luminosity.

HAMILTON, Richard (1922–), English painter. He has the reputation of being one of the instigators of **Pop Art**, although his role as a painter is of less importance than the example of the ideas he disseminated. He studied at the Royal Academy Schools and then at the Slade School. In association with the London Institute of Contemporary Arts he was responsible for the exhibition 'This is Tomorrow' at the Whitechapel Art Gallery in 1956. There Hamilton created an environment which forecast much Pop imagery, and showed the collage *Just What Is It that Makes Today's Homes so Different, so Appealing?* (1956, private collection) which could be described as the first mature Pop work. His work is rich in content though rather weak formally: *eg* . . . . *Coming Trends in Men's Wear* . . . . (1962, London Tate). Hamilton has been a considerable influence on **Blake, Richard Smith**, and **Hockney**. He has also been concerned with popularizing the work of Duchamp, producing a typographical version of the *Green Box* and a reconstruction of the 'Great Glass'.

HAPPENING, term describing a public performance or demonstration involving a number of the arts (painting, acting, poetry, music, the cinema, dancing) in an unconventional combination. The event may have a script, but it is essentially not repeatable, the value of the artistic experience lying in the combination of events as a whole, not the individual components. The original 'happenings' usually depended on their shock capacity as they tend to explore the boundaries of what is normally acceptable (or even legally permitted) for public entertainment. The public demonstrations of the Futurists, the Dadaists or Kurt Schwitters could all have been described as 'happenings', but the term as such is of more recent origin. The originator and most prolific creator of contemporary happenings is the American **Allan Kaprow**, who began in 1958 in New York; he was quickly followed by the German Wolf Vostell (1932–). The German Group 'Fluxus' was founded (1962) to further the art form. Many artists have devised or taken part in happenings, among them **Dine, Oldenburg, Rauschenberg** and **Warhol. Jean Tinguely**'s famous *Homage to New York* (1960) could be described as a happening. Activities at happenings have included **Action Painting** and **Collage** involving live actors (often naked), the painstaking reconstruction of an event *eg* a car crash, the slaughter of small animals and the wrapping-up of actors and audience in polythene sheeting, brown paper or

hessian sacks. In the late 1960s an altogether simpler type of happening has developed which is usually a manifestation of some aspect of **Conceptual Art**.

HARD-EDGE, term for a style which emphasizes the contours of forms at the expense of painterly handling. It is thus applicable to **Purism, Constructivism, Cubo-Realism** and other similar styles. It has also been used since around 1960 as a synonym for Post-Painterly Abstraction, though it properly only describes those artists who, like **Kelly** and **Frank Stella**, depend upon the precise perception of the boundaries between forms, and not those such as Albers, Noland, or most Op artists, whose boundaries are minimized or disappear as the result of the interaction of the fields separated by them.

HARE, David (1917–), American sculptor. One of the sculptors of the **Abstract Expressionism** era, he only took up art after graduating in Chemistry. His works, in welded metal, are freely dynamic in shape rather than formal and self-contained, and are Surrealist in their almost naive figurative suggestions and visual puns, *eg Sunrise* (1955, Buffalo, Albright AG). He took part in the 1957 São Paulo Bienãl.

HARTIGAN, Grace (1922–), American painter. She went to New York in 1945, and has lived there since. She has said that she is interested in an art that is neither abstract nor realistic, and that her subject is 'that which is vulgar and vital in American modern life, and the possibilities of its transcendence into the beautiful'. Her canvases are large and dense, with a rich pattern of strongly worked paint. Various figurative elements are included in the manner of **de Kooning**. She avoids any conventional composition which focuses attention on a central subject, *eg River Bathers* (1953, New York MMA). Her colour resembles that of Matisse, and her sense of balance gives her work affinities with the traditional 'well-made picture'.

HARTLEY, Marsden (1877–1943), American painter. He studied at the Cleveland School of Art, the Chase School,

New York, and later at the National Academy of Design. In 1909 he met Alfred Stieglitz, who presented his first one-man show of landscapes in an Impressionist style. *eg Mountain Lake, Autumn* (1908, Washington, Phillips Coll.). Through Stieglitz he saw the work of **Picasso** and **Cézanne** in 1911, and was immediately influenced by them. In 1912 he went to Europe for four years, visiting Paris and then Germany, where he met **Kandinsky** and exhibited with the Blaue Reiter. Kandinsky's influence drew him away from figurative Cubism towards complete abstraction, involving signs, figures and motifs from flags which he combined in tight but rich patterns. *eg Painting No. 5* (1914–15 New York, Whitney Museum). From Germany, he sent work to the **Armory Show** in 1913. He returned in 1916 to the U.S. and painted some totally abstract, almost Constructivist works. *eg Movement No. 2* (1916, Hartford, Wadsworth Atheneum). However, in 1919 he abandoned abstraction, returning to a highly simplified Cézannesque style which was intensified by a long stay (1921–9) in southern France. Hartley's last years were spent mainly in his native Maine where he painted landscapes and fishermen in a deliberately **Naive** style.

HARTUNG, Hans (1904–   ), German painter. He attended (1924–8) the academies at Leipzig and Dresden. He moved to Paris in 1935. Hartung won the Guggenheim Prize in 1956 and the International Prize for painting at the 1960 Venice Biennale. He is one of the most important European exponents of **Calligraphic Painting**. As early as 1922 he was producing works in which the paint and its application were more important than the figurative content. His more mature works were all completely abstract, and in the 1930s the first examples of the graphic line characteristic of his work appeared. By 1950 the line had become important, not so much as an element in a composition but as the record of the artist's emotions, the trajectory of the energy of his hand as he wielded the brush. The typical paintings of this period consist of a group of thick black marks on a monochrome background. From about 1960 graffito techniques occur in his

work more and more frequently, resulting in white scratched lines as well as black painted ones, and the colour range increases: *T.1966—H.28* (1966, Birmingham City Museum). Hartung has never named his pictures, rather he gives them a number accompanied by a letter indicating the medium and the date. He is one of the leading artists of the School of Paris and his style received a great impetus when the work of **Jackson Pollock** became known in Europe in the 1950s.

HAY, Alex (1930–   ), American artist. He attended Florida State University and moved to New York in 1959, becoming, like **Rauschenberg**, active in the theatre. Much of Hay's art is **Pop** making use of current images such as the toaster. In a few works however, such as *Paper Bag* (1968, New York Whitney Museum), he reproduces virtually featureless everyday objects on an enlarged scale in a way that relates him to Johns and also to Minimal Art.

HAYDEN, Henri (1883–   ), French painter, born in Poland. He began painting in 1905 after studying at the Warsaw Polytechnic and went to Paris in 1907. Until 1915 the predominant influence on his work was Cézanne. Upon meeting Lipchitz and Juan Gris, Hayden turned to **Cubism**, as in *Nature Morte à la Guitare* (1918, Auckland AG). His *Three Musicians* (Paris MNAM), exhibited in 1920, has superimposed forms typical of the simultaneist spirit of much of his work at this time. In 1922, he suddenly reverted to a direct and very realistic study of nature. His works became more stylized and brighter in colour, particularly during the 1950s when he began to paint glowing still-lifes, such as *Nature Morte à la Mandoline Rouge* (1957, Paris MNAM) and *The Chessboard* (1961, London Tate), somewhat influenced by Matisse and de Staël.

HECKEL, Erich (1883–1970), German painter. He was a self-taught painter and helped to found **Die Brücke** in 1907. He was by nature the gentlest and most lyrical of the Brücke painters, as can be seen in such works as the *Reclining Girl* (1909, Munich NG), although he was increasingly influenced by the jagged, forceful style of Kirchner, *eg The Con-*

valescent (1913, Harvard Busch-Reisinger Museum). After World War I Heckel developed a personal harmonious style, with rounded outlines and balanced forms, showing the influence of Gauguin and also of Oriental art, *eg Zoo in Autumn* (1920, Raleigh MA), *The Sleeper* (1932, Mannheim Kunsthalle). In his recent sensitive landscapes and flower-studies, he has used paler colours. The Erfurt Museum has a series of frescoes executed by him in 1922–3.

HEILIGER, Bernhard (1915–   ), German sculptor. He studied with **Maillol** in Paris, and developed his style after World War II in a series of allegorical bronzes. He began to introduce plant forms into his work and, more recently, bent sheets and blocks of metal in abstract shapes: *Flame* (1962, Berlin, Ernst-Reuter-Platz). His recent work is completely abstract and includes bars, tubes and other elemental shapes bound together in a pattern which suggests rhythmical movement: *Hanging Sculpture* (1967, Berlin, Reichstag). Heiliger was a considerable influence on post-War German sculpture.

HENRI, Robert (1865–1929), American painter and teacher. After studying at the Philadelphia Academy of Art, Henri attended the Académie Julian and the Ecole des Beaux-Arts in Paris (1889–90). Impressed by the art of Manet and of the Impressionists, he returned to Philadelphia, where he in turn influenced younger artists. He returned to Europe for four years in 1895 and then moved to New York, where he began an outstandingly successful career as a teacher, at the Chase school, the Art Students' League and in his own school. Henri, with his fellow members of the **Ash Can School**, was important as the first realist painter in America to employ the technique of contemporary French painters to portray the contemporary American scene. This he did principally in figure-studies such as *Young Woman in Black* (1904, Chicago Art Inst.). His influence as a teacher, however, was far greater than his example as a painter. He rejected the idea of the subject merely as a peg on which to hang technique, urging students to explore the subjects around them for their inherent value. He also promoted free discussion of modern trends, not only in painting but in all the arts. His pupils included Bellows, Davis, Dove, Hopper, Niles Spencer and Joseph Stella.

HEPWORTH, Barbara (1903–   ), English sculptress. After studying in Leeds and London, she went (1925) to Rome, where she learned the traditional Italian technique of marble carving. This technique, expressed with her craftsmanlike precision, was to become the mainstay of all her subsequent art. Her early works had much in common with those of **Henry Moore**, a fellow student at Leeds. They consisted of quasi-naturalistic figures, *eg Doves* (1927, Manchester City AG), but already showed her characteristic submerging of detail in a simple rotund form; these forms were then interrelated in lyrical, but precise ways. In 1931 she met the painter **Ben Nicholson**, who later became her second husband; through him she became aware of contemporary developments in Europe and of the implications of Cubism and Constructivism. In 1933 they joined the **Abstraction-Création** group and met most of the members of the **School of Paris**, including Arp, Brancusi, Gabo and Mondrian, all important influences on her work. Nicholson and Hepworth in turn led Gabo, Mondrian and Moholy-Nagy to come and live in England before World War II. Her work of this period included very simplified torsos, sometimes with profiles drawn Cubist-fashion on smooth stone, frequently pierced with round holes to intensify the effect of the carving as form. In the mid-1930s there were also a number of works closely related to **Constructivism**, both hard geometrical works and, more typical of the artist's character, constructions involving simple forms which were nonetheless softened and had slight irregularities like pebbles or other natural forms, *eg Discs in Echelon* (1935, New York MMA), *Three Forms* (1935, London Tate). In 1939 she moved with Ben Nicholson to Cornwall and her work became technically more complex, though still concerned with regular, classically conceived forms: she developed her earlier idea of the hole in sculpture, and made more play with the relationship between the outside and inside of a figure which would often be painted or threaded with string to link the two surfaces, as in

Pelagos (1946, London Tate). She became interested (*c* 1950) in anthropomorphic forms again and increased the scale of her work. *eg Dyad* (1949, Edinburgh Gallery of Modern Art); *Figure (Churinga)* (1952, Minneapolis Art Inst.). In 1950 she took part in the Venice Biennale, and in 1959 won the Grand Prix at São Paulo. Commissions began to pour in and the artist started working in metal as well as carving. *eg Meridian* (1958–9, London State House); *Winged Figure* (1962, London. John Lewis store); *Single Form* (1962–3, Dag Hammarskjold Memorial, U.N. Building, New York). Her most recent work, though diversified in material and scale, shows the same exquisite craftsmanship and Classical beauty. The largest collection of her work is in the Tate Gallery, London, but the Otterloo RKM has a varied collection interestingly displayed in and around a pavilion by the De Stijl architect, Gerrit Rietveld. She was awarded the D.B.E. in 1965.

HERBIN, Auguste (1882–1960), French painter. He exhibited at the Salon des Indépendants in 1906, and in 1926 he began to practise a style of total abstraction. He founded, with Vantongerloo, the **Abstraction-Création** group and published his theoretical work, *L'Art non Figuratif, non Objectif* in 1949. Herbin's mature work is mostly in gouache and consists of two-dimensional designs of

Auguste Herbin: Air-Feu *(detail, 1934, Paris MNAM); ph. Giraudon.*

geometrical figures painted in bright, but subtly combined colour. Often he used a simple word such as 'Oui' or 'Non' whose letters generated the shapes on which the composition was based. There are examples in London. *Nude* (1960, Tate), New York (MMA and Guggenheim), Chicago Art Institute. Paris, *Air-Feu* (1934, MNAM), and the Basle Kunstmuseum.

HERMAN, Josef (1911–), British painter born in Poland. He studied at the Warsaw School of Art, but had to flee to Belgium in 1938. Already an Expressionist by nature, he came under the influence of **Permeke** and painted, in the Borinage district, the peasants and miners who had inspired van Gogh's early work. In 1940 he went to Glasgow and then settled in the Welsh mining village of Ystradgynlais in 1944. Most of his paintings are of miners, in a heavy, sombre style, somewhat like early Cézanne. Sometimes the figures are treated in isolation with the same direct presentation as **Millet**, *eg Pruning the Vine* (1952, Cardiff National Museum). Sometimes Herman places them in the context of a realist genre setting as in *Miners' Canteen* (1960, Auckland AG).

HERON, Patrick (1920–), English painter. He studied at the Slade School but did no begin to paint full-time until 1945. His early work was influenced by Cubism generally and by **Braque** in particular, though it always showed a wholly personal gift for colour, as in *Anemones and Lemons* (1950, Leeds City AG). In 1956, influenced by **Abstract Expressionism**, he turned to abstract art, using simple shapes to study the relationship between colour and space, achieving extraordinary perceptual ambiguities which relate him to Rothko. *eg Green and Purple Painting with Blue Disk* (1960, London Tate). His works have a sure balance, *eg Complex Cadmiums and Carmines with Brown Luminous Disk* (1967, Leeds AG).

HEUZE, Edmond (1883–), French painter. A self-taught artist, he became a professor at the Ecole des Beaux-Arts and was elected (1948) to the Institut. He is best known for his paintings of circus life, done in a truculent style, somewhat influenced by Degas, *eg Ceratto dans sa Loge* (Paris MNAM).

HILAIRE, Camille (1916–), French painter. He studied at the Ecole des Beaux-Arts and in 1950 won the Prix Antral and the Prix de la Casa Velasquez. He also works in tapestry and stained glass (1963, Lisieux Cathedral). His pleasing but slightly trivializing style applies quasi-Cubist fragmentation and strong rich colour to a variety of subjects, including race-course scenes, nudes, orchestras and dancing, *eg La Femme aux Verrières* (Paris. MAMVP); *The Rehearsal* (1958, Princeton Univ.); these lack a sense of overall control.

HILLIER, Tristam (1905–), English painter born in Peking. He studied at the Slade School and then went to Paris where he studied under **André Lhote**, and lived in the south of France until 1940. His earlier style was abstract or Surrealist, although in about 1937 he devoted himself to representational painting: *La Route des Alpes* (1937, London Tate) is an example of the transition. Hillier's landscapes and still lifes are worked up in the studio, composed with scientific accuracy and painted with meticulous care in a clear hard light reminiscent of early Dutch and Flemish painting. Undoubtedly the still lifes such as *Bridle* (1943, Ottawa NG) and the landscapes containing a proliferation of still life objects, *eg Trinity Wharf* (1947, Sydney AG), are the most successful. The regular patterns made by the objects have a formal interest within the basic realist convention not unlike the Cubo-Realism of **Edward Wadsworth**, who was a fellow member of Unit One in 1933.

HILTON, Roger (1911–), English painter. Hilton studied at the Slade School and later in Paris at the Académie Ranson under Bissière. His works are abstract and extremely simple. At first he juxtaposed a few patches of strong colour in a collage-like style, *eg June 1953* (Edinburgh Gallery of MA). Since the late 1950s Hilton has made increasing use of a lyrical, calligraphic line across the broad areas of paint as in *September 1961* (London Tate); *March 1963* (Liverpool Walker AG). In his recent works he has turned to figure and animal subjects which are summarized with great economy, and without a radical alteration of style.

HILTUNEN, Eila (1922–), Finnish sculptor. After studying at the Art School in Helsinki, she travelled in the U.S., France and Scandinavia. Her first works, in a realistic style, consisted of war memorials, and busts and medals of Finnish public figures. Later she used metal, especially welded steel. Among her most notable works is *Under Water*, a monument for the town of Tampere. She also received the commission for the national monument to the composer Sibelius. Her expressive style, with its subtle use of space and broad, dynamic rhythms, is at its most typical in her transfiguration of men and animals into mythical beings.

HIQUILY, Philippe (1925–), French abstract sculptor. He began (*c* 1950) to use forged and welded iron as his main materials. Some of his works reveal the influence of Surrealism, *eg La Stripteaseuse* (1958, New York Guggenheim). Others employ rounded, heavy masses in various combinations, from which thin pointed stalks emerge, the whole reminiscent sometimes of the female body, sometimes of insect forms.

HIRSHFIELD, Morris (1872–1946), American painter, born in Poland. One of the most striking modern **Naive** painters, he emigrated to the U.S. in 1892. It was not until 1936, when a severe illness forced him to retire from tailoring, that he began to paint. His most frequent subjects were wild animals set in carefully-planted landscapes, looking as though they were modelling fur coats, *eg Tiger* (1940, New York MMA), and nudes, often looking at themselves in a mirror which reflected the back view, *eg Girl before the Mirror* (1940, New York MMA).

HITCHENS, Ivon (1893–), English painter. A student at the Royal Academy Schools under Sargent, he began to paint in a variety of styles. His work of the 1920s includes semi-abstract landscapes (a theme which was to continue throughout his work). They tended to be very formal, with regular hard-edged shapes influenced by Cézanne, *eg Underhill Farm* (watercolour, 1923, London Victoria and Albert M). He also attempted more complex still lifes in the manner of Matisse and even (*c* 1935) some pure abstracts in which his gift for striking and evocative colour contrasts first showed itself. Indeed, a work such as *Coronation* (1937, artist's collection) with its freely brushed washes of colour on the bare canvas anticipated **Abstract Expressionism**, a term which could be applied to the majority of his work since. However, Hitchens' métier emerged (*c* 1940) with a series of landscape compositions in a characteristic wide format and with a remarkable conception of space. At first these were fairly naturalistic, *eg Damp Autumn* (1941, London Tate), although very soon the brushstrokes were allowed their own, Calligraphic, expression as forms in themselves, the colour assuming the main representational burden, as in *Winter Walk No. 1* (1948, Toronto AG). In the most recent pictures, the natural forms are no longer to be identified and the colour schemes become more daring with the use of petrol blue, lime and canary, and yet the pictures in their overall balance still convey an impression of the English countryside. He has also done occasional figure compositions, *eg Interior, Orange Sunlight* (1960, Aberdeen AG), and the two types of painting are combined in the great mural *Day's Rest, Day's Work* (1960, Brighton, Univ. of Sussex).

HOCKNEY, David (1937–   ), English painter and etcher. He studied at the Bradford College of Art and at the Royal College of Art, where he was influenced by **R. B. Kitaj**, and **Richard Smith**, and exhibited at the 'Young Contemporaries' Exhibition in 1961. He has spent most of his time since then in the U.S. He was largely concerned at first with satirical figure subjects which, whether in oil or in a graphic medium, were drawn in an uncouth scribbled style similar to children's graffiti, though combined with areas of more realistic painting in imitation of **Collage**, *eg Alka Selzer* (1961, Oxford, Balliol College); *The first Marriage* (1962, London Tate). His frequent use at this period of commercial imagery related him to **Pop Art**. Since about 1966 his style has become more and more realistic and he is in considerable demand as a portraitist: *Mr. and Mrs. Clark and Percy* (1971, London Tate).

HODLER, Ferdinand (1853–1918), Swiss painter. He studied at the Ecole des Beaux-Arts, Geneva, under Corot's friend, Barthélemy Menn. Hodler began by painting labourers and craftsmen at work in a restrained, economical style recalling that of Holbein. He went (1891) to Paris, where he was influenced by the work of Cézanne, Gauguin and the Symbolists. His work became increasingly literary and symbolic, as in his idealized genre pictures, with chalky colours and hard outlines, *eg Tree-Feller* (1910, Bern Kunstmuseum), mystical works, *eg Day* (1900, Zurich Kunsthaus) and historical compositions, *eg Departure of the Students of Jena* (1909, Jena Univ.). His art was a fusion of French Post-Impressionist elements with **Secession** painting. He joined the Berlin Secession in 1899 and was given a retrospective exhibition at the Vienna Secession of 1904. His best works are portraits, which are direct and penetrating, and alpine landscapes, in which he depicts Lake Geneva and the Alps in a broad monumental style with a free use of colour. Hodler also wrote, but used an idealized style.

HOFER, Karl (1878–1955), German painter. He lived abroad, first in Rome and then in Paris (1908–13), during which time he painted in an idealized Neo-Classical style. His paintings after World War I contained a note of sadness and often anguish, *eg The Black Rooms* (1928, 1943, Berlin 20th C Gallery). He was awarded the Carnegie Prize in 1928. Hofer described himself as a 'thwarted Classicist', but his colour and robust modelling were influenced by Expressionism.

HOFLEHNER, Rudolf (1916–   ), Austrian sculptor. He studied architecture at Graz, before moving to the Vienna Academy of Art. It was not until the late 1940s that he began producing sculptures in iron using oxyacetylene and engineering techniques, not to smooth the material out, but to hew it into blocks like a quarryman blasting granite. All his sculptures are anthropomorphic and have a characteristic split down the middle, with an uneasy transition from one part to the other as in *Split Figure* (1957, Vienna 20th C Museum). In most of his works, however, he only presents a few parts which stand for the whole, generally forms reminiscent of legs and pelvis, with brutal erotic overtones, *eg Figure in Iron 11* (1961, Mannheim Kunsthalle). In his more recent work the forms are considerably softened, *eg Figure in Iron* (1963, London Tate).

HOFMANN, Hans (1880–1966), American painter. After studying in various schools in Munich, Hofmann went to Paris in 1904 and stayed there ten years. There he met Pascin, Delaunay, Picasso, Braque, Gris and **Matisse**, whose work made a lasting impression on him. Hofmann only made limited use of Cubism as in *Green Bottle* (1921, Leominster, Mass., Lane Foundation), but Cubist stylizations appear in many of his later near-abstract works. He returned to Munich at the outbreak of war and opened a school there. Thereafter a large part of Hofmann's time was spent teaching in Germany, on summer excursions to the Mediterranean, from 1930 to 1933 at the University of California, and from 1933 onwards in his own school which he opened in New York. Hofmann is one of the great teachers of the century and he influenced much of New York **Abstract Expressionism**, as well as later artists. The direct influence of his own painting, particularly his use of the drip-painting technique, which first appeared in his work in 1939, has also been of prime importance. It was borrowed and extended by Jackson Pollock, and provided the principal technique of **Action Painting**. Hofmann's post-War works are curiously varied in style and rarely have the amplitude of conception of his American followers. He uses strong primary or pure secondary colours, sometimes freely scumbled in compositions owing much to **Kandinsky** *eg Delight* (1947, New York MMA), sometimes laid on in flat areas like a Matisse collage *eg Magenta and Blue* (1950, New York Whitney Museum); sometimes applied in bold gestural strokes as in *Exuberance* (1955, Buffalo AG), sometimes in splashes and drips, *The Prey* (1956, New York MMA). But all his works have in common an exuberance and positiveness of expression which can be seen reflected in almost all American painting since World War II.

HOMER, Winslow (1836–1910), American painter. Originally trained as a lithographer, he earned a living throughout his career illustrating books and magazines. His style remained largely independent of European models, although some works painted after his trip to Paris (1866–7) show the influence of Boudin, *eg Long Branch, New Jersey* (1869, Boston MFA). Some of his open-air scenes such as *Breezing Up* (1876, Washington NG) have a freshness which parallels Impressionism, though their use of earth colours in shaded passages is essentially different. Many of Homer's subjects were genre scenes, and at least part of his importance lay in sustaining the myth of rural American life as an escape from an increasingly urban civilization, particularly in watercolours such as *The Pioneer* (1900, New York Metropolitan Museum). *The Fox Hunt* (1893, Philadelphia Pennsylvania Academy) is one of many pictures in which the subject has been removed from all distracting detail and locked into a deceptively simple composition, influenced by Japanese prints. His seascapes, both in watercolour and in oil, are probably his finest work with their perfect balance of pictorial design and evocation of the brute power of nature, *eg Early Morning after a Storm* (1902, Cleveland MA).

HOMMES TEMOINS, see **Realism**.

HOPPER, Edward (1882–1967), American painter. As a pupil of **Robert Henri** in New York (1900–6), he was encouraged to draw the city around him and subsequently became one of the pioneers of 20th century American **Realism**. Between 1900 and 1910, Hopper visited Europe three times, but it was **Manet** and the Impressionists who affected him, rather than current developments. His early work was rather Whistlerian in style, *eg Corner Saloon* (1913, New York MMA), but its lack of romanticism was not well received, and from 1915 to 1920 he practically gave up painting, concentrating on etching. His mature work is dominated by modern America: not the bustle of the commercial world nor the awesomeness of industrial development, but the odd backwaters trapped between railway lines and apartment blocks, as in *Manhattan Bridge Loop* (1928, Andover, Mass., Addison Gallery), the deserted streets, *eg Early Sunday Morning* (1920, New York Whitney Museum), or the lonely garage at dusk on the country road, as in *Gas* (1940, Minneapolis Walker Art Center) which approaches

Magritte in its eerie atmosphere. Although Hopper often used figures as a focus for the feelings (especially of loneliness) engendered by his settings, *eg New York Movie* (1939, New York MMA), it was the city itself and the material aspect of American life which were his main subjects. In his power to express so strongly the feelings evoked by the inanimate world, without any hint of Expressionism, Hopper anticipated in straightforward painting the work of many **Pop** artists, notably Wesselmann and George Segal.

HOYLAND, John (1934–   ), English painter. He studied at Sheffield College of Art and at the Royal Academy Schools. From the time he left college in 1960, his work has belonged to the new **Post-Painterly Abstraction** in the tradition of Rothko and Albers. In the 'Situation' exhibitions of 1960 and 1962 he showed huge canvases painted with horizontal stripes of vibrating colours. He soon abandoned this **Op Art** approach for a more informal distribution of the hard-edged colour areas on the canvas, *eg 20.2.62* (1962, London Tate). This informality has increased and his recent works often consist of little more than two or three rectangles of colour on an all-over ground. With this adoption of acrylic paint in 1963 the hues have increased in intensity and the colour relationships have been chosen with greater daring *eg 28.5.66.* (1966, London Tate). In his work of 1968 and 1969 Hoyland has made cautious use of **Action Painting** and drip techniques to give texture to certain areas as in *25.4.69.* (1969, London Tate). Although his work has not the machine-like finish of much contemporary American painting and seems to hold more to traditional values, it never dissipates its formal power by reference to landscape, emotion or conventional ideals of beauty and form.

HUMBLOT, Robert (1907–1962), French painter. A student at the Ecole des Beaux-Arts in 1931, he was a co-founder with Rohner and Jannot of the *Forces Nouvelles* group. In 1953 he won the Grand Prix at the Menton Biennale. His work, realistic in inspiration, depicts rocky landscapes, dessicated still lifes and angular nudes in a concentrated style in which the forms seem cut out against unified backgrounds. His uncompromising art, with its bitter clarity, attains dramatic, cold intensity.

HUNDERTWASSER, Fritz (1928–   ), Austrian painter, originally Friederich Stowasser. He studied in Vienna where he was influenced by the tradition stemming from Klimt via **Schiele**. He was later influenced by **Klee**. His earlier works were figurative and rich in colour, being composed like a flat patchwork quilt. In 1952 he adopted a decorative abstraction, and began to use characteristic bands or contours of adjacent contrasting colours, giving a maze-like effect, *eg Der Grosse Weg* (1955, Vienna 20th C Museum). The works of the 1960s combine these styles, but are more open and less hermetic in design. They are considerably more varied in colour, which comes out in larger areas with bolder contrasts. His work is partially figurative in subject, and frequently contains patches of Klimt-like gold and silver.

HUNTER, Leslie (1877–1931), Scottish painter. Although his roots remained in Scotland he emigrated with his family to California in 1890, and began his painting career in San Francisco. In 1904 he visited Paris, and in 1906 settled in Glasgow, although he returned to France and America several times during his life. His style is derived from Impressionism and Post-Impressionism. His fairly conventional treatment of form was coupled with an interest in rich harmonies of colour and textures of paint, *eg Kitchen Utensils* (*c* 1914, London Tate). His later works were lighter, using a more open brushstroke, and combine Fauve influence with a keen perception of the Scottish scene, *eg Reflections, Balloch* (*c* 1925, Edinburgh Gallery of Modern Art).

HYPPOLITE, Hector (1894–1948), Haitian painter. After travelling in the U.S. and Africa, he worked as a house painter and decorator in Haiti. He was also a Voodoo priest. Encouraged by **Wilfredo Lam**, he made use, through Naive art, of Caribbean folklore and a fine sense of curvilinear rhythm, *eg Composition* (Port-au-Prince Museum). He had considerable influence in his native country and participated in several **Surrealism** exhibitions abroad.

I

ICHE, Rene (1897–1954), French sculptor. He studied stone carving and architecture with Auguste Perret. He remained independent of contemporary trends, producing a vigorous body of work in stone and bronze. He was responsible for monuments at Puiseaux and at Carcassonne (1948), and for the entrance to the Palais du Travail at Narbonne (1951). His human figures were sculpted in a concentrated, powerful style, *eg Baigneuse* (1928, Paris MNAM), and *Lutteurs à Terre* (1945, Paris MNAM).

IMPRESSIONISM, term which is one of the best-known in the history of modern art and one of the most misunderstood. The name was originally given to the work of a small number of artists, led by **Monet**, who exhibited together in Paris for the first time in 1874. However, the term is frequently extended (especially in the form 'impressionistic') to describe any artist who paints the general impression of a scene without concentrating on its details, to any art in which the facts of the subject are less important than the artist's response to them, to painting which is blurred rather than focused. It is even used, quite unjustifiably, as an antonym for Expressionism. The word in popular use thus often depends on the point of view of the user. For this reason it is important to define the primary meaning of the term accurately.

The term was first used by a reviewer in *Le Charivan* of a picture by Monet entitled *Impression: Soleil levant* (1872, Paris Musée Marmoltan). It was exhibited (1874) in a large group show at the studio of the photographer Nadar, and Monet along with his fellow exhibitors **Cézanne**, **Degas**, **Pissarro**, **Renoir** and Sisley accepted it as the nickname for the movement which they felt they were initiating. There were seven other Group Exhibitions held in 1876, 1877, 1879, 1880, 1881, 1882 and 1886 respectively. Numerous other artists took part in each one, and only Pissarro, of the painters mentioned above, exhibited at all of them. Cézanne only showed at the first and the third; Renoir and Sisley took part in the first three and the seventh only; and Monet himself dropped out after the fourth, though he also showed at the seventh. Degas showed work at all the exhibitions except the seventh, though he was responsible for introducing a number of other artists at the last exhibition, whose presence considerably distorted the original aims. Gauguin was included for the first time in the seventh show, and Seurat at the last, although both artists, and indeed Cézanne himself, merely took Impressionism as the point of departure for their own styles. Thus it is impossible to arrive at a useful definition of the term even by concentrating on the work shown at the eight Impressionist Exhibitions.

There is, however, a much smaller body of work which can be said to characterize the style. Impressionism was pre-eminently developed by Monet from about 1870 onwards, and its essential principles were upheld by him throughout his life. It is also seen in the work of Sisley and Pissarro, who were closely associated with Monet from about 1870 to 1884, and in the landscapes and genre scenes of Renoir done about this time. The portraits of Renoir and the figure-paintings of Degas also show some Impressionist characteristics but to include them without reservation would be to extend the term beyond a useful point. Manet is often mistakenly numbered among the Impressionists. He did influence them considerably in their choice of subject-matter, and allowed himself in turn to be influenced by Monet to the extent of working with him at Argenteuil in the summer of 1874, *eg Monet Working in His Boat* (1874, Munich NG). Nevertheless he is distinguishable from the Impressionists by his use of black, his reverence for the Old Masters and his refusal to exhibit in their Group Exhibitions.

In choice of subject-matter, the Impressionists were Realists. Their willingness to record objectively what they saw opened up a vast range of new subject material which had not fitted into the idealizing conceptions of Academic painters. They painted the everyday life of the city, on the boulevards and in the cafés; they painted the railway stations, and resorts, such as Argenteuil, La Grenouillière and La Grande Jatte which the railways had opened up to the working classes for their weekend outings; they painted their fellow human beings both at work and in the dance-halls. **Realism** was not new in 19th century art, but the Impressionists' approach to it was less didactic than **Courbet**'s and less artificial than Manet's.

Claude Monet: The Charcoal Porters of Argenteuil *(1872, private collection); ph. Giraudon.*

Stylistically, these artists were solely concerned with painting what they saw rather than what they knew to be there. It was essential to paint out-of-doors and to take every change of the weather into account: indeed in picture-series like Monet's *Rouen Cathedral* (1892–5, *eg* Paris Jeu de Paume), the changing light forms the entire subject. *Plein-air* painting was not quite new, having been anticipated by **Daubigny**, but the Impressionists were the first to insist on finishing the entire picture in one session before the subject. In order to capture the effects of light they lightened their palette, banishing black and earth colours and restricting themselves on the whole to the pure hues as found in the spectrum. In order to be able to paint *'alla prima'* and to avoid too much mixing, and hence muddying, of the colours, they adopted a brushstroke in which paint was put on in a number of individual dabs of colour, or else in short strokes that contributed to the drawing of the object.

Two contradictory but equally mistaken assessments of the Impressionists are often put forward: one is that they were scientific, the other that they were totally naturalistic. Close examination of their pictures reveals that technique and choice of colour were far from consistent. **Seurat** and his followers, the Neo-Impressionists, did turn the instinctive practice of the Impressionists into an ordered system, but this approach cannot be applied to the older artists who were utterly unsophisticated in their approach ('I would like to paint as a bird sings,' said Monet). On the other hand, if it was the Impressionists' aim to achieve perfect naturalism with their painting it was a failure, for most of the pictures are patently unreal. So far from the individual brushstrokes blending together in the eye, they remain a fascinating flickering pattern when seen at any discernable distance, and one cannot help feeling that this was intentional. For whereas the Impressionists did undoubtedly introduce a new method of seeing, in which a scene was taken as a whole rather than being built up from a mass of detail, they did this in terms of paint on canvas. Their interest in **Japanese Prints**, their simplified drawing and the broken brushstrokes all tended to flatten the picture and emphasize the surface. Their use of touches of one colour in areas of another created a multiplicity of cross-references between colours in the picture and a close interlocking of the pattern, which was increased by the fact that many of the colours were chosen as complementaries to bring the most out of each other.

The Impressionists were (apart from the **Pre-Raphaelite Brotherhood**) the first major movement to arise in revolt against the artistic establishment, and that has been the pattern followed by most of the major movements of this century, such as Fauvism, Cubism and Dada. Impressionism was the starting point for the individual developments of Cézanne, Gauguin and van Gogh, and for **Neo-Impressionism**. The Impressionists' adoption of pure hues and their use of colour for its effect on the canvas (albeit without sacrificing the representation of the subject) made possible the total release of colour, in **Fauvism**, from any adherence to naturalism. The impact of Impressionism on many artists, *eg* **Robert Henri** and his pupils, was to give rise to a surge of realism in subject-matter without necessarily adopting Impressionist technique. This has been an important factor in the struggle of modern art to keep pace with the contemporary world. Furthermore, by recording things as they appear to the artist and by making paintings which have to be assembled and interpreted in the eye of the beholder, Impressionism is a *subjective* art, and thus anticipates the approach of **Expressionism**. Impressionism has given numerous later artists a language in which to express their own particular idea, *eg* the **Futurism** of Utrillo and Munch. Finally, there are the artists such as Corinth, Vuillard and above all **Bonnard** who have in one way or another continued to explore the ideals of Impressionism.

INDIANA, Robert (1928–   ), American painter, born Robert Clark. He studied in

Indianapolis and Utica, at the Chicago Art Institute and finally at Edinburgh College of Art (1953–4). He settled (1956) in New York, where he befriended **Ellsworth Kelly** who influenced his hard geometrical style. Although he has done some figure paintings, somewhat in the manner of **Sheeler**, Indiana specializes in geometric shapes emblazoned with stencilled inscriptions in strong billboard colours. They owe something to the 'poster portraits' of Demuth. Since the slogans on his works (*eg* 'EAT' 'DIE' 'ERR' 'KILL') are generally intended as a satirical challenge to the 'American Dream', Indiana could be classed as a non-figurative Pop artist as in *The Red Diamond, American Dream* (1962, Eindhoven van Abbemuseum).

INFLUENCES. Artists in the 20th century have formed their styles more in response to individual influences than as a result of a common tradition as in previous centuries. They have been essentially individualists, even revolutionaries, desiring to create new works by rejecting the past (**Futurism** went so far as to demand the destruction of all museums). However, nothing is born of nothing, and the range of influences acting upon artists today is extraordinarily wide. There has been a tremendous increase in the number of museums, galleries and exhibitions; scientific research has widened knowledge of the arts of all periods and civilizations; the number of art books and magazines has grown, the techniques of photographic reproduction, especially in colour, have improved immensely since World War II; and, finally, taste has widened to admit a broader definition of the word 'art'. The range of visual images, 'the museum without walls' in André Malraux's phrase, is of phenomenal size.

The first group of influences to be considered comprises those artists who brought about the modern pictorial revolution. The most significant of these have been the great masters of the 19th century: **Delacroix**, who initiated the cult of pure colour; **Ingres**, who was valued particularly in **Cubism** for his carefully calculated compositional technique; **Corot**, whose figure-paintings are held in particular esteem; **Daumier**, for his vivid response to the contemporary social scene; and **Courbet**, the genius of impasto. Painters of all countries have seen in **Paul Cézanne** (especially in his work of 1904–10) the most profound and perfect embodiment of their aspirations. Four other practitioners of **Post-Impressionism** have also exerted a decisive influence on modern art: **Gauguin** for his return to primitive art; **Seurat** for his attempt to found an art based on absolute rules of construction; **Toulouse-Lautrec** for his ability to combine realistic portrayal of the contemporary scene with purely pictorial design; and **van Gogh** for the tragic intensity of his colour and handling. Among the artists of the 20th century, some have exerted a considerable influence because of the sheer originality and audacity of their creations: **Picasso**, the creator of Cubism, whose astounding inventiveness has continued for sixty years is the most obvious example, but the impact of **Matisse**, and lately of **Bonnard**, has also been critical in certain developments of modern art. Moreover the promoters of abstract art, among them **Mondrian**, **Klee** and **Kandinsky**, can now be seen to have initiated a worldwide trend.

The influence of the painters of former times never remains static, but alters with shifts of emphasis in contemporary thought. In the present century, the Classical masters, Raphael, Titian, Rubens and Rembrandt have been to a certain extent superseded in the interests of artists and students by a great number of hitherto neglected artists whose work now seems to indicate solutions to modern problems. Chief among these is Vermeer of Delft, the master of pure colour, light and design, and also one of the greatest painters of genre, in whose works everyday objects seem to take on a greater reality, which parallels the importance given to them in **Surrealism** and, latterly, in Pop Art. The Surrealists have also been influenced by great figures such as Hieronymus Bosch, who created fantastic and nightmarish compositions, and **Goya** for his terrifying late works, as well as by a host of minor ones such as Arcimboldo, who painted human figures composed of fruit and other objects. The interest of several modern artists centres on the early 'primitive' Renaissance painters who had already been discovered in the 19th century by Ingres and the **Pre-Raphaelites**. Today, however, the rigorous geometricality of

the compositions of Uccello and Piero della Francesca are more influential than the lyricism of Botticelli or the Lippi. The Flemish and French primitives, the early Germans, to say nothing of the Byzantine mosaicists and the Roman fresco painters of the 12th century have come increasingly into favour. There are certain 16th century painters who are passionately admired by the painters of today, among them proto-Expressionist Grünewald and the Elder Bruegel. As far as French art is concerned, it was the taste for Romanesque art, in painting, sculpture, and architecture, which brought the removal of Gothic art from the pedestal on which it had been placed during the 19th century. Modern artists also favourably regard the art of the Merovingian period, and early Irish and Scandinavian art. An increasing interest in the art of other continents has also affected European art of the last 100 years. **Japanese Prints** were one of the chief influences on **Whistler**, **Manet** and most of the Post-Impressionists, and completely altered the traditional conception of pictorial composition. They were followed by Japanese Buddhist Nara sculptures (6th–8th centuries), and by Chinese bronzes and statuary; Oriental calligraphic art has also had an important influence since World War II. The strange, dramatic art of pre-Columbian America has also been responsible for a revolution in taste. Peruvian pottery and especially Mexican sculptures revealed a religious art of fantastic forms and great tragic expressiveness. Interest in ancient civilizations has tended to focus on the most ancient and most primitive forms of art. Thus Greek art, previously associated with Academicism, has again awakened interest, but especially in its Cycladic figures dating from 2000 BC. The discovery of Sumerian sculpture, which preceded Assyrian art, was very important for modern art, while the excavation of the tomb of Tutankhamen brought Egyptian painting and statuary back into prominence as an influence on contemporary art. The famous wall-paintings of Altamira, discovered in 1875, were not recognized as authentic until twenty years later, but the cave paintings at Lascaux were saluted as 'the Sistine Chapel of pre-history' as soon as they were found in 1940. The perfection of these animal figures, thought to serve a magical purpose and some tens of thousands of years old, was quite astonishing and effectively destroyed all theories of 'progress' in art. The strange and powerful style of pre-historic figurines such as the *Venus of Willensdorf* has deeply impressed modern sculptors. The arts of modern peoples of more primitive civilizations have been among the most important recent discoveries. **Derain** and **Vlaminck** are believed to have been (*c* 1904) the first artists to admire a Negro mask, and they were soon followed by Picasso, who employed this image in his famous *Demoiselles d'Avignon*. Negro art, which is essentially ritualistic, has produced fetish-statues, masks and decorative objects,

whose stylization is both beautiful and expressive. Its influence has, in the eyes of some Western artists, warranted the adoption of styles pre-occupied with abstract form and rhythm, both in painting and sculpture. Pacific art, still further removed from the canons of European art, interested the Surrealists in particular. Profoundly animistic, Melanesian and Polynesian art is the vehicle of an extremely complex mythology, and its stylization is probably the strangest ever invented. Maori art, the most highly developed of all Pacific styles, is characterized by an obsession with spirals and volutes of great power. The statues of magic divinities called the Tiki, the immense stone heads of Easter Island,

Pablo Picasso: Les Desmoiselles d'Avignon *(1907, New York MMA); ph. Hazan.*

the fairy-like feathery garments of Hawaii, have all contributed to the mysterious universe of many artists of the 20th century.

The general concern for a return to the sources of art has also led to the discovery of other areas which have hitherto been excluded from the fine arts. The decorative richness and the freshness of folk inspiration have been a revelation to modern artists. Following the enormous influence of **Henri Rousseau**, so-called 'primitive painting' has become widespread. Another form of **Naive** painting arousing considerable interest has been children's art. Baudelaire said: 'The child is intoxicated by the novelty of what he sees. Genius is a result of the will to recreate this vision.' The freshness, the imaginative grace and the fantasy of the works of children bring one near to the source of authentic art, although the element of personality is largely absent from them; the art of **Chagall**, Klee, **Dubuffet** and others comes close to child-like utterances.

The art of schizophrenics and others suffering from mental disorders has much intrigued artists. The whole question of the relationship between the artist's mental state and his art came to the fore at the beginning of this century. The cases of such painters as van Gogh, Séraphine and **Kubin** contributed to the idea, that art is a form of mental disorder. The 'Brutalist Art' movement, begun in 1947 by **André Breton**, Jean Paulhan and Jean Dubuffet, undertook a systematic enquiry into the works of mediums and of lunatics. The symbolism of their works, their development of an automatic style of painting and the hallucinatory quality of their inventions have been the object of research and even imitation, for example in the later work of **Tchelitchew**. Artists and writers, such as **Jean Cocteau** and **Henri Michaux**, have produced drawings of the most startling quality under the influence of narcotics. Their hope was to find, by this method, a new art of a direct intensity which had never been attained.

In addition to these specifically visual influences there is the question of the effect upon art of modern technology. It is not merely a question of subject matter (though artists such as **Duchamp**, **Léger**, and the Futurists have turned to the machine for inspiration and **Kinetic** sculp-

tors build what might be called 'aesthetic machines') but of the more subtle relationship between the 'fine' and the 'commercial' arts. The **Bauhaus** was founded to train designers to come to terms with the machine aesthetic. The resulting developments in design have naturally had their repercussions upon art. It is arguable that the rigid hard-edge painting style of **Constructivism** and of the **De Stijl** group would not have arisen had not the machine age set new standards of precision. It is certain that the application of these styles to commercial art has gradually made the public more responsive to developments in this direction. The fine arts have, in turn, admitted the influence of commercial art and made use of its imagery, notably in **Pop Art**.

Of modern inventions, photography has had the greatest influence on art. Photographs have been used by artists since the mid-nineteenth century as a means of gathering a wider range of visual material than would otherwise have been possible. **Bacon** bases many of his works on photographs and film stills, and **Rauschenberg** incorporates actual newspaper photographs into his works. Artists such as Corot and **Degas**, have sometimes tried to imitate photographic effects; at the opposite extreme, one of the main impulses of modern art has been the attempt to create things that could not be done better by photography.

Summing up, it can be said that modern art partakes more fully of life as a whole, influencing it, and being influenced by it, to a far greater degree than ever before.

INGRES, Jean Auguste Dominique (1780–1867), French painter. He was the unchallenged leader of the Neo-Classical school of French painting. This was in effect the approved academic style, although Ingres transcended routine academicism. Nevertheless the fact that most of the revolutionary movements in the latter half of the century (notably **Impressionism**) rejected academicism and found their inspiration more in Ingres' contemporary, **Delacroix**, has led to an inadequate estimate of Ingres' influence on modern art. While Delacroix can be said to have represented the Dionysiac in painting, Ingres' approach was Apollonian. His chief concern was a balance and order based on a thorough mastery of line. However, that line was exceedingly expressive, in reducing spatial poses of considerable complexity to two dimensions, and in using distortion to demonstrate more closely the relationship between forms and even to express some emotional or dramatic content. This is particularly true of late works such as *The Turkish Bath* (1863, Paris Louvre). **Degas** received advice from Ingres which had a continuing effect on his style. Ingres' technique of two-dimensional abstraction of form bore fruit in the drawings of **Matisse**, *cf La Danse* (Merion, Penn., Barnes Foundation), Picasso, Modigliani and even in the pure abstractions of artists such as Arp. Among the results of Ingres' search for Classical balance in a picture such as the *Odalisque with Slave* (1842, Baltimore Walters AG) was a remarkable telescoping of space and a use of non-realistic colour in discrete areas which influenced **Whistler**, the Impressionists, **van Gogh**, and **Gauguin** and his followers. Finally Ingres' treatment of patterned fabrics in late portraits such as *Mme. Moitessier Seated* (1856, London NG) anticipated many of the effects later artists tried to achieve through **Collage**.

IRWIN, Gwyther (1931–), English painter. He studied illustration at Goldsmith's College and fabric design at the Central School, London (1952–5). In 1957 he made his first collage, and this medium has occupied most of his output since. His works are non-figurative and he chooses his materials for their textures rather than for any associations they might have. He has worked with string, cardboard, wood shavings and the backs of old posters torn off walls. This last material gives a rich rusty texture, *eg Parade* (1961, London Tate). The materials are torn into small fragments and arranged close together in horizontal rows, making a recurring, flickering pattern that has much in common with **Op Art**. In 1963 he began to do pure paintings which were similar in form and showed the optical effects more strongly. There are works by him in the Albright-Knox Gallery and at Yale University.

ITTEN, Johannes (1888–1967), Swiss painter and teacher. After reading mathematics at Bern University, he went to Stuttgart to study art. He had his first exhibition at the Der Sturm Gallery in 1916, and became in 1919 the first teacher of the preliminary course at the **Bauhaus**. In 1923 he left the Bauhaus and ran a school of his own in Berlin from 1926 to 1934. He was director of the School of Applied Arts in Zurich from 1938 to 1967. Itten's own paintings were first influenced by **Der Blaue Reiter**. Later he developed a free **Calligraphic** style, ultimately exploring the expressive effect of Klee-like patchworks of coloured squares. But it was his influence as a teacher that was most remarkable and his account of his Bauhaus course in *Design and Form* (1963–4) is one of the most valuable documents of modern art. As well as systematically teaching his pupils to know their materials (the basic contrasts of line, form, colour and texture, the characteristics of different media and of different tools and methods of painting), he would develop their imagination through cultivation of the other senses, and through attempts at freeing the creative impulse by **Automatic Writing** and the expression of diverse mental states. He thus attempted to bridge the Constructivist and the Expressionist tendencies in contemporary art.

J

JACOBSEN, Robert (1912–), Danish sculptor. A self-taught artist, he executed his first wooden sculptures at the age of eighteen. In 1941 he was a member of the Surrealist-inspired Danish 'Host' group. Subsequently, he worked in polychromatic stone. He settled in Paris in 1947, at which time he began to employ metal and to create quasi-Constructivist works. In his recent work, he has used pieces of scrap iron, combined in open cages or globes.

JANSEM, Jean (1920–), French painter. born in Armenia. He went to France in 1931 and studied at the Ecole des Arts Décoratifs. He first made his living from drawings and cinema posters. In 1944 his painting *Le Violoniste* was accepted at the Salon des Indépendants. Jansem became one of the leading exponents of Miserablist art (see **Gruber**), painting large-scale pictures of working-class people. His style

Jean Jansem: Trois Femmes *(detail, 1960, Paris, Raymond Ventura Collection); ph. Cauvin.*

is characterized by thin sharp outlines which define the haggard figures of his subjects with a near-grotesque bitterness, emphasizing gnarled and coarse bare feet and hands, and thin limbs. He counteracts the outlines with brilliant colour and fashionable free treatment, giving his pictures an attractiveness at odds with the superficial pathos of his subjects.

JAPANESE PRINTS, one of the most significant influences on modern art at the end of the 19th century. Japanese prints of the 18th and early 19th centuries used to arrive in France with consignments of other goods, often being used as wrapping paper. Among the first artists to collect them seriously were Whistler, Degas and Manet: some can be seen in the background to Manet's *Portrait of Zola* (1868, Paris Jeu de Paume). Their influence derived from the example afforded by the techniques of the

Japanese artists in composing their subjects for the print, an essentially flat medium. They often tended to adopt unusual perspective, as if seen from a high angle, the objects furthest away from the observer being placed highest on the page. Typically, they avoided representing actions in depth, but when they did it would be indicated by a clear diagonal dominating the picture; the pictures were otherwise composed in planes parallel to the picture-place and to each other. The rectangular frame of the print was frequently emphasized by the use of dominant horizontal and vertical lines in the composition, or off-set by flowing curves on the picture surface. These characteristics were reflected in the portraits by **Whistler** and **Degas**. Equally important to Degas and the Impressionists was the Japanese printmakers' frequent device of 'misframing' the composition so that an apparently important figure or object would be cut off by the frame. This technique was adopted by **Toulouse-Lautrec**. All this provided the Impressionists and others with an alternative to Academic composition, an alternative, moreover, which was particularly suited to their aim of capturing the impromptu aspect of contemporary life. By acknowledging paper surface as being essentially flat, the Japanese artists, and those who followed them, repudiated the Academic convention that the picture frame was, in effect, a window on a three-dimensional world. This was crucial, for the concept of abstract and non-representational art depends upon manipulating the picture *as a picture*. From this point of view, the use of colour in Japanese prints (essentially restricted and therefore non-naturalistic) was a contributing factor, although this aspect was not imitated until later, by **van Gogh**, who made free copies of Japanese prints (Amsterdam Stedelijk M), by **Gauguin** and by the **Nabis**. More recently, other aspects of Japanese art and philosophy have influenced artists, notably **Tobey**, who have looked for parallels between their Abstract Expressionism and Oriental calligraphy.

JAVACHEFF, Christo (1935–   ), Bulgarian artist. After studying art in Sofia he moved to Paris in 1958 and settled in New York in 1964. He specializes in packaging anything from household objects to portions of the landscape. Although there are similarities to Dada, Christo's aim is constructive, since the wrapping up of a utilitarian object in paper and string suspends the usefulness of the object, but thereby enhances its artistic interest. His most ambitious projects have included packaging the Bern Museum for an exhibition (1968) and wrapping up a mile of Australian coastline (1970), which is an art using **Environments** on a huge scale. He has also made street barriers out of oil drums and, between 1963 and 1966, blanked-out shop windows.

JAWLENSKY, Alexei von (1864–1941), Russian painter. After 1896 he worked in Munich where in 1901 he founded the 'Neue Kunstler-Vereinigung' with **Kandinsky**, whose influence upon his style was critical. He joined Kandinsky in the **Blaue Reiter** movement of *c* 1910, and with Feininger and Klee, formed the 'Blue Four' (1924–9). In the early years of the century Jawlensky became interested in Matisse and, following a visit to **Pont-Aven** in 1905, in Gauguin and the Nabis. Thus, his early portraits and still-lifes shared some of the characteristics of French Fauve painting, though their rhythms were flatter and more supple, and the colour had a **Nabis** harmony rather than the Fauve éclat, *eg Girl with Peonies* (1909, Wuppertal Museum); *Girl with Green Face* (1910, Chicago Art Inst.); *Blue Jug and Figure* (1908, Cologne, Wallraff-Richartz-Museum). In 1917 he began a series of human heads which were to occupy him almost exclusively until his death. In these the features were simplified into the simple shape of a cross within an oval (a procedure probably influenced by Constructivism) so that they resembled an icon, with spiritual overtones, *eg Head of Christ* (1920, Pasadena AM). Colour became all-important in conveying an astonishing range of emotions through this simple form, as can be seen in the very late works such as *Winter Night, where the Wolves Howl* (1936, Wiesbaden Museum), in which the face shape has been almost completely replaced by colour as the expressive force.

JEANNERET, Edouard ('Le Corbusier') (1887–1965), French architect. As well as architecture, he practised painting and graphic art throughout his career. He was interested in Cubism, and, with his friend Ozenfant founded **Purism**, a reform movement which was to lead Cubism back from its tendency towards mere decoration. For several years he concentrated on still lifes, signing his canvases Jeanneret; these are Cubist in subject but more rigidly organized, *eg Still Life* (1920, New York MMA). In about 1929 he turned to figure painting and developed a flat style very much dependent on a continuous cursive line, *eg Bull III* (1953, London Tate). He has also executed some sculpture and produced 36 tapestry designs for the Aubusson workshop.

JENKINS, Paul (1923–   ), American painter. After studying at the Kansas City Art Institute and the Art Students' League in New York, he settled in Paris in 1953, although he makes frequent trips to the U.S. He was at first influenced by **Wols**, although his style has always been calmer and more mysterious. In the mid-1950s he developed a style of Chromatic Abstraction, probably influenced by **Louis**, making use of overlapping translucent veils of colour and the accidental effects of one wet colour merging with another. The pictures are wonderfully rich and strong in form, and convey great intensity of feeling, *eg Phenomena Blue Carries* (1962, New York Guggenheim Museum); *Phenomena Votive* (1963, Liverpool Walker AG).

JESPERS, Oscar (1887–   ), Belgian sculptor. The son of a sculptor, he studied at the Académie des Beaux-Arts in Antwerp. His early works were influenced by Negro and Primitive art, and tended towards an hieratic simplicity. After World War I his style came under the influence of **Expressionism**, but in a straightforward, almost naive way, *eg The Temptation of St. Anthony* (1934, New York MMA). After 1937 he employed sweeping curves which were both full and elegant. He had a retrospective exhibition at the 1960 Venice Biennale.

JOHN, Augustus Edwin (1878–1961), British painter, born in Wales. A student at the Slade School (1894–8) with his sister **Gwen John**, he was precociously talented. He travelled to France in 1900 and for several years thereafter, studying the Post-Impressionists and Rembrandt, who remained a constant influence on his portrait style, *cf Robin* (*c* 1936, Dublin Gallery of

Modern Art). He is responsible for many of the penetrating records of English personalities in the first decades of the century. His early style was much influenced by **Gauguin**, but by about 1920 he had adopted a more painterly treatment which produced portraits of great subtlety, *eg Joseph Hone* (*c* 1926, London Tate). His full-length portrait of the cellist *Madame Suggia* (1920–3, London Tate) is one of the classics of musical portraiture, expressing in the sweep of her gown and in the abandon of the pose the force of the player's personality and music. John also painted many successful genre pieces, which show Gauguin's influence most clearly, ranging from simple quasi-portraits, such as *Washing Day* (*c* 1912, London Tate), to large decorative panels of subjects taken from gypsy life in Ireland and Spain, *eg The Mumpers* (*c* 1911, Detroit Art Inst.).

JOHN, Gwen (1876–1939), British painter. The sister of **Augustus John**, she was his contemporary at the Slade School, but went to live in Paris in 1898, seldom returning to Britain. She studied for a while at Whistler's School in Paris, and became close friends with Rodin. Her work consists mainly of figure paintings and portraits in a simple direct style, at first very firm and realistic, as in *Self-portrait* (*c* 1899, London Tate). Later they became rather more painterly and combined harmonious compositions with simple background shapes, *eg Young Woman Holding a Black Cat* (*c* 1915, London Tate).

JOHNS, Jasper (1930–   ), American artist. He studied at the University of South Carolina before going to New York in 1952. He has been closely associated with **Rauschenberg** and has followed him in his development out of **Abstract Expressionism** towards **Pop Art**. His contribution to contemporary art is as important as Rauschenberg's, and has taken a different, more intellectual course. Johns' painting is more concise and uses simpler means. While Rauschenberg incorporates a wide variety of material in his works, Johns has been concerned with a very small range of subjects. Both artists have established a new relationship between art and the everyday object, but whereas Rauschenberg merely implies this, Johns examines the rules governing the relationship. To a significant degree Johns is an artist whose subject is art itself: using unconventional means to examine the nature of art. Johns owes something to Duchamp, and looks forward to **Conceptual Art**. His first mature paintings were the series of flags begun in 1954–5, and continued in one form or another up to the present day. He has added other subjects of a similar nature, for example targets, stencilled numbers, as *Zero through Nine* (1961, London Tate) and maps, as *Map* (1961, New York MMA). What these subjects have in common is extreme familiarity and simplicity; the flags (all Stars and Stripes) are presented flat on the surface, covering the whole canvas or set off against a simple border. At first sight they are pointless, merely flags hung up on a gallery wall; but on looking closer one sees what it is that makes these flags different: Johns' extraordinarily vibrant handling in encaustic (wax-based) paint. The ultimate result is to draw attention to the act of painting itself in a way that no less familiar subjects could do. Johns has achieved a complementary and possibly more significant result with his bronzes, begun in 1960. His *Painted Bronze* (1960, artist's collection), for instance, consists of a clutch of paint-stained brushes standing upright in an old coffee tin with the maker's name still legible. It is an extraordinary piece of *trompe l'oeil* for it looks like the real thing, but is in fact entirely of bronze, cleverly painted. Works like this not only draw attention to the work of the artist, but also focus on the object as a thing in its own right. By reproducing every quality of the original except for the practical one, Johns forces us to abandon our merely utilitarian attitude to objects around us, a change of outlook which he feels is essential to our survival as people in the modern world. Many of Johns' works are more complex than these and show great wit. *Drawer* (1957, Waltham, Mass., Rose AM) is painted all over in short brushstrokes of various shades of grey, giving a sensation of depth in the painted surface which Johns puns upon by incorporating a pull-out drawer front in the canvas surface. In a number of works he makes reference to the other senses, *eg Target with Four Casts* (1955,

New York MMA) consists of a target painting surmounted by four boxes each containing a plaster model of a head, showing mouth and nose but cut off below the eyes, the organs of sight. A number of works such as *False Start* (1959, private collection) contain the stencilled names of colours, red, yellow, grey, *etc*, superimposed on passages of free painting. These are in effect allegories of the painter's art, since the artist opposes two different methods of describing colour, specifying it and creating it, and shows that the two do not necessarily coincide. In recent years Johns' paintings have become rather more painterly and less concerned with the real object, but even more crammed with allegory.

JOHNSON, Ray (1927–), American artist. He studied at the Art Students' League, at Black Mountain College, and with **Albers** and **Motherwell**. Up to 1952 he worked in an abstract style, but then took up the medium of figurative collage. Many of his works use **Pop** imagery, such as the series of distorted pictures of *Elvis Presley* (1965, private collection). He has also founded the 'New York Correspondence School', a continuous **Happening** in which he corresponds with a number of people exchanging collage materials each of which forms an irrational association with previous items.

JONES, Allen (1937–), English painter. He studied at Hornsey College of Art and at the Royal College of Art (1959–60). He first made his name in a series of paintings in bright colours with a vivid sense of movement, conceived abstractly but later given a figurative context, such as his *Sun Plane* (1963, Liverpool Walker AG). In 1963, influenced by **R. B. Kitaj** and **Richard Smith**, he turned to figure painting, mainly of an erotic nature with an emphasis on underwear and pin-up figures, though studied afresh from life, *eg Hermaphrodite* (1963, Sunderland AG). But Jones is never content merely with the selection and juxtaposition of imagery like many other **Pop** artists; his works have great vitality in terms of painting and a formal interest which is never obscured by the subject matter. He won the Prix des Jeunes Artistes at the Paris Biennale of 1963, and exhibited at the São Paulo Bieñal in 1967.

JORN, Asger (1914–), Danish painter. He studied in Denmark and, in 1936–7, with Léger in Paris. His early works were brilliant in colour but were also influenced by late **Cubism**, with hard edges, although the handling of the larger areas of paint was freer. During World War II, he gradually achieved a more spontaneous style, and in 1948 he became a member of the **Cobra Group**. Although he treats his childlike imagery with great freedom of handling he is less of a Gesture painter than, say, Appel, *eg Le Timide Orgueilleux* (1957, London Tate). He has also been active as a ceramicist in Italy, and in 1959 produced a ceramic mural, 88 feet long, for the senior school in Aarhus, Denmark.

JUDD, Donald (1928–), American artist. He studied at the Art Students' league, New York and at Columbia University. He had his first one-man show in 1961 and he has since been included in all important exhibitions of **Minimal Art**. He started by painting very simple geometrical compositions, but soon began producing reliefs and then free-standing sculptures using wood, metal and plastic. Although his work is varied he has kept returning to the themes of tubes and of boxes (in this he was influenced by **Flavin**). In contrast to Robert Morris, he is only interested in regular, hard-edged forms, and in very simple arrangements of volumes and surfaces painted in uniform colours. He is particularly interested in the spatial effects of series of similar forms—for example a horizontal row of cubes projecting from the wall. In these works, however, he completely rejects conventional artistic composition, and groups his elements either completely regularly or according to a mathematical series.

JUGENDSTIL, the German name for **Art Nouveau**. The name is taken from the periodical *Jugend* ('Youth') first published in 1896.

K

KANDINSKY, Wassily (1866–1944), Russian painter. One of the foremost exponents and probably the first practitioner of abstract art, he influenced at least three prominent artistic movements: the **Blaue Reiter** of which he was co-founder, the **Bauhaus** of which he was assistant director, and post-War **Abstract Expressionism** which developed ideas he had sketched during World War I. Kandinsky is not easy to classify: his art has a richness which distinguishes it from the more austere abstract movements. On the other hand, its forms are too precise and the pictures as a whole too intellectual to be considered as a direct development of **Expressionism**.

Kandinsky's early training was in music, a life-long interest, and there are obvious analogies in his art with the formal organization of complex themes and patterns of music. Upon seeing an exhibition of the Impressionists in Moscow in 1895, he decided to devote himself to painting. In 1896 he settled in Munich, where in 1901 he founded the 'Phalanx Group' and met Gabriele Münter, with whom he lived until 1914. He travelled in Tunisia, France and Switzerland. He founded the *Neue Kunstler-Vereinigung* ('New Artists' Association') in Munich in 1909 and the Blaue Reiter in 1911 in association with **Marc**. His work progressed by way of paintings, in an Impressionist style, *eg Sunday* (1904, Rotterdam, Museum Boymans-van-Benningen), quickly becoming more highly coloured with thicker impasto and much simplified drawing, a development paralleling that of **Fauvism** in France, *eg Landscape with Tree* (1909, Dusseldorf Kunstmuseum). During this period he produced a number of works with large blocks of colour so simplified that although they contained figurative elements drawn from African or Russian life, they were given abstract titles such as *Improvisation 6* (1910, Munich Civic Gallery). In 1910 he executed his first completely abstract watercolours, and although the oil paintings continued to retain figurative elements, these became less and less significant, *eg Battle* (1911, London Tate), *Pastoral* (1911, New York Guggenheim). Most of the paintings of the following years developed the free linear elements of the first of these paintings with the flooded areas of merging colour of the latter. At times they were extremely complicated, as in *Fugue* (1914, New York Guggenheim). Figurative references were now excluded and Kandinsky's aim followed that set out in his book *Towards the Spiritual in Art* (1912). It was the work of this period that first earned the term 'Abstract Expressionism' and which was a forerunner of post-War developments. In 1914 he went to Russia where he became prominent as a teacher and museum administrator, founding the Academy of Arts in 1921. At this time he met Gabo and Pevsner and gradually became infected with the spirit of **Constructivism**. Under this influence his own work became harder and more precise, retaining his characteristic proliferation of ideas and colours, but introducing geometrical figures drawn with ruler and compass, *eg Composition VIII* (1923, New York Guggenheim). In 1922, he was appointed to the Bauhaus, where, with **Paul Klee**, he was largely responsible for giving the institution its undisputed place in the history of art. His own style became richer towards the mid-1920s, using deeper, more closely harmonized colours and relying heavily on the circle as his principal formal unit, *eg Several Circles* (1926, New York Guggenheim). He joined Klee, **Feininger** and **Jawlensky** in the 'Blue Four' group in 1924, and in 1926 published a new theoretical work *Point and Line to Surface*. He became a member of the 'Cercle et Carré' and **Abstraction-Création** groups in Paris in 1930 and 1931 respectively. From then until the end of his life his compositions, though still remaining complex and clearly-defined, began to make more use of amoeboid and other curvilinear shapes, *eg Composition IX* (1936, Paris MNAM), *Dominant Curve* (1936, New York Guggenheim). By the end of his life, these had become anthropomorphic in suggestion.

KANE, John (1860–1934), American painter, born in Scotland (see **Naive Art**).

KAPROW, Allan (1927–   ), American artist. Shortly before an exhibition of his **Abstract Expressionism** paintings at the Reuben Gallery, New York, in 1958 Kaprow decided to make the show more interesting by suspending curtains of torn canvas and concealed lightbulbs in front of each painting. The resultant efforts of the public to reach the paintings made the first **Happening**, an art form which Kaprow has developed since in conjunction with many of the Pop artists.

KELLY, Ellsworth (1928–   ), American

painter. After studying (1946–8) at the Boston Museum School, he transferred to the Ecole des Beaux-Arts in Paris, and lived there until 1954. Kelly was thus out of America during the crucial years of **Abstract Expressionism**, and when he settled in New York in 1954 he had considerable influence on those painters who were reacting against the freedom of the prevailing style and who were already painting in the 'hard-edge' manner later to be termed **Post-Painterly Abstraction**. Although the formal influences on his style are European, notably Neo-Plasticism, the constructions of Hans Arp, and the late *papiers coupés* of Matisse, Kelly differs from even these artists in his courage to stake everything on a single bold statement. He uses only primary or pure colours, and never more than two or three on a canvas. Similarly there are never more than one or two large hard-edged forms against a plain background, or two or three interlocking areas of flat colour, *eg Broadway* (1958, London Tate), *Black Island No. 2* (1961, Pittsburgh Carnegie Inst.). In his works of 1962–5, Kelly takes a single colour contrast, for example, in *Red White* (1963, San Francisco MA), an area of red almost filling a white canvas, and adjusts the shape of the boundary between the colours to make the most out of it, avoiding symmetry, avoiding unwanted optical illusions, perfectly balancing figure and background. In 1965 he began painting canvases of a single flat colour, both irregular and rectangular, to be hung alone or in groups. Some of these single-colour works, which are the clearest statement of **Minimal Art** in painting, are made of sprayed metal sheets, which may be bent so as to stand on the floor or project into the room like a sculpture, *eg Green* (1968, Minneapolis Walker AG). Kelly was a painter at the Pittsburgh International Exhibition of 1963, and exhibited at the Venice Biennale in 1966.

KEMENY, Zoltán (1907–65), Hungarian sculptor. Despite his training at the School of Decorative Arts, Budapest, he did not take up full-time work in the fine arts until 1942, when he moved to Zurich. His earlier work was **Collage** of various materials but in 1955 he executed his first 'Images in relief' in metal. These were made of elements in relief fixed in a rhythmical pattern on the surface of a picture, presenting an image which changes slightly as the observer moves past it. Each work was a variation of a basic shape: clusters of raised T-shaped elements in *Ombre du Miracle* (1957, New York MMA); open rectangular boxes in *Banlieue des Anges* (1957, London Tate); and leaves of 'pages' of metal in *Petit Soir le Matin* (1959, Chicago Art Inst.).

KEPES, Gyorgy (1906–), American painter. He studied at the Royal Academy of Fine Arts in Budapest. Kepes wrote essays on design and form, and is known for his interdisciplinary approach to art and science and his concern to develop an art relevant to society. He was the first artist to use neon tubing on a large scale as a light mural in the U.S.

KIDNER, Michael (1917–), English painter. See **Op Art**.

KIENHOLZ, Edward (1927–), American sculptor. He had no formal education and his earlier years were spent in a variety of jobs, most of which are reflected in his later work. Settling in Los Angeles in 1953, he began to make wooden reliefs using bits of junk ('the left-overs of human experience') roughly painted over. These gradually became more complex until by about 1958 he was in effect working in sculpture. In 1961 he exhibited 'Roxy's', a number of female figures in a carefully reconstructed brothel, the first of his many **Environments** which he refers to as 'tableaux'.

Within the context of Pop Art, Kienholz comes closest to **Oldenburg** and **Segal**, except that his works have a deliberate crudity of construction and a harshness in them that is unique: the horrific *Hospital* sums up Kienholz' experience as an attendant in a mental hospital; *Portable War Memorial* (1968, private collection) places conventional heroic sculpture in the setting of a seedy café. Juxtapositions such as this strongly reflect **Surrealism**; *Beanery*, a reproduction of a Los Angeles bar is peopled by figures having stopped clocks for heads. Although Kienholz' work is often amusing, its power lies in being able to force the observer to face things which might otherwise be hidden.

KIKOINE, Michel (1892–), Russian

painter, member of the School of Paris. He studied at the art school at Vilna and the Ecole des Beaux-Arts, Paris, where he met Soutine. His style is akin to Soutine's, but less Expressionist with delicate colours and rich impasto, *eg Bunch of Field Flowers* (1935, Paris MNAM).

KINETIC ART. Although Kinetic Art itself is only concerned with physical motion, the representation and study of motion has always been of great concern to the artist. An implied sense of movement is the principal characteristic of the Baroque style which flourished in all the arts in the 17th century. In our own century, **Futurism** was the first movement to develop a new pictorial language for the depiction of motion. The painters Matisse, Miró, Klee and Kandinsky, and the sculptors Brancusi and Gabo, were all concerned with representing or suggesting movement in a large number of their works. **Gesture Painting** takes this even further, since the marks on the canvas are the literal record of the spontaneous movements of the painter. Finally, many works of **Pop Art**, although static in themselves, give the illusion of motion to a passing observer.

The term is generally used in art to refer to works with movable parts. The pioneer in this field was **Marcel Duchamp** (who had already anticipated Futurism in his work of around 1911) with his *Rotary Glass Plate* (1920, Stockholm Moderna Museet). Also in 1920, Gabo made his *Kinetic Sculpture* (London Tate) in which a wire is set in vibration so as to appear as a three-dimensional volume.

Alexander Calder began creating motorized sculptures around 1930. Modern motorized sculptures can be divided into those in which the mechanism is visible and carries the main interest of the work, and those in which a concealed motor is merely the means of rearranging formal elements. Pre-eminent among the first group are the extraordinary machines of **Tinguely**; many of the works of Medalla are in a similar vein. **Takis** also leaves the mechanism visible, but his works have the interesting paradox that it is the moving elements themselves which make visible the power source, the invisible field of magnetic force. The most remarkable of the concealed-motor artists is **Pol Bury** whose works have an irrational and faintly

menacing character. This is also true of the *Pulsating Walls* of Colombo which stand up miraculously, although the individual blocks of which they are composed seem to strain out of their places. Artists such as von Graevenitz and Wynter use concealed motors merely as a way of achieving random rearrangements of formally conceived works.

Many kinetic works use light, either as one element in a sculptural construction, or else projected by a concealed mechanism on to a screen to make a 'kinetic painting'. **Moholy-Nagy**'s *Light Space Modulator* (1922–9, Harvard Busch-Reisinger Museum), the first major work in this field, can be viewed either as a moving sculpture, or as the pattern it throws on a screen when illuminated. Liliane Lijn, the wife of Takis, often uses light to illuminate moving drops of water and objects in water. Schoeffer and Malina have made kinetic paintings with a constant play of colour. This idea was originally suggested as a musical device by the composer Scriabin. Besides making motorized sculptures, Calder invented the **Mobile** in which the parts are set in motion by random breezes in the air. Among his most direct followers are the Englishmen Chadwick and Kenneth Martin and the Brazilian Julio Le Parc.

Finally there are works with parts which do not move themselves but which require the participation of the spectator. This field in its more complex aspects borders on **Happenings**.

KING, Philip (1934–   ), English sculptor. King is probably the best-known of the pupils of **Anthony Caro** at St. Martin's School of Art where he studied in 1957–58; he was also assistant to **Henry Moore** for two years and represented Britain at the 1968 Venice Biennale. His style is also very varied including both the open constructions in coloured sheet metal influenced by Caro, *eg Dunstable Reel* (1970, London Tate), and almost architectural arrangements of geometrical volumes, *eg Span* (1967, Victoria NG). Much of his work, although abstract, has also a Surrealist air as *And the Birds Began to Sing* (1964, London Tate).

KIRCHNER, Ernst Ludwig (1880–1938), German painter. One of the leading German exponents of **Expressionism**, he trained as an architect in Dresden. His early painting was in a highly coloured style, first influenced by Divisionism and then becoming much more individual, *eg The Street* (1907, New York MMA). He founded **Die Brücke** in 1905 with Heckel and Schmidt-Rottluff. His paintings of the period show increasing simplification of drawing and colour, but remain comparatively lyrical, as in *Nude with Hat* (1911, Cologne Wallraf-Richartz-Museum). In 1911 Kirchner began spending his summers on the island of Fehmarn and his pictures show the influence of **Cubism**. He attempted greater distortions of space and developed a characteristic angular type of figure, *eg The Street* (1913, New York MMA), *Estate in Fehmarn* (1912, Hamburg Kunsthalle). His interest in Cubism was concerned with its distorting, expressive powers. His work after World War I was simpler, *eg Self-portrait with Cat* (1918, Harvard Busch-Reisinger Museum), and included some fine landscapes, *eg Moonlit Winter Night* (1918, Detroit Art Inst.).

KISLING, Moise (1891–1953), French painter, born in Poland. He began painting at the age of 15 at the Cracow Academy. His teacher introduced him to **Impressionism** and encouraged him to visit Paris, where he arrived in 1910; he took French citizenship in 1915. He became friendly with **Modigliani** and **Soutine**; his art has a similar melancholy quality, *eg Polish Woman* (1928, Paris MNAM). Kisling's style was derived from that of **Cézanne** but it was softer in atmosphere and placed less emphasis on volume, *eg La Charrette* (1924, Merion, Penn., Barnes Foundation). He was also a fashionable portraitist, his charm lying in a naive objectivity influenced by Henri Rousseau *eg Colette de Jouvenel* (1933, Marseilles MBA).

KITAJ, Ronald B. (1923–), American painter. A student (1951–2) at the Cooper Union, New York, and in Vienna, he entered the army in 1955. On his discharge in 1958, Kitaj went to England to study at Oxford and at the Royal College of Art. His knowledge of American art (such as that of **Johns**), coupled with the example of **Richard Smith**, influenced the British artists from the Royal College who exhibited with him at the 'Young Contemporaries' exhibition in 1961, Boshier, Hockney, Jones and Phillips. He now lives in England. His work is figurative, but eclectic in its sources. He has a characteristically firm drawing style with strong colour and little or no modelling, and figurative elements in his works; he used near abstraction in one picture. He also uses **Collage** and silk-screen techniques, and even in works which are pure painting he may juxtapose diverse images in the manner of a collage. Many of his works have a literary or left-wing political theme, *eg The Red Banquet* (1960, Liverpool Walker AG), *Isaac Babel Riding with Budyonny* (1962, London Tate), *The Ohio Gang* (1964, New York MMA). Kitaj has also collaborated with **Eduardo Paolozzi** on several works.

KLEE, Paul (1879–1940), Swiss painter. Klee's remark that 'Art does not render the visible, but renders visible,' is a useful definition of non-representational art and is also the best introduction to his own work. Although he almost always used figurative elements in his works, he used them in the manner of an abstract artist to portray inner sensations, dreams, intellectual concepts and even jokes.

Klee spent most of his working life in Germany. His father was a music teacher and encouraged Klee's early interest in music. He decided to become a painter and studied (1898–1900) in Munich where he lived until 1921, with trips to Italy, France and elsewhere. Klee struggled to find his style, working in pen, water-colour and etching; all his work, however, shows a characteristic preoccupation with expressive line, *eg Young Woman on a Chaise-longue* (1909, Bern Kunstmuseum). In 1911 he met Kandinsky and Marc who encouraged him to take part in the **Blaue Reiter** exhibitions. Like the other artists of the group he was impressed by Cubism and visited Paris again in 1912. A trip to Tunis with **Macke** in 1914 crystallized his style, and he began painting simplified landscapes composed of patchworks of luminous coloured squares and triangles, *eg Föhn in Marc's Garden* (1915, Munich Civic Gallery). A similar style also provided the framework for compositions springing purely from the imagination, as in *With the Eagle* (1918, Bern Kunstmuseum). He

Paul Klee: In the Meadow *(1923, private collection); ph. Giraudon.*

began to use oils in 1914 and at the same time produced countless drawings experimenting with the properties of line, imitating children's drawings, making use of Calligraphy, often with imaginary scripts. He explored the potential of long continuous lines, building pictures up with a limited range of pen strokes, *eg Bird Drama* (1920, New York Guggenheim), *They're Biting!* (1920, London Tate), *Christ* (1926, Bern Kunstmuseum). He also united these with his patchwork painting style in a varied series of paintings, in which comparatively large forms were broken up into coloured patches, as in *A Young Lady's Adventure* (1922, London Tate). Others consisted of brightly coloured small forms, quite unrelated by ordinary logic, in a mysterious setting, *eg Fish Magic* (1925, Philadelphia MA); others again were simple drawings on a painted background, *eg Twittering Machine* (1922, New York MMA). He even used the shapes of the letters of a poem to generate an abstract painting (an important contribution to **Concrete Poetry**) in *Once Emerged from the Grey of Night* (1918,

Bern Kunstmuseum). Many more pictures were built up of signs closely resembling script, rather like an embroidered sampler, as in *Pastoral* (1927, New York MMA).

Klee was appointed to the staff of **Bauhaus** in Weimar in 1921 and remained there until 1924. He also visited the Bauhaus at Dessau and taught at the Dusseldorf Academy from 1931 until he was dismissed by the Nazis in 1933, when he fled to Switzerland. His work as a teacher was of the greatest importance, and he has published many of his ideas in the *Pedagogical Sketchbook* (1925). The paintings of Klee's last years were broader and bolder, the fine draughtsmanship being replaced by heavy black lines and combined with fewer and simpler areas of colour. Some examples are *Revolution of the Viaduct* (1937, Hamburg Kunsthalle), *A Sheet of Pictures* (1937, Washington Phillips Collection) and *The Drummer* (1940, Bern Kunstmuseum).

KLEIN, Yves (1928–62), French painter. He was one of the most revolutionary of recent French artists and had a profound influence on many young European artists, co-members of the Nouveaux Réalistes, among them **Raysse** and **Tinguely**. He studied Oriental languages, jazz and judo, but was a self-taught painter. In 1946 he began to paint seriously, aiming at the representation of space and infinity, by paintings entirely in monochrome, which were first shown in 1950 in London. In 1952–3 he visited Japan. In 1957 he exhibited eleven paintings, all of the same size, all covered evenly with 'International Klein Blue': *Monochrome Bleu* (1957, Krefeld Kaiser Wilhelm Museum). In 1958 he gave an exhibition on the subject of 'The Void' consisting of entirely empty rooms. At the same time he was working on murals for the Opera House at Gelsenkirchen, two of which consist of reliefs made out of sponges. He continued to work with sponges in the following years, *eg L'Accord Bleu* (1960, Amsterdam Stedelijk M). In 1960 he exhibited his first 'Monogold' painting, which involves surface texture as well as the all-over gold colour, *eg Triptych* (1960, Louisiana Museum). He also showed a number of 'Cosmogonies', paintings which had been completed by exposure to the rain, wind or fire, as *Pluie Rouge* (1961, Stockholm Svensk-Franska Gall.). He went on to develop the fire theme by means of walls and fountains comprised of jets of flame, and by paintings executed with a flame-thrower, *eg Fire-Colour-Picture* (1962, Louisiana Museum). In 1960 he also started his 'Anthropometrics', a novel kind of **Action Painting** in which nude models covered themselves in blue paint and pressed themselves against a plain canvas at Klein's direction, while an orchestra played his 'Monotone Symphony', several minutes of a single held note, followed by an equal period of silence. Klein also used the models as stencils, spraying paint round them to form a silhouette on the canvas. Klein was an important contributor to the **Minimal Art** movement.

KLIMT, Gustav (1862–1918), Austrian painter. Klimt's importance as a seminal force in 20th century Austrian and German painting, not to mention his influence further afield through the Vienna **Secession**, is unquestionable. Although certain aspects of his work may find parallels in

French art, he was nonetheless a completely original painter who forged a personal style of the utmost richness. He founded a studio of mural painting with his brother in 1883 and undertook several important commissions. From 1898 to 1903 he presided over the Vienna Secession. In 1902 he executed a frieze on the theme of Beethoven for the Secession House (now Vienna, Osterreichische Galerie). In 1911 he completed his masterpiece, the diningroom of the Palais Stoclet in Brussels. All these works received considerable adverse criticism.

Klimt's oeuvre contains a number of landscapes and portraits in a style influenced by Impressionism and later by van Gogh: *Garden Landscape*, (*c* 1909, Pittsburgh Carnegie Inst.); the rich texture of many of these pictures with a mosaic of coloured forms was characteristic of his decorative pictures. Almost all of his mature figure paintings were flat in conception, with the figures treated more or less naturalistically but set in parallel planes of the richest texture of paint and gold leaf, sometimes recalling mosaic, peacock or butterfly wings, or a lush floral texture; but these patterns were usually abstract. The influences on this style were numerous, **Whistler** and **Art Nouveau** being two examples, but nothing equivalent had been attempted on such a scale before. Klimt was often criticized for superimposing his decorative schemes upon the real world (as opposed to deriving them from observation of reality, as did Toulouse-Lautrec, a similar painter in many respects). There is some truth in this, but Klimt's drawings, especially of the human figure, show a high degree of observation and disregard for convention, that link them directly to the work of **Kokoschka** and **Schiele** and to Expressionism as a whole. The poses of his best figures, such as *Danae* (1907, private collection), *The Kiss* (1907, Vienna Osterreichische Galerie), *Judith II* (1919, Venice GAM) and *Adam and Eve* (1917–18, Vienna Osterreichische Galerie), are both original and startlingly true. Finally, he undeniably possessed a remarkable facility to balance detail within a larger structure.

KLINE, Franz (1910–62), American painter. The son of a German immigrant, he trained in art at Boston University. For some years he painted in a figurative, though Expressionist style. In about 1946 he turned to abstract painting and by 1949 had reduced his work entirely to black and white, and was painting on a very large scale. These works relate to the black and white works produced around the same time by Motherwell, de Kooning and Pollock, but in Kline's paintings the element of **Action Painting** is far less significant than the monumental statements of form he made often with the simplest means, *eg Chief* (1950, New York MMA). In 1955 he began to introduce colour gradually as in *The Bridge* (1955, Utica Art Inst.) and developed a style of greater complexity, but without softening or confusing the force of his earlier paintings, *eg Cupola* (1958–60, Toronto AG); *Meryon* (1960, London Tate).

KOHN, Gabriel (1910–   ), American sculptor. He has made sculptures since the 1940s using strips and blocks of wood laminated together and polished to give patterns of light and shade as on a parquet floor. All his recent sculptures consist of single massive forms with the play of slight curves on their edges contrasting with the lie of the laminated wood: *Acrotere* (1960, New York MMA).

KOKOSCHKA, Oskar (1886–   ), Austrian painter. As a student (1905–9) at the School of Decorative Arts, Vienna, he was influenced by the *Jugendstil*, as can be seen in a poster, *Pietà* (1908, Vienna Museum of Applied Art), for one of a number of plays he wrote at this time; it also shows a violent **Expressionism**. More important was the influence of **Klimt**, from whom he learned to couple realism with expressive distortion in his style of drawing, and an ability to devise startling poses. His *Children Playing* (1909, Duisburg Museum) refuses to idealize yet exercises understanding, and also shows, despite a more genial outlook, a similarity to Schiele. He went to Berlin in 1910 where he exhibited at Der Sturm Gallery. He began to paint the first of his many portraits of famous men, using a frank style in which the figures were set against a heavily-worked textured background, and in which Kokoschka captured and exaggerated the telling feature or gesture, as in *Professor and Mrs. Tietze* (1909,

New York MMA). These works set the norm for realistic Expressionist portraiture. He also did a number of subject pictures of great evocative power, *eg The Visitation* (1911, Vienna Osterreichische Galerie), *Tempest* (1914, Basle Kunstmuseum), and from about 1916 a number of works in a bolder style with a linear impasto derived from van Gogh, *eg Knight Errant* (1915, New York Guggenheim), *Friends* (1918, Linz Neue Galerie). In 1917, he settled in Dresden, where he began a series of landscapes, at first in a rather flat style with the picture divided into clearly-defined areas, as in *Dresdner Neustadt* (1921, Detroit Art Inst.), later in a style involving a shimmering atmosphere and a fine mesh of multicoloured detail, *eg London, Tower Bridge* (1925, Minneapolis Art Inst.). These landscapes, which he continued to paint during many years of travelling, are, with his portraits, the finest part of his oeuvre. Although frequently choosing a high viewpoint his views do not become guide-book maps, but, by means of subtle distortions and choice of colour and emphasis, powerfully capture the spirit of a place: *Biarritz Beach* (1925, Harvard Fogg Museum); *Lyon* (1927, Washington Phillips Collection); *Polperro* (1940, London Tate); *Hamburg Harbour* (1951, New York MMA). Kokoschka also designed stage sets, illustrated books and painted two large triptychs, *Prometheus* (1950) and *Thermopylae* (1954), both privately owned. He fled to London in 1938 and took British nationality in 1947. He has divided his time between London and Salzburg, where he runs a summer painting school for amateurs, whom he prefers to professional artists 'because of the freshness of their vision'.

KOLLWITZ, Käthe (1867–1945), German sculptor and print-maker, born in Russia. One of the principal forerunners of German Expressionism, she studied in Berlin and did not travel much outside Germany except for holidays and a journey (1927) to the Soviet Union. Most of her work depicted proletarian life and its struggle against oppression; it was stark and bitter but compassionate. Her principal series of prints (etchings and lithographs) was *The Weavers* (1897), *The Peasants' War* (1906–8), *War* (1922–3) a woodcut series with a deliberate return to a harsh

mediaevalism, and *The Proletariat* (1925).
Her sculptures owed much to **Barlach**,
with whom she worked on the satirical
magazine *Simplizissimus*, eg *Pietà* (1937,
Berlin NG).

KOLOS-VARY, Sigismond (1899–   ),
Hungarian painter. Settling in Paris in
1926, he gradually progressed towards an
abstract style. His compositions, in which
colour is applied in rectangular patches,
have been influenced by **de Staël** in that
they are derived (somewhat at a distance)
from natural subjects eg *Joie Triste* (1962,
Paris MNAM).

KOONING, Elaine de (1920–   ), American painter, wife of Willem de Kooning.
She is associated with the New York
School and is an Abstract Impressionist,
rather like Guston. Her abstract portraits
attempt to capture the essence of the sitter;
she uses broad brushstrokes and can
finish a portrait in a couple of hours.

KOONING, Willem de (1904–   ), American painter, born in the Netherlands. He
attended the Rotterdam Academy of Art,
an establishment run on Bauhaus lines. In
1926 he went to the United States, since
then his home. He met **Gorky** in 1927 and
the work of the two artists developed
along parallel lines for many years. De
Kooning primarily painted still lifes and
figure subjects in muted colours and in a
basically realistic style counterbalanced
by a tendency to fragment and accentuate
line derived from Cubism. He worked with
Léger (1935) on a mural for the French
Line Pier, New York. In 1946 he started a
series of abstract paintings in black and
white house paint, similar to those of
Pollock and **Kline**, but more controlled
because de Kooning has always been a
prolific and precise draughtsman, eg
Painting (1948, New York MMA). Gradually elements of colour began to return to
these abstracts, at first only in small
patches, as in *Ashville* (1948–9, Washington Phillips Collection), *Excavation* (1950,
Chicago Art Inst.). At the same time he
began to return to figurative themes,
notably a series of 'women' treated in a
style somewhat resembling children's art
(strangely similar to the art of his compatriot, Appel) and painted with such
freedom as to render them almost abstract,

eg *Woman* (1949, Chapel Hill, Univ. of N.
Carolina); *Two Women* (1952, Chicago
Art Inst.); *Woman and Bicycle* (1953, New
York Whitney Museum). The exuberance
of these paintings led to a resurgence of
full colour in his abstracts, which were
often very complex, eg *Abstraction* (1955,
York Guggenheim). Since 1956, however,
he has gradually simplified these, painting
large-scale abstracts based on freely-
brushed areas of strong colours (often
with a suggestion of some landscape
motif) which are among the finest products of **Abstract Expressionism**, eg
Visit (1966–7, London Tate).

KREMEGNE, Pinchus (1890–   ), Rus-
sian painter. A member of the School of
Paris after 1912, he was influenced by
Fauvism, and later by the art of Soutine.
He uses heavy impasto and a rich, restricted
palette.

KRICKE, Norbert (1922–   ), German
sculptor. He began to develop his personal
style in 1949 after leaving the Berlin Academy. All his subsequent works have been
extensions of the same basic approach.
Fascinated by the structure of the wire
armatures used for clay modelling, he made
'space sculptures' out of bent and painted
rods which explore and define space, eg
Space Sculpture (1952, Dusseldorf Kunstmuseum). The first examples were simple
and regular, but later he began to use
curved shapes built out of bundles of rods,
a much more dynamic concept, eg *Space
Sculpture Mannesman* (1958–61, Dusseldorf, outside Mannesman Building). In
1956 he developed two-dimensional sculptures out of parallel rods set adjacent to each
other. Such a work was made in 1957–9 for
the façade of the Gelsenkirchen Theatre.
His subsequent work returns to the more
complex three-dimensional spaces, but
uses the rods in planar groups rather than in
bundles as in '*Grosse Kasseler*' *Skulptur*
(1958–9, Leverkusen). Kricke's work,
though independent, is akin to that of
David Smith and **Caro** in its concern with
space.

KROHG, Per (1889–   ), Norwegian
painter. Among his works are mural decorations (eg Town Hall, Oslo), done in a style
combining popular inspiration with sophisticated construction. His easel paintings,

mostly of genre subjects, reflect the influence of **Munch**, *eg Buying Pearls* (1928, Stockholm National Museum).

KRUSHENICK, Nicholas (1929–), American painter. He began his formal art training at the Art Students' League. Later he studied with Hans Hofmann, who did not, however, influence his style which is neither figurative nor literal. He organized the Brata Gallery with his brother John in 1957. In the early 1960s Krushenick's work was often identified with Roy Lichtenstein's comic-strip paintings; hence, his work appeared in many **Pop Art** exhibitions. His work is not subject-oriented, it is hard-edge and abstract.

KUBIN, Alfred (1877–1959), German draughtsman. A student in Munich, after 1903 he produced a large number of drawings, prints, book illustrations, and a few paintings. His characteristic style depended on a fine, apparently casual scribble with almost caricatured details and unexpected contrasts of scale. This expressed a fantastic imagination, making him an early Expressionist and a precursor of Surrealism. He associated with the artists of the **Blaue Reiter**, but did not adopt their style.

KUHN, Walt (1880–1949), American painter. The son of a German immigrant father and a half-Spanish mother, he grew up in New York. In 1899 he began to make money from the sale of drawings and in 1901 went to study at the Académie Colarossi in Paris. After a year, he went to the Munich Academy before returning (1903) to the U.S. For many years he worked as an illustrator and also part-time in theatres and revues, painting pictures in a bold style influenced by **Fauvism**, *eg Sleeping Girl* (1922, Ogunquit, Maine, MA). He was the main organizer of the **Armory Show**. In 1925 he suffered an almost fatal stomach ulcer and began to devote himself with a new intensity to his painting, producing the still-lifes and pictures of circus personalities which made him famous. These were more tightly knit than his earlier paintings, presenting the figures against a plain background though in a variety of formally satisfying poses in which every detail contributed to the overall rhythm, *eg Clown with Black Wig* (1930, New York MMA). While being absolutely objective, the best of these pictures have a deeply compassionate insight into the figures as people, *eg Trude* (1931, Santa Barbara MA).

KUPKA, František (1871–1957), Czech painter. After training in Prague and in Vienna he went to Paris in 1894, and settled some years later in Pateaux, France. His early work was influenced by the Vienna **Secession** style; this contact with the *Jugendstil* was reflected in his interest in curvilinear rhythms even in his most austere abstract work. He gradually came under the influence of French Post-Impressionism and adopted a palette akin to the Fauves, *eg Waterfall* (1906, London Tate); *Yellow Scale* (1907, Paris MNAM); *Red Gigolette* (1909, Paris MNAM). In 1908, however, he began a development which was to be critical in the history of abstract art. Kupka attempted a picture of a nude, *Girl with a Ball* (1908, New York MMA; another version Paris MNAM), but abandoned it because it failed to capture the essential movement in the subject. He then explored the movements of the girl and the trajectory of the red and blue ball in a series of drawings and studies paralleling developments in **Futurism** (mostly New York, MMA), culminating in a totally abstract summation of the essential relationships, the great *Fugue for two Colours* (1912, Prague NG). The interlocking circles which provide the formal structure of this work were probably influenced by **Delaunay** (Kupka exhibited with the Orphists in 1912); but Kupka's picture is more austere, using only hard-edged forms of red, blue, white and black. It is concerned with defining a precise situation as opposed to the more vague sensations of Delaunay's works. Several variants of this theme followed. Kupka also worked on a number of other series of equal importance. A picture of 1909 entitled *Piano-keyboard/Lake* (Prague NG), in which the painting of a piano keyboard at the bottom of the canvas, with an A major chord played on it, generates vertical forms that reorganize the movements in the more conventional lake scene above, led to further study of the relationship between musical and colour harmony by using interlocking vertical bars of colour: *Vertical Planes 1* (1912–13, Paris MNAM); *Mme. Kupka among the Verticals* (1920, New York MMA). A further series studied the properties of lines and of pictures dominated by a single colour, *eg Form of Vermilion, Form of Orange* (1919–24, Paris MNAM). He also produced a series in which the circular forms have a specific mechanical significance, which are among the finest evocations of the machine age, *eg Working Steel* (1927–9, Paris MNAM). His later works were purely abstract and often consisted of a group of very simple rectilinear elements held in perfect balance (as pure as that achieved by Mondrian), but with a lyricism that was Kupka's own *eg Abstract Painting* (1930, Prague NG); *Autonomous White* (1951–2, Paris MNAM).

L

LACHAISE, Gaston (1882–1935), American sculptor. He studied at the Ecole des Beaux-Arts, Paris and settled in the United States in 1906, living in Boston, and then in New York. He executed a large number of busts, *eg* of the poet Cummings and the painter John Marin, and low reliefs for the New York Telephone Building. He is best known for his female nudes, of which the most famous is the *Standing Woman* (1932, New York MMA). The rounded, massive forms of this vibrant athletic figure are in questionable taste, but the work has an energy which was influential in drawing American sculpture away from cold academicism.

LAETHEM-SAINT-MARTIN, an artist's colony (after *c* 1900), where many of the important figures in Belgian art have worked, located in a small Flemish village on the river Lys. The first to arrive were the painters Valerius de Sadleer (1867–1941) and Gustave van de Woestjne (1881–1947) and the sculptor Minne. Much impressed by the simple vision of the local self-taught painter Albin van der Abeele (1835–1919), they cultivated a style of the greatest simplicity. The 'Second School of Laethem' formed after World War I around the painters Permeke, van der Berghe and the brothers Gustav and Léon de Smet. These painters still clung to simplicity of form but

Roger de la Fresnaye: Still Life *(c 1912, private collection); ph. Giraudon.*

used darker colours and distorted shapes to Expressionist effect.

LA FRESNAYE, Roger de (1885–1925), French painter. In 1930 he enrolled at the Académie Julian, where he became friends with Segonzac, and in 1908 went to the Académie Ranson, where he was taught by Sérusier and Maurice Denis. In 1910 he was attracted to Cubism, and exhibited with the Cubists at the Salon des Indépendants, and also with the Section d'Or. After World War I his output decreased and he concentrated on red chalk drawings and watercolours. La Fresnaye's style is basically realistic, but simplifies the subject into geometrical forms given a bold but not bright colouration, eg *Le Cuirassier* (1910, Paris MNAM), *Le Mappemonde* (1913, Washington, Phillips Collection). This style was derived from Cézanne (*Meulan*, 1912, Philadelphia MA) but not taken as far as Cubism; La Fresnaye retained a single viewpoint. See illus. p. 131.

LAM, Wilfredo (1902–), Cuban painter. He went to Paris in 1937 and to the United States during World War II; he now lives in Italy. His work is Surrealist and his strange, pointed forms, inspired by primitive art, detached from a mysteriously dark, empty background, are hallucinatory in their effect, as in *The Jungle* (1943, New York MMA) and *Ibaye* (1950, London Tate).

LANDOWSKI, Paul (1875–1961), French sculptor. His many official monuments, of undeniable power though rooted in academicism, include *The Sons of Cain* (1906, Paris, Place du Carrousel), *Reformation Monument* (1917, Geneva), and the *Christ* (1931) on the mountain overlooking Rio de Janeiro.

LANYON, Peter (1918–64), English painter. Most of his life was spent in Cornwall. In 1938 he was encouraged by **Ben Nicholson** and Naum Gabo, both of whom deeply influenced his method if if not his style. He won the Critics' Prize in 1954 and was represented at the São Paulo Bieñal in 1961. Lanyon's work of the 1950s was complex. The painting *Porthleven* (1951, London Tate) was the first of a series of near-abstract landscapes comprising numerous aspects of the same subject including related studies of nudes

used as landscape motifs. Besides making sketches for it, Lanyon built numerous three-dimensional constructions in the manner of Gabo, to study the spatial problems it posed; after months of preparatory work the painting itself was executed in four hours. In 1959, Lanyon joined a gliding club and many of his later pictures such as *Thermal* (1960, London Tate) explored the sensations of flight and movement, and the nature of air and the other elements. These last paintings, large and ample with broad strokes of highly personal colour, show Lanyon's kinship with Abstract Expressionist artists, notably Motherwell and de Kooning.

LA PATELLIERE, Amédée de (1890–1932), French painter. His painting is characterized by its rather decorative realism, massive forms, and dark palette with occasional areas of bright colour. He painted the nude, landscapes, still lifes, and scenes of country life, eg *La Vachère* (1928, Paris MNAM).

LAPRADE, Pierre (1875–1931), French painter. At the beginning of his career, he was slightly influenced by Fauvism, but very quickly established his own graceful style which recalls the atmosphere of 18th century art. His landscapes have a particular charm, eg *Florence, Boboli Gardens* (1908, Paris MNAM).

LARDERA, Berto (1911–), Italian sculptor. He has lived in Paris since 1947, and specializes in metal scuplture. He works exclusively with flat plates, perforated and indented at the edges. Sometimes these are arranged in a single plane but in such a way as to give the impression of three dimensions, eg *Two Dimensional Sculpture* (1947, Paris MNAM). More often they are composed into three-dimensional constructions of great monumental power, as in *Broken Rhythm VIII* (1955–6, Dallas MFA), *Love for the Stars II* (1959–69, Racine, Jonson Foundation). In his *Toy for Adults* (1963–4, Krefeld, Kaiser-Wilhelm Museum and Montreal MFA) the nine parts can be rearranged in countless combinations.

LARIONOV, Michel (1881–1964), Russian painter. Initially influenced by Cubism (*Nocturne*, 1910, London Tate), he founded

Henri Laurens: Woman with Bird *(1943, Paris, Louis Carré Collection); ph. Louis Carré.*

Rayonism in 1910. He took part in the Blaue Reiter movement in 1912, and two years later settled with his wife Natalia Gontcharova in Paris, where he produced numerous decors for the Ballets Russes. Primitive art also played a large part in his work, *eg Soldier on a Horse* (1908–11, London Tate).

LASSAW, Ibram (1913–   ), American sculptor. Born in Egypt of European parents, he came to America in 1921. He began by making grid-like structures in metal, not unlike three-dimensional versions of Mondrian's later work. By the 1950s, coinciding with the rise of Abstract Expressionism, the uneven blobs of brass and silver on these grids had given them a vital flickering character similar to the painting of Tobey, *eg Kwammon* (1952,

New York MMA). The later works, although still open in construction, are freer in design and more ornate: *Procession* (1956, New York, Whitney Museum).

LATHAM, John (1921–), English painter. He originated 'Skoob' Art ('Books' spelt backwards). This consists variously of painting on books, cutting up books, building book towers, and burning books, whether on film or in **Happenings**: *Film Star* (1960, London Tate); *Shem* (New York MMA).

LAURENCIN, Marie (1885–1956), French painter. Her art deals mainly with the idealized female figure with elongated, pure forms, and a colour-range of delicate pastels. Cubist influence superimposes a structure on her pictures, but it is never allowed to interfere with their lyricism, *eg Two Girls* (1915, London Tate). Her poetic sensitivity possesses a subtle charm of its own, especially in the early works.

LAURENS, Henri (1885–1954), French sculptor. He began as a student of the decorative arts, and his first sculptures were done for buildings. In 1911 he joined forces with Braque and embraced **Cubism**. He used collage and polychromy to create geometrical compositions with objects from real-life as a starting-point, *eg Petit Construction* (1915, Paris MNAM), *Guitar* (1918, Paris MNAM). After this geometrical period, he became more interested in curved, naturalistic forms, taking the female body as his theme, as in *Bather* (1931, London Tate); this development closely parallels that of Picasso. Also in 1937, he executed several high reliefs, including *Earth and Water* for the Sèvres pavilion at the Universal Exhibition, and *Life and Death* for the Palace of Discovery. He then concentrated exclusively on the curve, and sculpted several massive pieces which developed the theme of the curve in an increasingly abstract way, *eg Crouching Figure* (1941), *Sleeping Woman* (1943, both Paris MNAM). In 1950 he shared the Grand Prix of the Venice Biennale with Matisse, and he won the Grand Prix at São Paulo in 1953. See illus. p. 133.

LAWSON, Ernest (1873–1939), American painter. Although a member of the **Ash Can School**, he avoided the urban realist subjects painted by most of the others in favour of suburban landscapes painted in a very fresh and well-composed Impressionist style, *eg Spring Night, Harlem River* (1913, Washington, Phillips Collection).

LE BROCQUY, Louis (1916–), Irish painter. In 1938 he went on a tour of European galleries, studying and copying. He had his first one-man show when he settled in London in 1947, represented Ireland at the 1956 Venice Biennale, where he won an international prize, and settled in the south of France in 1958.

Le Brocquy's first mature pictures were of tinkers and gypsies, painted in a Cubist style between 1945 and 1949, *eg Tinkers Resting* (1946, London Tate). From 1950 to 1955 he more or less renounced colour, painting highly simplified figure compositions set in spaces enclosed by large grey planes, *eg Tired Child* (1954, Belfast, Ulster Museum). In 1956 he entered his 'white period', painting mostly nudes in heavy white impasto and mixed media on a white background. The artist christened some of those ghostly figures 'presences'. This describes well figures that are built from the inside out, without outlines, and with strange visceral splashes of colour visible through the impasto as in *Woman* (1959, London Tate); *Isolated Being* (1962, Dublin Gallery). These figures, and especially Le Brocquy's recent series of heads, show a technical similarity to Bacon's work.

LE FAUCONNIER, Henri (1881–1946), French painter. He studied at the Académie Julian, Paris, and in 1908 went to Brittany. His thoughtfully-constructed style is not unlike early Cubism; he was soon to become a member of that movement. During World War I, he was in Amsterdam, where he produced a number of Expressionist paintings which considerably influenced Dutch art.

LEFRANC, Jules (1887–), French painter. A **Naive** artist, he was first encouraged by Monet and began to give more time to painting, devoting himself entirely to it in 1938. His subjects are almost exclusively machines and industrial scenes, depicted with extreme clarity and with classical balance. They include *Railway Lines with Eiffel Tower* (Paris MNAM), *Ship's Propellers* (Saint-Denis Museum).

Fernand Léger: The Mechanic *(1920, private collection); ph. Giraudon.*

LEGER, Fernand (1881–1955), French painter. An architect's apprentice in Caen, he went to Paris in 1900 where he was initially employed as an architectural draughtsman. In 1903, he enrolled at the Ecole des Arts Décoratifs, also studying at the Ecole des Beaux-Arts and the Académie Julian.

His early productions owe much to **Impressionism** eg My Mother's Garden (1905, Biot, Musée Léger). He met Braque and Picasso and took part in Cubist exhibitions, showing Nudes in the Forest (1910, Otterloo RKM) at the Salon des Indépendants in 1910. The conception of this picture owes much to Rousseau, but all the forms are simplified, in Cubist fashion, into cylinders and cones. It should be noted that Léger's process at this time is a literal interpretation of the famous remark of Cézanne (see **Cubism**): although he simplifies the forms in his subjects, they are not rearranged as in a true Cubist work. However he soon began to attempt such rearrangement, for example in Three Figures (1910–11, Milwaukee Art Center) and The Smokers (1911, New York Guggenheim). The latter shows both the increas. gly bright colour he used and, in the incorporation of a village street scene into the picture, the lingering traces of Impressionism.

During the years 1912–14 he adopted a style using black outlines and spots of colour separated by white, as in The Staircase (1913, Zurich Kunsthaus), Woman in Red and Green (1914, Paris MNAM). In 1917 he began to paint in a new geometrical, tubular style, eg The Game of Cards (1917, Otterloo RKM). His colours became extremely bright and, influenced by **Purism**, he began painting works in which pictorial elements were excluded, the material being drawn from city buildings and machinery expressed by simple sign-symbols, human figures being included only if treated as machines, eg The Propellers (1918, New York MMA), The City (1919–20, Philadelphia MA). He did, however, also attempt some non-mechanical figure compositions in which the figures are frozen into rotund monumentality, as in Three Women (1921, New York Guggenheim). His style became purely static and so simplified that it approached abstraction, particularly in his still-lifes, eg Composition (1925, New York Guggenheim). He continued to develop, and took as his subject-matter isolated objects such as keys, a compass, a leaf, or indeed a woman's body, detaching them from their surroundings and re-disposing them in empty space, often on a gigantic scale, eg Still Life (1928, London Tate), Mona Lisa with Keys (1930, Biot, Musée Léger).

In 1925, with Robert Delaunay, who influenced him to some extent (cf Disks, 1918. Paris MAMVP), he decorated a pavilion at the Exposition des Arts Décoratifs. In 1929 he taught, with Ozenfant, at the Académie Moderne, and then at the Académie de la Grande-Chaumière. In 1940 he taught at Yale University, and painted a series of compositions containing acrobats, cyclists and divers, eg Big Julie (1945, New York MMA). He returned to France at the end of 1945 and received a commission for a mosaic for the Church of Our Lady at Assy. With his strong political convictions, he turned increasingly to the common people, the workers, for his subject-matter, as in Les Constructeurs (1950, Biot, Musée Léger), The Great Parade (1954, New York Guggenheim). His figures became very realistic, and resembled popular images surrounded by mechanical objects such as ropes and chains, again returning to the inspiration of Rousseau. Towards 1954 he began to separate colour and form, adding large rectilinear patches of transparent colour over a black and white drawing, eg Two Women holding Flowers (1954).

There is a Léger Museum at Biot, which is decorated with enormous ceramic panels of his own design. Léger's style results from a highly individual synthesis of **Realism** and Cubism, and its considerable impact on modern art is due to its decorative power, its diverse use of media, and the simple, blunt, and rather dry view it takes of modern art.

LEGUEULT, Raymond (1898–   ), French painter. He is a poetic Realist working in the tradition of Impressionism and of Bonnard. At first he used subdued lilac tones, and subtle greys and greens, as in Solitude (1933, Paris MNAM), La Chéminée Noire (1937, Helsinki NG). Later he began to use lighter, more vivid colours which seem to shimmer and melt, and his drawing became more delicate and spontaneous, exact in the depiction of figures, but freer in the handling of backgrounds and objects. He frequently depicts one or two female figures set among a luxuriant mass of plants, still life objects, furniture and hangings.

LEHMBRUCK, Wilhelm (1881–1919), German sculptor. His early work was naturalistic, but tender in feeling, eg Bather (1905, Dusseldorf Kunstmuseum). Towards 1910 his style became more robust (*Woman's Head*, 1910, London Tate) but after his stay in Paris from 1910–14 it changed to a more mannered, elongated style, influenced by Modigliani, Archipenko, and Brancusi, though still more realistic in feeling than the Parisian artists. Works from this period include *Kneeling Girl* (1911, New York MMA), *Seated Youth* (1918, Duisburg Cemetery).

LE MOAL, Jean (1909–   ), French painter. He studied under Bissière at the Académie Ranson in Paris, together with Manessier and Singier. His early works were figurative, though heavily stylized in Cubist fashion, and Surrealist in implication. He has continued the bright colour of these works, though from about 1950 expressed through a shimmering grid on the surface of the canvas in a completely abstract composition. In his more recent works the dark grid has disappeared leaving a rich mosaic of merging blobs of colour, rather like the work of Nay, *eg Ocean* (1959, Paris MNAM).

LE PARC, Julio (1928–   ), Argentinian sculptor. After studying in Buenos Aires he moved to Paris in 1958 and in the following year helped to found the Groupe de Récherche d'Art Visuel. He works exclusively in **Kinetic Art**. Much of his output consists of fairly trivial devices for disorienting the spectator (distorting glasses, spring-loaded shoes *etc*). However, he has made a number of very fine **Mobiles** whose metallic elements scatter the light in a particularly interesting way: *Continuel—Mobile, Continuel—Lumière* (1963, London Tate). He was the grand prizewinner at the 1966 Venice Biennale.

LESLIE, Alfred (1927–   ), American painter. A member of the New York school of Abstract Impressionists, his technique makes use of frequent runnels and splashes of paint. The surface of his work conveys the impression of a constant state of flux, by means of his 'paint-blockout-paint' method, using vivid colours.

LEVINE, Les (1936–   ), Canadian painter and sculptor. A New York based artist, he is concerned with providing an environment in which the potential of a material can be released. He encourages chance in art and incorporates conceptual elements into his work. Using plastics, industrial tools and processes, he is in the forefront of artists trying to come to terms with technology in art.

LEWIS, Wyndham (1884–1957), English painter and author. A pupil of the Slade School and a member of the Camden Town Group, he founded **Vorticism** in 1914, and was chief editor of the journal *Blast*. A work of this period is *Vorticist Composition* (1915, London Tate). His paintings, both representational and abstract, are constructed on a vertical axis, and are very precisely drawn, in a somewhat hard, metallic style. His important *Red Scene* (1933–6, London Tate), painted in subdued colours, has a complicated, geometrical composition revealing several perspectives. He owes his considerable influence as much to his writing as to his painting.

LEWITT, Sol (1928–   ), American sculptor. See **Minimal Art**.

LHOTE, André (1885–1962), French painter. A self-taught artist, he worked as an apprentice for ten years in a commercial sculptor's studio. In 1906 he began to buy Negro carvings, and, inspired by what he had seen of Gauguin's work, devoted himself to painting. In 1909 he became friendly with Dufy and Jean Marchand. His experiments with construction led him to **Cubism**, and he concentrated on port scenes and sporting events, *eg Harbour* (1913), *Rugby* (1917, both Paris MNAM). The figures in his paintings became progressively more schematized and simplified, and his palette became bright and acidulous. Except in his later works, which are more lyrical in feeling, his drawing is always complicated, rhythmically very well-ordered and precise almost to the point of being dry. His colour is extremely vivid and full of contrast and it is used to destroy the unity of the painting's surface. This produces a decorative art which is clever, stylized and sometimes a little artificial, as in *Homage to Watteau* (1918 study in London Tate). He founded a college of art of his own in 1921, and through it exerted considerable and prolonged influence on modern art, on both French and foreign artists.

LIBERMAN, Alexander (1912–   ), American painter and sculptor. He began to study under André Lhote in Paris at the age of 17; after being harshly criticized for a Pointillist still life he left and studied architecture for a time. In 1937, his realistic paintings earned him a prize at the Paris Exhibition. His work changed radically in the 1950s and he began to study a basic element, the circle. His sculpture, generally machine-made to his designs, explored the same motif. Recently he has concentrated on the triangle. He is regarded as a pioneer of **Hard-edge** abstraction, although the forms in his recent works have again become more painterly.

LICHTENSTEIN, Roy (1923–   ), American painter. Probably the best known artist of the **Pop** movement, he is certainly one of the most uncompromising. His adoption, in 1961, not only of the subjects of commercial art but also of its techniques, the round dots and primary colours of cheap printing processes being blown up to an enormous scale in his paintings, made a decisive break with Abstract Expressionism and with his own earlier work. His technique has not been imitated by any major artists, but his subject-matter has been extremely influential, not only on other painters, but also on popular taste and on the very commercial world that he is imitating.

Lichtenstein is above all a painter and a genuinely creative artist. If his comic strip pictures, for example *Whaam!* (1963, London Tate), look like mechanically enlarged plagiarisms, that is evidence of his skill. All his works, whatever their source, start as small-scale freehand drawings which are then projected onto the canvas while he works. Even the pictures which are fairly close to an actual model are considerably altered, both in the preliminary drawing and upon the canvas, when a large-scale rearrangement of elements takes place. His technique involves great simplification and clarification, and thus he is constantly paring the picture down to its essentials. What remains is a transformation of the material into an image which can stand examination by all the Classical criteria of form.

Lichtenstein's subject-matter of 1961–4 included many everyday objects such as exercise books, balls of twine and golf balls. They share with the works of Johns and Oldenburg the paradox of being like the objects they represent, and yet different, thus emphasizing both the qualities of the object and the artist's own contribution. The famous cartoon images of the same years refine a crude medium into a concentrated expressiveness, and there is the similar paradox that the very fact that the emotion of the originals was so synthetic emphasizes by contrast the true values of a real situation. In 1964 he began a series of Classical Temples, which further extended his delicate sense of rhythm and form, and a series of landscapes, 'subjectless' pictures, in which the representational techniques themselves were allowed to generate their own interest, as in **Op Art**. At the same time he began to use a wider variety of materials, and to work in sculpture. Since 1966 he has been concerned with abstract works reinterpreting the decorative style of the 1930s (for example, cinema architecture) and his various *Modern Sculptures* (1967) in bronze, velvet, marble and chrome perfectly sum up the style and yet exist as extraordinarily satisfying objects in their own right.

LIEBERMANN, Max (1847–1935), German painter. He is sometimes known as 'the father of German Impressionism'. His early work consists mostly of conventional rather Academic genre scenes, *eg Memorial Service* (1888, London Tate). He gradually came under the influence of French Impressionism, however, and by the 1890s his work was altogether lighter in touch, brighter in colour and more airy in atmosphere. Nevertheless he continued to prefer scenes from life to pure landscapes, *eg Parrot Walk in the Amsterdam Zoo* (1902, Bremen Kunsthalle), *Terrace of the Restaurant Jacob* (1903, Hamburg Kunsthalle). He was also a successful and sensitive portraitist, *eg Professor Richard Cassirer* (1918), *Self Portrait* (1934, both London Tate). As President of the Berlin Secession, his influence was considerable at the beginning of the 20th century.

LIJN, Liliane (1939–   ), American sculptor. See **Kinetic Art**.

LINDNER, Richard (1901–   ), American painter, born in Hamburg. He studied in

Nuremberg and Munich. After living in Paris during the 1930s he escaped to the U.S. in 1941. As an illustrator, Lindner worked for *Harper's Bazaar* and *Vogue*. He is a Pop artist who is constantly intrigued by unusual clothing, often brutal or fetishist, which he shows, with or without figures, in harshly-coloured quasi-mechanical drawings recalling Duchamp: *Stranger No. 2* (1958, London Tate).

LIPCHITZ, Jacques (1891–), French sculptor, born in Poland. He arrived in Paris in 1909 and studied at the Ecole des Beaux-Arts. His development roughly parallels that of Cubism, though at a slight remove. His *Woman with Serpent* (1913, Philadelphia MA), though basically naturalistic, shows a simplification of volumes and lines like that of early Cubism. *The Bather* (1915, Merion, Penn., Barnes Foundation) is evidence of a brief period of Analytic Cubism, though by this time he was already producing works corresponding to Synthetic Cubism, *eg Man with Guitar* (1916, New York MMA). *The Head* (1915, London Tate) shows the influence of **Brancusi**.

In the mid-1920s his style completely changed. He became more interested in open forms, and in the volumes defined around him, rather than in the volume of the material itself, *eg Pierrot escapes* (1926, Zurich Kunsthaus), *Nude with Guitar* (1928, London Tate), *Mother and Child* (1930, Cleveland MA) all show a gradual return to solidity within this style. In 1941 he went to live in the United States and began to experiment with tormented forms in a spirit akin to the Baroque, *eg Prometheus Strangling the Vulture* (1944–53, Philadelphia MA), *Study for a Monument* (1953, London Tate). Not all his later work is so tortured, however, and he has produced several variations on a womblike, enfolding motif, notably *Blossoming* (1941–2, New York MMA) and the *Virgin* (1948) for the Church of Our Lady at Assy.

LIPPOLD, Richard (1915–), American sculptor. He worked as an industrial designer, and taught industrial design at the University of Michigan from 1937–44. He

Jacques Lipchitz: Girl with Plait (1913); ph. Larousse.

took up sculpture and in 1942 began to execute abstract constructions in wire influenced by Gabo. Lippold's sculptures in metal wire, nickel, chrome, gold and silver, are remarkable for their diaphanous, yet entirely ordered quality, *eg Primordial figure* (1947–48, New York, Whitney Museum). His large-scale sculptures, such as *Flight* (1962, New York, Pan American Building), which stretch wires across large spaces so that they dissolve in the light, assume an entirely new relationship between sculpture and architecture.

LIPSI, Morice (1898–   ), French sculptor, born in Poland. He studied at the Ecole des Beaux-Arts, Paris. His early work is more or less naturalistic but he gradually moved towards abstraction. In 1946 he began to depict the structure of natural objects like leaves and snail-shells. He prefers monumental forms executed in stone, *eg St. Christopher* (La Billette, Charente, France). His most recent works are extremely simple, elemental blocks with clear-cut edges, *eg The Wheel* (Mannheim, Städtisches Hochbankamt).

LIPTON, Seymour (1903–   ), American sculptor. A self-taught artist, he began sculpting in 1932, and from 1935–45 practised representational wood carving. Later, working in metal, he followed the Surrealists in using the forms of natural organisms as a point of departure for abstract works. He used sheet steel, chiselling, bending and brazing it to suggest movement around an empty space. His sculptures which have a jagged regularity about them express an underlying violence, *eg Jungle Bloom* (1954, Yale Univ. AG). His later works are less angular, *eg Sorcerer* (1958. New York, Whitney Museum).

LISSITZKY, Lasar El (1890–1941), Russian painter. He joined the Constructivist movement in 1919, and began a series of drawings and paintings called *Proun*. These are purely abstract works characterized by the presence of space-defining elements shown in perspective as if standing out from the canvas ground, *eg Proun 12 E* (*c* 1920, Harvard, Busch-Reisinger Museum), *Proun* (1922, New York MMA), *Proun L. N. 31* (*c* 1924, Yale Univ. AG).

He was appointed professor in Moscow in 1921, but had to leave Russia when official policy hardened against modern art. He went to Berlin, and then to Switzerland. In 1924 he designed the periodical *Merz* for Kurt Schwitters. In 1925, with Arp, he published *The Isms of Art*. His style rests on a very individual concept of space, which gives three-dimensional objects a two-dimensional form, in conformity with ideas expressed in his *History of Two Squares*, which was published in 1920. Lissitzky's influence on the development of abstract art and on typography in Europe has been very important, not least because of its effect on **Moholy-Nagy** and, through him, on the Bauhaus.

LORJOU, Bernard (1908–   ), French painter. He was a self-taught artist; in 1948 he took part in the realistic and representational Hommes Témoins exhibition. In the same year he shared the Critics' prize with Bernard Buffet. He has never ceased to be the centre of scandals and lawsuits in his role as the scourge of abstract art and the art establishment. Lorjou's painting, which is based on vigorous draughtsmanship, is characterized by its strident colours and rich impasto. His still lifes, *eg Canard de Barbarie au Crochet* (Paris MNAM) have richness and breadth and his other compositions, which are sometimes so energetic as to be confused, are tragic and monumental in feeling.

LOUIS, Morris (1912–62), American painter. He studied at the Maryland Institute of Art and worked in Washington. In the early 1950s he developed a style of 'colour imagism' in which all the emphasis was to be placed on colour, and not on the shapes in which it happened to be presented. He influenced Kenneth Noland in this direction, and both artists were themselves influenced by the work of **Helen Frankenthaler**, which they saw in 1953. From her, Louis learned the technique of staining unprimed canvas with acrylic dye. He used to work with unstretched canvas, pouring the colour on from cans and controlling the flow with great accuracy, by a process which nobody has been able to imitate.

In the earlier works the various colours overlap in veils, creating an effect of great depth. Around 1960, however, he began his paintings known as 'unfurleds', separating the colours and pouring them in diagonal ribbons across the corners of the white canvas, *eg Alpha-Phi* (1961, London Tate), in radial pattern like the petals of a flower, or in vertical columns as in *Partition* (1962, London Tate). These works are all very large in scale and, despite the predominance of the white ground in the later paintings, very sensual in effect, since Louis would often use more than a dozen different colours on one canvas.

LOWRY, Laurence Stephen (1887–), English painter. He received a conventional training at Manchester College of Art. In 1909, however, he moved with his parents to Salford, and he began gradually to paint the industrial landscape and its inhabitants. The subject occupied him all of his life, causing him to travel from one English industrial town to another in search of material, with his eye constantly alert for the odd, the pathetic, and even the ugly.

The first of his many exhibitions at the Lefèvre Gallery in London was held in 1939. The first of his pictures to be bought (1930) by a public collection *An Accident* (1926, Manchester City AG), early illustrated the characteristic features of his style. Painted mainly in white, besmirched by the smoke of the chimneys and the dark caverns of the tenement doorways, the buildings of Salford are laid out like little dolls' houses, the space between them emphasizing the loneliness of the environment. In the square in front are numerous little black figures, shuffling along in heavy boots, muffled in cheap clothes, some walking, some running towards a crowd already gathered in one corner. It does not matter that one cannot see what has happened. Lowry's detached attitude anatomizes the scene and comments both on universal human nature and on the bleak lives of these particular people. His matchstick figures (comparable to Chaplin's little man of the silent films) can be used to express a wide variety of human situations from tragedy to celebration, as in *VE Day* (1945, Glasgow Kelvingrove)

Lowry's paintings may seem naive at first glance, but in fact he chose a naive style as the best way to express a variety of ideas of great poignancy. His post-War pictures tended to concentrate on the human element than on the landscape, and his figures, while becoming more detailed, were painted with wilful but expressive distortions of form, *eg The Cripples* (1949, Salford AG).

LUCE, Maximilien (1858–1941), French painter. After studying under Carolus Duran, he became friendly with Pissarro, Signac and Seurat, and adopted a Divisionist style under their influence. He spent some time in Belgium in a mining community and this experience introduced him to the life of the working classes, and the industrial landscape of factories, workyards, and docks. His compositions were original, and well constructed. He later turned to a more Impressionist style, using a rich palette to gain subtle, luminous effects.

LUKS, George (1867–1933), American painter. Of all the members of the **Ash Can School**, he was the most radical in his choice of subjects, painting scenes from working-class life in a style influenced by Frans Hals, *eg The Wrestlers* (1905, Boston MFA).

LURCAT, Jean (1892–1966), French painter and tapestry designer. He went to Paris in 1912. **Cubism** influenced him strongly from about 1920, and in his subsequent development he often resembled Braque. Long stays in Spain (1923), the Sahara and Asia Minor (1924) were partly responsible for his vision of nature as a desert scattered with ruined monuments. Around 1930, a journey to Arcachon produced a series of tragic maritime landscapes. His canvases of this period owed much to **Surrealism** (Lurçat was in fact a member of the Surrealist group) *eg Le Gros Nuage* (Washington NG). His paintings are a curious mixture of the decorative and the fantastic, with unexpected elements such as veils, sticks and painted panels appearing from nowhere. He went to New York in 1928 and began to paint pictures of mysterious hieratic beings. Fourteen such works are in the Amsterdam Stedelijk M.

His most important achievement was his revival of the art of tapestry. His interest in the subject dated from 1915, and his first tapestry design, *Les Illusions d'Icare*, was woven at the Gobelins workshop in 1936. The decisive point in his career was his appointment to a post in the Aubusson workshop, where from 1939–41, collaborating with Gromaire, he gave new life to the medium by his revival of the technique of 'gros point', and his use of numbered colours and designs. In twenty-five years, he produced a thousand tapestry designs,

Jean Lurçat: Tapestry with Cock *(1953, Neuilly, Gimpel Collection); ph. Giraudon.*

the most famous perhaps being *Le Tapisserie de l'Apocalypse*, 56 metres square, for the Church of Our Lady at Assy (1948), his tapestries for the Musée de Vin, Beaune (1947), the *Homage aux Morts de la Résistance et de la Déportation* (1954, Paris MAMVP) and *Le Chant du Monde*, a group of panels covering 500 square metres, woven between 1957 and 1963.

Lurçat's tapestries are as original in theme as in technique. He used insects, vegetation and the natural elements as his subject matter, fixing them in their strangest aspects and giving them a symbolic significance. Momentous events such as man's conquest of space, or Hiroshima, were also taken as visual material and combined with extensive written inscriptions.

M

MACDONALD-WRIGHT, Stanton (1890–), American painter. During a trip to Paris (1907) to study at the Académie Julian and the Ecole des Beaux-Arts, he encountered Fauvism, Cubism and Orphism. With Russell he founded Synchromism, an abstract style using Cubist-faceted forms to achieve rich colour juxtapositions, eg Synchromy in Green and Orange (1916, Minneapolis Walker Art Center). He was represented at the Armory Show in 1913 by several of these paintings. Macdonald-Wright settled in California in 1916. Representational elements gradually came back into his painting, though it was still diffused by an abstract screen of coloured facets, as in Far Country Synchromy (1920, Detroit Art Inst.). He became interested in Oriental Art and in Zen Buddhism, visiting Japan in 1937. The Oriental influence led Macdonald-Wright to a naturalistic style, with Calligraphic forms replacing the formerly angular ones, eg Yin Synchromy (1930, Santa Barbara MA). In 1954, however, after a further two years in Japan, he reverted to abstract painting, not unlike his early style, but more clearly focused and with a greater sense of rhythm.

MACKE, August (1887–1914), German painter. A student at the Dusseldorf Academy, he travelled extensively abroad. During several trips to Paris after 1907, he came into contact with Fauvism and Cubism. He was a member of the Expressionist Blaue Reiter group, in the company of his friends Marc and Kandinsky, whom he met (1909) in Munich. When he was in Paris in 1912 he visited Delaunay, who had a profound influence on him. Following the example of Cubism and Futurism, Macke arrived at a stylization of objective reality by what he called 'simultaneous contrasts' of light colour. His work was figurative, except for some abstracts painted in the years 1913–14. He often depicted scenes from contemporary life, eg Illuminated Shop Window (1912, Hanover Landesgalerie).

Macke's painting recalls Cubism in that forms are simplified and space subdivided into rectilinear faceted elements. In handling and colour, however, it is bolder than French work of the period. It possesses a certain elegance and, in the watercolours done on a visit to Tunisia with Klee in 1914, a remarkable limpidity, eg Kairouan I (1914, Munich NG). These qualities, coupled with his close observation of modern life, place Macke in a special position among the German Expressionists.

MacTAGGART, William (1903–), Scottish painter. The grandson of the painter William MacTaggart, he was educated at home and encouraged by his family to take up art. He studied part-time at the Edinburgh College of Art, and first exhibited at the Royal Scottish Academy in 1921. He made regular winter visits to the Mediterranean coast of France from 1922–39 for health reasons. His paintings of this period were mostly landscapes, highly simplified under the influence of Cubism. In 1931 he was greatly impressed by a Munch exhibition in Edinburgh, and this influence on his work towards richer paint and stronger colour increased after 1937. In the 1950s he became influenced by Rouault and, ceasing to work directly from nature, began to treat landscape themes in an imaginative way each expressing a particular mood, eg Duet (1958, London Tate); Nocturne (1963, Edinburgh, Gallery of Modern Art). Many of these paintings, with their intense colours glowing under a dark sky, are almost mystical in feeling, and are close in mood to the works of his compatriots Maxwell and Redpath. MacTaggart was elected President of the Royal Scottish Academy in 1959 and knighted in 1962.

MAGNELLI, Alberto (1888–), Italian painter. A self-taught artist, he first exhibited in 1911 at the Venice Biennale. Magnelli was influenced by both the Futurists and the Cubists during his visit to Paris in 1913. When he returned to Italy, his painting was marked by extreme simplification, as in The Orange Seller (1914, Zurich Kunsthaus), which led him in 1915 to pure abstraction, using very bright colours. In 1918, he adopted a semi-figurative, violently expressive style which was to form the basis of his painting for another fifteen years. Back in Paris in 1933, he returned to an Abstract Expressionism, beginning with a so-called 'stone' period, during which he painted forms resembling shattered rocks on tarred paper. By about 1937 he had developed a flatter style, with areas of rather dull colour separated by ribbons of light and dark paint, *eg Ronde Océanique* (1937, Paris MNAM).

MAGRITTE, René (1898–1967), Belgian painter. **Surrealism** interested him from 1925 and he became friends with many of its leaders during a stay (1927–32) in Paris. His own style was remarkably consistent, although he experimented for a while (1939–46) with bright colours and a looser handling. Magritte's Surrealism differed from that of, for example, Dali, in that he was concerned less with exploring the hinterland of the emotions (dreams and mentally-disturbed states) than with examining the nature of reality. His basic method was to paint objects, figures and landscapes in a realistic style, simplifying them to give them an aura of eternal significance. Many of his works contain unexpected juxtapositions or alterations of scale: even the simplest such as *The Empire of Light* (1950, New York MMA), which shows a night scene with a street lamp and lighted windows silhouetted against an afternoon sky, can be most disturbing.

One element can be exchanged for another, as in numerous works in which the sky appears composed of solid blocks, or as in *The False Mirror* (1928, New York MMA) which shows an enormous eye with sky painted in place of an iris: these lead one to question one's preconceptions about the world. Sometimes Magritte merely presented a few objects or a figure in a still landscape, *eg La Liberté de l'Esprit* (1948, Charleroi Museum); in other works, the objects were drawn from a small repertoire of everyday things (a tuba, sleighbells, a rose, leaves, *etc*) which, whether drawn out of scale or not, seemed to have a special significance. In these works he was probably closer to the **Metaphysical Painting** of De Chirico than to Surrealism.

Magritte was always an intellectual artist: it is the ideas in his paintings which are so disturbing, as in *Time Transfixed* (1930, London Tate) which shows a steaming railway engine thrusting through the fireplace in a bare room with a clock on the mantelpiece above. He regarded painting as the art of creating illusion, using it as a metaphor to explore a larger reality. An early work, *Le Trahison des Images* (1928, New York private collection), shows a realistic painting of a tobacco-pipe with the inscription 'This is not a pipe'; other works show a view through a window with a canvas placed on an easel in front of it in such a way that the view painted on it exactly replaces that portion of the landscape which it blots out; finally there are a number of reworkings of famous paintings, *eg Perspective* (1950, Ghent Museum, based on Manet's *Balcony*), in which the figures are replaced by coffins. These paintings anticipated a similar questioning of reality in the work of Jasper Johns, Jim Dine and George Segal. Magritte, between 1951 and 1953, worked on a huge circular fresco in the Casino of Knokke-le-Zoute entitled *Le Domaine Enchanté* which could be said to be an anthology of all his principal motifs.

MAILLOL, Aristide (1861–1944), French sculptor. He went to Paris in 1881 and studied at the Ecole des Beaux-Arts under Gérome and Cabanel, from whose studios he was subsequently dismissed. In 1893 he joined the circle of the **Nabis** and took up painting *eg The Wave* (1898, Paris, Petit Palais): the few canvases he produced in later years were more closely related to this period of art than to his subsequent development. He then turned his attention to tapestry, designing in a style derived from late Gothic. He set up a tapestry studio at Banyuls, where he chose the wool and used natural dyes. A serious eye accident forced him to give up this work, and he turned to sculpture, having previously produced ceramics influenced by Gauguin, whom he had met in Brussels in 1894. He began as a woodcarver and took up modelling in 1900. At Marly-le-Roi he built the studio where he worked for the rest of his life, except for his summer sojourns at Banyuls. Thus his vocation only became clear when he was forty, and his personal style suddenly emerged fully formed.

Maillol's style was closely allied to Classical Greek treatment of the nude (a little more round in some works, perhaps, a little more naturalistic in others), a direct continuation of the tradition and making

Aristide Maillol: Venus *(Algiers MBA);*
ph. Giraudon.

no concessions to the distortions of con-temporary art. His approach was not sterile, rather he was drawn to this style because it seemed best to represent the humanity of his subjects. However, during his only visit to Greece in 1908, he attacked the academicism of Praxiteles' *Hermes,* saying that it was 'carved in soap'. In 1905 he received the commission for a monument to the revolutionary Blanqui, for which he sculpted *Action in Chains*, a gigantic female figure striding forward with her hands tied behind her back (Paris MNAM; casts of the torso in London Tate and New York MMA). His other monuments are also treatments of the nude, *eg Monument to Cézanne* (1911–16, Paris Tuileries Gardens) and *Monument to Debussy* at St.-Germain-en-Laye. The male nude is seldom treated by Maillol, but there is one example: Le *Coureur Cycliste* (1904). This is the figure of a young boy, poised and graceful; despite its title this too is Classical in inspiration.

Maillol did not invent new poses as, say, Rodin did: his *Venus with a Necklace* (1918–28) and *The Three Nymphs* (1930–8, examples of both in the London Tate) are based on a Hellenistic bronze and on the Hellenistic *Three Graces* group res-pectively; his *La France* (1930) is derived from the *Venus de Milo* and his *Woman with a Thorn* (1920) is a female variant of the famous *Spinario*. His busts were rare: there exist several excellent busts of women, in an understated style, and a moving portrait of *Renoir* (1907, cast in New York MMA), with whom Maillol had so many affinities. He was also an excellent draughtsman in pencil, red chalk and crayon, and produced many book illustra-tions in a style which fused Classicism of outline with a Gothic directness. In 1964 a dozen of his sculptures were placed in the Tuileries Gardens, Paris.

MALEVICH, Kasimir (1878–1935), Rus-sian painter. He was first influenced by the Fauves, and lived in Paris in 1911. Malevich was a member of the 'Jack of Diamonds' group, and exhibited works in a style owing something to Cubism and Léger, *eg Woman with Buckets* (New York MMA). In 1913 he exhibited his *Black Square on a White Background* in Moscow. This was the first example of **Suprematism** and caused a sensation. In 1914 he produced a purely geometrical work, which established him

K

as a pioneer of abstract art, the *White Square on a White Background* (New York MMA). He was appointed to the professorship of applied art in Moscow, but in 1922 the reactionary attitude of the Soviets to art brought his removal to Leningrad, where he continued to teach but was forbidden to exhibit. He went to Germany in 1925 to publish (at the Bauhaus) his book, *Die Gegenstandlose Welt* (*The World without Objects*).

MALFRAY, Charles (1887–1940), French sculptor. He went to the Art School at Orléans, then to the Ecole des Beaux-Arts, Paris. In 1920, he won the Blumenthal Prize. At that time, he was working on monuments to those killed in World War I at Pithiviers (*L'Effroi*) and Orléans. The latter, over 40 feet high, was violently criticized, but Malfray refused to change it. He was not prolific, and many of his works are fragments, *eg Torse de Nageuse* (1936, Lyons MBA), *Femme s'essuyant les Pieds* (1928, San Francisco MA), *La Danse* (1937, Paris MNAM). His work is in the Classical tradition, not unlike that of Maillol, but characterized by greater vigour of modelling, and by a stronger sense of movement, leading to striking asymmetric poses, *eg L'Eveil*, 1938, Algiers MBA. His most important sculptures are in the courtyard of the Petit Palais in Paris, and at Orléans (MBA).

MALINA, Franz (1912–), American engineer and artist. He was largely responsible for the design of the first American space-probe rocket in 1945, and since then has been President of the International Academy of Astronautics. Since 1953, when he moved to Paris, he has been working as a Kinetic artist, developing various forms of 'light box' in which changing patterns and colours are formed on a glass screen by handpainted moving and fixed elements within the box.

MANES, Pablo (1891–), Argentinian sculptor. After studying in Italy, he went (1914) to Paris, where he was one of Bourdelle's students. He won the silver medal in the Exposition des Arts Décoratifs in 1925. After 1926 he was active both as a diplomat and as a sculptor. His earliest works showed the influence of Lipchitz, *eg Le Guitariste*. His later constructions

were lighter in style, *eg Les Acrobates* (1925), and he evolved a dynamic quasi-abstract manner, *eg Fall of Icarus* (1933). His work has varied from airy allusiveness to prosaic realism. *La Danse*, which unites these elements, is a confident composition in broad rhythms.

MANESSIER, Alfred (1911–), French painter. He studied first at Art School in Amiens, and then at the Académie Ranson, Paris. He began exhibiting at the Salon des Indépendants in 1933, and later at the Salon des Tuileries, and formed a group with the painters Le Moal and Bertholle, and the sculptor Etienne-Martin. After staying at La Trappe in 1943 his paintings took on a religious character, expressed in abstract form, *eg Barabbas* (1952, Eindhoven, van Abbemuseum). In 1953 he won the São Paulo Bienal Prize for Painting. His output includes large-scale decorations, *eg* the Railway and Air stands at the Exposition Universelle in 1937, theatre sets and, in particular, a large body of stained glass work, *eg* the church of Brisseux and All Saints at Basle.

His paintings are sometimes inspired by an atmospheric, mysterious view of nature, as in *Espace Matinal* (1949) and *Le Port Bleu* (1948), both in Paris MNAM. More frequently his mysticism is translated into subtly combined geometrical forms and rich colour contrasts resembling stained glass. Manessier emphasizes the spiritual element in his art: 'Non-figurative art seems to me to be the modern painter's means of arriving at his own reality. If the question of spiritual value is the main one in man's life, external appearance is only significant if it contains the spiritual.' Manessier contributed much to the modern revival of religious abstract art. The Carnegie Institute at Pittsburgh and the Toronto Art Gallery have examples of his work.

MANET, Edouard (1832–83), French painter. Manet's **Realism** influenced the subsequent development of art, particularly because of his power of isolating an image either against a plain background, or in a subtly rearranged composition of compressed planes, *eg The Dead Toreador* (1864, Washington NG), *Un Bar aux Folies-Bergère* (1881, London Courtauld Galleries). This suggested to later artists a means of handling images from modern

Alfred Manessier: Games in the Snow *(New York Guggenheim); ph. Giraudon.*

life while avoiding complete naturalism. In his subject-matter he anticipated the Impressionists to a certain extent. However, Realism was only one aspect of Manet. He received a formal Academic training at the studio of Couture and, although he was soon rejected by Academic circles, many of his pictures were based closely on Old Masters (Goya, Velázquez, Titian and even Raphael), and a large number were attempts to recreate traditional subjects in modern terms. Although his broad *alla prima* technique and his deliberate simplification of light and shade influenced the Impressionists, Manet was never one of them (being unwilling, among other things, to give up his use of black), except for a short period in 1874 when he was painting with **Monet** at Argenteuil, *eg In a Boat* (1874, New York MMA).

MANGUIN, Henri (1874–1949), French painter. A student of Gustave Moreau, he was associated with **Fauvism** and exhibited *La Sieste* at the celebrated Salon of 1905, in the Fauve Room. He regularly went to stay in southern France, especially at St. Tropez. Manguin's work was characterized by flowing draughtsmanship and a rich bright palette. In the intensity of his colours, Manguin was a Fauve, but his art did not exploit violent distortions. Rather he tried to convey the intensity of his experience (landscapes soaking up the sun, nudes with flesh almost capable of engulfing the touch, still life objects seeming to light up their entire environment), though at times this tended to be rather artificial. He was an eclectic painter: his landscapes were influenced by Monet or Cézanne, many of his figure studies were akin to those of Matisse and his harbour scenes were reminiscent of Marquet. However, in a few works, notably his portraits, *eg Claude Manguin* (1907, Cologne, Wallraff-Richartz-Museum), and still lifes, *Nature-morte aux Huitres* (1908, Geneva Modern Art Foundation), he achieved a discipline of colour and simplicity of form without sacrificing the essential spirit of the rest of his oeuvre.

MANOLO, see **Martinez Manuel Hugues y.**

MANZU, Giacomo (1908–   ), Italian sculptor. He worked first with an engraver and gilder, then with a stucco craftsman. He studied for a short time at the Art School in Verona. He went to Paris in an abortive attempt to meet Maillol and to study the work of Rodin, but collapsed from hunger and returned to Milan, where he has lived since, becoming a professor at the Brera in 1940. He first made his reputation with portrait busts in wax or bronze, but also created an astonishing variety of sculptures and reliefs in various media of religious and secular subjects. These show the influence of Hellenistic and *Quattrocento* sculpture as well as of Rosso, Rodin and Maillol, *eg* the bronze *Susanna* (1942, London Tate). Probably his first masterpiece was the *Large Portrait of a Lady in a Dressing-gown* in bronze (1946, New York MMA, second cast) which showed Manzù's ability to create monumentality out of a pose which was naturalistic, informal and completely original.

Throughout his career he produced figure sculptures which endowed new poses with Classical qualities; examples are the *Young Girl on a Chair* in bronze (1955, Toronto AG) or the marvellous series of *Dance Steps* which might be called variations on the vertical (1953, Antwerp, Middelheim Museum; 1954, Mannheim, Kunsthalle; 1963, forecourt of Gas Company Building, Detroit). These, and almost all his mature works were in bronze, cast either from wax or clay originals, and retaining the finger-marks and little ridges made by smoothing or scraping away the soft material in order to give the characteristic Manzù surface to the finished cast. Manzù has since been increasingly occupied with religious works. In the late 1940s and 1950s he produced a series of *Cardinals*, seated or standing, with

their robes treated in a manner reminiscent of Donatello, giving the forms volume and a clear-cut discipline (1948, London Tate; 1951, São Paulo Modern Art Museum; 1954, Cologne Wallraff-Richartz-Museum). Some of these works are solemn and heiratic, others witty, almost caricatured, but with great humanity. His most important commissions, however, were the *Portal of Love* for Salzburg Cathedral in 1958, and the *Portal of Death* for St. Peter's Rome, finished in 1964. Both works employed a new, rather mannered, style of sketchy drawing on very low relief. The Salzburg door consists of scenes from the lives of the saints. The Rome work, however, combined traditional subjects such as the Death of the Virgin, with scenes from contemporary history (the Second Vatican Council) and genre scenes showing various aspects of death, and includes a most moving portrait of Pope John XXIII; they indicate a considerable range.

MARC, Franz (1880–1916), German painter. The son of a painter, he studied art in Munich and went on several occasions to Paris. In 1903 and in 1907 he encountered van Gogh's work, and in 1912 he worked with Robert Delaunay. In 1910 he met Macke and Kandinsky, and published the **Blaue Reiter** almanac with them. He was influenced successively by Pointillism, Fauvism, and Cubism, interpreting these styles with energy and an individual sense of colour. His great passion was the animal world, and his aim was to discover the essential form (*Wesensform*) which would express the innocence and nobility of wildlife. His masterpiece, the large *Blue Horses* (1911, Minneapolis Walker Art Center), is a landmark in 20th century art. In 1913 he painted several large mythological canvases evocative of Henri Rousseau, whom Macke much admired, as in *Animal Destinies* (1913, Basle, Kunstmuseum). The influence of his friend Delaunay induced him to paint in a more abstract manner, *eg The Tyrol* (1913–14, Munich NG), suggesting the struggle between the elements of the cosmos. His last works are noticeably more abstract, *eg Battling Forms* (1913, Munich NG) and evoke the theme of organic growth. Marc's death during World War I deprived modern German painting of one of its most brilliant exponents.

MARCHAND, André (1907–   ), French painter. He began sending works to the Salon d'Automne in 1932, and to the Salon des Indépendants in 1933. While in Algeria in 1933 he painted *La Jeune Fille et le Paralytique*, which won the Paul Guillaume Prize in 1937. He then began to paint in Provence, landscapes and street scenes at first, and later, compositions which were less and less realistic. The works of the 1940s employ a rather spiky drawing style, with branches of plant stems criss-crossing in front of the picture so that the whole appears rather flat. The colour gradually increases in intensity, making use of rich harmonies such as blue-turquoise-green or scarlet-orange-amber, often set against a predominant background colour giving a stained-glass effect, as in *La Bouteille et les Fruits* (1948, Paris MNAM). Then, in the 1950s, the criss-crossing lines assumed a calligraphic life of their own, all pretence of spatial organization ceased, and the colour became far less closely confined to discrete areas. Although he is an original artist of considerable power, Marchand's work is unfortunately not well known.

MARCHAND, Jean (1883–1940). French painter. He studied at the Ecole des Beaux-Arts in 1908 and was loosely connected with the Cubist group. He exhibited at the Salon des Indépendants in 1908, at the Salon d'Automne and at the Tuileries. His early work consisted principally of landscapes and town views which were simplified and given a firm architectonic construction rather in the manner of Cézanne, *eg Toits Rouges* (1913, London Tate). Later his style became softer (in the manner of Marquet) although he retained simplicity and discipline of composition, *eg Coup de Mistral* (1927, London Tate).

MARCOUSSIS, Louis (1883–1941), French painter, born in Poland as Louis Markous. He studied at art school in Cracow, and then with Jules Lefèvre in Paris in 1903. Influenced by the Impressionists until about 1907, in that year he exhibited at the Salon d'Automne, and then allied himself with **Cubism**, and in 1912 with the **Section d'Or**. In 1920 he exhibited in Der Sturm in Berlin, and in 1933 at Chicago. His style represented a vigorous continuation of Synthetic Cubism, with delicate but intense colours, notably hot reds and subtle colour contrasts, *eg Nature Morte au Damier* (1912, Paris MNAM); *La Pluie No. 1* (1927, London Tate); *Table on a Balcony* (1928, Glasgow, Kelvingrove).

MARIN, John (1870–1953), American painter. Having worked as an architect, he began to paint seriously in 1889. He arrived in Paris in 1905, and sent 10 watercolours to the Salon d'Automne in 1910. On returning to New York, he exhibited at Stieglitz' Gallery 291, and took part in the **Armory Show** of 1913. He established himself as a modern painter of importance with an exhibition at the Museum of Modern Art, New York, in 1936 and with a retrospective exhibition of his work at the 1950 Venice Biennale. He was influenced first by Whistler and then **Cubism**, whose fractured planes he found particularly suitable for the staccato rhythms of American cityscapes, *eg Lower Manhattan* (1922, New York MMA). In contrast to the French Cubists, however, he tended to use the planes as a frame for comparatively naturalistic painting. He also painted concurrently a number of altogether freer works, usually of natural subjects, in a sensitive Expressionist vein: those towards the end of his life approach Abstract Expressionism. He was perhaps at his best in watercolours, *eg Maine Islands* (1922, Washington, Phillips Collection); *Downtown, New York City* (1923, London Tate).

MARINI, Marino (1901–   ), Italian sculptor. He studied at art school in Florence and Paris (1928–9) then settled in Milan, taught sculpture at Monza (1929–40), and then at the Brera, Milan. He was one of the first in Italy to attempt to forge a modern idiom from the style of Classical and pre-Classical sculpture. In consequence almost all his works have a spare, self-contained quality with the individual features greatly simplified. Only the rough surface quality of his work and the expressions of his figures which, though stylized, portray an astonishing depth and often violence of feeling, reveal him as an artist essentially of the 20th century. His work consists principally of nude figures, *eg Pomona* (1940 Brussels MBA) and portrait busts, *eg Igor Stravinsky* (1950, San Francisco MA), though many pieces have religious overtones, *eg Archangel* (1943, Basle, Kunstmuseum). Since World War II he has become more and more absorbed with the subject of *Horse and Rider*. He has developed this theme from its Classical origins to a more vigorous treatment which is closer to the spirit of primitive art (examples are in London Tate; Minneapolis, Walker Art Center; New York MMA).

MARQUET, Albert (1875–1947), French painter. Ill-health as a child resulted in a withdrawn and timid manner and the life of a recluse. He settled in Paris with his mother in 1890, entered the Ecole des Arts Décoratifs where Matisse befriended him, and then studied under Gustave Moreau at the Ecole des Beaux-Arts. He copied Poussin, Claude and Corot at the Louvre, and exhibited at the Weill Gallery and in the Salons, most notably with the **Fauvism** group in 1905. The Belgian painter Evenepoel introduced him to the galleries of the Rue Lafitte, where he became interested in the works of Monet, Cézanne and van Gogh. As a result he began to make wider but restrained use of pure colour, *eg Portrait d'André Rouveyre* (1904, Paris MNAM), *La Plage de Fécamp* (1906, Paris MNAM), *Le Sergent de la Coloniale* (1904, Paris, private collection). When his mother died in 1907 he moved to an apartment in the house in which Matisse lived. Here Marquet painted the wharves and Notre Dame from a high window, in all seasons, *eg Le Pont-Neuf* (Washington NG). His palette brightened and became subtler and he achieved a direct, sober and spacious style. His canvases are peopled with lively little figures for which he did many drawings from nature. Between 1910 and 1914 he executed a series of female nude studies remarkable for their astringency and plastic force, *eg Nu à Contre-jour* (1911, Bordeaux MBA). By this time he was becoming well known and, during frequent journeys to Holland, Romania, Sweden and Italy, he produced a large number of paintings, specializing in harbour scenes and seascapes; *eg Harbour at Bougie* (1922 Glasgow, Kelvingrove). His style underwent further change during his stays in Tunisia, Morocco and Algeria (from 1920). his colours becoming richer, but his later work was somewhat superficial. In 1931 he moved into an upper apartment at the corner of the Rue Dauphiné and the Quai

Albert Marquet: Portrait d'André Rouveyre *(1904, Paris MNAM); ph. Giraudon.*

des Grands-Augustins, from which he again painted the Pont-Neuf at night and by day, on canvases of extraordinary breadth and solidity.

Marquet was a painter who realised his limitations and turned them to his own advantage. He painted water scenes to the exclusion of almost all other subjects, but he gave new life to this theme through his subtle and profound feeling for nature, space, the atmosphere of the changing seasons, and the effects of light, air and snow. His technique, despite (or perhaps because of) his contact with Fauvism, was simple: his drawing concise and understated, his colour (after the early years) tonally unified and limpid, and his handling fluid and restrained. There is an important collection of Marquets at the Bordeaux MBA, his birthplace.

MARTIN, Kenneth (1905–   ), English painter and sculptor, husband of **Mary Martin**. While working as a designer, he studied part-time at the Sheffield School of Art and in 1929 went to the Royal College of Art. He painted direct from nature until 1948 and then continued with abstract painting. His sculptural constructions, dating from 1951, include a number of **Mobiles** based on clear spatial concepts, eg *Small Screw Mobile* (1953, London Tate). Martin's approach is essentially Constructivist, being based on the clear statement and logical elaboration of simple principles, often borrowing rhythmic ideas from mathematics and from music as in *Oscillation* (1962, London Tate). His mobiles are less fanciful than those of Calder, by whom he has been influenced.

MARTIN, Mary (1907–1969), English artist. Studying at Goldsmith's College and at the Royal College of Art, she married **Kenneth Martin** in 1930 and her interest in the principles of Constructivism has paralleled his. She painted her first abstract picture in 1950 and almost immediately began constructing reliefs in painted wood based on regular permutations of simple geometrical motions eg *Spiral Movement* (1951, London Tate). Her later work, using mirror-faced steel half-cubes, introduced subtle patterns of reflected light; *Cross* (1969, Liverpool AG). She also created a number of reliefs using subtly-coloured rectangles in the manner of Pasmore.

MARTINEZ, Manuel Hugues y, known as Manolo (1872–1945), Spanish sculptor. He spent his early years in Spain before going in 1904 to Paris where he met Picasso, and was quickly accepted by the Bohemian group at Montparnasse. Self-taught, he copied at the Louvre and the Musée de Cluny, taking up sculpture in 1910 at Céret, influenced by Gauguin and Maillol. The so-called School of Céret developed around him, and included his friends Picasso, Braque and Juan Gris. He did not adopt Cubism, creating instead little animated figures broadly and confidently carved in stone. He returned to Spain in 1928.

MARTINI, Arturo (1889–1947), Italian sculptor. An early interest in ceramics was replaced by sculpture in 1905. In 1921 he joined the **Valori Plastici** movement. His huge monument to the *Italian Pioneers of America* was finished in 1928, and erected at Worcester, Massachusetts. He won the Grand Prix for sculpture at the first Quadriennale in Rome in 1931 and became the official sculptor of the Fascist regime. Martini was technically highly skilled, but most of the works in his huge and varied oeuvre are merely facile. His style betrayed numerous and often contradictory influences simultaneously. His aggressive monumental works such as *Victory of the Air* (1934, Milan GAM) have a historical value in capturing the spirit of the Fascist régime. Some of his genre scenes in high-relief, however, create interesting effects in the relation of figures to background rather akin to Pittura Metafisica, eg *Moonlight* (1931, Antwerp, Middelheim Museum). There are works by Martini in the New York MMA and in Pittsburgh, Carnegie Institute.

MASCHERINI, Marcello (1906–), Italian sculptor. A life-long resident of Trieste, he studied at its Industrial Institute. Mascherini attracted attention in 1933 with his statue *Icarus* at the Milan Triennale; in 1938 he was given a room at the Venice Biennale, where he won the Sculpture Prize in 1950. His style, somewhat in the spirit of Martini was inspired by Etruscan work of the 15th century and is distinguished by its chaste, elongated forms and delicate outlines, which reveal an imagination at once fantastic and ironical, eg *La France* (Otterloo RKM).

MASSON, André (1896–   ), French painter. He studied in Brussels, then in Paris from 1912, where he studied fresco painting at the Ecole des Beaux-Arts, but was also influenced by the paintings in the Louvre. He was a friend of Juan Gris and was influenced by Cubism. In 1922 he met Kahnweiler, whose constant support enabled him to devote himself entirely to painting. André Breton admired the symbolical paintings in his first exhibition of 1924, and from then until 1929 he was a member of the **Surrealism** group, although continuing to paint works in a Surrealist vein at intervals thereafter, *eg In the Tower of Sleep* (1938, Baltimore MA). From 1934 to 1936, he worked in Spain painting bullfights, insects and tortured landscapes, *eg Ibdes d'Aragon* (1935, London Tate). He was in the United States from 1941 to 1945 where he had widespread influence. Masson attempted to portray matter in its eternal state of fusion and decomposition, and the forces which act upon it, *eg Combats de Poissons* (1927, New York MMA) symbolizes human conflicts. His technique is characterized by interweaving lines and ambiguous forms, and in an effort to gain intensity he practised **Automatic Writing.**

MASTROIANNI, Umberto (1910–   ), Italian sculptor. After studying in Rome, he settled in Turin. His earliest work to attract attention (at the 1936 Venice Biennale) was representational but under the influence of Cubism and of Futurist sculpture he began to experiment with forms built up in large angular masses. Most of his works, although non-representational, are based on the human form, treated in a rhythmic and energetic way, *eg Conquest* (1954, Otterloo RKM). There are also several portraits and heads with the features simplified to block-like forms but still recognizable, as in *Mask* (1957, Elat MMA). Many of his most important works are in public squares, *eg Lovers* (1955) in front of Rotterdam station, and the Partisan Monument (1946) in Turin. He won the Grand Prix of the Venice Biennale in 1958.

MATHIEU, Georges (1922–   ), French painter. He began to paint in 1942, settling in Paris in 1947. He has exhibited all over the world and has organized important exhibitions of American contemporary art in Paris. His style is related to Action painting: paint is rapidly applied either by squeezing it direct from the tube onto the canvas, or by drawing with fine threads, drips and splashes of paint in a manner akin to Calligraphic art, although very free. His works represent a reaction against excessive formalism in abstract painting, although they are relatively simple beside those of, for example, Jackson Pollock. They often employ subtle formal effects of apparent depth, colour harmony and the interplay of fine point-traces with larger, more regular elements. Many of his abstract works, often of vast size, have resounding historical titles, *eg Les Capétiens Partout* (1954, Paris MNAM); *Le Couronnement de Charlemagne* (1956, Urbana, Illinois, Krannert Museum); *Pompe Funèbre du Coeur de Condé en l'Eglise Saint-Paul-Saint-Louis* (Liège MBA). Mathieu has also developed his theories in several books.

MATISSE, Henri (1869–1954), French painter and sculptor. While a lawyer's clerk in Saint Quentin he went to evening classes at the Ecole Quentin-Latour. When he received permission to go to Paris, he studied at the Ecole des Arts Décoratifs, at the Académie Julian, and finally at the Ecole des Beaux-Arts, where he worked under **Gustave Moreau** who recognized his pupil's ability. Among his friends were Rouault, Camoin, Piot, Manguin, Dufy and Friesz. In his early works he drew from nature, and was a frequent visitor to the Louvre, where he copied Champaigne, Poussin, and Chardin. His painting at this time was traditional, with grey tones and muted atmosphere, *eg Le Tisserand Breton* (1896, Paris MNAM). In 1898 he exhibited *La Desserte* at the Société Nationale des Beaux-Arts; he produced several very different versions of this theme. In a few works of this period, notably the *Still Life with Oranges* (*c* 1899, St. Louis, Washington Univ.), his love of bright colours in bold contrasts began to assert itself, but for the most part he painted figure studies and townscapes in a more restrained vein, *eg Notre Dame* (1900, London Tate).

In 1900, he entered Carrière's studio and took up sculpture. His style continued to develop and he was fascinated by Cézanne. In 1903 he participated in the first Salon d'Automne, and in 1904 held his first one-man show at Vollard's. He spent that summer with Signac and Cross and briefly practised Divisionism, as can be seen in the famous *Luxe, Calme et Volupté*, shown at the Salon des Indépendants in 1905. His own personality finally emerged clearly in **Fauvism** and Matisse became the acknowledged leader of that school. He simplified by avoiding tonal modelling, instead denoting the object in flat areas of strong colour which were either juxtaposed and contrasted, or separated by black outlines or the white of the canvas. He rejected perspective and illusionism, and his colour contrasts do not suggest space so much as light, *eg Landscape at Collioure* (1906, Leningrad, Hermitage); *Portrait of Derain* (1905, London Tate). In 1908 he published 'Notes d'un peintre', a manifesto of his ideas, in *La Grande Revue*, and sent paintings to several exhibitions abroad.

This period was marked by the first of his paintings in a Neo-Classical style, such as *Bathers with a Turtle* (1908, St. Louis AM) in which the figures are painted in a Greek vase style, the landscape muted and still further simplified, and the whole composition quite flat. His style developed rapidly during a stay in Morocco (1911–12) and the paintings of that period were close to Cubism, *eg Yvonne Landsberg* (1914, Philadelphia MA). They became increasingly simplified, austere in tone with blacks, greys and ochres predominating and disciplined and angular in line: some have the effect of semi-abstract collages of motifs, *eg The Moroccans* (1916, New York MMA), while others approach total abstraction.

After 1917 Matisse spent his winters at Nice. His subsequent work was less urgent in character. This may have been the result partly of his success, partly of the

Henri Matisse: Odalisque with Draught Board *(1928, private collection).*

Mediterranean atmosphere, and perhaps also of the general euphoria of the immediate post-War years. His colour was brilliant as it had been in his Fauve period, but less violent, his line sinuous and dominating, and he made more use than hitherto of modelling. He preferred interior scenes with open windows and graceful figures of women, especially odalisques as in *Interior at Nice* (1921, Chicago Art Inst.). In 1931 he returned to his Neo-Classical manner in *The Dance*, a mural for the Barnes Foundation at Merion, Pennsylvania (first version in Paris MAMVP), in which the simplification is quite masterly, the picture containing nothing to disturb the surface yet filled with a refined sense of movement and grace. This simplification continued, less markedly, in his easel paintings, *eg Music* (1939, Buffalo AG), the ten versions of *La Blouse roumaine* (1939–45) and reached its logical conclusion in the chapel at Vence. There, between 1947 and 1956, Matisse produced designs for stained glass windows and drew three compositions on white-enamelled terra-cotta. He also produced, during his last years when he was too infirm to use a brush, a number of 'gouaches découpées' (large collages made from shapes cut from paper previously painted all over in a single bright colour). He said of them: 'Cutting into living colour reminds me of the sculptor's direct carving.' These last works seem the perfect culmination of Matisse's style. The greatest of them, such as *L'Escargot* (1953, London Tate) and *Memory of Oceania* (1953, New York MMA), though almost completely abstract, show a perfect discipline of form, and exhibit his love of simple line and bold colour contrasts at their purest.

Matisse made a large number of pen and pencil drawings. Some of his nude studies came dangerously close to banality, but he was most successful in rendering unexpected silhouettes and attitudes with a few brief, spontaneous strokes. He made over five-hundred engravings (etchings, woodcuts, and lithographs) and illustrated a number of books. He also produced a large number of sculptures in bronze, most of them female figures which are curiously tense and expressive, and show little trace of the graceful arabesques of his painting. The series of four bronzes, *The Back* (1909–29, London Tate), shows Matisse's

Henri Matisse: La Blouse roumaine *(1940, Paris MNAM); ph. Giraudon.*

power to transform an image from a naturalistic representation to a form of almost architectural solidity. Matisse was an articulate writer and formulated the theories which had made him the leader of a whole school of painting. He once declared: 'I cannot distinguish between the feeling I have for life and my manner of expressing that feeling. A design should possess a force of expansion which vivifies the things that surround it.' (*La Grande Revue*, 1908). Matisse has perhaps had more influence on 20th century art than any other master of the School of Paris, except Picasso. His bold logic, and his inventiveness in line and colour, have stimulated almost all painters since.

MATTA, real name Roberto Matta Eschaurren (1912–   ), Chilean painter. A student of architecture under Le Corbusier in Paris, he began to paint in 1938 and after moving to New York in 1939, he joined **Surrealism**. Matta called his pictures of this period 'inscapes', and they possess visionary qualities, in which totem-like forms (inspired by a visit to Mexico in 1941) loom in an indeterminate space created by clouds of shifting hue, *eg Here Sir Fire, Eat* (1942, New York MMA). The works of the succeeding years, *eg Vertu Noir* (1943, London Tate), also contain passages of very free handling (anticipating Abstract Expressionism) with sweeping calligraphic lines and eerily glowing scribbles like the 'white writing' of Tobey. In 1945, under the influence of his friend Duchamp, he introduced strange quasi-mechanical personages into his work, combining human and machine-like features in a nightmare space with apparently limitless perspectives. These works strongly influenced **Gorky**. Recently he has also executed sculptures.

MAURER, Alfred (1868–1932), American painter. The son of the German immigrant painter and lithographer Louis Maurer, he also trained as a lithographer. He was in Paris from 1897 to 1914 and studied briefly at the Académie Julian, but thereafter worked alone. His style at this time was naturalistic, influenced by Whistler, and his *Arrangement* (1901, New York, Whitney Museum) won the Gold Medal at the Carnegie Institute (1903). He was much influenced by the Fauves in 1905, and thereafter turned his back on naturalism, *eg Flowers* (1912, New York, Whitney Museum), gradually losing the popularity he had gained. In the 1920s, having returned to the US, he painted a number of rather melancholy figure paintings, such as *Self Portrait* (1927, Minneapolis, Walker Art Center), gradually moving towards Cubism, *eg Still Life with Doily* (1930, Washington, Phillips Collection).

MAXWELL, John (1905–62), Scottish painter. He studied at the Edinburgh College of Art and then in Paris, under Léger and Ozenfant. His mature style, however, inhabits the world of the imagination, in total contrast to the measured aesthetic of those artists. Certain recurrent themes (bouquets of flowers, birds, circus figures) are very similar to Redon and to Chagall, and yet Maxwell's heavy impasto, and rich jewel-like colour is his own, although other Scottish painters such as Philipson and Redpath have similar characteristics, *eg The Circus* (Glasgow Univ.), *Butterflies and Rose* (1959, Aberdeen AG).

MEADOWS, Bernard (1915–), English sculptor. He studied at the Norwich School of Art and then at the Royal College

of Art both before and after World War II. From 1936 to 1939 he was assistant to Henry Moore. He has exhibited at the Biennales of Antwerp, São Paulo and Venice (1952 and 1964). He became Professor of Sculpture at the Royal College of Art. Most of his work is in bronze and treats the human figure in heavy, chunky forms, with the torso being given much more bulk than the limbs, as in the work of Armitage and Butler. He has also used stylized animal motifs, *eg Four Reliefs* (1958, London Tate). His recent works often contrast highly polished round forms with the heavier bulky shapes of his earlier style.

MEDALLA, David (1942–), Filipino artist. Since coming to London in 1960, he has been extensively involved in Kinetic Art. His works tend to be unconventional in principle, very rough in manufacture, and to have an air of Dada. They include machines for pumping out clouds of foam, for making patterns in sand, and for painting with sponges dipped in mud.

MEDLEY, Robert (1905–), English painter. While studying at the Slade School (1924–6) and then in Paris, he painted in a somewhat Impressionist style, although using a very restricted palette, *eg Top Floor* (1929, Newport, Mon., AG). Much of his work before World War II was devoted to theatre design. Most of Medley's post-War work starts from a naturalistic subject and uses it to create a vital complex of tensions around and through the large empty spaces in the middle of the canvas, *eg The Perambulator* (1954, Birmingham City AG). In the early 1960s under the influence of American painting, he abandoned direct representation, working out his pictures solely in terms of patches of brightly coloured paint, set off against larger areas of less-defined painting as in *Figuration on White* (1963, London Tate). His recent work is **Hard-edge** and is concerned with spatial ambiguities: *Three over Four* (1970, London Tate).

MERZ, MERZBILDER, see **Schwitters.**

MESTROVIC, Ivan (1883–1962), Yugoslavian sculptor. He worked first as an apprentice with a stonemason in Split and then studied at the Vienna Art School until

1905. He spent the years 1907–9 in Paris, where he met Rodin and exhibited at the Salon d'Automne. When he returned to Yugoslavia, he settled in Zagreb. His sculpture celebrated the legendary heroes of his country and also religious themes. His *Monument to the Poet Botic* (1905) is at Split, and the *Statue of Bishop Stross-mayer* (1926) at Zagreb. His abstruse style, occasionally sentimental or given to over-statement, was nevertheless capable of epic monumentality, as in his *Monument to Yugoslavian Independence* with its figure moving forward into the wind in a manner recalling the *Winged Victory of Samothrace*. His *Self Portrait in Plaster* (1915) is in the Tate Gallery, London.

METAPHYSICAL PAINTING, see **Pittura Metafisica.**

METELLI, Orneore (1872–1922), Italian painter. He began to paint merely as a hobby. His large output consists mainly of town squares, bands and processions which, though Naive in their detail and inconsistencies of scale, generate an intense atmosphere in their design and restricted colouring not unlike that of De Chirico.

METZINGER, Jean (1883–1956), French painter and writer. Having begun as a follower of Neo-Impressionism and then of Fauvism, he joined **Cubism** in 1908 and concentrated on the geometrical aspects of painting. In 1911 he exhibited with the Cubists at the Salon des Indépendants, and also sent paintings to the exhibitions of the Section d'Or. With **Gleizes** in 1912 he published the first work on the new aesthetic, called 'De Cubisme', which brought him considerable notoriety. The best of his earlier work was closely related to Synthetic Cubism, bold, geometrical and having a subject clearly identifiable, *eg Still Life with Melons* (1916–17, Bremen, Kunsthalle). His objects were often surrounded by flat planes which were used to articulate the space in the picture: generally his colouring was strong, but this did not preclude subtle variation, as in *Woman with a Coffee-Pot* (1919, London Tate). Some of his earlier works also used Divisionist techniques, *eg Dancer in a café* (1912, Buffalo AG) which has much in common with the Futurism of Severini.

MEYER-AMDEN, Otto (1885–1933), Swiss painter. He worked for a time as a photographer's apprentice and studied at technical high school in Zurich. In 1912 he moved to the artists' colony of Amden. His composition and relation of light to surface planes show the influence of Cubism, and he was fond of domestic interiors with all the family present, or classes at the orphanage recollected from his childhood. His crayon drawings are perhaps his most expressive works: they depict almost exclusively the melancholy and mysterious environment of the family and other human groups suggesting that the group simultaneously protects and imprisons those who belong to it. Among his best works are *Woman Weaving* (1917–18, Zurich, Kunsthaus) and *Young Girl with Cups* (1918, Basle, Kunstmuseum).

MICHAUX, Henri (1899–), Belgian poet and artist. Best known as a Surrealist writer, his poems and paintings capture, snapshot fashion, his dreams and imaginative meanderings. His 'automatic' works in oil, watercolour, and pencil have had some influence on other artists. A feature of his style is his use of little splashes of ink which suggest an animated crowd of tiny people. Michaux has experimented with hallucinogens, such as mescalin. His creations sometimes achieve a unique obsessive quality.

MILLARES, Manola (1926–), Spanish painter. Starting as a landscape painter, he turned to Surrealism in 1948, and his work became completely abstract in 1949. His work has gradually developed in the direction of Abstract Expressionism. He uses unusual materials, such as sand, and torn and stitched canvas in conjunction with paint, in a similar fashion to Tapiès, *eg Painting 150* (1961, London Tate).

MILLES, Carl (1875–1955), Swedish sculptor. He was a carpenter's apprentice in Stockholm, but by 1899 he was exhibiting in Paris, where he lived from 1897 until 1904, and received lessons from Rodin. He taught at the Art School in Stockholm from 1920 to 1930, and then left for the United States. There, he received commissions for the *Peace Monument* for the City Hall in St. Paul, Minnesota, and for *Nature* for the Time and Life Building in

New York. He executed portraits of historical figures: realistic busts and slender alert,
rather academic, male studies. Two studies
for large fountains (*Europa and the Bull*,
Folke Filbyter, both 1924) are in the Tate
Gallery London, but the largest museum
collections of his works are at Gothenburg,
Kunstmuseum, and in his house in Lidingo,
near Stockholm.

MILLET, Jean François (1814–75),
French painter. He settled in the village of
Barbizon in the forest of Fontainebleau,
becoming one of the chief painters of the
'Barbizon School' (see **Daubigny**). However, in contrast to his companions,
Daubigny and Theodore Rousseau, he was
more concerned with portraying the country
people than the landscape. A peasant
himself, Millet produced unsentimental
works showing peasants at work in the
fields. His influence can be seen in the
work of van Gogh, Seurat and in the
approach to similar subjects by many
Expressionist painters. Although realistic in
treatment, Millet's works were not completely objective, for they generally carried
religious or allegorical overtones as though
illustrating a Biblical parable. Many of
Millet's late landscapes anticipated Impressionism in their light colouring and broken
brushstrokes.

MINAUX, André (1923–), French
painter. His early works, sombre in colour,
included a series of butcher's shop interiors.
A realist in intention, he turned to still lifes,
eg The Chair (1951, London Tate) and to
country scenes in gayer colours, with the
paint applied thickly in clearly outlined
areas.

MINIMAL ART, term coined in 1965 by
the American critic Richard Wollheim to
describe the most simple products of Pop
Art, such as the Brillo boxes of Warhol or
the exercise books and sheets of paper
painted by Alex Hay. He intended to
signify that these objects had minimal
value as works of art in themselves, but
were important in defining an attitude of
mind in the artist and spectator; it is thus
virtually synonymous with Conceptual Art.
The term has since proved applicable to
other art, having nothing to do with Pop,
produced in the 1960s. A number of artists
have recently been refining their formal

language so that each work comprises only
one or two essential elements which might
be machine-made (and often are). They
show no trace of the artist's 'workmanship',
but when arranged by the artist for exhibition, they make simple and possibly profound statements about space, volume,
light, colour, texture or material. These
works are a development of **Constructivism**. Because of its rejection of the
painterly, Minimal painting can be classed
as an aspect of **Post-Painterly Abstraction**. The most influential artists are
Barnett Newman and especially Ellsworth
Kelly, particularly in his monochromatic
works. The monochrome and black paintings of Ad Reinhardt and the near-
monochrome works of Jo Baer are the
successors of this. Similarly the simpler
works of Kenneth Noland and his followers
are related to this tendency. An example
was set in France by Dubuffet's texturo-
logies. The art of Yves Klein is also
Minimal, in its concentration on a single
technique and a single colour in each group
of works.

It is however, in sculpture that Minimal
Art has developed as a widespread move-
ment. The work of Anthony Caro and his
pupils in England, who include David
Annesley (*Orinoco*, 1965), Michael Bolus
(*Nenuphar*, 1963), Philip King (*And the
Birds began to sing*, 1964), and William
Tucker (*Memphis*, 1965; all four works in
London Tate), has given sculpture a new
simplicity and directness of means. The
real leaders of the school, however, are
Robert Morris and Donald Judd. Ronald
Bladen, Robert Grosvenor and Tony Smith
are all concerned with large, uncompromisingly simple, monumental solids, which
totally transform any room in which they
are placed. Carl Andre and Dan Flavin also
transform and articulate the gallery environment, but in an ephemeral way; Andre
arranges plain metal plates or bricks in
regular groupings on the floor; Flavin uses
ordinary commercial fluorescent tubes, fixed
at intervals to walls or floor. Sol Lewitt and
Robert Smithson are interested in series
works, incorporating permutations of simple
basic elements. Lewitt makes modular
open-grid constructions; Smithson is concerned with the rearrangement of solid
parts within a work or group of works.

MINNE, Georges (1866–1941), Belgian

Joan Miró: The Wall of the Moon *(ceramic panel, 1957, Paris UNESCO Building); ph. Giraudon.*

sculptor. In 1897 he sculpted *Agenouillé* (kneeling figure), an angular study of adolescence, and cast it in bronze for fountains at Brussels and Ghent. He went (1899) to live in Laethem-Saint-Martin, where he became the leader of a colony of artists who were interested in an idealistic style of painting. Under Constantin Meunier's influence, his art became gradually more realistic during the years 1908–22, eg *Le Débardeur* (1912). As a refugee in England in 1914, he expressed his anguish at the plight of his country in a series of *Pietà* drawings, and especially in a series of sculptures on the *Mother and Child* theme. In 1937 one of these became the monument to Queen Astrid at Antwerp. His work is characterized by sober, quasi-geometrical surfaces and his treatment of the human figure is hieratic, compassionate and dignified. The Folkwang Museum in Essen has a large collection of his works.

MIRO, Joan (1893–), Spanish painter. He studied at Barcelona Art School and then at the Galí Academy. His first canvases were painted around 1914 in a dramatic Expressionist style, whose convulsive linearity reflected the work of the Fauves. He met Picasso and the two became friends. After 1920 he spent the winters in Paris. At this time his style

resembled the simplified naturalism of Maria Blanchard; *The Ear of Corn* (1922, New York MMA) is an extreme example. *The Farmer's Wife* (1922, private collection) shows realistic elements beginning to combine with abstract ones and by 1924 he had arrived at his own individual style with the paintings *The Ploughed Field* (Pennsylvania, private collection) and *Catalan Landscape* (1924, New York MMA). In both works realistic and imaginary elements are portrayed in a spiky drawing style set against self-coloured backgrounds which are sometimes used to suggest space, sometimes flat planes. There are resemblances to **Surrealism**, and in fact he joined the group the following year. He continued to develop and refine this style until all objects were denoted by a type of filigree or by amoeba-like shapes.

After a journey to Holland in 1928, he painted the famous series of *Dutch Interiors* (one of which is in New York MMA); these transformations of 17th century Dutch originals provide, as it were, an excellent glossary of Miró's methods of transforming reality into symbol. In the following year he made a number of collages, reminiscent of Schwitters. The inspiration of Miró's art had been becoming more metaphysical and the links between the various symbol-

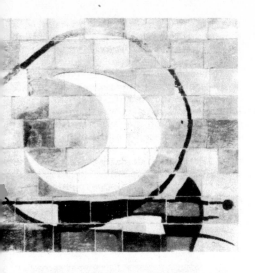

objects in his pictures were to be found less in the expression of any spatial or physical reality, than in a connection of ideas, often involving the contrast or comparison of several different elements: *Dog Barking at the Moon* (1926, Philadelphia MA) is an early example, and *Femmes, Oiseau au Clair de Lune* (1949, London Tate) a more recent one. He occasionally included words and phrases in his paintings, *eg Painting-poem: 'Une Etoile Caresse le Sein d'une Negresse'* (1938, New York, Pierre Matisse Gallery) which is related to **Calligraphic Painting**. In about 1940, when Miró returned to Spain, his paintings became more complicated, whether covering the entire picture surface in a network of signs as in the *Constellations* series (1940, several examples in the Pierre Matisse Gallery, New York) or in caricature figures set against an impalpable background, as in *Woman and Birds in Front of the Sun* (1942, Chicago Art Inst.).

In 1944 he produced his first ceramics and in 1945 a number of sculptures in terra-cotta, a medium he was to return to during the years 1956–62 (several examples in the Pierre Matisse Gallery, New York). As early as 1937 Miró had had a mural commissioned for the Universal Exhibition in Paris, and from about 1946

onwards his style gradually became broader and larger in scale. In 1947, on his first visit to the United States, he executed a mural at Cincinnati; another for Harvard University followed in 1950, and in 1957 he worked on two immense tiled walls for the UNESCO building in Paris, *The Wall of the Sun* and *The Wall of the Moon*. In the 1950s he frequently abandoned his spiky drawing style for a broad handling more akin to cave painting, as in *An Opening in the Sky Gives us Hope* (1954, New York, Pierre Matisse Gallery). His most recent work includes, together with painting and ceramics closer to his earlier style, huge canvases, which are completely abstract variations on a single colour, *eg Blue II* (1961, New York, Pierre Matisse Gallery). In Miró's art, as in Picasso's, one can see a reaction to most of the main artistic movements of the century, although the dominating force in his style is probably Surrealism, as Picasso's is Cubism. Unlike Picasso, Miró develops but has not changed his style. Each departure bears the stamp of his personality, although preventing him from sharing the other's genius.

MOBILE, a type of Kinetic sculpture. Mobiles are usually operated by natural draughts of air, but occasionally are motor-driven. The concept was introduced by **Alexander Calder** in 1932 and practised by other artists, notably Lynn Chadwick and Kenneth Martin.

MODERSOHN-BECKER, Paula (1876–1907), German painter. She had brief periods of art study in London and Berlin, and went to Paris four times from 1900 onwards, visiting the Académie Julian. In 1900 she married the painter Otto Modersohn. The principal influence on her art was the style of Gauguin and the Nabis, although she always retained her own muted colour, *eg Still-life with Blue and White China* (1900, Hanover, Landesgalerie). Her finest works were produced at the lonely heathland village of Worpswede, near Bremen. She painted simple compassionate portraits of peasants, with large melancholy features, as in *Old Peasant Woman* (1903, Hamburg Kunsthalle). These pictures used simple settings and clearly defined colour areas, but she became (*c* 1905) influenced by the painters of Die Brücke and adopted a bolder, more Expres-

Amedeo Modigliani: Paul Guillaume *(1915); ph. Lenoir.*

using the Cubist interest in surface as a means of obtaining that pure, flat line which characterized his later work.

He became addicted to alcohol and narcotics and was forced to sell for a few sous at café tables large numbers of quickly executed but wonderfully sensitive and expressive drawings. The dealer Zborowski gave him enough money to stay alive and in 1917 organized an exhibition of his work at the Berthe Weill gallery. Modigliani met Jeanne Hébuterne, a student at the Ecole des Arts Décoratifs, in 1918, and she bore him a child. Several painters were his friends, including Soutine, Pascin, and above all **Kisling**, with whom he worked and produced his series of large nudes. His

sionist style, while still retaining her natural objectivity, *eg Poorhouse Woman* (1907, Bremen Kunsthalle).

MODIGLIANI, Amedeo (1884–1920), Italian painter. He visited all the most important galleries in Italy with his widowed mother, who had him enrolled at art school in Florence, and then in Venice. His earliest paintings showed great technical skill in a Classical style. He went to Paris in 1906 where his work, consisting chiefly of figure studies, was influenced by Picasso and Toulouse-Lautrec. In 1907 he met Dr. Alexandre, who bought his first paintings, and he exhibited five paintings at the Salon des Indépendants, in a Cézannesque style, the next year. His friend **Brancusi** stimulated an interest in sculpture. This interest was short-lived, and most of his carvings in wood, marble and stone were left unfinished (*Head*, 1910, Washington NG; *Head*, 1912, New York, Guggenheim; *Head*, 1913, London Tate). These works, inspired to some extent by Negro sculpture and obviously influenced by Brancusi, are elongated, with the features indicated by clear-cut angular lines. Modigliani's painting style during this period was influenced by Cubism, *eg Bride and Groom* (1915, New York MMA), although he was already

Amedeo Modigliani: Nude *(1918); ph. Larousse.*

health deteriorated and he went to live (1918–19) in Nice and Cannes but, on his return to Paris, a prey to tuberculosis, he was admitted to hospital, where he died prematurely.

Modigliani concentrated almost exclusively on the human face and figure, and his work consists of portraits of women, children and young people, both working-class, *eg The Little Peasant* (1918, London Tate), and from the world of artists and writers, *eg Chaïm Soutine* (1917, Washington NG). He also painted several decorative figures, *eg Cariatide* (1912, Paris MNAM), not always very convincingly, and a series of large nude studies, such as *Seated Nude* (1912, London, Courtauld Galleries); *Seated Nude* (1917, Antwerp MBA). In these nudes his style was essentially linear, remarkable for its continuous flowing curves drawn with astonishing

elegance and precision, and with a predominance of ochre in the palette. Analogies have been suggested with earlier Italian painters, most obviously Botticelli. Modigliani, however, often used unexpected asymmetries and breaks in the line to set off its purity, and all his paintings exploited subtle spatial ambiguities and slight anatomical distortions to bring out the essential form in a manner developed from Cézanne, *eg The Large Nude* (1919, New York MMA). His portraits were far more varied in their means, although they almost all employed frontal poses which allowed the artist to achieve the same linear simplicity as in the nudes. Each painting conveys a deep insight into the personality of the sitter, and it was this, combined with the range of his subjects, which made Modigliani's portraiture probably the most important part of his work.

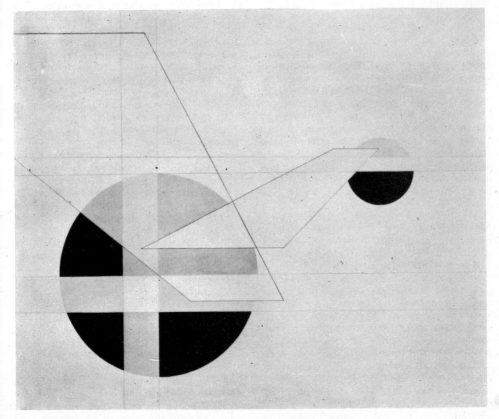

Laszlo Moholy-Nagy: composition.

MOHOLY-NAGY, Laszlo (1895–1946), Hungarian sculptor. He began by painting abstracts and then took up sculpture, both strictly Constructivist in theory, *eg K VII* (1922, London Tate). An exhibition of his work at the Der Sturm gallery in Berlin in 1922 led to his appointment by Gropius to teach at the **Bauhaus**. In 1932 and 1936 he took part in the Abstraction-Création exhibitions in Paris, and in 1937 he went to live in Chicago, where he founded the Institute of Design. The essentials of his teaching were contained in his book *Von Material Zu Architektur* (1929) in which he spoke of the necessity of getting away from the old distinction between 'fine' and 'applied' arts, and substituting an approach to art to be based on an understanding of the basic sensations of sight, touch, sound and smell, of the individual qualities of the materials used by the artist and craftsman, and of the tools and machines which he might employ to fashion them.

Moholy-Nagy's interest in light and movement led him to produce several Kinetic sculptures consisting of spirals and blocks of transparent material through which light bulbs projected images on to a wall (the Paris MNAM has a good example). His interest in space, and in the way in which paintings could create space, led to a series of *Space-Modulators*, combinations of paintings with semi-transparent three-dimensional elements, often interchangeable (New York MMA). After 1940 he produced sculptures in Plexiglass, *eg Double Ribbon* (1946, Munich NG), perforated by holes and lit by projectors. See illus. p. 161.

MONDRIAN, Piet (1872–1944), Dutch painter, originally Pieter Cornelis Mondriaan. He studied at the Amsterdam Academy (1892–5). Until 1906 he painted landscapes in a traditional, rather melancholy style dominated by grey and green tones. During this period, he led a solitary existence, following his passionate interests, religion and theosophy. In 1908 he met the painter Toorop, who introduced him to Divisionism and encouraged him to lighten his palette, *eg Hayricks* (1908, New York MMA). He went to Paris in 1911 and was fascinated by Cubism. His development at this stage was crucial to his later style. As early as 1909, as in *Church Tower at Domburg* (The Hague, Gemeente-

museum), he had set objects quite realistically painted against a background of sky subdivided in rectilinear areas, which seemed to follow a rhythm generated by the central object itself. In a series of paintings of trees, the same motif was transformed from the brightly coloured picture of a tree with branches silhouetted against the sky in the manner of van Gogh, *eg The Blue Tree* (1909, The Hague, Gemeente-museum), through works in which the branches could be conceived of as dividing the sky into interlocking fragments, to pictures such as *Flowering Trees* (1912, The Hague, Seggar Gallery) in which the sky had become the main subject, the sectioning branches being reduced to thin black lines similar to those in a Cubist painting and the colour similarly reduced to greys and ochres. In this short space of time, Mondrian apparently formed his basic philosophy of art, which was to reveal the underlying structure of the universe as something indicated by, but independent of, the objects which happened to be before his eyes (a philosophy, incidentally, which might be said to define Classicism in terms of 20th century art). He returned to Amsterdam in 1914, and in a number of seascapes, *eg Pier and Ocean* (1915, Otterloo RKM), he gradually reduced everything to a pattern of crossing horizontal and vertical lines on a near-monochrome background of great subtlety.

In 1917 Mondrian founded the review **De Stijl** with his friend van Doesburg; in it he published essays propounding the doctrines of abstract art, one of which, entitled 'Natural Reality and Abstract Reality', is basic to any study of the subject. For the rest of his life his pictures were expressions of an underlying structure of the universe in its purest form, horizontal and vertical lines which were conceived of as extending beyond the boundaries of the frame, and solid elements represented by rectangles of the three primary colours, red, blue and yellow; grey vanished from his work in 1922. He returned in 1919 to Paris, where his Neo-Plasticism influenced Léger and Baumeister, and his ideas on the subject were set out in *Neo-Plasticism* (1920), published by the Bauhaus in German in 1925. He set high aims for abstract art: 'Pure beauty is identical with what used in the past to be termed "the divine"; we poor human beings need it in order to live and retain our sense of balance.' He stopped contributing to De Stijl in 1924, considering the **Elementarism** of van Doesburg heretical. This in itself was proof of Mondrian's single-mindedness: van Doesburg had begun to employ diagonal lines in place of vertical and horizontal ones, in effect rotating a Mondrian picture by 45 degrees. If one considers Neo-Plasticism simply as a decorative device for dividing up the picture surface, such an alteration might seem insignificant, but for Mondrian the lines were essential structure revealed, but not created, by him as though each picture were a window upon absolute reality. His studio was frequented by a cosmopolitan group of artists and intellectuals including Moholy-Nagy, Marinetti, Arp, Pevsner, Gabo, Gropius and Katherine Dreyer. The latter introduced Mondrian's work to the United States in 1926, and Ben Nicholson did the same in Britain, where Mondrian lived for a time after 1938. In 1940 he went to New York, where he found many admirers and his style changed slightly: black was no longer used, and the paintings contained more yellow, red and blue lines, dissected into little rectangles, eg *Broadway-Boogie-Woogie* (1942–3, New York MMA).

The finish of Mondrian's paintings is so high that the slightest variation in the composition possesses great significance. During certain periods, in the rectangular paintings from 1929–32 for example, Mondrian frequently used large red rectangles which occupied two-thirds of the area of the canvas, sometimes leaving only an empty space filled with black lines and occasional areas of colour. The slight asymmetry of his compositions and his personal touch in applying the paint were the subjective elements in his style reflecting something of the restless quality of Mondrian's own mind. He is justly regarded as the greatest and most single-minded exponent of pure abstract art. Examples of his mature work are to be seen in Chicago (Art Inst.), Philadelphia (MA) and Yale University (AG), as well as in New York (MMA), London (Tate), and in Dutch and other European galleries.

MONET, Claude (1840–1926), French painter. The importance of Monet as an influence on 20th century art cannot be overestimated. It springs not only from his position as founder of **Impressionism** but also from the fact that he alone of the group showed a clear, single-minded development of its principles. Right up to his death in the second quarter of this century he continued to produce works which carried deeper and deeper his researches into light and colour, in strong contrast to the facile and picturesque work of many of his erstwhile colleagues. These later works, it is true, did not have a significant influence on the principal avant-garde movements at the beginning of the century (the art of **Fauvism** was probably the last which could be seen as a direct development of Impressionism), but their profound exploration, almost approaching abstract art, acted as an inspiration to many much later artists, especially the Abstract Expressionists. But these late works are perhaps a special case. The function of Impressionism in its heyday (1874–86), and of Monet's art in particular, was not only to extend the range of subjects open to the artist, thus continuing the battle for Realism against Academicism fought by **Courbet** and **Manet** but also to insist on a new method of seeing, and hence of painting, a sharp departure from academic techniques and preconceptions. Cézanne's famous comment, 'Monet is no more than an eye; but, my God, what an eye!', is relevant; Monet saw things which otherwise would not have been noticed, and in doing so opened the way to all sorts of further experiment into the relationships between colours and shapes, whether or not they were carried out with Monet's fundamentally representational aim.

As a boy in Le Havre Monet's drawings were sold in a local stationer's and noticed by Eugène Boudin who gave him lessons. In 1856 he went to study in Paris, where he met Pissarro, Renoir, Sisley and Bazille at the Ecole des Beaux-Arts. He used to paint in the forest of Fontainebleau, and in the summer at Sainte-Adresse on the coast, where he met Jongkind. His work of this period revealed a feeling for contemporary scenes akin to that of Manet or Courbet. His style, too, was related to Manet's broad handling and light bright colours laid side by side in flat areas, in a palette reminiscent of Corot's. His first major work, *Le Déjeuner sur l'Herbe* (1865, destroyed, but fragment in Paris Louvre; second version Moscow, Pushkin Museum), is obviously influenced by Manet's picture of the same name, though Manet ridiculed Monet's insistence on painting literally in the open air. Monet's style had a far greater lightness, freshness and open-air feeling, which remained its principal characteristics. In 1870 Monet went to London, where he was impressed by the work of Turner and in 1871 visited Holland. His paintings of this period generally employed much brighter, often garish, colours juxtaposed in broad brushstrokes like bars or slashes, *eg Houses at Zaandam* (1871, Frankfurt, Kunstinstitut). This new boldness went hand in hand with a greater emphasis on the picture surface and hence a flattening effect. Both may have been the result of an interest at about this time in Japanese prints. *eg La Japonaise* (1876, Boston MFA). Gradually his brushstrokes became smaller and more easily adapted to representing anything from the shimmer of light on water, as in *Argenteuil Bridge* (1874, Paris Louvre), to the effect of light filtered through the steam in a railway station, as in *Gare Saint-Lazare* (1877, Harvard, Fogg Museum); this was his Impressionist period proper.

Monet quarrelled with Degas in 1880 and did not show in any further Impressionist exhibitions, except that of 1882. From this time onwards he began the systematic development of his researches into colour which characterized his later years. His brushstrokes tended to become still smaller, and the range of colours used in building up an effect became wider and more unexpected. Many of the works of this time were of cliff scenes, *eg The Cliff Walk* (1882, Chicago Art Inst.); *La Manneforte* (1883, New York Metropolitan). However, from about 1890 he concentrated on definite series of paintings in which the same subject was painted again by different lighting conditions: the most famous were *Poplars* (1890–1, examples in London Tate, Edinburgh NG of Scotland and New·York Metropolitan), *Haystacks* (1889–93, examples at Cardiff National Museum and Farmington Hill-Stead Museum), and the façades of Rouen Cathedral of 1894 (large group in the Louvre, Paris and also in Boston MFA). In 1890 Monet had bought a property at Giverny and from 1899 to the end of his life (with the exception of a series of paintings of Venice and of

Claude Monet: Waterlilies *(detail, 1914–18, Paris, Orangerie).*

London) he concentrated almost exclusively on paintings of the waterlily garden there. The earlier paintings of this subject, such as *Le Bassin aux Nymphéas* (1899, London NG), did not mark any sharp break in his style, but gradually the perspective frame of the banks and the little bridge were cut down, the water surface became indistinguishable from the surface of the canvas, and that in turn seemed to dissolve in a constant shimmering of water, reflections of flowers and glimpses below the surface. The best of this series is in the specially-designed (but not very flattering) room in the Orangerie, Paris, but there are examples in New York (MMA), Chicago (Art Inst.) and elsewhere. These huge canvases cease to be merely a representation of something for the viewer to look at, but an experience of light and colour acting upon him and defying rationalization of what is being done to him and how.

MOORE, Henry (1898–   ), English sculptor. He lectured and then became a professor at the Royal College of Art (1926–39). His first one-man exhibition was held in 1928, when he was commissioned to sculpt a stone bas-relief, *The North Wind*, for the headquarters of the London Underground near St. James's Park. In 1940 he made a famous series of drawings in the London underground stations, which were being used as air-raid shelters, and the bulky, reclining, highly-draped forms of the sleepers recur frequently throughout his later work (the process of metamorphosis can be seen in a coloured drawing of 1940 in the Ashmolean Museum, Oxford). He won the Sculpture Prize at the Venice Biennale in 1948, and at São Paulo in 1953.

Henry Moore is undoubtedly the greatest sculptor working in Britain today. Although his work shows the influence of pre-Columbian art, Brancusi, Archipenko and Picasso, it is remarkably consistent. Although many of his works verge on the abstract, they are always based on one of a few simple anthropomorphic ideas. Whether there is an explicit human subject or not, Moore's sculptures also have a deliberate affinity with landscape and with natural shapes. His studio is full of pieces of bone and pebble which he has picked up and which give him ideas for his work. His work is seen best in open-air settings: the most striking example is the setting of one of the copies of *King and Queen* (1952–3) high up on a Scottish Moor above Dumfries. By far the most frequent of Moore's subjects has been the reclining figure, a pose with a tradition extending both from Roman river-gods and Mexican sculpture. Early examples such as *Reclining Woman* (1929, Leeds AG) or *Reclining Woman* (1930, Ottawa NG) are in one piece, solid and fairly naturalistic, although the head of the Leeds figure shows Cubist influences, and both owe something to the Neo-Classical phase of Picasso. A later group (examples in Buffalo AG, 1935; London Tate, 1938; Detroit Art Inst., 1939) introduces the characteristic Moore interplay of solid and void, with the figure pierced by holes. More recently these figures have been in two or three pieces

Henry Moore: Family *(bronze, 1950, British Council Collection).*

(examples at St. Louis Airport and Buffalo AG, 1959; Edinburgh Gallery of Modern Art, Otterloo RKM and New York MMA, 1960; Gothenburg Kunstmuseum MFA and Syracuse, Everson Museum, 1961; Leeds AG, 1962; and New York Lincoln Center, 1963–5). Each element is self-contained, like a pebble or piece of bone, but the group as a whole suggests a reclining figure.

Another theme which has developed in much the same way is that of *Mother and Child* which occurs both in nearly naturalistic versions (1924, Manchester City AG) and in abstracted versions, the idea being represented simply by a large and a small form, one fitting into the other, as in *Two Forms* (1934, New York MMA). There is also a 1939 version (in the artist's own collection) in one piece, in which the two 'heads' are connected together by wires, a technique exploited by Moore during the years 1937–40 (*cf The Bride*, 1939–40, New York MMA). A work which is also related to the maternal theme is *Internal and External Forms* (1954, Buffalo AG, small versions in Toronto AG, Basle Kunstmuseum and Providence, Rhode Island,

School of Design), in which a smaller shape nestles inside a big one which seems to enfold it protectively. This idea of interlocking pieces has recently become very important to Moore and most of his recent work employs rings, vertebrae or other shapes which fit together. Two fine examples of this are to be seen on the Thames Embankment in London, not far from the Tate Gallery, the *Locking Piece* (1963–4, near Vauxhall Bridge) and the *Knife-edge Two-piece* (1965, opposite the House of Lords).

MORANDI, Giorgio (1890–1964), Italian painter. He studied at art school in Bologna where he spent most of his life. He began to paint in 1911, at first influenced by reproductions of Cézanne, an influence which lasted all his life in his protracted search for Classical harmony in countless rearrangements of simple elements. His work up to about 1915 was also influenced by Cubism, *eg Still life* (1914, Paris MNAM). There were also a few landscapes, at this time as well as later in his career, in a restrained ochre and green palette, and with a balance of simple forms reminiscent of Corot, *eg Landscape* (1936, Rome GAM). Morandi's principal subject, however, was still life, generally arrangements of simple bottles and jars on a table-top, seen just below eye-level and painted against a plain background. From 1918 to 1922 when he belonged to the **Pittura Metafisica** and **Valori Plastici** groups, Morandi's still lifes had the hard-edged drawing associated with De Chirico, *eg Still Life* (1918, Leningrad, Hermitage). For most of his career he clung to the same style which he constantly refined, a cool palette of pale colours, a group of simple round objects with soft outlines, washed by a gentle raking light which brings out the forms and produces delicate modulations of colour. The *Still Life* of 1938 (New York MMA) is an unusually bold and freely painted example; the *Still Life* of 1946 (London Tate) and still more the *Still Life* of 1956 (Winterthur, Kunstmuseum) show what purity he could obtain. But to appreciate fully Morandi's constant research into the relationship between form and light, (a study as obsessive as Monet's paintings of haystacks), one has to see a large number of his works together in an exhibition in which the slight variations

have the effect of opening one's eyes to a new way of seeing.

MOREAU, Gustave (1826–98), French painter. Although he has influenced the course of 20th century art through the enlightened teaching and encouragement he gave to his many pupils, including Matisse, Marquet and Rouault, and although his influence extends to the present day, it is still difficult to classify his work. Moreau studied first at the Ecole des Beaux-Arts and later with Théodore Chassériau in 1848. Through Chassériau he was influenced by the style of Ingres, but also by the richer colour and freedom of handling of Eugène Delacroix. Moreau's earlier works, such as *Oedipus and the Sphinx* (1864, Paris Louvre) and *Salome Dancing before Herod* (*c* 1870, New York Hartford Collection), combined these influences and showed, too, characteristic passages of apparently vague painting with little clots of significant detail, reflecting the influence of Rembrandt. Moreau's public works such as these were almost all of literary subjects, portrayed imaginatively, as if in a dream, where every detail seemed to be the symbol of some concept enriching the picture. This feature of his work aligned Moreau with so-called **Symbolism**, and considerably influenced the **Nabis**. However, Moreau also produced a large number of watercolours and oil sketches which were never exhibited and which can now only be seen in the Moreau Museum, Paris. They show Moreau in a completely different light—as a plastic artist and technical innovator, as opposed to a *littérateur* who just happened to express himself in paint. The studies are mostly compositional sketches which show the general disposition of light and colour in the boldest possible way; some are completely abstract. The subject-pictures in water-colour, *eg* the comparatively restrained *Europa and the Bull* (Hartford, Wadsworth Atheneum), contain extraordinary juxtapositions of colour and a broken slashing technique; in some he even squeezed paint directly from the tube.

Finally, there are about 200 oil sketches which are just abstract patterns of colour and paint, all of which were handled with the greatest freedom and the paint in some even pulled about by the artist's fingers. It is not known what Moreau meant by these works, although he considered them important enough to mount and frame.

Nonetheless their influence, whether on Surrealism, Tachism or Abstract Expressionism is indisputable.

MORRIS, Robert (1931–), American sculptor. He studied at the Kansas City Art Institute, then in San Francisco, moving to New York in 1961 to study Art History. His first one-man exhibition was in 1963 and he took part in the 1968 Venice Biennale. Morris' output consists equally of works which relate him to **Conceptual Art**, such as the closed wooden box containing a tape recorder perpetually replaying the sounds of the box being made and of simple geometrical sculptures which have made him the leading sculptor of **Minimal Art**. Most of his works of the periods 1961–2 and 1964–6 consist of large-scale hard-edged polyhedrons in wood or metal in a style similar to that of Donald Judd. These are usually painted grey and may be resting on the floor, suspended from the ceiling or fastened on to the walls of a room in such a way as to alter its spatial properties; a few works also contain concealed lights, *eg Untitled* (1966, New York, Whitney Museum). In 1963 and 1964 he made a number of lead reliefs and other objects influenced by Jasper Johns, but without his highly personal execution so that the pieces appear solely as clear statements of ideas; *eg Three Rulers* (1963, private collection) which is a group of 36" rulers all of different lengths!

In 1967 Morris began making sculptures in heavy felt, coloured, cut into strips and hung from the walls or laid on the floor, *eg Felt Piece* (1967, London Tate); he intended these to be a sculptural equivalent of Morris Louis' paintings which are also formed by colour obeying the laws of gravity. At the same time he began to increase the range of materials used for his geometrical sculptures; there are examples, all untitled, in wire-mesh (1968 Oberlin), steel (1967, New York, Guggenheim) and fibreglass (1968, London Tate). Morris does not confine his energies merely to the making of art objects, however: in 1971 he created a kind of obstacle course in the Tate Gallery, London, in which participants could test their sense of balance, and could clamber up ropes or slide down pipes; he then created an Observatory for the International Sculpture Exhibition at Sonsbeez in Belgium—a kind of Stonehenge made by building great dykes of piled earth and reinforced concrete, orientated towards the rising of the sun.

MORTENSEN, Richard (1910–), Danish painter of the School of Paris. Influenced by Kandinsky, he produced his first abstract paintings in 1933, *eg Spatial Composition in Blue* (1933, Copenhagen, Statens Museum). He went to Paris for the first time in 1937, settling there permanently in 1947. His paintings during the war years were tormented and harsh, *eg Night Sacrifice* (1945, Copenhagen, Stateus Museum). In more recent years, however, he has produced large canvases in which the colours interlock in a flat pattern of straight lines, somewhat resembling the later *papiers coupés* of Matisse, though containing some subtle spatial allusions. His colour-schemes are varied, but always dry and refined, *eg Corneilles* (1956, Aarhus, Kunstmuseum).

MOSES, Anna Mary Robertson (1860–1961), American painter, known as 'Grandma' Moses. She was a servant at the age of twelve, became a farmer herself in Virginia, and, after 1905, ran a dairy farm north of New York. In 1930 when her hands became too stiff for embroidery she began to concentrate on painting. An exhibition of her work in a chemist's shop attracted the attention of a collector in 1938, her work was reproduced on Christmas cards in 1946, and she became well-known. Grandma Moses' paintings depict local customs and scenes of her childhood, as in *Making Maple Syrup* and *Thanksgiving* (1955). Her paintings consist principally of vast landscapes, dotted with rural houses and peopled with figures and animals. Her art is fresh and unsophisticated, resembling that of the Elder Bruegel, and she shared many of his most valuable qualities. She had the same ability to relate detail to broadly-conceived mass, the same remarkable sensitivity to changes in the seasons and weather, the same sense of colour, brilliant but never garish, and the same panoramic views, not only of landscape but also of humanity, which she observed with a detachment neither supercilious nor patronising. She was the most famous American **Naive** painter. However, it must be admitted that, despite these real qualities, her success in the United States lies partly in the fact that her paintings evoke a nostalgia for the 'good old days' in American life.

MOTHERWELL, Robert (1915–), American painter. One of the leaders of **Abstract Expressionism** in New York, he has pursued a perfectly consistent development in the last decade. He is remarkable for the range of his style and technique, which has included brilliant colour and austere monochrome, Hard-edge Painting and **Action Painting**, and figurative, collage and abstract approaches. Yet each work shows a boldness of execution and a sense of importance as to content. Motherwell graduated at Stanford University. He travelled to Europe in the summers of 1935, 1938 and 1939, and became interested in Delacroix. In 1940 he went to New York and attended Columbia University. His interest in Surrealism was reinforced by meeting many European expatriate artists, and in 1941 he worked in Mexico with Matta. He first exhibited in the International Surrealist Exhibition in New York in 1942. His work of this period belongs to near-abstract Surrealism, and is generally a collage or painted juxtaposition of contrasted passages, some with a figurative implication and some without, eg *The Joy of Living* (1943, Baltimore MA); *Pancho Villa, Dead or Alive* (1943, New York MMA). In these works Motherwell consciously looks beyond Surrealism to Symbolism both in his use of combinations of evocative, if irrational images, and in his great dependence on colour, an influence he acknowledged in *Mallarmé's Swan* (1944–71, Cleveland MA). This awareness of tradition is characteristic of Motherwell, and from 1944 to 1951 he was editor of the important series of reprints of the manifestoes of Modern Art, *The Documents of Modern Art*.

In 1948 he opened an art school with Baziotes, Newman and Rothko. He began to paint a few more nearly geometrical paintings (somewhat influenced by Klee) without figurative reference, eg *Western Air* (1946–71, New York MMA). On the other hand, in 1948 he also began a series of paintings

in black and white called 'Elegy to the Spanish Republic', eg *Elegy IV* (1955–60, Cleveland MA). These paintings, which continued alongside his other work for several years, anticipated the similar work in black and white begun around 1950 by Pollock, Kline and de Kooning. These pictures are large and very simple, consisting of a few broad bands of black linked by black ovals of equivalent scale, forming a balanced image which is both monumental in form and also a symbol of the relationship between life and death. Motherwell has done several other black and white series since, exploring the techniques of Action Painting. At the same time, he has continued his interest in collages, though making them simpler and more painterly, eg *N.R.F. Collage No. 2* (1960, New York, Whitney Museum). Since 1955, he has made regular trips to Spain and Italy, and the experience gave rise to a number of very large paintings in bright contrasted colours rather like the late collages of Matisse; only the flag shapes suggest that there is some political or ethical idea in the artist's mind, as in *Dublin 1916 with Black and Tan* (1964, artist's collection). Motherwell's recent *Open* series marks a new simplicity in his work and consists of large fields of a single colour with only one or two smallish rectangular areas separated off, eg *Open 122, in Scarlet and Blue* (1969, London Tate). In 1958, he married **Helen Frankenthaler**.

MOYNIHAN, Rodrigo (1910–), British painter of Irish-Spanish descent. After a childhood in England, the U.S. and Rome, he settled in London in 1928 and studied at the Slade School. He became a member of the London Group in 1933, and was Professor of Painting at the Royal College of Art from 1948 until 1957, when he went to live in France. The bulk of Moynihan's work is figurative, though he produced non-representational works in the 1930s, eg *Objective Abstraction* (1935–6, London Tate) and returned to abstraction again in 1956. His painting is rich in colour and texture and, as he says, derives from Impressionism in that it grows out of the paint-and-canvas rather than as an attempt to impose a preconceived idea. This is especially true of his abstract work, eg *Yellow and Violet* (1957, London Tate).

In recent years Moynihan has practised a form of Tachism.

MULLER, Otto (1874–1930), German painter. At first an apprentice lithographer, he studied at the Academy in Dresden. Up to about 1920 his style resembled that of the painters of **Die Brücke**, to which he belonged from 1910 to 1912. Most of his works at this time were female nudes which he painted in idyllic settings, eg *Nudes in the Dunes* (1911, Hamburg, Kunsthalle), and with a happy lyricism totally different from the paintings of his Expressionist contemporaries. Müller's people, whether in paintings or in his numerous prints, shine with a quiet enjoyment of life and a non-prurient sexuality that is most appealing. From about 1920 he began to paint gypsies more and more frequently; his colours became deeper and richer and his handling more firm. These works, in which an interest in colour pattern took over from the airy space of his earlier pieces, were obviously influenced by Gauguin, eg *Gypsies and Sunflower* (1927, Saarbrücken Museum), *Gypsy Madonna* (1927, Darmstadt Landesmuseum).

MUNCH, Edvard (1863–1944), Norwegian painter. He enrolled at the School of Arts and Crafts, Oslo, and was soon leader of a young group of revolutionary painters. On a visit to Paris in 1885 he was deeply impressed by the Rembrandts he saw in the Louvre, but when he returned there in 1890 he became interested in van Gogh, Seurat, Gauguin and Toulouse-Lautrec: under their influence, his palette became lighter and more vivid. An important exhibition of his work held at the request of the Artists' Society of Berlin, where he lived from 1892 to 1895, provoked such an outcry that it had to be closed the day after the opening; but this episode made him well-known. His obsession with tragic subjects had already been apparent in *The Sick Child* (1885–6, Oslo NG; version in London Tate) and was later confirmed in such paintings as *The Room of Death* (1894–5, Oslo NG) and *The Dead Mother* (1900, Bremen Kunsthalle). Such pictures are generally considered among the parent works of **Expressionism**, and yet it is important that in these, as indeed in most of his works, the emotion is implicit rather than explicit. Munch used a palette composed of rather acid colours contrasted with heavy blacks; his paint was sometimes overworked, sometimes loosely handled, but always with a prominent surface texture; his perspective was tilted so that the figures, disposed in planes parallel to the frame, seem unnaturally close to the observer yet not close to each other, as though seen through a telephoto lens; finally, his asymmetric composition and trick of separating the figures into unconnected planes makes one conscious of the atmosphere surrounding them, very often in terms of an almost tangible silence (compare later, **De Chirico** and **Delvaux**). Munch's most famous work, *The Cry* (1893, Oslo NG; also in lithograph), again made use of the metaphor of sound, though this was one of the comparatively few works in which the sound, and hence the emotion, was made explicit. Munch explained, however, that the title refers to 'the great cry I feel throughout Nature' and that the woman was just a symbol of this, an explanation linking him with **Symbolism** and with the use of symbols by Ibsen and Strindberg.

A sense of an impalpable power in nature added overtones to a number of paintings which were not explicit, such as *The Voice* (1893, Boston MFA), and to the landscapes without figures he painted around 1900, eg *Summer Night at the Shore* (1902, Vienna, Kunsthistorisches Museum), especially as they exploited the curious half-light of the Scandinavian summer evening. Many of these subjects were painted as part of one of a number of series entitled *The Frieze of Life* ('a poem of life, love and death'), executed between 1893 and 1906. By this time he had numerous followers in Germany including Kirchner, Nolde and Kokoschka. In 1908, however, a serious nervous crisis led to his return to Norway where he spent six months in a clinic. He never again left his native country. From 1909–11 he was occupied in painting symbolical mural decorations, dominated by a huge sun, for Oslo University. These, and his other works at this time, were much more luminous, executed in bright colours juxtaposed in a manner owing a lot to van Gogh and to the Fauves. During his last year, however, Munch painted a series of self-portraits, one of which, *Wandering in the Night* (1939, Oslo, Munch Museum) was as violently Expressionistic as his early work. The tortuous, linear compositions of many of Munch's works may superficially resemble Art Nouveau, but he used line and colour expressively, not as mere decoration. Despite his view that natural forms often symbolized malevolent or dreamlike qualities, Munch was a real painter, and his subjects were expressed primarily in plastic terms.

MUNTER, Gabriele (1877–1962), German painter. She studied in Munich, first at small art schools, then with Kandinsky, with whom she lived until 1914. Although a member of the **Blaue Reiter** movement, she did not enter fully into the development of its style along Cubist lines. Her best works were Expressionist in their simplified drawing and strong, flat colours, but she also had a strong sense of form and a feeling of repose both in her choice of subjects and in her colour harmonies, *eg Still life in Grey* (1910), *Meditation* (1917), both in the Civic Gallery, Munich.

MUSEUMS. Only within the last 150 or 200 years has the idea of the public museum of art arisen. Most of the great galleries of the world developed from the nucleus of a private collection, to which other pictures have been added. The Louvre in Paris, for example, contains the art treasures of the French crown, together with works confiscated by Napoleon during his conquests in Italy and elsewhere. As a museum gains reputation, private collectors become more willing to bequeath works, both as a posthumous proof of their ability as collectors and because they know the pictures will be respected. The situation alters, however, with 20th century art. There are many private collections, but in most cases the original owners are still alive and there is no ready-made equivalent of the royal collections to act as a nucleus for gifts and bequests. In some cases, a private collector has built his own museum and opened his collection to the public: this is the origin of the Maeght Foundation at Vence and the Solomon Guggenheim Museum in New York. Other collectors have entrusted their collections, not to established galleries, but to other institutions which will put them on display: the Courtauld Collection in the University of London is a case in point. By and large, it has been the responsibility of far-seeing national and municipal authorities to found modern art museums and buy works for them. Most modern art museums are of fairly recent origin and have a long way to go before they could be said to have formed really representative collections. A few exceptional public collections do exist, notably in New York, Philadelphia, London, Amsterdam, Basle and Zurich, but not all the major works by a modern artist are in public institutions, as would be the case with a Renaissance or Baroque artist.

For many artists at the beginning of the century, museums were mausoleums of the past and an impediment to progress: the Futurists wanted to burn them down. Other artists, however, such as Cézanne, while seeing a distinction between the 'art of the museums' and that of the present, wanted to reconcile the two. Today, the directors of the most successful museums of contemporary art see the necessity to make these live, rather than dead, institutions. A great example was set by the Stedelijk Museum at Amsterdam which, under its former director, Sandberg, pioneered a series of developments of layout and lighting, and a policy of catering for all sections of the community. Similarly, the Museum of Modern Art in New York conceives its responsibility to extend to all branches of contemporary art, including cinema, photography and theatre, and the wealth of its amenities makes it resemble a large club.

MUSIC, Antonio (1909–), Yugoslav painter born in Italy. His abstract style developed from a series of landscapes in which the hills were treated schematically as striped rounded forms; from about 1950 these forms and related shapes were deployed on a plain background. The painting gradually became softer and by 1955 the entire picture surface had taken on a vaguely striated or globular texture with subtle colouring which gives the impression of a natural material. In the last few years the landscape motif has become explicit once more, and horses are frequently introduced into the paintings. Musič, who lives in Venice, has won several prizes at the Biennale there.

N

NABIS, The (Hebrew, 'prophets'), name given by the poet Cazalis to a group of young artists of the last decade of the 19th century who had a considerable influence on 20th century painting. **Sérusier** met Gauguin in September, 1888, and on the latter's advice produced a painting on board, *Bois d'Amour* (Paris, private collection), which juxtaposed areas of pure colour. Sérusier showed this picture to friends at the Académie Julian, **Bonnard**, Ibels, Ranson and **Maurice Denis**, and it became the 'Talisman' of the Nabis. It inspired Denis' definition '. . . before being a charger, a nude or an anecdote, a picture is essentially a flat surface covered by colours arranged in a certain order.' Several students from the Ecole des Beaux-Arts, including Vuillard, Roussel and Piot, Verkade, Vallotton, Maillol, and Rippl-Rónai also joined the group. The entire group met every Saturday in Ranson's studio, which became known as 'the temple', where they were sometimes joined by Gauguin. They also held meetings in Père Tanguy's shop, where they saw paintings by Cézanne and van Gogh, and at the house of their own dealer Le Barc de Boutteville. They held exhibitions on the premises of the *Revue Blanche* (1891–7), also visited by Toulouse-Lautrec and the Symbolist writers. The Nabis aesthetic extolled flat application of colour, a style of composition influenced by Japanese prints (Bonnard was known as the 'Nipponizing Nabi'), and a full, flowering use of outline which had affinities with the style of Art Nouveau. These painters, from middle-class backgrounds, tended to paint scenes of family and city life. The Nabis heralded a revolution in decorative art and their work in the fields of book illustration, stage design and stained glass, was highly significant. Yet another characteristic of the group was the mysticism of certain of its members, especially Sérusier and Maurice Denis. Verkade became a monk and Maurice Denis devoted the latter part of his career to reviving religious art, working with the monks of the Abbey of Beuron. The Nabis are sometimes rather superficially regarded as a link between Neo-Impressionism and Fauvism, but this does scant justice to their inspiration.

NADELMAN, Elie (1885–1946), American sculptor, born in Poland. He worked in Munich and Paris before settling in the United States in 1914. His early style, based on Classical and pre-Classical Greek models, had an elegant smoothness. He did, however, produce a few works in a more chunky style, *eg Standing Bull* (1915, New York MMA). In 1915 he exhibited *Man in the Open Air* (New York MMA), an elegant figure whose smooth lines are broken only by a bowler hat and bow tie. The wit of this work links it with the American Dada movement, but he went on to develop a refined Classical yet unmistakably contemporary, even urbane style. This he used for portraits and many models of dancers and athletes.

NAIVE ART. In the twentieth century, considerable interest has been shown in the work of non-professional painters who, by the freshness of their vision, have shown artists of more conventional upbringing how to free themselves from traditional preconceptions. The term 'naive' is unsatisfactory; even more so is the description 'primitive' as this creates the possibility of confusion with the art of peoples whose society is less 'civilized' in the Western sense of the word. There is, in fact, no adequate objective term; even 'amateur' is inaccurate as many of these artists came to make a living from painting once they had established a reputation. Some of the artists even had a conventional art school training, but without losing their primitive vision. It is not possible to write a meaningful history of naive art as each artist is essentially solitary. Artists who are identified with the genre are those who happen to have been discovered and the amount of critical attention given to different artists and different nationalities is not often reliable as a guide to quality. Value judgments are suspect, as is the term 'naive' itself: such artists are not 'naive' themselves—their standards are merely different from those of the 'professional' art world.

It was in France that interest in naive painting first developed. The earliest painter to achieve fame, and the best known was **Henri Rousseau** who was taken up by Gauguin, Picasso and many of the avant-garde. The critic Wilhelm Uhde met him in 1907 and began to write about his work and about that of the other primitives he

Camille Bombois: The Strongman *(c 1930, Paris MNAM); ph. Giraudon.*

Louis Vivin: Cathédrale Notre-Dame de Paris *(c 1930, Paris MNAM); ph. Giraudon.*

discovered, among them Séraphine de Senlis, Bombois, Bauchant and Vivin. In Britain there has been less interest in naive painting, although one artist, Alfred Wallis, has had a considerable influence since his discovery by Ben Nicholson and Christopher Wood, and his adoption by the St. Ives School. The Glasgow painter Scottie Wilson has also had success with his Klee-like hieroglyphic painting. There have been comparatively few naive artists to emerge from Italy, perhaps because an awareness of the national cultural heritage forms part of the birthright of every Italian. However the work of Orneore Metelli is also of exceptional quality. Whereas most French and European primitives were painting within a highly cultivated milieu, the tradition of painting in the United States dates from the first settlers, among whom the painter was a humble craftsman, for example the builder or the cabinet maker. Nonetheless certain artists continued in this tradition alongside others working in a European style. Of these, the most important was Edward Hicks (1780–1840) who portrayed an idealized America in which man and all species of animal could co-exist happily (he did many versions of The Peaceable Kingdom). His popularity stems from the importance of the vision he brought to American mythology as well as from his undeniable technical ability. In the 20th century the best known include 'Grandma' Moses, Hirshfield and Pippin. The humanitarianism of John Kane (*Self-Portrait*, 1929, New York MMA) and the extraordinary technique and fine detail of Joseph Pickett (*eg Manchester Valley*, 1914–18, New York MMA) are also notable. In different ways the folk art of other countries has given rise to local strains of naive art, for example in Haiti where a group of artists has grown up around Hyppolite.

By attempting a complete record of their subject without the benefit of a traditional training, naive artists often invent new ideograms for things which, in turn, suggest new departures. Their frequent use of boldly contrasting colours parallels Fauvism. They sometimes represent what they know as opposed to what they see, showing several aspects of an object superimposed, a practice of interest to the Cubists. The inconsistencies and inconsequentialities of many of their paintings are in effect a kind of Surrealism. Painters such as Walkowitz, Lowry and Dubuffet consciously imitated naive painting in order to achieve intellectually controlled effects. Undoubtedly the finest primitives, *eg* Rousseau and Hicks, have been those who have brought to their painstaking portrayal some outstanding quality of imagination. Their reverence for the qualities of the object as a thing with its own identity has appeal for Dada artists, exponents of Pop Art and other modern realistic movements.

NAKIAN, Reuben (1897–   ), American sculptor. The son of Armenian immigrant parents, he made a living from 1912 doing lettering and posters. In 1916 he became an apprentice of the sculptor Paul Manship whose assistant, Gaston Lachaise, taught him a variety of sculptural techniques. His early work, which became very popular, consisted mainly of animal sculptures, stylized in the manner of Brancusi, *eg Seal* (1930, New York, Whitney Museum). In 1932 he began a series of portrait busts which are realistic yet have far greater spatial complexity, as *'Pop' Hart* (1932, New York MMA). In 1935 he met Gorky and in 1937 de Kooning, possibly encouraged by them, he took a completely new direction in his work and explored the area between figurative sculpture and Abstract Expressionism. Most of his post-War works are grouped in series: first as fairly naturalistic drawings on paper or scratched on the surface of terra cotta, then treated three-dimensionally in terra cotta or plaster. The distortions of the forms are derived from Rodin and Rosso; the final works are generally executed on a gigantic scale in curved steel plates welded onto a network of rods. There may also be a series of near-abstract wash drawings exploring the ultimate relationship of the shapes but making use of chance effects at the drawing stage. Various stages of this evolution can be seen in the studies for *The Rape of Lucrece* (1955–8) at the New York MMA, and in those for *The Duchess of Alba* (1959) at the County Museum, Los Angeles.

NASH, John (1893–   ), English painter. Unlike his elder brother **Paul Nash**, he did not formally prepare for a career in art. He began to paint and draw on his own and first exhibited in 1913, with his brother. He was a member of the London Group and Official War Artist. His true métier is as a landscape painter, both in oil and watercolour. Many of his paintings are in the tradition of Constable, but they are generally arranged more formally with large, clear shapes, sometimes glowing with an unexpected almost mystical light, *eg Cornfield* (1918, London Tate), *Upper Water* (1933, Leeds City AG).

NASH, Paul (1889–1946), English painter. He studied at the Slade School, London and was an Official War Artist in both World Wars. His varied talent was applied to painting in oils and watercolour, to textiles and ceramics. His mystical turn of mind reveals the influence of William Blake. His paintings of World War I are fairly realistic, and sum up with unrivalled power the utter desolation of the devastated battlefields, as in *In the Year of Our Lord 1917* (Ottawa NG), *We are making a New World* (1918, London, Imperial War Museum). After the War he painted a number of landscapes which approach abstraction, *eg Winter Sea* (1925, York City AG), *Nostalgic Landscape* (1928–9, Fredericton, New Brunswick, Beaverbrook Art Gallery), *Voyages of the Moon* (1934, London Tate). After this last picture, one of his few pure abstracts, he returned to more naturalistic landscapes which combined disparate images in a Surrealist manner (he exhibited with the Surrealists in 1936 and 1938), *eg Landscape from a Dream* (1938, London Tate), *Landscape of the Megaliths* (1937, Buffalo AG), *Monster Field* (1939, Durban AG). These culminated in his masterpiece *Totes Meer* (1940–1, London Tate) in which the whole landscape seems to be made of wrecked German aircraft, covered with ice and lit by the wan moon. Nash excelled as a war artist, his other works being of secondary importance, but he had a considerable influence on other British artists, among them Sutherland and Piper.

NAY, Ernst Wilhelm (1902–   ), German painter. From 1925 to 1928 he studied with Hofer, whose influence contributed towards a short period of **Surrealism**. Nay's real development began however, in 1936–7 when he was painting in

Norway. In a number of seascapes, *eg Fishermen's Departure* (1936, Hanover, Landesgalerie) and even more in the landscapes of the Lofoten Islands, he employed a stark style derived from German Expressionism, the colour element achieving a great measure of independence from the motif represented. This was developed in the mid-1940s in a series of works in which a Cubist figuration provided an armature for the colour, *eg The Source* (1947, Hamburg, Kunsthalle); *With Blue Dominant* (1951, Hanover, Landesgalerie). By the mid-1950s all external structure had disappeared, his pictures being formed of patches of pure colour, as in *Flaming Yellow* (1956, Bremen, Kunsthalle). Nay then developed a personal Abstract Expressionism, somewhat similar to the style of Sam Francis, but quite independent.

NEO-CLASSICISM, stylistic term used to describe a return to the principles of Greek and Roman art. Although the Classical spirit has, in one way or another, informed the art of many periods, notably that of the Renaissance, the term 'Neo-Classicism' is generally used of art which makes a clear-cut reaction against the prevailing style of its time in favour of greater simplicity and nobility. The term is mostly used of the work of some later 18th and early 19th century artists (for example Flaxman and Ingres) coinciding with the rediscovery of Classical Greek, as opposed to Roman, art. It is often also applied to a tendency in modern art shortly after World War I.

Most of the revolutionary movements in modern art occurred during the first 15 years of the century, and this period was followed generally by a period of retrenchment. Although most Constructivist artists, having already broken through to a style of extreme simplicity, were able to continue in the same direction, many other artists returned to the figurative image and developed a monumental style, purged of irrelevancies. This was particularly true of Picasso, in such works as *Seated Woman* (1923, London Tate) and *Two Seated Women* (1920, New York MMA); Braque was influenced to a certain extent, *eg Nude.*(1925, London Tate). The other main exponent of this style in France was Derain, but most of the artists who had flirted with Cubism moved in a similar direction.

It is also notable that it was in this climate that the mature style of Modigliani and that of several sculptors such as Maillol, Bourdelle and Despiau, was able to develop, although in none of these cases was there any question of a reaction against a previous revolutionary phase. A considerable influence on the French artists was Italian art, not only of the past but of their contemporaries. **De Chirico** had always proclaimed himself a Classical painter, and this became more clear in his figure paintings of the 1920s. He was followed by Casorati, Campigli, Carrà and Severini.

NEO-IMPRESSIONISM, term used by the critic Fénéon in the Brussels review *L'Art Moderne* in 1886 to describe the movement founded by **Seurat, Signac** and their friends. The article was enlarged and published in 1887 as *Neo-Impressionism*. The movement began as a revolt against Impressionism. Its aim was to introduce scientific exactitude to art by the minute study of optical phenomena. The tenets of the movement are further described under **Divisionism**. The masterpiece of this new doctrine was Seurat's *Un Après-midi à la Grande Jatte* (Chicago Art Inst.), exhibited at the last Impressionist exhibition in 1886. It graphically illustrated the gulf which had opened between the 'romantic' and the 'scientific' Impressionists (to use Pissarro's terms). The Neo-Impressionists first exhibited as a group at the second Salon des Indépendants (1886). Apart from Seurat and Signac, it included Henri Delacroix (Cross), Charles Angrand, Dubois-Pillet, Camille Pissarro, who adopted Neo-Impressionism for a period, and his son Lucien Pissarro. In 1887, the Neo-Impressionists were invited to exhibit with the Société des XX in Brussels, where they converted van Rysselberghe and Henry van de Velde, while in France the group was joined by Petitjean, Maximilien Luce and Lucie Cousturier. The movement was equally successful in Italy, where its followers Segantini, Previati and Morbelli exhibited in Milan in 1891. An Academic Divisionism was practised by such painters as Henri Martin and Le Sidaner, who attempted to popularize and sweeten the style. After 1900, pure Divisionism was only practised by Signac and some of his friends. But the movement led directly on to **Fauvism**; Matisse adopted a Pointillist style when he was painting with Signac and Cross at Saint-Tropez in 1904. The contribution of the other members of the movement did not reach Seurat's level, their claims to an art of scientific exactness soon being repudiated by later movements.

NEO-PLASTICISM, name given by Mondrian to his style of painting in 1920; more generally applicable to all work produced by the **De Stijl** movement. It can be seen as an extreme development of Analytical Cubism and is based on the suggestion that if the complexities of a motif can be analyzed in straight lines and interlocking planes, they can be expressed more simply by an even more severely limited vocabulary of horizontal and vertical lines only, which might more clearly reveal the underlying harmony in the motif. Further, this harmony (revealed by rigorous analysis of the motif) could be expressed with no reference at all to the motif. Mondrian tried to express a harmony of elements giving the greatest possible contrast to each other, using only horizontal and vertical lines, the three primary colours red, blue and yellow, and three non-colours, black, grey and white. These ideas had lasting influence, especially on the applied arts, but Mondrian and his immediate followers such as Diller were the only ones to continue to apply them in this pure form.

NEVELSON, Louise (1900–), American sculptor, born in Russia. She has studied at the Art Students' League in New York, with Hans Hofmann in Munich, and in Mexico with Diego Rivera (1932–3). She had her first show in New York in 1936. By 1941 she was experimenting with Kinetic sculpture and with light and sound in the presentation of her works. Her 'Sculpture Montages' date from 1944 and are **Assemblages** of wooden junk. As well as rough unfinished timber, she uses balusters, table legs, chair backs and seats, *etc.* They are assembled in low relief in a number of shallow boxes, fitted together vertically to make a wall, and painted uniformly in black, white or gold, *eg Black Wall* (1959, London Tate). At the Venice Biennale in 1962, Nevelson exhibited works of one colour altogether, filtering the lighting in each room to create a different environment in each case. These walls are impressive and rather disturbing when seen in large units; the shock as one recognizes the source of individual components contrasts strangely with the mysterious depths of the relief and the neutralizing effect of the painting. More recently she has made much more open walls using hollow forms that one can see through as in *Atmosphere and Environment I* (1966, New York MMA) and in 1967 exhibited some *Ice Palaces* in engraved clear Plexiglass, returning to the purity of Neo-Plasticism: *Transparent Sculpture V* (1967, Otterloo, Kröller-Müller Museum).

NEVINSON, Christopher Richard Wynne (1889–1946), English painter. He studied at the Slade School and the Académie Julian, Paris, where he shared (1912–13) a studio with Modigliani. He met Marinetti in Paris and became the chief English disciple of **Futurism**, publishing with him the manifesto *Vital English Art*. He also exhibited with the Vorticists. The most striking work of this period was *The Arrival* (1913, London Tate), a simultaneous composition of various aspects of a steamer and pier, obviously influenced by Boccioni, though more geometric in composition. In 1917 he became an Official War Artist and produced a number of broadly realistic works full of disillusionment, *eg A Taube* (1918, London, Imperial War Museum). The most impressive paintings were those made while still under the influence of Futurism, the jagged pattern of which increases the force of the grim reality represented, as in *La Mitrailleuse* (1915, London Tate). In 1919 and 1920 he visited the U.S., producing paintings which powerfully express the loneliness of big cities, *eg Wall Street* (1919, Birmingham City AG). Much of Nevinson's subsequent work was more lyrical, and by 1925 he had almost completely dropped Futurist stylizations.

NEWMAN, Barnett (1905–1970), American painter. He studied at New York City College, Cornell University and the Art Students League. In 1948 he joined Baziotes, Motherwell and Rothko in founding an art school in New York. Newman is utterly uncompromising and remarkably detached. He rejected the ties of geometrical painting, calling them a hang-over from World War I; he also rejected the extremes of

Gesture Painting, although he is one of the most important of the Chromatic Abstractionists within **Abstract Expressionism**. His compositions are determined entirely by the shape of the canvas, which is painted in nearly uniform colour, often of red-brown, and divided into two or more rectangular fields by vertical stripes of a second colour, eg *Adam* (1951–2, London Tate); *The Stations of the Cross* (1965, New York, Guggenheim Museum). These paintings are the strongest possible statement of the Abstract Expressionist idea of composing 'all-over', *ie* locating the image entirely in the surface of the canvas. Although they are restrained works which do not give up their secrets at first glance, their huge scale, as the artist said, 'invites the participation' of the beholder. Newman also produced occasional pieces of sculpture, on a huge scale, *eg Broken Obelisk* (1970, Houston, Rothko Chapel).

NICHOLSON, Ben (1894–   ), English painter. The son of the painter Sir **William Nicholson**, he was at one time married to the sculptress **Barbara Hepworth**. He studied at the Slade School, London, and in California. In the early 1930s he visited Paris several times and met Picasso, Arp and Mondrian among others. At that time he was painting figurative still lifes using pearly restricted colour, flattened space, and simple Cubist forms, *eg Au Chat Botté* (1932, Manchester City AG), *Le Quotidien* 1932, London Tate), *White Relief* (1935, London Tate), *Painting* (1937, London Tate). In 1933 he joined the **Abstraction-Création** group and produced completely abstract paintings including the first 'white reliefs', wood carved in regular superimposed forms and painted white, slightly influenced by Arp, and paintings influenced by Mondrian, though more subtle in colour. In 1937 he edited the periodical *Circle* with Gabo and Leslie Martin. In 1949 he moved to St. Ives in Cornwall where he took up landscape painting. He won the Carnegie Award in 1952 and the Guggenheim Prize in 1956. After World War II, his painting followed the same themes, treating them with greater complexity and colour range, *eg Feb. 1952; Carafe* (1952, Minneapolis, Walker Art Center). Nicholson is undoubtedly the finest Classicist in. English painting, responding particularly to the balanced, half stated visual fact. But his grey, blue and pearl colour schemes (in this he may have been acting on advice given to him by the primitive, Alfred Wallis), and his frequent use of suggestive textures created by scraping at old paint with a razor blade, betray a lingering Romanticism which is characteristically English.

NICHOLSON, William (1872–1949), English painter and designer, father of **Ben Nicholson**. He studied in Bushey and at the Académie Julian, Paris (1889–90). He and his brother-in-law James Pryde designed posters (in a style related to Art Nouveau) under the name of 'The Beggarstaff Brothers' (1893–c 1900). He also worked as a stage designer. His painting is entirely figurative, but he developed a very free handling and considerable awareness of the effects of light, influenced by the Nabis, *eg Silver* (1938, London Tate). He was knighted in 1936.

NIEDERHAUSERN, Rodo (1865–1913), Swiss sculptor, originally Auguste de Niederhäusern. He studied under Falguière at the Ecole des Beaux-Arts, and was Rodin's assistant for eight years. He did a bust of his friend Verlaine (1902–4, Luxembourg Gardens Paris). His statues are mainly symbolic or allegorical and were influenced by Impressionism *eg L'Avalanche* (1892, Bern, Kunstmuseum), *Les Initiés*, *Amertum* (Geneva Musée d'Art).

NIELSEN, Kai (1882–1924), Danish sculptor. He studied at Art School in Copenhagen. His style was mainly Classical, but some later works have a fine sense of movement in space, *eg Zeus and Io* and *Leda* (Copenhagen, Statens Museum).

NIVOLA, Constantino (1911–   ), American sculptor. A native of Sardinia, he studied with Marino Marini in Italy. He was commissioned to work on the Milan Triennial mural in 1933, and the Italian Pavilion at the Paris Exhibition (1937). After moving to the United States, he served as art director of *Interiors* magazine (1941–5) and later became director of design workshop at Harvard University. He is widely respected as an educator and an innovator in design.

NOGUCHI, Isamu (1904–   ), American

sculptor, born in Japan. Encouraged by his American mother to renounce Japanese citizenship, he went to the U.S. for his education and studied sculpture in New York. In Paris on a Guggenheim Fellowship in 1927, he became Brancusi's assistant; he also helped Calder with his *Circus*. He studied Orientalia and visited China and Japan (1930–1), returning to New York in 1932. He has worked in Japan several times since World War II. Noguchi's work reflects these varying influences; he has been in the vanguard of abstract art since 1930. However, the range of his imagination and his Oriental approach to art as being as much a mystical symbol as a plastic idea, means that he has not carried out a logical development of a single style. His early work owes much to Brancusi, with its rounded dynamic forms, as in *Miss Expanding Universe* (1932, Toledo, Ohio, MA), but he was also making purely abstract experiments in space, using wire and sheet metal, as well as modelling portrait heads, *eg Ruth Parks* (1929, New York, Whitney Museum). In the 1940s Japanese traits became more important in his works, frequently built up of a number of separate bone-like parts, interlocking loosely together like a three-dimensional hieroglyph, *eg Kouros* (1945, New York MMA). Noguchi later achieved more powerful expression with greater economy of means as in *The Cry* (1962, New York, Guggenheim Museum). Alongside these, however, he has produced some extremely concise works conceived of as single unified forms, *eg The Self* (1956, London Tate); *Mu* (1952–8, New York MMA); *Integral* (1958, New York, Whitney Museum). Recently he has been making interesting works in coloured aluminium which stand directly on the floor, forming a type of environmental sculpture: *Man Walking* (1959, Chicago Art Inst.). Noguchi has also had a long and successful career as a landscape gardener and as a stage designer.

NOLAN, Sidney (1917–), Australian painter. He attended night classes at Melbourne National Gallery Art School (1934–8). Reproductions of Picasso, Klee and Miró influenced his work and from 1936 until about 1941 he painted in an abstract calligraphic style, also executing collages, many with a Dada intent. In the 1940s he turned to figurative painting of scenes from Australian life, in a deliberately naive style. From about 1946 onwards, many of Nolan's paintings were concerned with the myth surrounding the Australian bandit Ned Kelly, who is generally shown in his makeshift iron helmet and breastplate, which Nolan uses as a device for half-abstracting the figure. Nolan depicts him in the kind of desert landscape painted by Russell Drysdale, although he combines this with abstract devices, as in *Kelly at Glenrowan* (1955, New York MMA); *Glenrowan* (1956–7, London Tate). The subject of most of his paintings is the isolation of the individual. In 1951 and from 1953–8, he lived in Europe, returning from Australia to London in 1960. In a series of pictures of *Leda and the Swan* (*eg* 1958, Sydney AG) in the medium of PVA, he achieved a mottled colour effect, in a heavy dark setting like those of Arthur Boyd. In 1963 he did a number of evocative pictures of African animals in their natural habitat, and in 1964 he painted some Antarctic subjects.

NOLAND, Kenneth (1924–), American painter. He studied at Black Mountain College, North Carolina under Josef Albers and with Ossip Zadkine in Paris (1948–9). Until 1961 he taught in Washington where he met Morris Louis in 1953. They were influenced by the work of **Helen Frankenthaler** and adopted her staining technique. This has enabled Noland to flood the canvas with luminous colour so that his work can be considered as the interaction of pure colour-signals, rather than patches of coloured paint. The sophistication of his colour derives from, and parallels, that of Albers. The early works, which continued up to 1962, were concentric 'target' paintings on a large scale, with three or four bands of colour on a plain ground. These differ from Albers' work in the crucial respect that the circle, unlike the square, is an unstable form; the eye cannot 'keep its place' on the circumference of a circle and, if painted without any modelling, the target appears weightless. Thus when Noland employs the effect of colour vibration and induced aftereffects (see **Op Art**) the eye continually passes from the centre to the circumference and in again, the circles seem to change colour or to vanish completely, the targets seem to expand and contract both in size and apparent depth, and the beholder can no longer distinguish the actual from the imagined, *eg Gift* (1961–2, London Tate).

However, his paintings are varied, and can induce an almost trance-like state of mind which remains with the beholder even when the initial stimulus has worn off. In 1962 he began to use oval shapes as in *Hover* (1962, Harvard, Fogg Museum) and in 1963, he abandoned the concentric formats. The shapes that succeeded these, roughly classifiable as chevrons (1963–4), double chevrons (1964–5) and striped lozenge shaped canvases (1966–8), marked a strikingly new approach. Noland's scale, already large, increased still further; the stripes are separated by bands of white and isolated in a vast white field, or if they are adjacent, they are of colours which contrast clearly rather than the hallucinatory halo-like colours of the target paintings. The resulting monumental paintings have much in common with Minimal Art. In 1968 Noland reverted to paler colours used in thin horizontal stripes; with these paintings there is no longer a feeling of a single unchanging format being used for each colour variation, but by varying the spacing and grouping of the stripes Noland shows himself a master of form as well as of colour.

NOLDE, Emil (1867–1956), German painter, originally Emil Hansen, who took the name of his birthplace. He was a teacher of drawing and lived in Saint-Gall, Munich, Paris and Copenhagen. A member of **Die Brücke** when in Berlin in 1906, in 1912 he was closely connected with the **Blaue Reiter**. He travelled extensively in the Far East. His art was pronounced degenerate by the Nazi regime in 1933 and he was forbidden to paint in 1941. His style was very broad with strong colour heavily applied; the forms, though much simplified, are rarely distorted except to suggest the effect of movement, as in *Wildly-dancing Children* (1909, Kiel, Kunsthalle). Biblical and other figure paintings such as the *Legend of Maria Aegyptiaca* triptych (1912, Hamburg, Kunsthalle) and *Christ and the Children* (1910, New York MMA) suggest an influence from wood carving and folk art. He also collected primitive masks. His flower studies, *eg Sunflowers*, 1934, Detroit Art Inst., and his near-abstract studies of

sea and sky, *eg The Sea B* (1916, London Tate) are among his most striking works. The largest collection of Nolde's work is preserved in his former home at Seebüll.

NUCLEAR ART, see **Baj, Enrico.**

O

OBJET TROUVE, phrase meaning 'found object' used by the Surrealists for an everyday object incorporated in a picture, or preserved by itself for its evocative qualities. These may be enhanced by various alterations from the artist, and a number of objects can be used to compose a new one; this technique is found in the work of Dali, Ernst and Miró. Outside the Surrealist context, the term is also used for everyday objects used in art, whether in 'ready-mades' as in the case of Duchamp, or as an ingredient in collage or assemblage. The gathering of objets trouvés however is the chief activity of many Conceptual artists. Certain artists such as Arp and Henry Moore have also used accidentally found objects as inspiration for abstract forms.

O'BRADY, Gertrude (1901–   ), American painter of the School of Paris, originally Gertrude MacBrady. She began to paint in Paris (1939), when she produced her first watercolour during an excursion to Bougival. Three one-man shows in Paris between 1945 and 1948 brought her work to the attention of a number of art lovers. Her favourite subjects are drawn from everyday life, and her paintings, thronged with busy little figures, are original and charming. The high finish, rich colouring and plastic relief on her work make her one of the best Naive painters.

O'CONOR, Roderic (1860–1940), Irish painter. He studied briefly in London and Antwerp, then went to live in France in 1883. He began visiting Pont-Aven in 1892, and was influenced by Gauguin in his vivid approach to colour and in his use of cloisonnism, although his palette was original. He tended to adopt a very painterly handling, using juxtaposed stripes of colour, possibly his own version of Neo-Impressionism, *eg Still Life with Bottles* (1892,

London Tate); *The Glade* (1892, New York MMA). He gradually adopted a more subdued manner, using filtered lighting, owing much to Bonnard and to Cézanne, *eg Still Life* (1924, London, Courtauld Galleries).

O'KEEFE, Georgia (1887–   ), American painter. She studied at the Chicago Art Institute and at the Art Students' League, New York, then became a teacher. In 1916 she was given her first show by Alfred Stieglitz, whom she later married. Until about 1920 her work consisted of abstract paintings often in watercolour, somewhat influenced by Oriental art, and close to nature in its curving rhythms: *Blue No. 11* (1916, New York, Brooklyn Museum). In the 1920s the landscape motifs which had always underlined her paintings became explicit, altɦough they were still greatly simplified and painted with an almost mystical rhythm of line and harmony of colour: *Red Hills and the Sun* (1922, Washington, Phillips Collection). In 1929 she visited New Mexico for the first time, and this has continued as a subject for her paintings, *eg Black Cross, New Mexico* (Chicago Art Institute). Other subjects include bones and the petals of flowers seen in close-up: *Black Iris* (1926, New York MMA). Alongside these subjects, however, she painted a number of skyscraper pictures (1926–29) and, from about 1930 to the present day, pictures of simple architectural motifs which have something in common with Cubo-Realism, but contain much of the melancholy poetry of De Chirico: *Patio with Cloud* (1956, Milwaukee Art Center). Although her early art paralleled that of Kandinsky and the Orphists, O'Keefe was important in being one of the first Americans to evolve an original abstract style independent of Cubism.

OLDENBURG, Claes (1929–   ), American sculptor, born in Sweden. Having settled in Chicago in 1936, he studied at Yale University and at the Chicago Art Institute, and moved to New York in 1956. With Allan Kaprow he has been the leading American instigator of **Happenings**. His contribution to the Pop Art movement has been to extend to a wide variety of subjects the concern for the 'object-as-object' shown by **Jasper Johns**. Like Johns, Oldenburg makes replicas of common

objects, reproducing their principal characteristics, but either in incongruous materials, such as stuffed fabric or enamelled *papier-mâché*, or on an enormous scale *eg Giant Three-way Plug* (1970, London Tate). His techniques derive from advertising and display procedures—the shop window hamburger, for example, that is totally uneatable (*Dual Hamburger*, 1962, New York MMA)—but their effect is to divorce form from function and to enable one to understand each better: *eg Soft Typewriter* (1963, private collection); *Soft Drainpipe—Blue (cool) version* (1967, London Tate). As an extension of this Oldenburg has recently been designing monuments for public places, a giant ice-lolly for Park Avenue, for instance, or an enormous beer barrel blocking the Thames.

OLITSKI, Jules (1922–   ), American painter, born in Russia. He went to the United States in 1924. An Abstract Expressionist, his paintings explore the action of painting. His early works were often thick with impasto. Recently, he has been covering large areas with coarsely-sprayed colour using contrasting hues of close value to create an optical surface tension on the canvas. His work was included in the 'New York Painting and Sculpture: 1940–1970' exhibition at the New York Metropolitan Museum.

OP ART, an abbreviation coined (in irrelevant assonance with Pop Art) for art which makes use of optical illusions to achieve its effects. Artists have always taken the peculiarities of the human eye into account, and many artists over the past eighty years have made considerable use of optical illusions (for example at the Bauhaus), yet it is only since about 1960 that there has been a widespread interest in art in which these retinal effects constitute the principal means of expression. Op Art is an attempt to break away from the concept of form as something which is confined to the arrangement of elements on the canvas surface, and to substitute an art which only exists, subjectively, in the eye of the beholder. It can be classified within the general trend of **Post-Painterly Abstraction**, since it substitutes calculated control on the part of the artist for the freer procedures of Abstract Expressionism, and replaces the painter's subjective expression with a subjective experience for the beholder, the artist himself remaining detached. Several Abstract Expressionists, such as Rothko, have achieved rather similar effects on the beholder, though approaching from the opposite direction.

Although some of the most important work today is being executed in black and white, it was colour and its optical effects which were first investigated systematically by Chevreul in 'La Loi du Contraste Simultané' in 1839. He discovered that an area of bright colour tends to induce a halo of its complementary colour around it. By extension, this means that certain juxtapositions of colour have particularly strong effect: complementaries enhance each other, slightly different colours tend to clash, while others may merge to produce a third colour. These principles were used by the Neo-Impressionists and by the Fauves. Herbin and Vasarely have used colour contrasts together with formal effects to give an added impact to their art. Much of the post-War work of Albers has been devoted to a study of subtle colour interactions; and colour illusions are an important part of the work of Noland. Larry Poons and Frank Stella produce works which, though not exclusively optical, depend very much on colour relationships for their effect. In England, Hoyland Sedgley and Michael Kidner (*Orange and Violet*, 1961, London Tate) have worked largely with non-objective colour images.

The inter-War works of Jean Arp frequently involve the 'figure-ground' illusion, a state of ambiguity between what is to be taken as motif, and what as background; Jeffrey Steele makes use of similar effects. The *Graphic Tectonics* executed by Albers in the 1940s make use of linear patterns seeming to indicate a third dimension, but which elude logical resolution by changing course unexpectedly; Hannes Beckmann is interested in similar phenomena, *eg Neither Nor* (1961, Boston MFA). Most Op Art is based on the fact that the eye has difficulty in focusing on a regularly repeated geometrical pattern, but groups and regroups the elements in a constant state of dynamic uncertainty; this principle is explored in its purest form by Bridget Riley. It also occurred in some of the work of Mondrian, *eg Pier and Ocean* (1915, Otterloo RKM), and is an important factor in the recent work of Lichtenstein and Gwyther Irwin. In such

a system, very slight alterations of the shape or scale of some elements can have a great effect on the dynamics of the system; this approach is adopted frequently by Vasarely, and by the American Richard Anuskiewicz. Finally, many artists make use of optical devices in reliefs and three-dimensional works to achieve the effect of **Kinetic Art**, using only the movement of the spectator or random changes in the lighting. The commonest illusion employed is that which can be observed while walking past two parallel fences, for example, and looking at something through them. This underlies much of the work of the Venezuelans Soto and Carlos Cruz-Diaz, while the paintings of Agam and Yvaral, painted on prismatic surfaces, change as the observer moves by them. The reliefs of Camargo and Mary Martin appear to move as the pattern of the light on them changes. These various trends were united for the first time at the important exhibition at the Museum of Modern Art, New York, in 1965, aptly entitled 'The Responsive Eye'.

ORLOFF, Chana (1888–), Russian sculptress, originally Chana Orlova. She went to Paris (1911), where she met Joseph Bernard, Apollinaire and the Cubists. Her earliest works were woodcarvings. Her art embodies elements of Cubist stylization, but her treatment of the human figure is mainly realistic, direct and lively, as in *Femme Accroupie* (1924, Paris MNAM). After 1945 her style became increasingly supple and graceful, and the forms more elongated.

OROZCO, José Clemente (1883–1949), Mexican painter. After working as an architectural draughtsman, he studied at the San Carlos Academy. About the time of the Revolution in 1913, he became a caricaturist and was a friend of Rivera and Siqueiros. Many of Orozco's works deal with the heroic past of his country, *eg Zapata* (1930, Chicago Art Inst.) and *Zapatistas* (1931, New York MMA). The style of such works is bold and dramatic with large figures set against a simplified landscape background. His palette was based on primary colours as in the painting of primitive people, but his characteristic iridescent modelling is more reminiscent of El Greco. An affinity with Goya is seen in his ability to use the exaggerated drama of his compositions to distil a deep pathos. However, Orozco's art is also concerned with the modern world; two pictures in the New York MMA demonstrate this: *The Subway* (1928) with its profound understanding of the loneliness of big cities, and the horrifying *Dive Bomber and Tank* (1940). The latter work is in fresco, a medium used by Orozco all through his life; two examples are *Prometheus* (1930, Claremont, Calif., Pomona College) and the dome of the Hospicio at his home in Guadalajara, painted in 1938 and generally considered his masterpiece.

ORPEN, William (1878–1931), Irish painter. A student at the Metropolitan School, Dublin and at the Slade School, London, he was a successful portrait painter. At first, he employed a rather Academic manner, *eg The Mirror* (1900, London Tate). Later, under the influence of the **Nabis**, he achieved a beautiful, airy style with light shimmering colour, *eg In the Studio* (Leeds City AG).

ORPHISM, a movement which developed out of Cubism in the years 1910–14. The initial impulse came from **Duchamp**, **Villon** and other members of the short-lived Section d'Or group who were exploring the possibility of introducing, into a Cubist framework, the ideas of colour harmony and proportion propounded by the Nabis. The principal artists of the movement were **Delaunay** and **Kupka**. Chagall and Léger were also strongly affected, though retaining their own distinctive styles. Orphic art is distinguished from Cubism by a wider colour range and by a conscious effort to achieve harmony of colour and form. The term 'Orphism' was coined by Apollinaire, partly as a pun on *Section d'Or*, but largely in reference to Orpheus, symbol of the lyrical view of nature which these artists pursued.

OUDOT, Roland (1897–), French painter. A student at the Ecole des Arts Décoratifs, he later worked with Léon Bakst for the Ballets Russes and has exhibited at the Salon d'Automne since 1919. His earlier easel paintings include still lifes and portraits, and are rather influenced by Cézanne, *eg Loisette* (1929, New York MMA). He has also produced a number of genre scenes from country life with a feeling rather akin to Millet, and

figure paintings which have the knack of catching an unexpected and revealing expression, *eg Folies-Bergère* (1957, Vevey, Musée Jenisch). His colour has gradually become brighter and in some of the recent landscapes reaches travel-poster intensity.

OZENFANT, Amédée (1886–1966), French painter and critic. He studied in Saint-Quentin and then studied art and architecture in Paris. He founded the review *L'Elan* in 1915, in which he expounded a new aesthetic doctrine, **Purism**, applying the term to Le Corbusier. In 1918 the two artists published their theories in the review *L'Esprit Nouveau* (1921–5). In 1931 Ozenfant began a huge composition containing more than a hundred figures entitled *Life* (Paris MNAM). He founded an art school in Paris (1930), and later the Ozenfant School in New York, where he lived after 1938. In his early style he took real objects such as jugs as points of departure, eliminating all accidents of form until an essential grouping of large shapes was achieved, as in *The Vases* (1925, New York MMA). His compositional technique had musical affinities frequently underlined by such titles as *Fugue* (Chicago Art Inst.). Later, his painting became more austere and atmospheric, evoking many themes including the movement of heavenly bodies.

P

PAOLOZZI, Eduardo (1924–), Scottish sculptor of Italian parentage. He studied at the Edinburgh College of Art and at the Slade School. He worked in Paris (1947–50), where he met Giacometti. He won the Bright Foundation Sculpture Prize at São Paulo in 1957. His earlier work in cast metal is abstract in form, and was somewhat influenced by Klee's later work, *eg Two Forms on a Rod* (1948, London Tate). In 1956 he exhibited with Richard Hamilton in the 'This is Tomorrow' exhibition and was thus associated with the **Pop** movement from its inception. Most of his work since then has been **Assemblage** of mechanical objects, grouped into monumental anthropoid forms and cast in metal, *eg Cyclops* (1957, London Tate).

In about 1964, however, he abandoned these monumental cast forms and executed a number of looser aluminium sculptures resembling lengths of exhaust-pipe or the coils of a large brass musical instrument, *eg Neo-Saxeiraz* (1966, Amsterdam, Stedelijk M). He has also made several very simple works in chrome-plated steel: references to mechanical forms are no longer explicit and the sculptures can be appreciated entirely in formal terms. Paolozzi has explored the theme of related human and mechanical forms (derived from Duchamp and Picabia) in photographic collages, in silk-screen prints and in his animated film *History of Nothing* (1962).

PARIS, School of, term first used in the early 20th century to refer to artists, many of them Jews from central Europe, who emigrated to France and lived in Montparnasse. The most important of these were Chagall, Pascin, Kisling, Soutine and Modigliani; later the Polish artists, Eugène Zak, Krémègne and Gottlieb, the Ukrainian Mintchine, and the Lithuanian Max Band were added to the group. All these artists practised a form of Expressionism centred on the human figure and stylistically remote from the experiments of the Cubists. Their individualistic art differed considerably from most other forms of Expressionism. Thereafter, however, other foreign artists working in Paris, such as Picasso, Juan Gris, Foujita and van Dongen were also said to belong to the School of Paris, and later still, the term was extended to include all French artists who were members of the modern movement, including Matisse, Derain and Dufy. Several writers have criticized this broad application of the term, but it seems an obvious and logical usage.

PASCIN, Jules, originally Julius Pinkas (1885–1930), American painter, born in Bulgaria. He studied in Vienna and in Munich, where he contributed to the satirical journal, *Simplicissimus*. He went to Paris in 1905 and to the United States in 1914, becoming an American citizen in 1920. During his stay in Munich Pascin had been influenced by the painters of **Die Brücke**, and their unflattering and frank attitude to the human body remained with him, though he soon lost their angularity of style. The principal influence

on his work, however, was **Degas**, both in choice of subject and technique, *eg Claudine Resting* (1923, Chicago Art Inst.) and *Young Girl* (1924, Paris, Petit Palais). The pale colour of these works, the subtle modelling by light and the technique of drawing on the canvas and then filling in vague areas with soft colour show Degas' influence clearly. Pascin's pictures often look as though they are being seen through a veil of mist, and his colour is generally cooler than that of Degas, *eg Nude with Green Hat* (1925, Cincinnati AM). He did not share Degas' characteristic of seeing his sitters entirely objectively; there is always some comment, some relationship implied, whether it is the erotic provocation of works such as the *Girl in Boots* (1927, Cincinnati, Hebrew Union College), the physical repulsion of *Standing Woman* (1928, London Tate, Sainsbury Loan), or the humour of *Socrates and his Disciples Mocked by Courtesans* (1921, New York MMA).

PASMORE, Victor (1908–   ), English painter. He took up art in his spare time. His work of this period was at first realistic, as *The Bradman Still Life* (1929, Leeds City AG), but he became influenced by Fauvism, *eg Tea Gardens* (1935, Bury AG) and moved towards abstraction. In 1938 he founded the Euston Road School with **Coldstream**. At this time he returned to an objective figuration, influenced by Impressionism, *eg The Flower Barrow* (1938–42, Adelaide NG). He adopted a conspicuous **Pontillism** as a decorative effect (see **Vuillard**) rather than as a realistic technique. This has remained a recurring feature even of his abstract style, *eg The Thames at Chiswick, No. 3* (1946–7, Melbourne NG). In 1948 he returned to abstract art and painted a number of works in which the entire canvas was animated by van Gogh-like spirals as in *The Wave* (1949–50, Ottawa NG) and *The Coast of the Inland Sea* (1950, London Tate). In 1951 he began to execute collages, *eg Square Motif in Brown, White, Blue and Ochre* (1949–53, New York MMA) and three-dimensional constructions. These are very much in the tradition of De Stijl and are composed of clean-cut projecting planes of wood and Perspex, animated by characteristic off-centre effects and touches of unusual colour as in *Abstract in White*,

Black, Maroon and Ochre (1957, Liverpool Walker AG). He continued painting at the same time, and some of his most original works are those which combine painterly and Constructivist techniques. In the last decade, when most artists have rejected painterly qualities (see **Post-Painterly Abstraction**), Pasmore has included progressively freer passages in his work, but using their very freedom as yet another force to be held in a constructivist balance; for example, the red field stabilized by the incursion of a solid white bar in *Red Abstract* (1960, Buffalo AG), or the two black bars that seem to compress and animate the cloud of Pointillist dots in *Black Abstract* (1963, London Tate).

PEARLSTEIN, Philip (1924–), American painter. Although not a Pop artist, Pearlstein's particular form of almost photographic realism has been made possible by Pop painters such as Rosenquist. He paints mostly nudes which are treated in a bold, non-idealized style and with compositions which cut the figures off by the frame thus fixing and depersonalizing the sitters.

PECHSTEIN, Max (1881–1955), German painter. A student in Dresden (1900–6), he became (1906) a member of **Die Brücke**. In 1908 he visited Paris and his style became closely influenced by Matisse, thus being slightly more elegant than that of his fellow painters, *eg Young Girl* (1908, Berlin, 20th C Gallery). He taught at the Berlin Academy (1923–33, 1945–55).

PEPLOE, Samuel (1871–1935), Scottish painter. He went to Paris, where he studied under Bouguereau, and returned to France from 1910 to 1913 and again in 1928. The principal influence on his work was **Cézanne**, which gives his landscapes and still lifes an intellectual discipline not found in the work of his contemporary and friend **Hunter**, *eg Still Life, White Roses* (Glasgow Kelvingrove). Nonetheless he handled the style with a Scottish love of colour, probably influenced by Fauvism. Among the most impressive of his works are the views of Iona, *eg Iona* (c 1924, Glasgow Univ.) in which the landscape is conjured up by a few blocks of blue paint on the almost plain canvas, capturing an atmosphere which belongs uniquely to the Scottish coast.

PERMEKE, Constant (1886–1952), Belgian painter and sculptor. He studied in Bruges and Ghent. In 1909 he went to live at Laethem-St.-Martin, where he founded the influential second school of **Laethem-St.-Martin**. After World War I he settled at Jabbeke, near Bruges; his studio there became the Permeke Museum after his death. Regarded as the master of Flemish Expressionism, his style, however, was first influenced by Impressionism, *eg Winter in Flanders* (1912, Antwerp MBA). This early phase was succeeded by a more vigorous manner with jagged black outlines and a pictorial construction influenced by Cubism, though still basically realistic. By the mid-1920s, he had developed his own characteristic style which he applied principally to studies of country people and life. His work is quite different from German Expressionism. Permeke's palette was darker and had a brooding quality emphasized by occasional flashes of colour. Instead of pinching and distorting his figures, he magnified them to heroic, monumental size; above all his emotion was not self-centred but was derived from a profound understanding of common humanity. The robust plastic qualities of his later works explain why Permeke was drawn to sculpture after 1936, *eg Niobe* (Brussels MBA). Few of his works are outside Belgium though there are examples in the Tate Gallery, London, such as *The Harvest* (1927), and in the Edinburgh Gallery of Modern Art, *eg Winter in Flanders* and *Female Head* (bronze).

PEVSNER, Antoine (1886–1962), French sculptor, born in Russia. He studied art in Kiev and St. Petersburg, visiting Paris twice during the years 1912–14. There he was impressed by **Cubism**, and even more by the Eiffel Tower whose latticework of metal, beautiful yet logical, was to influence his later work. His paintings of the period include some which are abstract or nearly so, *eg Head of an Italian Woman* (1915, Basle, Kunstmuseum). Although obviously influenced by Cubism they are bolder and more architectural, the many facets of a Cubist picture being reduced to a few which interlock in the picture plane to create something of great solidity. In 1915 he went to Oslo, where his brother **Naum Gabo** was staying; the latter interested him in sculpture, and together they developed **Constructivism**, an art founded on the idea of articulating depth in space. In 1917 he was appointed Professor at the Moscow Academy, alongside Kandinsky and Malevich. In 1920 he signed with his brother the 'Realist Manifesto', which proclaimed the principles of Constructivism. In 1923 he left Russia, visited Germany and settled in Paris permanently, becoming a French citizen in 1930.

As a youth, Pevsner had been impressed by an icon in the monastery at Novgorod and had realized that the secret of the figure's power was the feeling of limitless depth in the eye-sockets. This experience seems to have provided the basic principle for all his sculpture: instead of volumes encased within unbroken, impregnable surfaces (as in conventional sculpture) he created his works out of transparent and perforated materials such as wire and Perspex, which would reveal the inherent spaces. This can be seen clearly in such comparatively realistic works as *Torso* (1924, New York MMA) and *Portrait of*

Antoine Pevsner: Dynamic Projection at 30° *(1951, Paris MNAM); ph. Giraudon.*

Marcel Duchamp (1926, Yale Univ. AG). Although many of his works were based, ultimately, upon human proportions, they were rarely as obviously anthropomorphic in later years, *eg Bas-relief* (1932, New York, Guggenheim); even *Dancer* (1927–9, Yale Univ. AG), which is important as one of the first of Pevsner's works to make use of implied movement, achieves its effects not by any great similarity to a figure in motion, but by the feelings aroused as the eye travels over the smooth curves cut in the metal. This principle of implied movement, and of the sculpture exploring space by scanning it, or setting up a number of patterns of movement through it, formed the basis of the rest of Pevsner's work, and in 1936 there appeared the first of the *Developable Surfaces* (two examples, 1938 and 1941, Peggy Guggenheim Collection, Venice), which are perhaps his most characteristic works. These consist of sheets of metal, with their edges forming parabolas, spirals or other regular curves and with their surfaces marked by ridges or grooves which radiate outwardly as tangents to the basic edge-curves. The whole effect is reminiscent of a mathematical function plotted in a graph. Nevertheless, the basic impulse of these works is not to define a self-contained mathematical statement, but to explore outside themselves. Although not always large, these works are thus enormous in effect, because each curve and each tangent demands to be extended into the surrounding space, creating relationships capable of infinite development. (The principle was similar to the Neo-Plasticism of **Mondrian**, who was, with Pevsner, a founder-member of the **Abstraction-Création** group in 1931.) Many of the works are composed of sheets of wires soldered together so that the directional effect of the sculptures is more marked, *eg Developable Column* (1942, New York MMA). Indeed, the first ideas for these sculptures were usually expressed by a few wires delineating the main curves and soldered together into an open basket, as can be seen in *Liberation of the Spirit* (1952, London Tate), the maquette submitted by Pevsner as his entry for the competition for a monument to the Unknown Political Prisoner. Not all Pevsner's sculptures were free-standing: a number, misleadingly called *Frescoes, eg Fresco for a Cathedral* (1943–4, Chicago Art Inst.),

took the wall as the starting point for their explorations of space. Many of these later works used colour in a very subtle way, and were made with a silversmith's attention to finish. There is an entire gallery devoted to Pevsner in the MNAM, Paris.

PEYRONNET, Dominique (1872–1943), French painter. A printer by trade, he only began to paint when he was almost fifty. His style, though Naive, was very intricate and he treated a variety of subjects, including figures, *eg Reclining Woman* (Paris MNAM), landscapes, *eg Ferryman of the Moselle* (1936, New York MMA), and seascapes. His drawing was precise and his colours vivid, but harmonious.

PHILIPSON, Robin (1916–), British painter. Although born in England, his artistic links are almost entirely with Scottish painting, and he is, with Anne Redpath, John Maxwell and the late Joan Eardley, a leading exponent of the extreme painterliness and love of colour which characterize the school. He studied at the Edinburgh College of Art under MacTaggart and Gillies and returned to teach there in 1947. He is a figurative painter, but uses countless abstract devices to add meaning to his pictures. His early figure-studies and cityscapes show the influence of Kokoschka which led him to give the colour and paint substance a freedom independent of, but reflecting the subject, *eg Edinburgh in Summer* (1956, Liverpool, Walker AG). He has continued this in several series, using the qualities of the paint to intensify the emotion inherent in the subject, *eg* the violence of the fighting cocks, or the deep peace of the cathedral windows, *eg Cathedral Interior* (1960, Glasgow Kelvingrove). Recently he has painted a series of religious polyptychs, *eg Golgotha Altarpiece* (1965, Glasgow Kelvingrove), a fantastic example of watercolour technique on a large scale containing images from Philipson's past work and new motifs from modern warfare.

PHILLIPS, Peter (1939–), English painter. After studying at the Royal College of Art he exhibited with the 'Young Contemporaries' in 1961 (see **Kitaj**). His work of that date, influenced also by Richard Smith, and through him by Johns, uses the fruit-machine image as the frame for various Pop vignettes, some handled with great freedom. In recent years he has become more concerned with the striped formats of Op Art, although he has not eliminated realistic passages, *eg Random Illusion No. 64* (1968, London Tate).

PICABIA, Francis (1878–1953), French painter. After studying under Cormon at the Ecole des Beaux-Arts he exhibited at the Salon des Indépendants in 1903, and until 1908 painted landscapes in an agreeably polished manner reminiscent of Impressionism, *eg Notre-Dame* (1906, Leeds City AG). He was next influenced by Cubism, and in 1911 exhibited with the **Section d'Or**. In the following year he took up Orphism, *eg Catch as Catch Can* (1913, Philadelphia MA). He then went to the United States, where he exhibited at the **Armory Show**. At this juncture he painted two of his most important works, *Udnie (Jeune Fille Americaine, ou la Danse)* (1913, Paris MNAM) inspired by the dancer Napierkowska, and *Edtaonistl* (1913, Chicago Art Inst.), which are near-abstract compositions of forms and colours. He had already painted one completely abstract work, *Caoutchouc* ('Rubber', 1909, Paris MNAM). His friendship with **Marcel Duchamp** coincided with a number of works in which inappropriate subjects were treated in the style of an engineering drawing, *eg L'Enfant Carburateur* (1915, New York, Guggenheim). He went in 1916 to Barcelona and, in founding the *Revue 391*, provided a vehicle for his own caustic wit. In 1918 Picabia encountered Arp and Tzara, the founders of **Dada**, in Switzerland, and on his return to Montparnasse served as a link between the Dadaists in Zurich and Paris, producing such works as *A la Memoire de Léonard de Vinci* (1919, London Tate). He took part in the scandal-provoking demonstrations organized by

Pabla Picasso: Guernica *(1937, New York MMA); ph. Hazan.*

the Dadaists, and made his provocative 'ironic machines', in which mechanical bits and pieces were assembled in witty fashion. After exhibiting for a period with the Surrealists, he abruptly broke off all contact with them and returned to a resolutely representational style of painting. During World War II he painted a series of academic nudes to sell in Algeria, but in 1945 he returned to abstract painting and created his 'Surirrealiste' works with such aggressive titles as *I Don't Want to Paint Any More, You'll Never Sell It* and *What Do You Call That?* An eccentric and volatile artist, he produced a succession of uncompromisingly useless, whimsical and absurd creations, and, although technically limited, he was a vital part of the history of the Dada movement.

PICASSO, Pablo (1881–1973), Spanish painter and sculptor, originally Pablo Ruiz Blasco. Although Picasso was probably best

known for his association with **Cubism**, which he invented and which brought him world-wide fame, his creativity spanned many schools, and he is impossible to classify. Although almost all his working life was spent in France, Picasso was nonetheless Spanish, by birth and in character; this shows in the violence, contradictions, ornamental exuberance, quixotic audacity and tragic pathos of his work.

Picasso was an infant prodigy who by the age of thirteen was producing canvases of such high standard that his father gave up painting and handed him his brushes. In 1895 he entered Barcelona Art School and in 1897 he received a commendation at the Madrid Exhibition of Fine Art for a large composition *Science and Charity*, painted in an astonishingly capable, naturalistic style. Picasso spent his early years in Barcelona haunting the 'Four Cats', the centre of literary, artistic and anarchist groups. Several of his drawings were published in the revue *Arte Joven*, which he helped to found. After several stays in Malaga and Madrid, where he had a brilliant career at the Academy of San Fernando, he left for France in 1900. He spent the next four years in Paris in complete poverty. Vollard organized his first exhibition in 1901, which failed; at the same time he began to sign himself simply Picasso (his mother's name). He had several writers among his friends, including Apollinaire, who became Picasso's staunch defender. In 1904 he began to attract several foreign patrons, including Kahnweiler, who became (1907) Picasso's principal dealer. In 1908 he met Matisse, Derain and **Braque**, founding the Cubist movement with the latter. His financial position improved, and he became famous. He made several excursions to the south of France, painted at Cadaqués, Spain, with Derain in 1910, and at Céret (1911–13) with Braque and Juan Gris. During World War I, he went with Cocteau to Rome and worked with the Ballets Russes, designing the sets and costumes for Satie's *Parade*. His contact with Italy had a profound influence on his art, and he adopted a Neo-Classical style.

After 1923 he returned with increasing frequency to the Côte d'Azur, Antibes, Monte Carlo and Juan-les-Pins. In 1928 he took up sculpture after a break of fourteen years and also began engraving.

He returned to Spain in 1934 and in 1936 was appointed director of the Prado by the revolutionaries and in 1937 he presented his famous *Guernica* at the Paris Universal Exhibition. An important retrospective exhibition of his work was held in New York in 1939. During World War II Picasso lived quietly in Paris. A large group of his works was shown at the Salon d'Automne after the Liberation: this was the first Salon exhibition Picasso had ever had. He joined the Communist Party organized by the Movement de la Paix, and despite a reluctance to travel, he went to Warsaw, and created his famous poster with the dove of peace. In 1946 the Musée Grimaldi at Antibes (now a Picasso Museum) was offered to him as a studio, and when he left it he also left all the works he had produced during his stay there. In 1947, at Vallauris, he began to produce ceramics, and over a period of years created a body of work which has become famous. He took part in the Venice Biennale in 1950, and important retrospective exhibitions were held in Rome, Lyons, and São Paulo in 1953. He was by then living almost uninterruptedly in southern France. At that time he executed several large decorative projects, including the *War and Peace* panels for an inter-denominational chapel at Vallauris, and a huge panel for UNESCO. Every year he produced a new series of paintings, which were often variations on masterpieces by Delacroix, Manet or Velazquez. Age made no difference to his prodigious creativity and he was as active in the fields of engraving and sculpture as in painting.

Perhaps the most conspicuous feature of his style was its extreme diversity. Every year he seemed to undergo a complete regeneration, but his work can be divided into a number of successive periods. There is nothing comparable to the protean variety of Picasso in the history of art. It is easy to detect influences on his style, and he himself said that it is necessary to copy others, but tragic to be reduced to copying oneself. His earliest work was not especially notable for its originality, and the influence of Toulouse-Lautrec and Impressionism was evident, *eg The Flower Seller* (1901, Glasgow Kelvingrove). But in his 'blue' period (1901–4), Picasso had found a very personal mode of expression, an unadorned style which allowed him to depict human poverty with great subtlety and insight. Some critics claim Picasso never surpassed the 'blue' period work, *eg The Funeral of Casemagas* (1901, Paris MAMVP), *La Vie* (1903, Cleveland MA). During the 'pink' period (1905–7), he concentrated primarily on circus scenes and his style was more free, subtly lyrical, but with a sharp pathos, as in *Woman in a Chemise* (1905, London Tate), *The Family of Acrobats* (1905, Washington NG).

Cézanne's influence was visible in a series of paintings with dominant greens, combined with the influence of Iberian sculpture as in *Les Demoiselles d'Avignon* (1907, New York MMA). This was painted after the artist had spent several months making preparatory drawings and studies. This strange composition marks a decisive moment in Picasso's development. The artist here abandoned the grace of his 'pink period' and turned to bold research into purely plastic problems. The angular forms and the simultaneous profile, front and back views of the bottom right figure, showing the influence of African carved masks, were features which led directly to Cubism. Nonetheless, the entirely new style of this work initially disconcerted his friends. Matisse thought that Picasso meant to ridicule the modern movement, and even Braque at first disliked the work. Picasso left the canvas rolled up in his studio and it only became known to the public when exhibited in 1937 at the Petit Palais.

From 1912 until 1914, he produced collages and paintings using all sorts of unusual materials, *eg Still Life with Chair Caning* (1912, private collection), to decorative effect. His work as a designer for the ballet led to large compositions such as *Three Musicians* (1921, versions in New York MMA and Philadelphia MA). He then became a convert to **Neo-Classicism**, evidently an influence on the series of calm, balanced, monumental figures, including *Standing Nude* (1922, Hartford, Wadsworth Atheneum) and *Seated Woman* (1923, London Tate). In 1926, determined to avoid the Academism to which his virtuosity might have led him, he turned briefly to **Surrealism**, and occasionally used a pure abstract style which embodied strange, disjointed shapes. These canvases, like his earlier Cubist work, aroused a violent storm of protest, *eg The Studio* (1928, New York MMA).

Pablo Picasso: Woman Crying *(1937, London, Mrs. Miller-Penrose Collection).*

In 1936 he was again painting violently expressive and rhythmically disjointed figures; the culmination of this style was *Guernica* (1937, New York MMA). This was inspired by the bombardment of the little Spanish village of Guernica by the

German Air Force during the Spanish Civil War. It expresses the violent emotions felt by the artist, who ardently supported the Republicans. The picture contains a number of figures, human and animal, each with a specific meaning. The various distortions are almost an anthology of Picasso's style, *eg* the elongated head of the moving figure with the lamp, the screaming mouths with their spearlike tongues and the abrupt changes of tone which replace conventional modelling. The illuminated bare window and naked light bulb represent a bomb explosion. The work could be said to belong to Picasso's Expressionist period, yet horror is not the only emotion in the picture: there is also great pity. *Guernica* is the masterpiece of 20th century politically-engaged painting, and is all the more remarkable because it is almost the only example in Picasso's work. After 1940 the brutal deformation and dislocations of Picasso's art are an expression of the feeling of the time, as in *L'Aubade* (1942, Paris MNAM) and *First Steps* (1943, Yale Univ. AG), and the garishly coloured, monstrous figures are probably the works by which he is best known to the general public. But it must be stated that Picasso's treatment of the familiar objects and personalities around him had an underlying consistency, sincerity and emotional content

After 1945 Picasso seemed to withdraw from contemporary movements to plunge into a kind of retrospective re-working of many of his former inventions. Picasso's intense visual curiosity allowed him to ransack a vast store of images, from Primitive Art, which he was one of the first to appreciate, to the Old Masters of European painting, *eg Les Demoiselles des Bords de la Seine* (1950, Basle Kunstmuseum), after Courbet. Still lifes and studies of the human figure supplied him with material for inexhaustible variations. One of his favourite subjects was the bullfight which has never been treated with more expression or authority. His furiously rapid execution revealed the urgency and the energy of his creative gift. Picasso defined his own aim as 'a lifelong struggle against reaction and the death of art'. Once, while he was visiting an exhibition devoted to children's art, he said: 'I could draw like Raphael when I was their age, but it took me a lifetime to learn how to draw like them.'

PICKETT, Joseph (1848–1918), American painter. He was a grocer and owner of a rifle range before he took up painting at the age of sixty-five. See **Naive Art**.

PIGNON, Edouard (1905–), French painter. A miner's son, he worked in the mines when he was fifteen. He went to Paris in 1927, attended evening classes at the Ecole des Arts Appliqués and exhibited at the Salon des Indépendants in 1932. He was at first influenced by Léger and Picasso, and painted vast compositions of working-class life in a dynamic, robust style, though his drawing and some of his smaller works often have a deep pathos, *eg The Miner* (1949, London Tate). Pignon has treated a wide variety of themes: southern landscapes, threshing scenes, cock fights and sea scenes. Recently his handling has become much freer, and his graphic style pushed close to abstraction. He is rather similar to the Cobra group in his use of the techniques of **Action Painting** within a basically figurative framework.

PIPER, John (1903–), English painter. Beginning relatively late, Piper at first painted works strongly influenced by Synthetic **Cubism**. After a number of landscapes making use of an adventurous collage technique, he painted (1935–7) a series of rigid, disciplined abstracts (example of 1935 in London Tate). These, however, are exceptions in his complete oeuvre, which is figurative, even representational. Many of his works are collages using newsprint and coloured papers of various textures as a basis on which to paint, *eg Monument, Boxted* (1947, Toledo, Ohio, MA). Even those works done in a conventional medium are influenced by the **Collage** technique to the extent that they employ little flecks of detail which are independent of the contrasting broad areas of paint which make up the picture surface, leaving the viewer to reconcile the two, as in *Stone Gate, Portland* (1950, Washington, Phillips Collection). The other feature which permeates all Piper's work is a strong sense of theatre: his pictures often look like dramatically lit stage sets waiting for the actors, *eg Stourhead* (1940, Manchester City AG). His favourite subjects have been related to architecture, to which his keen perception of the relationship between detail and overall effect is most suited, *eg Seaton Delaval* (1942, London Tate). He may be said to have initiated a whole new style of illustration in the architectural press. During the War he was commissioned by the British government to paint ancient monuments damaged by bombing, such as *Coventry Cathedral* (1940, Coventry AG). There were also many beach scenes and a remarkable series of Welsh mountain landscapes in which his graphic style became exceptionally free, *eg Rock Face, Cwm Tryfan* (1950, New York MMA).

Piper has also had considerable success as a stage designer, in particular working on the sets for almost all Benjamin Britten's operas. Recently, he has produced a number of Venetian views, making use of a shimmer of little blobs and trails of paint, in effect reconciling Action painting with his firm architectural sense. He has also been increasingly occupied with stained-glass-making in collaboration with Patrick Reyntiens: major examples of their work can be seen at the Roman Catholic Cathedral, Liverpool, and in the great baptistery of Coventry Cathedral (1957–62).

PIPPIN, Horace (1888–1947), American painter. One of the most powerful of modern American Naive painters, his oil paintings date from 1930, and include war scenes, religious compositions, and scenes from the life of his native Negro people. His work was distinguished by an intense dramatic feeling and striking harmonies of sombre colour, *eg John Brown on the Way to Execution* (Philadelphia, Pennsylvania Academy).

PISIS, Filippo di (1896–1956), Italian painter. Interested in both literature and painting, as an art critic he published *Modern Painting* (1918). In painting, his earliest allegiance was to Futurism; later in Ferrara with De Chirico and Carrà, he adopted a Metaphysical style. In 1920 he became a member of the **Valori Plastici** group. He went to Paris in the same year and stayed there until 1940. He spent the last years of his life in a sanatorium in Rome. The art of di Pisis was basically traditional and close in spirit to the Venetian School of the 18th century, although there is evidence of French Impressionist influ-

ence. His landscapes, painted with a light palette, characterized by alert brushwork and subtle effects of light, and populated with numerous little figures, were original, elegant and full of life, *eg La Salute* (1943, Rome, private collection). He also composed refined interior studies, *eg The Soldier in the Studio* (1937, Milan, private collection) and delicate still lifes (often in fact seascape foregrounds containing shells and other small objects painted in a highly finished manner).

PISSARRO, Camille (1830–1903), French painter. He was the oldest practitioner of **Impressionism**. He and Degas were the only two artists to take part in all eight Impressionist exhibitions. Although influenced in turn by Corot, Monet and Seurat, his soft restrained style remained his own. He was not an innovator and his direct influence on 20th century art was only slight. The son of a Jewish merchant and a Creole mother, Pissarro was educated in Paris before returning to the West Indies; it was not until 1855 that he settled in Paris as a painter. His early work was rather in the manner of Courbet, with deep colours and a broad touch, *eg Still Life* (1867, Toledo, Ohio, MA), although the principal influence on his style was Corot who allowed him to exhibit as 'a pupil of Corot'. Gradually he began to lighten his palette and his touch, producing soft landscapes in a range of ochres, pinks, slate blues and dull greens very similar to Corot's late work, though rather brighter in key, and with a stronger and more simple sense of composition than Corot showed in his later years. The works of this period (early 1870s) are arguably his finest paintings, *eg Penge Station* (1871, London, Courtauld Galleries), *Pontoise, the Road to Gison in Winter* (1873, Boston MFA). In 1874 he took part in the first Impressionist exhibition and his style began to change: he increased his colour range, but without ever achieving the lightness of Monet, and used smaller broken brushstrokes, sometimes giving his pictures a messy effect, as in *Woman and Child at a Well* (1882, Chicago Art Inst.), *The Pork Butcher* (1883, London Tate). In 1885 he introduced **Seurat** into the Impressionist group and for some years imitated his Divisionist style, but without the same discipline of colour or of composition, *eg The Lacroix, Rouen* (1888,

Camille Pissarro: Red Roofs *(1877, Paris, Jeu de Paume); ph. Giraudon.*

Philadelphia MA, John G. Johnson loan). Finally he returned to a broader version of his earlier style. His sons Lucien, Georges and Ludovic were also painters.

PITTURA METAFISICA, name given by **De Chirico** to his painting from about 1911 onwards. It also applies to the work of Carrà and Morandi, who associated themselves with him in 1917. Much of the theoretical basis of the movement was propounded in the first numbers of the magazine *Valori Plastici* in 1918 by the poet Savinio, De Chirico's brother. The word 'Metaphysical' was used to indicate a deeper significance behind the places and objects represented. In this sense of mystery generated by inanimate objects, Pittura Metafisica was an important precursor of **Surrealism**. The formal sources of the style were early Renaissance painters: the hieratic solidity of Giotto's figures, and the clearly defined spaces of artists dis-covering linear perspective for the first time. Perspective is an important element in all these paintings, both expressed apparently simply as in De Chirico's *Delights of the Poet* (c 1913, New York MMA) and in the often self-contradictory complexity of the later works. Latterly, De Chirico, Carrà and Morandi achieved the same effects with still life objects, often grouped entirely illogically, *eg* De Chirico's *The Great Metaphysician* (1917, New York MMA). The influence of Pittura Metafisica and of the related **Neo-Classicism** found at the same time in artists such as Picasso, was considerable, for example on Magritte and Delvaux, Hofer and Schlemmer, and on the American realists.

PLUMB, John (1927–   ), English painter. One of the pioneers of **Post-Painterly Abstraction** in Britain from 1960 onwards, his earlier works often have a flaglike or emblematic appearance and frequently use

PVA tapes in conjunction with paint, *eg Edgehill* (1962, London Tate). His later work became notably simpler, probably in response to American influences, especially that of Louis, and they employ the technique of parallel colour stripes stained into the raw canvas, *eg Untitled, August 1969* (London Tate).

POINTILLISM, term, often ambiguously used, referring to the technique of painting in separate dots or touches of colour. It has been popularly used as a synonym for **Divisionism**, as well as an inaccurate description of Impressionism.

POLIAKOFF, Serge (1906–69), Russian painter of the School of Paris. He worked as a guitarist, went to Paris in 1924, and attended the Slade School in London from 1935–7. His meeting with Kandinsky and Delaunay in 1938 was an important event in his gradual development towards an abstract style of painting. After 1938 he exhibited at the Salon des Indépendants and elsewhere. In 1948 he won the Kandinsky Prize. Poliakoff's style was geometric and abstract, employing a mosaic of large two-dimensional forms, frequently organized around a focal point. His flat areas of boldly handled pigment, often with one colour breaking through the one above, bear a certain resemblance to the work of de Staël. However, Poliakoff's work lacks the figurative implications of de Staël's and his colour harmonies are closer and often more emotive. There are *Abstract Compositions* in New York (1948, Guggenheim; 1956, MMA) and in London (1956, Tate).

POLLOCK, Jackson (1912–56), American painter. A farmer's son, he enrolled (1925) at the Manual Art School, Los Angeles. In 1929, he went to study with Benton in New York. He discovered the painting in sand of the American Indians and the Mexican fresco painters and copied the masters of the European Baroque. After 1936 he painted a number of violently Expressionist pictures, and took part in the **WPA Project**, which brought him into contact with the technique of fresco. By 1940 he was painting a number of mythological works in a style somewhat reflecting the influence of Picasso, *eg The She-wolf* (1943, New York MMA) *Guardians of*

the Secret (1943, San Francisco MA). Although these works contain figurative elements, there are many passages consisting merely of swirls of paint which could be either random marks or hieroglyphics of some significance. They also show a construction typical of Pollock, in which a central area is paved by an outer border with marks overlapping the canvas.

Pollock then began to experiment with the techniques of **Automatic Writing** and by 1947 had arrived at his very personal style of 'handwriting'. He invented several techniques to which the name **Action Painting** is generally applied. He dispensed with palette and brushes, and instead threw or dripped his paint onto a long roll of canvas lying on the floor, which might then be cut up as required. Many of his pictures are very long as a result of this, *eg Number Two* (1949, Utica Art Inst.). Both Max Ernst and Hans Hofmann claimed to have invented this technique, but Pollock developed it, and, in his hands, it produced its most significant results, as in *Full Fathom Five* (1947, New York MMA) and *Autumn Rhythms* (1950, New York Metropolitan). These gigantic canvases present a vast confusion of lines of varied thickness which cover the whole surface

Jackson Pollock: abstract *(c 1950); ph. Oliver Baker.*

LMA

N

and suggest furiously energetic movement. Sometimes the combination of colours implies a spatial relationship between various layers, and Pollock often intensified this by including aluminium paint, thereby altering the lighting effect, *eg Cathedral* (1947, Dallas MFA). The last works of this series, painted on glass, incorporate objects such as shells, nails and wire mesh. From 1950–2, Pollock painted a series of ecstatically lyrical works in black and white; *Number 23* (1948, London Tate) is a slightly earlier example. He then returned to coloured paint applied thickly in circular forms, giving a much heavier effect than his earlier work, as in *Ocean Greyness* (1953, New York, Guggenheim).

Jackson Pollock was of highly-strung temperament, subject to periods of desperate self-doubt and inactivity, and he finally committed suicide in his car. This temperament, however, accounted for much of the power of his painting. Pollock wrote: 'My painting is direct. The method of painting is the natural growth out of a need: I want to express my feelings rather than illustrate them.' He also said: 'When I am *in* my painting, I'm not aware of what I'm doing. It is only after a sort of "get acquainted" period I see what I have been about.' His work embodies something of the frenetic nature of American civilization, as well as intoxicating vistas of its landscape. As one of the founders of the New York School he helped to make American painting aware of its independence.

POMPON, François (1855–1933), French sculptor. He spent some time at Art School in Dijon before going to work in Paris as Rodin's assistant in 1874. Apart from a number of busts, he executed numerous animal statues, *eg Poule d'Eau* (1911 Paris MNAM); *Duck* (New York MMA), which are rhythmical, full of life, and characterized by an expressive understatement. He also produced such very large pieces as *Le Taureau* (1933, Paris, Place Saulieu).

PONT-AVEN, School of, term referring to the group of painters around **Gauguin** when he arrived at the Breton village of Pont-Aven in 1886, and, more specifically, when he returned in 1888 after a trip to Martinique. Since the 1860s Pont-Aven had been a well-known artists' colony, attracting both Academic and more progressive painters, and preserving Breton folklore traditions. The most important of Gauguin's friends at Pont-Aven was **Emile Bernard**, who contributed greatly to the development of the characteristic style, **Cloisonnism**. **Sérusier** also worked there with Gauguin, and founded the **Nabis** on the basis of the experience. Other artists who came into contact with Gauguin included Emile Schuffenecker, Armand Séguin, Roderic O'Conor and Cuno Amiet.

POONS, Larry (1937–), American painter, born in Tokyo. Having studied at the Boston Museum School, he had his first exhibition in New York in 1963. Influenced by the American works of Mondrian, he has created a remarkable variety of Op Art in which little dots or ellipses of colour are scattered over a uniformly coloured field. The dots are arranged in several superimposed series, each of one colour, their exact position determined by a grid used by the artist in planning the work. Although the artist starts from a firm formal conception, he dematerializes the forms almost completely by reducing them to dots, which seem to exist in a space quite apart from the actual canvas surface, attracting one another, and giving the illusion of being in constant dynamic tension. It is Impressionism distilled to the last degree of abstraction. From about 1967, Poons used larger and more freely brushed marks in place of dots, *eg Cut* (1967, London Tate). His most recent works have abandoned the grid structure and consist of more assertive brushmarks of varying sizes with considerable contrasts of light and shade, *eg Untitled* (1969, Cleveland MA).

POP ART, often called 'New Super Realism' or 'New Objectivity', is a widespread movement which grew up during the late 1950s. It is international in scope although it first developed on an Anglo-American axis. It has involved a new attitude towards subject-matter and a break-down of the distinction between subject and object, that is, between the content of a work and the manner in which it is executed. (This idea also underlies the philosophy of Marshall McLuhan, summed up in his famous phrase 'The Medium is the Message!') In consequence, the range of technical procedures used by the Pop artist has been extended far beyond the conventional, thus questioning the nature of the artist's creative activity. The term 'Pop Art' was coined in 1954 by the English critic Lawrence Alloway for manifestations of popular culture in general; it did not at that time apply to the fine arts. In 1956, at the exhibition 'This is Tomorrow' held at the Whitechapel Gallery, London, **Richard Hamilton** exhibited *Just What is it that Makes Today's Homes so Different, so Appealing?*, which may be considered the first Pop Art work. It is a little collage of an interior made out of furniture advertisements, filled with 'quality' consumer goods, and inhabited by a male physique pin-up and a female nude; through the window can be seen a cinema advertising *The Jolson Story*. The next year Hamilton further defined Pop Art as 'popular, transient, expendable, low-cost, mass-produced, young, witty, sexy, gimmicky, glamorous, and Big Business'. This tongue-in-cheek definition may be trivial when applied to some of the works produced within the Pop movement, but it is a fair description of Pop subject-matter.

The aim of .Pop Art is to extend the boundaries of art to achieve something more in tune with modern urban life; this involves both a new iconography and new art-forms, more open and more complex. The subject-matter of Pop concentrates on commercial art (advertisements, wrappers, packages, *etc*), the styles of the cinema and television (particularly the mythology surrounding the big stars such as Monroe and Presley), the art of the comic strip, newspaper photographs, pin-up magazines, signs and badges, stencilled lettering, machinery and mechanical drawing, and trivial everyday objects. These things are the familiar common property of all, not merely accessible to those with a knowledge of art history. In this sense Pop is a genuinely popular art, although the sophistication of some of its processes may only be appreciated by a minority. There is nothing new in these subjects; they occur in the collages of Picasso and of Schwitters, and in the work of all Dada artists. In fact Pop is often dismissed as Neo-Dada, which is misleading, since it has shown itself a far more constructive movement, and in any case Dada needs to be repeated afresh for each successive generation. Nonetheless Pop owes many of its concepts to these earlier movements: it looks to **Cubism** for the invention of collage, which is its principal technique, and to **Marcel Duchamp** for the invention of the 'ready-made'. This approach to subject-matter is also prefigured by American realists such as Stuart Davis, Demuth, Sheeler and Hopper. Indeed, since it was in America that the new consumer society was first developed, and since similar changes in other countries today are generally thought of as 'Americanization', it is inevitable that Pop should have an American bias. Thus, many non-American artists give the disturbing impression of wearing American iconography like borrowed raiment (this is true, for example, of Hamilton himself), except for the few (such as Peter Blake) who have found an indigenous popular style, or those for whom (like Allen Jones and Richard Smith) the subject is less important than their own formal style.

The one technical feature which all Pop artists have in common (and which distinguishes them from other realists) is a rejection of the idea of the canvas as a window on the world. There are no Pop works which consist solely of the realistic painting of an arranged motif. Although realism is crucial to Pop, the artificial technique of realist painting is an anomaly in a world in which information is conveyed by photographs, by advertising copy, by window display techniques, by banners and slogans. There are two reactions to this. One is to employ the technique normally associated with the subjects in their commercial incarnation; for example, Warhol uses a silk-screen photographic technique, Rosenquist draws on his experience as a painter of hoardings, Indiana uses sign-lettering, Fahlstrom and Collins use comic-strip technique, Lindner employs the style of mechanical drawings and Lichtenstein and Caulfield employ the primary colour dots used in cheap printing. The other approach is to conduct a dialogue between art and life, for example, between painting and the real object, or between painting and words. This approach was pioneered by Rauschenberg and Johns; and Dine, Hay, Oldenburg, George Segal, Wesselmann, Tilson and Richard Smith continue it in various ways. Artists such as Rivers, Thiebaud, Kitaj, Blake, Boshier and

Allen Jones use Pop imagery in conjunction with painting of a more traditional sort, and the associations of the Pop elements add new tensions to a picture whose organization is mainly in terms of form. At the other extreme, some artists reject painting and modelling altogether, and use collage (Hamilton), photomontage (Paolozzi), or assemblage (Stankiewicz, Paolozzi).

The principal barrier which has been broken down by Pop Art is the concept of the self-contained, hermetic art work. Not only does the subject-matter claim a new familiarity with the public, but many Pop works (such as those of Kienholz) refuse to stay quietly on the wall and instead invade the beholder's own space, creating environments rather than isolated works. For the same reason, the rise of Pop was associated with the increasing occurrence of **Happenings** in which many of the leading artists took part.

Many other artists beside those mentioned have contributed to Pop, and the movement has spread to other countries (Raysse and Télémaque are notable exponents in France, for example). Although it means something different in the hands of each practitioner, Pop Art has had the general effect of promoting new thought as to the place of art in the modern world and has produced some telling comments on man in his environment.

PORTINARI, Cândido (1903–   ), Brazilian painter. Portinari studied art in Rio de Janeiro, won a travelling scholarship and stayed in Paris (1928–30). He became a university teacher in Brazil (1936). He is now only known abroad as a participant in the Venice Biennale, and for the two large panels offered by Brazil to the United Nations, *War and Peace* (1953–5), and for his frescoes in the Library of Congress, Washington (1942). His vast murals contain many brightly-coloured figures, broadly but precisely painted. Portinari's style, at first calm and peaceful, later developed a dramatic form of Expressionism, *eg Burial in a Hammock* (1944, São Paulo Modern Art Museum). He is regarded as the most important modern painter in South America.

POST-PAINTERLY   ABSTRACTION, term coined by the American critic Clement Greenberg to describe the common element in the work of a number of artists in the U.S. and elsewhere who in the late 1950s and 1960s have reacted in different ways against **Abstract Expressionism**. The terms 'Hard-edge', 'Geometrical Abstraction' and 'Cool Art' have also been given currency, but they do not completely describe the phenomenon. Abstract Expressionism, emphasizing direct self-expression through the free handling of paint, is the epitome of a personally-involved style, but many subsequent artists wished to take themselves completely out of the picture, and to present a work which exists only as an object in itself, or as a signal, in response to which the beholder can react. Although the artist is entirely dispassionate in his presentation, the works themselves may, and often do, evoke profound feelings. This approach, in general, marks a return to the principles of **Constructivism**.

Although the movement as a whole did not begin to gather momentum among younger artists until the late 1950s, there were certain artists within the Abstract Expressionist circle, such as Rothko, Newman, Reinhardt and Frankenthaler (*ie* the 'Chromatic Abstractionists') and certain others who for one reason or another had never been included, *eg* Albers, Louis, Noland, Kelly and Youngerman, who could be taken as models. The movement was paralleled by some of the tendencies within Pop Art, *eg* the work of Lichtenstein and Warhol, as opposed to that of Rauschenberg or Johns. And there were many artists, especially in Europe, who had never been affected by Abstract Expressionism, and whose influence became especially important, notably Vasarely and Herbin, Matisse (latterly) and Ben Nicholson.

One of the concomitants of the new movement was a keener interest in colour: the painterly style does not permit pure colour relationships. This is particularly true of the painters who came into contact with Greenberg himself: Frankenthaler, Louis, Noland and Frank Stella. These painters all stain the canvas with poured-on dye, a highly impersonal technique. Thus the non-painterly criterion applies even to those works which are not also 'hard-edge' such as the earlier work of Frankenthaler, that of Louis and Jenkins, and Jules Olitski, another Greenberg contact. A group of 'hard-edge' painters was formed in Washington around Noland, using colour in clear-cut forms, but with great subtlety: it includes Thomas Downing who uses clusters of circles, *eg Shamrock* (1964, Washington Gallery of Modern Art), Paul Reed, who uses irregular shapes, more like those of Matisse, as in *No. 17* (1964, Washington Gallery of Modern Art) and Gene Davis, who uses stripes like Louis and Noland although his development was independent.

In England a number of young painters organized the 'Situation' exhibitions of 1960 and 1962: although their work was not all non-painterly, it had its large size and minimal content in common with the American developments. Among those who exhibited were Bernard and Harold Cohen, Denny, Hoyland, Irwin, Plumb, Richard Smith, Stroud and Turnbull. No doubt the rise of other non-painterly movements in the last decade or so, such as **Op Art**, **Kinetic Art** and **Minimal Art**, stems from the same general reaction against over-involvement, and the phenomenon certainly has a parallel in the 'cool' philosophy of the 1960s.

POUGNY, Jean (1894–1956), French painter, born in Russia. Despite a musical heritage, he devoted himself to painting. He went to Paris in 1910, studied at the Académie Julian, and then travelled in Italy. He returned to Russia and joined the Union of Youth founded by Larionov and Malevich. He went back to Paris in 1914, exhibited at the Salon des Indépendants, adopting a Cubist manner. He then returned to St. Petersburg, where he organized several avant-garde exhibitions (including *Tramway V* and *0.10*), and was co-signatory with Malevich of the **Suprematism** manifesto. His works, incorporating elements of sculpture and collage, were mainly abstract at this time. He soon left Russia again and travelled in Germany before settling permanently (1923) in Paris. From that date onward he abandoned his experiments with abstract painting and developed an intimate representational style on small elongated canvases, using liquid blobs of extremely rich colour, recalling Vuillard's style before 1900. But Pougny's colour had a stronger element of fantasy, his paint was applied more boldly, and his forms were less precise.

POUPELET, Jane (1878–1932), French sculptor. A pupil of Rodin and Schnegg, she produced comparatively little, but her finished works are remarkable for their purity of style and all-round accomplishment. Some of them are female studies, such as *Femme à sa Toilette* (1906, Paris MNAM), posed with great concentration of effect and very accurately observed; others are statuettes of animals full of life.

POUSETTE-DART, Richard (1916–   ), American painter. He began painting full-time in 1940, executing intricate abstract designs influenced by Picasso and similar to Jackson Pollock's work at the time. As the design element became simpler and the rough surface texture of white and coloured paint took over the weight of the expression, Pousette-Dart moved into the mainstream of **Abstract Expressionism**, *eg The Magnificent* (1950, New York, Whitney Museum). His more recent works contain no drawing and are just all-over fields of mottled colour.

PRAMPOLINI, Enrico (1894–1956), Italian painter. He studied at the Art School in Rome, and after 1912 took part in the Futurist exhibitions. He published manifestos entitled *Chromophony* (1913), *Atmospherostructure* (1917) and *Spiritual Architecture* (1922). His liking for new materials led to the *Polimaterici* assemblages, while his interest in mechanical gadgets attracted him to the field of stage design for theatre and ballet. His experiments resulted in the non-figurative *Plastic Itineraries*. In 1935 he belonged to the **Abstraction-Création** group. His paintings, *eg Interview of the Gods* (1926), *Space Diver* (1929), *Speed-charmer* (1930, Paris, Petit Palais), frequently attempt to show the metamorphosis of one element into another, or the inter-relation of matter and the universe, but they are more interesting as metaphysical ideas than as works of art.

PRECISIONISM, alternative term for **Cubo-Realism**.

PRENDERGAST, Maurice (1859–1924), American painter. After an apprenticeship to a draper, he visited Europe several times, studying at the Académie Julian, Paris, and visiting Venice, which he painted in a bright Impressionist style, using a Divisionist brushstroke, *eg Ponte della Paglia* (1899, Washington, Phillips Collection). His development paralleled that of French Post-Impressionism, and he was influenced by the Fauves (especially in his watercolours, *eg The Balloon*, 1910, Andover, Mass., Addison Gall.), and the Nabis, *eg The Promenade* (1913, New York, Whitney Museum). Although, at Davies' suggestion, he was invited to join the **Ash Can School**, he was never a realist nor a particularly 'American' artist.

PRE-RAPHAELITE BROTHERHOOD, The, name secretly adopted in 1848 by a group of English painters including William Holman Hunt (1827–1910), John Everett Millais (1829–96) and Dante Gabriel Rossetti (1828–82). Their aims were to reject Academic tradition and to avoid the trivializations of early Victorian genre painting, by painting only ideas which had some moral value, studying directly from nature, and rethinking their subjects in realistic terms. Their work at first shocked the established art world, but from about 1851 onwards, with the powerful advocacy of John Ruskin, they gradually achieved great popularity. The style of the movement can best be studied in the work of Holman Hunt, in that of Millais up to about 1856 and in that of Rossetti until about 1852, though to a certain extent the pictorial ideas continue in the work of Rossetti's pupil Edward Burne-Jones (1833–98) and in the moral attitude and approach to natural decoration of William Morris (see also **Art Nouveau**).

Although the movement is now considered reactionary, in its own time it was one of the first great revolutionary movements in 19th century art. The emphasis on realism parallels that of Courbet, especially when given socialist overtones in the work of Ford Maddox Brown (1821–93). The aim of direct study from nature anticipates that of the Impressionists as does the greatly intensified colour-range which results from it; but reference to a painting such as Millais' *Ophelia* (1852, London Tate), with its fantastic wealth of scrupulous detail, will demonstrate the crucial difference that the Pre-Raphaelites looked at nature close-up, while the Impressionists were concerned with the general aspect of a scene. Nonetheless even this has had considerable influence on many Realist movements today. One remarkable feature of Pre-Raphaelitism is its ordering of space in a number of parallel planes which are arranged above, rather than behind, one another: although true of the earlier works such as Rossetti's *Annunciation* (1850, London Tate) it is especially so of Burne-Jones. Thus this movement has also contributed to the general compression of space which is such a feature of modern art.

PRIMITIVE ART, a phrase with two meanings; at times, it is used to describe the work of contemporary untrained painters whose freshness of vision has appealed to artists and connoisseurs; some examples are discussed under the heading **Naive Art**. It is correctly applied, however, to the art of more primitive peoples, either the ancient forerunners of Western civilizations, or else contemporary communities which have remained relatively removed from international civilization. The influence of the art of both types of peoples has been one of the most powerful forces in the present century, and is further discussed under **Influences**.

PURISM, a movement inaugurated (1920) by **Ozenfant** and Le Corbusier (**Jeanneret**). They had collaborated in an essay entitled 'Après le Cubisme' (1918) which criticized the decorative art into which the Cubism of Picasso and Braque had degenerated as opposed to the more rigidly organized work of Juan Gris. In 1920 they founded the magazine *L'Esprit Nouveau* as the organ of the new movement, which aimed to restore Cubism to something more in tune with modern technology. All Impressionist (*ie* romantically pictorial) elements were to be removed; subject-matter was to be confined to a few common, mass-produced objects; colour was to be cut down to the minimum and used structurally; and formal design of the painting was to be made tighter. Purism was an important influence on the development of Léger.

PUY, Jean (1876–1960), French painter. He studied architecture in Lyons, then studied art at the Ecole des Beaux-Arts, Paris from 1903, under Jean-Paul Laurens. He also worked in Carrière's studio. He exhibited in the famous Fauve room at the

Salon d'Automne of 1905 and became a close friend of Matisse and Derain. His style, however, remained basically realist, despite its bright colour. He painted figure studies, landscapes and still lifes in a broad and harmonious style. His *Paysage de Saint-Alban-les-Eaux* (1903–4) and *Au Lit* (1923) are in the MNAM, Paris.

Q

QUIZET, Alphonse (1885–1955), French painter. A self-taught artist, after 1903 he painted mainly landscapes of the Pré-St.-Gervais, the Canal Saint-Martin and Montmartre. He met and advised Utrillo, a solitary figure like himself, whose style was somewhat similar. Quizet's painting, despite its apparent gaucherie, was not that of a Naive artist. His rich impasto, and vivid, sometimes acid colours, gave his painting much plastic energy. He was able to transform well-known parts of Paris, and even waste ground, into something static with a calm, intimate atmosphere, *eg Quai de la Seine* (1912, Geneva, Chez Foundation), *Pré-St.-Gervais* (1927, Paris MNAM).

R

RANSON, Paul (1864–1909), French painter. A student (1888) at the Académie Julian, he was one of the most active members of the **Nabis** group, which met on Saturdays in his studio in the Boulevard du Montparnasse. His own painting was symbolic and decorative in spirit, and he also produced tapestry designs. He is best remembered for the Academy he founded in 1908.

RAUSCHENBERG, Robert (1925–   ), American artist. Rauschenberg is one of the most influential figures in contemporary art. Together with **Jasper Johns**, though slightly preceding him in development, he has been responsible for starting a departure from Abstract Expressionism leading directly to **Pop Art**. Yet to describe Rauschenberg's own works solely as Pop both belittles their value as painting, and risks an over-literal response to their highly inventive conjunctions of subject-matter. For Rauschenberg's invention of the 'combine painting', though a development out of collage and assemblage, has enormously widened the range of devices available to the abstract artist and has opened up a new approach to subject-matter.

Between 1946 and 1950 Rauschenberg studied in Kansas City, in Paris, at Black Mountain College with Josef Albers and finally at the Art Students' League, New York. His first paintings, from 1949 to 1951, were 'white paintings', divided up into compartments by lines scratched on the surface, and often with inscriptions or numbers on them. In 1952 and 1953 he gradually widened his range, painting in black and red, using bolder brushwork like that of **de Kooning** (always the chief influence on the painterly aspects of his work) and used **Collage** for the first time. In 1954 the collage element became predominant, and he began a series of works which included photographs, reproductions, posters, bits of fabric, household objects and even other paintings. In *Interview* (1955, private collection) the basis of the work is a cupboard with a hinged door, while *Untitled* (1955, private collection) includes a stuffed hen, and horizontal mirrors to reflect part of the work in another plane. *Bed* (1955, private collection) is a full-size made-up bed, turned on end and painted over in a manner bringing out its abstract qualities without obscuring its original function. After the exuberance of the first year, Rauschenberg's combines have become less confused in content, though no less inventive, making possible more telling links of meaning and suggestion between the various ingredients, *eg Ace* (1962, Buffalo AG). In 1962 Rauschenberg became concerned about the possible loss of power resulting from the destruction of the picture surface with real collage elements. Having tried **Frottage** techniques to incorporate objects in a way more compatible with his own painting, he then adopted Andy Warhol's technique of making silk-screens of photographs and stencilling them on to the surfaces. At first he used only black and white as in *Almanac* (1962, London Tate) and later a limited range of colour, but there is no doubt that these are the subtlest of his works to date. He won the first prize at the Venice Biennale of 1964 with these paintings.

Rauschenberg has also been active in other fields, notably as a designer, stage-manager and even a dancer for the Merce Cunningham Dance Company, as a promoter of **Happenings** and as a creator of environmental works. His principal work in this vein, *Soundings* (1968), is a hall of mirrors in which microphones pick up the spectators' talk and trigger the projection of changing images onto the back of the mirror surfaces.

The sources of Rauschenberg's art can be found in Cubist collage, and in the work of Schwitters, but these do not share the seductive quality of his painting nor his concern with preserving the original meanings of his ingredients. In *Studio Painting* (1961, private collection), for example, which contains relatively little collage, the work consists of large patches of Abstract Expressionist colour, dark on the left and light on the right. Visual forces are set up between the two sides of the picture, but Rauschenberg, by painting the work in fact on two canvases, abutting at a central vertical join and held together by a string attached to the one, passing over a pulley on the other and weighted with a sandbag, provides a physical metaphor for these visual forces, thus greatly intensifying them.

In the collage pictures Rauschenberg deliberately chooses his material to avoid obvious story-telling or overt symbolism. Only in his set of thirty-four combine drawings illustrating Dante's *Inferno* (1959–60, New York MMA) does he allow oblique reference to anything outside his painting itself. Although there are precedents for his work in Dada, his conjunctions are not destructive. Instead the different parts of each work link up into an evocative and complex metaphor, sometimes by subconscious association, sometimes with deliberate wit, sometimes by formal links only. Whereas the usual response to anecdotal art is to recall one's own responses to the actual thing represented, as though the work of art had not existed, Rauschenberg takes these responses and, without denying them, returns them enriched by creating something new around them by the artist's traditional means, colour and form. He has summed it up very well: 'Painting relates to both art and life. Neither can be made. I try to act in the gap between the two.'

RAY, Man (1890–   ), American painter and photographer. After studying mechanics, architecture and industrial draughtsmanship, he turned in 1907 to painting. Overwhelmed by the **Armory Show** of 1913, he very soon adopted an abstract style, which was both imaginative and caricaturist. In 1917 he met Marcel Duchamp and Picabia in New York, and together they inaugurated the **Dada** movement in the United States. In 1920 he founded the Société Anonyme to assemble a collection of modern works to be made available to public galleries for exhibition. He joined other exponents of Surrealism when he went to Paris in 1920, and also participated in the De Stijl movement, while earning his living by portrait photography. In 1922 he invented the 'Rayogram', a form of art making use of photographic techniques. After returning to the U.S. (1940), he spent ten years making Surrealist films, and then returned (1951) to Paris.

Man Ray has strenuously avoided repetition in his work. His first inspiration was Cézanne, but he quickly developed a style influenced by Cubism with Dadaist ingredients, *eg The Rope-dancer Accompanies herself with her Shadows* (1916, New York MMA), one of the only American works of the decade to be more than a provincial copy of French Cubism. His Surrealist paintings juxtapose unexpected objects, as in *Observatory Time* (private collection), in which two enormous lips are imposed on a background of evening sky, or *A Woman and her Fish* (1938, London Tate). Man Ray's principal qualities are perhaps his fantasy and his ingenuity.

RAYONISM, a movement founded (1911–12) in Moscow by **Larionov**, whose guiding principles were set out in a manifesto which appeared in 1913. To suggest a fourth dimension, the painter was to use crossed or parallel rays of colour. The importance of the paintings of the two exponents of Rayonism, Larionov and **Gontcharova**, lies in the fact that they were among the first purely abstract paintings, rather than in their intrinsic merits as works of art.

RAYSSE, Martial (1936–   ), French artist. The leading French exponent of **Pop Art**, he is one of the most original artists working in this field. His first exhibition was in 1957 in Nice. He has exhibited numerous times in Europe and America, notably the Venice Biennale of 1966. His art is iconoclastic and deliberately inhuman, in order to create a purer, more innocent vision. At first he used advertisements for beachwear and toilet preparations as an image of this hygienic purity. Then about 1964 he began to use reproductions of Ingres, or models photographed in a similar style, silk-screened on to the canvas in the manner of Warhol but in unnatural colours, the unreality often emphasized with neon, as in *High-tension Painting* (1964, Amsterdam, Stedelijk M). He has also made whole sculptures out of neon. His works are varied in subject and technique, the best using unexpected materials to build up a new vision of subjects usually consigned to the background.

REALISM. Although the art of the 20th century is primarily notable for the evolution of abstract art, realistic painting has retained a place. Indeed, it has opened up certain new areas of artistic expression not accessible to non-representational art. Several of the great 20th century movements have operated from a basically realistic point of view. Realism is the foundation for **Expressionism**; even when Expressionist artists distort, it is usually in the manner of the caricaturist, to call attention to detail. This was especially true of the work of Grosz, Dix, Kokoschka and Schiele, and to a lesser extent, since it was tempered by a delight in the plastic qualities of painting, in the work of Soutine, Kisling and Gruber. **Dada** also made use of realism. **Pittura Metafisica** is essentially a distillation of a reality almost approaching hallucination. And the most important aspect of **Surrealism** is its use of realistic techniques to portray a suggestive, disturbing or inconsistent world. This category includes the work of Dali, Magritte and Delvaux, much of the work of Max Ernst and, to a lesser extent, Balthus.

Many artists who paint realistically do so out of a social commitment, a desire to record generally neglected facts of life and force an adequate public response to them. This could be said of the earliest work of van Gogh: it was an important tool in the religious painting of Stanley Spencer and Desvallières; and it is certainly the case of Fougueron, Guttuso and Herman. This doctrine of Socialist Realism has been forced on artists in eastern Europe for propaganda purposes. The consequent weakening of the artistic impulse has produced, paradoxically, paintings which, however admirable technically, however photographic, are so obviously contrived that they cannot conceivably be called 'realist' in any meaningful sense.

Realism has always had a special place in American art. Having no indigenous artistic tradition, many American painters have attempted to create a new art from an unprejudiced portrayal of the American scene, particularly subjects drawn from the new urban civilization. The most influential was **Robert Henri** both as leader of the Ash Can School, and as a teacher. Later artists have concentrated on different aspects of their environment: Stuart Davis and Joseph Stella were concerned with modern buildings and modern life; Hopper and Burchfield portrayed the loneliness of the big city; and the so-called 'Regionalists', Benton, Burchfield, Grant Wood and Hartley (in his later works), attempted to capture the evanescent traditions of country life. A similar view of life was expressed by American Naive artists such as 'Grandma' Moses and Pickett. The so-called Cubo-Realists such as Sheeler and Demuth used realism to explore new and more intricate formal qualities; the English painters Wadsworth and Hillier had similar aims. Even today, artists in the U.S. and in Britain, such as Wyeth, Lowry and Freud, can use realism as a deliberate contrast to modern styles, as a means of maintaining the detachment necessary to convey a searching and poignant view of life.

The Hommes Témoins group, formed in Paris after World War II, included Buffet, Rebeyrolle and Minaux; English painters with realistic aims, including John Bratby and Edward Middleditch, emerged in the early 1950s. Such developments were paralleled in other art forms during the 1950s, in literature and the so-called 'New Wave' cinema, undoubtedly the product of a new and valid desire to produce an art more in touch with contemporary realities than the fine arts were thought to be.

The realist urge is responsible for some of the most exciting developments of art in the 1960s. On the one hand there are a number of artists, such as Dine, Oldenburg and especially Jasper Johns, who use realist techniques to question the nature of reality itself. On the other hand, the more general phenomenon of **Pop Art** has arisen through a desire to come to terms with the detail (even the trivial detail) of modern society. Finally, the success of Pop Art has made possible a resurgence of realistic painting of a wider range of subjects, particularly the work of American artists such as Rivers, Pearlstein and Thiebaud.

REBEYROLLE, Paul (1926–   ), French painter. A student at the Grande-Chaumière, he won the Prix de la Jeune Peinture (1950), Prix Fénéon (1951), and exhibited with Buffet and Minaux. His style was at first realistic and rather stark. However, he moved quite rapidly via pictures using ever-brighter colour, *eg Trout* (1956, London Tate), to large canvases which combine figurative elements with passages of exuberant painting.

REDON, Odilon (1840–1916), French painter and engraver. He created a very individual style, the clearest visual expression of the Symbolist movement. Having failed an architecture examination, he went to Paris in 1858 and studied under Gérôme at the Ecole des Beaux-Arts. He was more deeply influenced by the romantic engraver Bresdin, whom he met in Bordeaux and who introduced him to etching. At the Louvre, he copied both Old Masters and Delacroix, *eg* his copy of the latter's *Lion Hunt* (1870, Bordeaux MBA). He also studied lithography with Fantin-Latour. In 1879 he published his first album of lithographs, *Dans le Rêve*. He held two small exhibitions of charcoal drawings and in 1884 he was one of the first exhibitors at the Salon des Indépendants. He took part in the eighth Impressionist exhibition (although he never approved of Impressionist painting as such, considering it too limited) and at the Salon d'Automne in 1904, a whole room was devoted to his work. By the end of his life, he had considerable influence on such young painters as **Emile Bernard**, the **Nabis** and **Matisse**.

Redon's work can be divided clearly according to technique and period. Until the age of fifty, his work consisted principally of five or six hundred charcoal drawings, all on tinted paper, produced in his lonely house at Peyrelebade, where he lived until 1897. He used the subtle chiaroscuro of the charcoal medium to suggest an imaginary, visionary world: landscapes, *eg Two Trees* (1875, Chicago Art Inst.), or more often fantastic or tragic subjects, as in *Witch with Cauldron* (1875, Chicago Art Inst.), *Don Quixote* (1880, Harvard, Fogg Museum), *Fallen Angel* (1885, Otterloo RKM), *Crucifixion* (1895, Yale Univ. AG). The inspiration for these works sometimes came from writers such as Edgar Allan Poe, and was penetrated by a feeling of desperate and poignant sadness. Redon said: 'My originality consists in making incredible beings live according to credible laws, in placing the laws of the visible at the service of the invisible.' Redon's engravings, especially lithographs, are numerous and it was his book illustrations which were first to be appreciated by collectors. Redon's first excursion from black-and-white was made with pastels.

Odilon Redon: illustration for La Tentation de Saint Antoine *by Flaubert (1888); ph. Larousse.*

His subjects in this medium were portraits of his friends, *eg Mme. Arthur Fontaine* (1901, New York Metropolitan), religious themes, *eg The Crown of Thorns* (1895, London BM), *Christ of the Silence* (1895, Paris, Petit Palais), allegorical subjects, *eg Orpheus* (1903, Cleveland MA), and flowers, *eg Field Flowers* (1912, Paris, Jeu de Paume), *White Vase with Flowers* (1916, New York MMA). It was through his flower studies that Redon caught the attention of the general public. He took to oils in 1890, with *Les Yeux Clos* (Paris, Jeu de Paume; also version of 1895 in Northampton, Mass., Smith College) which is full of mysterious religious feeling. His use of colour gradually increased in intensity, without sacrifice of nuance or subtlety, and his subjects became less fatalistic, *eg Pegasus and the Hydra* (1907, Oterloo RKM), *Apollo's Chariot* (1907, Yale Univ. AG).

Redon's originality lay in his scrupulous attention to observed reality and the natural shape of things. Especially in his pastels, he combined natural objects with passages of pure colour in unexpected ways, producing works which pointed the way towards abstraction by abandoning conventional construction. These qualities in his work, which can be regarded as the epitome of **Symbolism** also commended Redon to the Surrealists, though he was less artificial.

REDPATH, ANNE (1895–1965), Scottish painter. As a student at the Edinburgh College of Art, she became interested in 14th century painting. Something of this primitive quality can be seen in all her work, which is extremely direct, *eg In the Church of St. Jean Tréboul* (1954, Edinburgh Royal Scottish Academy). Like many Scottish painters she owed much to the influence of Matisse, *eg Pinks* (Glasgow Kelvingrove), but she also adopted a richness of paint handling seemingly Scottish in character which lent her landscapes (especially those of Mediterranean scenes) the utmost vigour, *eg Poppy Field* (1963, London Tate). Her work is characterized by a strong sense of colour harmony and an original use of strong colour in unexpected contexts.

REED, Paul (1919–), American painter. See **Post-Painterly Abstraction**.

REICHEL, Hans (1892–1958), German painter. After meeting Klee in Munich (1919), he concentrated on painting, although he remained a musician and a poet. He went to Paris in 1928 and worked in Bissière's studio at the Académie Ranson, practising a romantically-inspired form of abstract art. His best works were watercolour, and they show a response to nature similar to that of Klee, though more contemplative, and a utilization of individual cells spread out over the paper, *eg Untitled* (1950, Paris MNAM).

REINHARDT, Ad (1913–67), American painter. From 1937 onwards, Reinhardt painted regular **Constructivism** abstractions with rectangular forms parallel to the canvas edges. During the 1940s he loosened his style, via abstract collage, to a free brushwork derived from abstract Surrealism and having much in common with Abstract Expressionism, *eg Number 18* (1949, New York, Whitney Museum). In the 1950s, however, he gradually returned to an even stricter geometrical style than before, using only a very few colours in each work. His final *Black Paintings* of the 1960s (a kind of riposte to Malevich's *White Paintings*), built up of rectangular black areas modulating by the minimum amount, have been influential on **Minimal Art**, although they contain a depth and sense of mystery foreign to that movement.

RENOIR, Pierre Auguste (1841–1919), French painter. Renoir and Monet were the only Impressionists who painted important work after 1900. Renoir alone among the Impressionists was notable both as a figure and as a landscape painter. The son of a poor tailor, he was encouraged by his teacher at the local school and became a decorator in a porcelain works, painting flowers on white backgrounds. By 1858 he was painting fans, copying Watteau and Boucher, whom he always admired. His industry and ability had earned him a small amount of money and he was enrolled (1862) at the Académie des Beaux-Arts in Gleyre's studio. There, he met Monet, Sisley and Bazille. He was refused by the Salon in 1866 and 1867 for *The Huntress Diana* (Washington NG), but his *Lise à l'Ombrelle* (Essen Museum) was accepted in 1868. At this time his painting was still soberly realistic in a style recalling that of

Auguste Renoir: Le Moulin de la Galette *(1876, Paris, Jeu de Paume); ph. Larousse.*

Courbet, although his peculiarly graceful sensuousness was already apparent, as in *The Sisleys* (1868, Essen Museum). His landscapes of this period show the quiverings of atmosphere on a hazy day, *eg Le Grenouillère* (1868–9, Stockholm Nationalmuseum).

He took part in the first **Impressionism** exhibition in 1874, exhibiting *La Loge* (London, Courtauld Galleries). At this point, he began to produce that astonishing series of masterpieces which were probably his best works: *Rising Path* (1874, Paris,

Jeu de Paume), *La Première Sortie* (1875, London NG), *The Swing* (1876, Paris, Jeu de Paume), *Woman at the Piano* (1875, Chicago Art Inst.) and *Le Moulin de la Galette* (1876, Paris, Jeu de Paume). The paintings of this period were luminous and richly modulated and he found support from several collectors and soon began to attract widespread admiration. He was then painting studies of young women, enveloped in light and painted with marvellous freshness, *eg Girl Reading* (1876, Paris, Jeu de Paume). He frequently worked in

Bougival and *La Danse à la Ville* (Boston MFA), and *Les Grandes Baigneuses* (1884–7, private collection) which was inspired by a bas-relief by Girardon.

Renoir lived intermittently in the south of France, and stayed for a time with Cézanne at the Jas de Bouffan. Towards 1900 he abandoned his linear style and acid palette, and returned to a supple, expansive manner, his 'mother-of-pearl' period, in which he concentrated almost exclusively on the nude, using women, girls and children as his subjects, eg *Bathers Playing* (1897, Cleveland MA), *Bather Arranging her Hair* (1900, Washington NG). Bouts of rheumatism, which had begun in 1898, forced him to move permanently (1903) to Cagnes. In 1904 an important retrospective exhibition of his work was held at the Salon d'Automne. His health deteriorated after 1912, and his brushes had to be placed for him between his fingers, by this time rigid with arthritis. But his work during this period was remarkably rich and abundant, and his palette, dominated by reds, particularly sumptuous.

Renoir's oeuvre, extremely abundant and not entirely consistent in quality, can be seen as a continuation of the tradition of the French masters of the 18th century, for whom he professed so much admiration, but he had a great deal more than their sweetness or naughtiness. He had a realist's eye for modern life which was evident in his Impressionist period when he painted Paris life, and he had a profound feeling for nature and for light, enabling him to suggest a mysterious accord between the human body, vegetation, and the atmosphere. He also had a voluptuous relish in the use of paint which he developed steadily from the divided brush stroke of his Impressionist pictures to the dazzling chromatic modulations of his last paintings. For Renoir, colour and form were intimately connected, and his linear experiments in his 'Ingresque' period led him to consider the problem of volume in painting. Indeed, it is significant that Renoir produced a remarkable body of sculpture in the last years of his life, eg *Venus Victorious* (1914) and *Washerwoman* (1917), both represented at the Tate, London, and executed under his direction. His efforts to achieve solidity, analogous to those of his friend **Cézanne**, drew painting away from the luminous mirages of Impressionism;

the open air on the banks of the Seine, painting large compositions such as *Le Déjeuner des Canotiers* (1881, Washington, Phillips Collection). His style changed about 1880, his colours became brighter and less subtle, and his drawing became sharper. This tendency was accelerated by a visit (1881) to Italy, where he was deeply impressed by the Florentines and the frescoes at Pompeii. This was the so-called 'Ingresque' period, of which the best examples are *Les Parapluies* (1882–3, London NG), the two large panels *Danse à* it re-emphasized the importance of relief, which was judged essential by Delacroix, one of Renoir's favourite painters. But the essence of Renoir's art was in the artist's instinctive and spontaneous feeling for life, and in his sensual and sensitive treatment of the human body.

RICHARDS, Ceri (1903–71), Welsh painter. An immensely varied artist, he defies classification. The constant factor in his art is content rather than style: he treated one subject exhaustively over a period of months, subjecting it to metamorphoses ranging from literal figuration to complete abstraction. The two most frequently recurring themes are the human figure and music. Richards studied at the Swansea School of Art and at the Royal College of Art. His work before World War II was influenced by Arp and Ernst, frequently executed in **Collage**, combining a variety of objects in a witty relief with Surrealist overtones. The forms were generally anthropomorphic as in *Two Females* (1938, London Tate). Many of his works after World War II were more representational: a few are isolated images, *eg The Deposition* (1958, Leeds City AG), but more often they were to be the starting-point for a series. For example the theme of the *Cycle of Nature* (1944, Cardiff, National Museum) originally inspired by seed-packets, was developed in abstract works, eventually being transmuted into a *Rape of the Sabines* series. A similar development can be seen by comparing two versions of *Trafalgar Square* (1950, London Tate; 1951, Liverpool, Walker AG) which also illustrates his brilliant colour and fluent drawing, both reminiscent of Matisse. In his last years Richards painted a number of works based on Debussy preludes, of which the most extended series was *La Cathédrale Engloutie* (1959–65, example in Belfast, Ulster Museum), which ranges from a free representation of the visual ideas in the prelude, rather as in the paintings of Debussy's contemporaries, the Symbolists, to taut abstract compositions which capture in another medium a single phrase or mark of expression in the Debussy score.

RICHIER, Germaine (1904–59), French sculptor. A pupil of Guigues at the Montpellier Art School, then an assistant in Rodin's studio, she went to Paris in 1925 as a private pupil of Bourdelle. Her early work comprised busts and torsos done in a vigorous Classical style. In 1936 she won the Prix Blumenthal. During World War II she began to produce somewhat Surrealistic sculptures in which nude figures were subtly metamorphosed to suggest animals, insects, or natural elements, *eg The Toad* (1940), *The Locust* (1946), *The Hurricane* (1948–9, Paris MNAM), *Water* (1953, London Tate). She had a predilection for sharply accented angles and slender points from which wires were stretched, increasing the impression of elongation. Her abandonment of Classical anatomy produced mutilated, visceral figures which were violently criticized. Her *Christ* (1950) for the Church of Our Lady at Assy had to be removed from the choir. She emphasized hollows and perforations and scored and gouged out the surface of her sculptures. Her half-human, half-animal figures express an occult and vaguely maleficent power, as in *La Tauromachie* (1953). After 1956, her work moved away from her Surrealistic style. She began to make very high, slender lead statues set against painted backgrounds made by other artists such as Vieira da Silva and Hartung. She also made a number of small figurines in gilded bronze, set against gold backgrounds and decorated with enamels. In 1952 her love of colour led her to use coloured glass in her lead sculpture, and to create large works in polychrome plaster.

RIJ-ROUSSEAU, Jeanne (1870–1956), French painter. An associate of Signac, the Nabis and Juan Gris, she began to paint in 1895. About 1908, she invented a theory of art, called 'vibrism', influenced by a methodical study of colour and by the practice of Oriental artists, which defined the relationship between colour and sound, and their psychological effects. It had a perceptible influence on Juan Gris and Cubism. Generally, her paintings dealt with modern subjects, *eg Football Players*. These were broken down into simplified planes in the Cubist manner. Her palette was very vivid and she was fond of broad effects of light.

RILEY, Bridget (1931–), English painter. One of the leading protagonists of **Op Art**, she studied at Goldsmith's College,

London and then at the Royal College of Art. She originally practised figure painting in an Impressionist manner, but in 1959 became interested in the work of **Seurat** and adopted a Pointillist style. In about 1960 she began to study the optical effects of juxtaposed dots and lines (as found in Seurat), but on an abstract level. She confined herself at first to black and white and to the simplest repetitive patterns. Nevertheless, these patterns were developed instinctively and the shape of each component very carefully controlled to give a direct and obsessive effect upon the optic nerve of the beholder, *eg Fall* (1963, London Tate). In 1967 she started to work in colour, used first in repeated stripes on a white ground, and most recently in more subtle configurations, and in combination with greys and half-tones. These works retain all the electric effect of the black-and-white paintings, but the colour seems to add a new dimension. She has said: 'I try to organize a field of visual energy which accumulates until it reaches maximum tension.' She won the painting prize at the 1968 Venice Biennale, the first British artist to do so.

RIOPELLE, Jean-Paul (1924–), Canadian painter. He studied mathematics at the Montreal Polytechnic, but was already painting extensively in a figurative style influenced by Surrealism. After World War II he turned to abstract art and settled (1947) in Paris, where he quickly became, together with Wols, Mathieu and Hartung, a leading European exponent of **Gesture Painting**. Riopelle's canvases are covered with a dense pattern of paint blobs in richly harmonious colours, worked with a knife into quasi-geometrical patterns of interlocking bars, *eg Perspectives* (1956, London Tate). Although his paintings are closely ordered (though perhaps rather tame compared with those of his American contemporaries) he has acknowledged the influence of Monet's *Nymphéas* series.

RIPPL-RONAI, József (1861–1927), Hungarian painter. He studied in Munich before going to Paris, where he was one of the Nabis group. He had a preference for vivid colour and a broad clear style of drawing and was a particularly incisive portraitist. Most of his works are in Hungary.

RIVERA, Diego (1886–1957), Mexican painter. He studied at the School of Art of Mexico, visiting Europe in 1907. Rivera worked in Paris, associating with the Cubists: *Still Life* (1916, London Tate). After travelling in Italy, Germany and Russia, he returned (1921) to Mexico, where he received government commissions for large mural decorations for public buildings, dealing with the working life of the Mexican people and the peasants' revolutions. The most important of these is the decoration for the National School of Agriculture at Chapingo (1926–7). The earlier of these works, based on the style of Giotto, were direct in appeal and deceptively simple. His later frescoes, especially those in North America (*eg* at the Detroit Art Inst., 1932) were considerably more complex, attacking the vast structure of capitalist civilization, often with devastating force, as in *Frozen Assets* (New York MMA), though he retained a simpler style when dealing with Mexican genre themes, *eg Women at Market* (1935, St Louis AM). All Rivera's art was patriotic and revolutionary in intent, and he was the leader of the revival of Mexican social realism between the World Wars, creating a direct and vividly coloured monumental art.

RIVERS, Larry (1923–), American painter. A professional saxophonist and student at the Juillard School of Music, New York, he began to paint in 1945 and studied (1947–9) with Hofmann and Baziotes. His painting style remains in the **Abstract Expressionism** tradition of his teachers, but he is closest to de Kooning in his free, vividly coloured, handling of figurative motifs. Rivers has been eclectic in his choice of subject-matter: cigarette packets, bank-notes and advertisements jostle with copies of the Old Masters. His *Dutch Masters and Cigars II* (1963, private collection), for example, takes the composition of an open cigar-box, but returns to Rembrandt's 'Syndics' for the picture on the lid. He has been associated with Pop Art through his choice of material, but the subject is secondary to the treatment he gives it (probing, stripping down and building up again in a fantasy of paint) and he is quite capable of genuine heroic statements as in *Washington Crossing the Delaware* (1953; second version 1960, New York MMA). A number of his works, *eg The Vocabulary Lesson* (1961, London Tate), show a figure with the various parts of the body labelled with stencilled names; Rivers repeats Jasper Johns' trial of painting versus language, coming down, perhaps, even more firmly on the side of painting. He has also executed a number of sculptures.

ROBERTS, William (1895–   ), English painter. While studying at the St. Martin's School of Art and at the Slade School (1910–13), Roberts became interested in Cubism. He joined forces with Wyndham Lewis, becoming one of the principal exponents of **Vorticism**. Some works of this period were abstract, but on the whole Roberts has used the language of Cubism in his work as a means of building complex patterns out of figurative subjects, patterns which at their best crackle with a jagged rhythm, *eg The Diners* (1919, London Tate). Since then Roberts has steered an uneasy course between Cubism and representational painting; the brutal force of his Léger-like figures gives a strong impact to the witty social comment in some pictures, as in *T.V.* (1960, Aberdeen AG), but too often they suffer from heavy-handedness and a tendency for the individual to be lost in the pattern, *eg Italian Peasant* (1964, Newport AG).

RODCHENKO, Alexandre (1891–   ), Russian artist. He began painting abstract works in 1913, and by 1915 had become one of the leaders of abstract art in Russia. In 1917 he linked up with Malevich and Tatlin thus originating **Constructivism**; his *Non-objective Painting, Black on Black* (1918, New York MMA) is in obvious homage to Malevich's 'white' paintings, but has a clumsiness that is typical of Rodchenko. In 1919 and 1920 he made a number of solid constructions in wood and metal, and after 1920 gave up painting and worked entirely in typography and photography.

RODIN, Auguste (1840–1917), French sculptor. A precocious gift for drawing led to his enrollment at the Ecole Nationale des Arts Décoratifs. Refused entry to the Ecole des Beaux-Arts three times, he worked with a master mason and house painter. He was in turn decorator, plasterer

Auguste Rodin: The Age of Bronze *(1877, Paris, Rodin Museum); ph. Giraudon.*

and stone-carver, acquiring great manual dexterity. He was taught (1864) by Barye at the Natural History Museum, Paris, and sent his first work *L'Homme au Nez Cassé* to the Salon; it was rejected. From 1864 until 1871, he worked in the studio of Carrier-Belleuse, and in 1871, was given work to do in Brussels. He spent seven years there, working on many buildings in the city: the Stock Exchange, the Palais des Académies, and several private residences on the Boulevard Anspach. He visited Florence and Rome (1876), becoming a devotee of Michelangelo. He wrote to Bourdelle: 'It was Michelangelo who freed me from Academicism.'

He sent his first masterpiece, *The Age of Bronze*, to the Salon in 1877. It provoked a scandal: he was accused of having cast the statue from the live model. An official enquiry was set up, but Rodin was subsequently vindicated; a bronze cast of the work was acquired by the government at the Salon of 1880. Thereafter, Rodin drew increasingly on Gothic art, as in *St. John the Baptist Preaching* (1878). In 1880 he received a state commission for the door of the future Musée des Arts Décoratifs, *La Porte de l'Enfer* (1880–5), which occupied him for the rest of his working life as he returned incessantly to the same motifs, *eg The Thinker, The Three Shades*, and never completed. This vast work, full of movement breaking across the frames of the door and almost dissolving the panels, was his most Baroque conception: he said at the time that movement was the most important factor in sculpture. Success began to come to him: a large studio in the Rue de l'Université was made available to him by the government. He began a series of busts in 1882: *Jean-Paul Laurens, Alphonse Legros, Dalou, Antonin Proust, Mme. Vicunha, Puvis de Chavannes*. His monuments to *Claude Lorrain* at Nancy, and *Victor Hugo* in the gardens of the Palais-Royal were of this period, as were several other passionately expressive works such as *The Prodigal Son* (1888), *The Kiss* (1886, London Tate), *The Eternal Idol* (1890, Harvard, Fogg Museum), *Orpheus and Eurydice* (1893, New York Metropolitan). These dates are approximate, as Rodin always took a long time to finish his statues, and would occasionally continue to work on them even after they had been exhibited; many were also produced in several different versions. In 1895, his group *The Burghers of Calais* was unveiled after he had spent ten years working on it. His work continued to arouse violent controversies, for example, the *Balzac*, which was rejected by the literary group by whom it had been commissioned in 1898, and was not erected until 1939.

In 1900 the sculptor moved to a studio at Meudon, where he executed the splendid final version of *The Thinker* (1904), and *Walking Man* (1907). In 1900 he organized a retrospective exhibition of his own work in a pavilion in the Place de l'Alma during the Exposition Universelle. His genius had by then been universally accepted. At the end of his life he produced a series of remarkable studies of dancers in motion, often in the most complex poses. Bourdelle and Pompon were among his numerous studio assistants. Two remarkable aspects of his oeuvre are his busts, *eg Berthelot, Bernard Shaw, Clemenceau, Benedict XV, Clémentel, Mme. Russell, La Comtesse de Noailles*, and his allegorical studies, *eg The Secret, The Hand of God, The Creation of Woman, The Cathedral* and *Océanides*. In 1907 he moved to the Hôtel Biron, which became the Rodin Museum after his death, containing the most important and the most finished of his works. A large number of others can be seen in his old studio, the Villa des Brillants at Meudon, which has also become a national museum. The Hôtel Biron also houses the collections enthusiastically assembled by the sculptor, which include works by Monet and van Gogh.

Rodin's work is an overwhelming torrent, the power of which dominated his age. It is marked by all the ephemeral developments in taste of the period, from the coyness of the Second Empire to the naturalism of the end of the century, via **Symbolism** and **Impressionism** (see also Rosso). But Rodin's personality, his profound sense of the pathos inherent in the human form, his furious sensuality, his sense of the tragic and epic qualities of human life, as in *The Cry, The Prodigal Son, The Danaid* (all Paris, Musée Rodin), and his social awareness (he had planned an immense *Tower of Work*) imparted to all his works, even those left unfinished, a lyrical grandeur which was a final flowering of the Romantic spirit in French art. Rodin's art, however, was consciously indebted to the great sculpture of the

O

past, principally to Donatello and Michelangelo, to the Middle Ages and even to Indian statuary. A fervent experimenter in formal design, Rodin was an immensely productive draughtsman who left a great number of sketches and wash drawings depicting movement with dazzling economy and precision. These drawings were in fact only discovered and appreciated after Rodin's death. Most of Rodin's sculpture was designed to be cast in bronze, and casts exist in many principal museums, of which the Musée Rodin, Paris, the Rodin Museum in Philadelphia, and the Tate Gallery, London, have outstanding collections. Only works in stone have here been mentioned with their locations.

ROSAI, Ottone (1895–1957), Italian painter. He produced (1913–14) a small number of Futurist paintings and collages based on café subjects. In 1919, however, he began to develop his own style, not unlike that of Soffici. His most typical works are landscapes, with sharply etched buildings painted in white and red, rather similar to those of De Chirico, though much more painterly and without metaphysical overtones, eg *Piazza del Carmine* (1922, Florence GAM). In his ability to create poetry out of the bend in a road or the juxtaposition of two bleak buildings, Rosai's work resembled that of Utrillo, yet placed figures in his landscapes with a pathos and sense of isolation beyond the range of the French masters.

ROSENQUIST, James (1933–), American painter. He studied at the University of Minnesota (1955), and then part-time at the Art Students' League, New York, while painting hoardings for an advertising company. This direct experience of advertising work distinguishes him from other Pop artists. He was very much struck by the effects of the enormous scale of his work, and by the fact that one seemed to drown in one part of the painting without being able to see it all at once. Rosenquist's paintings, therefore, are huge in scale (some of the recent ones are nearly 90 feet long) and are painted in an Academic commercial style reducing everything to a similar unreal texture, whether it is an image from American domestic life or a horrific war subject, presented in juxtaposition.

ROSSO, Medardo (1858–1928), Italian sculptor. He began as a student of painting, but later turned to sculpture. He enrolled in 1882 at Brera Academy, but was expelled the following year for instigating a revolt against traditional methods of teaching. He went to Paris in 1884 for some months as an assistant to Dalou. By 1889 several members of the avant-garde, including Degas and Zola, had become enthusiastic about his work. Rodin became his friend, and even exchanged one of his torsos for Rosso's *Petite Rieuse* (1890, Bargio, Rosso Museum). But when Rodin completed his *Balzac* (1893), a lasting dispute arose, each artist claiming to have been the first to translate **Impressionism** into sculpture. Rosso returned to Italy, where his reputation continued to grow.

A significant body of his less adventurous works are in the Musée Rodin, Paris, but the most important displays of his sculptures are those in the National Gallery of Modern Art, Rome, and in the Rosso Museum. Even in his earliest works as a sculptor, Rosso was interested in treating figures from everyday life, eg *The Hooligan* (1882, Rome GAM), *The Unemployed Singer* (1882, Rome GAM), *Kiss under the Lamp-post* (1882, private collection). He was also interested in the effects of light and his modelling was governed by a desire not so much to imitate the volumes of the model as to capture the play of light and shade. It is not surprising, therefore, that he was strongly influenced by Impressionism, and to a far greater extent than Rodin, who was a more traditional, and greater, artist. Many of his works seem direct equivalents of Impressionist subjects and carry to the limit the power of sculpture to suggest, rather than define, form: *Impression in an Omnibus* (1883–4, destroyed); *Conversation in the Garden* (1893, Rome GAM); *Bookmaker* (1894, New York MMA); *Yvette Guilbert* (1894, Venice GAM); *Impression on the Boulevard at Night* (1895, destroyed). Rosso usually worked in plaster, often covered with wax which could be scored and further modelled to break up the solidity of the underlying form. His approach to the portrayal of modern life had a considerable influence on **Boccioni**, who sent him a copy of the Futurist Manifesto of 1912.

ROSZAK, Theodore (1907–), American sculptor, born in Poland. A student of art in Chicago (where he later taught) he took up sculpture in 1930, while working as a lithographer and painter. His early works were rather coldly Academic paintings in which an atmosphere of fantasy predominated; *Fisherman's Bride* (1934, New York, Whitney Museum). For a few years, he adopted Moholy-Nagy's theories of **Constructivism** and produced wood reliefs and threadlike structures based on the straight line and the cone. He concentrated exclusively on metal sculpture after 1945, his mastery of welding techniques and the making of alloys being responsible for the creation of a series of dramatic, spiky forms in a highly personal style. A group of these were shown at the Venice Biennale in 1960. Fantasy combines with vegetable and animal reminiscences, as in *Ghost of Kitty Hawk* (1945–7, New York MMA), *Nantucket Whaler* (1952–3, Chicago Art Inst.), *Monument to the Unknown Political Prisoner* (1952, London Tate). Although a Surrealist feeling of horror is never absent from Roszak's work, he tempers this with a free lyricism, *eg Sea Quarry* (1949, West Palm Beach, Norton Gallery).

ROTHENSTEIN, William (1872–1945), English painter. He studied at the Slade School and the Académie Julian in Paris, where he met Degas and Whistler, who considerably influenced his early, rather dark style, *eg The Doll's House* (1899, London Tate). He returned to London in 1895. Between 1904 and 1907 he painted a series of Jews, comparable in approach to the earlier work of Rembrandt, *eg Aliens at Prayer* (1905, Melbourne NG). He was a war artist in France during World War I producing objective pictures with a strong sense of design, such as *The Ruined Church at Bourlon* (1918, Manchester City AG). He returned to numerous academic and official appointments and was knighted in 1931. Rothenstein was also a well-known portraitist.

ROTHKO, Mark (1903–70), American painter, born in Russia. He went to the U.S. with his parents in 1913. In 1925 he settled in New York and, although he had not had much contact with the visual arts previously, he began to draw and paint. His work during the 1930s was figurative and Expressionist in character, and was not exhibited widely. In the 1940s his painting, while still biomorphic, moved rapidly towards abstraction. He worked frequently in watercolour and works such as the *Baptismal Scene* (1945, New York, Whitney Museum) strike a perplexing balance between humanoid shapes and suggestions of Surrealist symbols on the one hand, and the random effects of loosely applied colour washes on the other; these are not very different, in their medium, from the work of Pollock in the early 1940s. By 1948 he had adopted a completely non-figurative style in which the whole canvas is brushed over with colour washes, one colour sometimes blending into another, sometimes isolated from it in hazy rectangular forms, as in *No. 12* (1948, Washington, Phillips Collection). By 1950 these rectangles typically occupy the full width of the tall canvas, and the pictures generally consist of from two to four such rectangles of different heights placed one above the other on a uniform background, *eg Light Red over Black* (1957, London Tate). At first the colour areas were sharply contracted; but more recently Rothko used very similar colours which would normally clash with one another but which he used constructively to set up tensions informing the entire canvas. At the end of his life, Rothko had been concentrating on paintings designed as series. There is a group in the Tate Gallery, London, originally painted for a large dining room, and a further 14 paintings were executed in 1970 for a specially-designed chapel in Houston, Texas.

As all his pictures are very large and as Rothko completely avoided hard-edge in painting, it is not possible to stand back and look at the pictures as form. Instead, the beholder is drawn in to the picture until the colours seem to be swimming before him. The result is a subjective sensation of space or movement, of activity or calm, totally unlike that created by conventional means. Rothko was one of the foremost exponents of **Abstract Expressionism** of the New York School, although his avoidance of painterly techniques for their own sake, and his aim of expressing himself *through* rather than *in* his painting, have made him an influence much respected by the succeeding generation of Post-Painterly Abstractionists.

ROUAULT, Georges (1871–1958), French painter. He can be regarded as the greatest French exponent of **Expressionism** and as France's most important contemporary religious painter. From the age of fourteen he worked with the stained glass designer Hirsch on the restoration of medieval stained glass, and went to evening classes at the Ecole des Arts Décoratifs. He entered the Ecole des Beaux-Arts in 1891, studying under Gustave Moreau, in whose studio he met Matisse, Marquet and Lehmann. He was Moreau's favourite pupil, and was encouraged by him to enter for the Prix de Rome. He failed, but in 1894 won the Chenavard Prize with his *Jesus among the Doctors* (Colmar, Musée Bartholdi). On Moreau's advice he left art school and until 1901 sent religious and mythological works, as well as landscapes and bathers, to the Salon. His style of this period was monumental, inspired by Rembrandt and, to a certain extent, by the Renaissance, and was characterized by solid drawing, mysterious backgrounds, and symbolic melancholy overtones, as in *The Ordeal of Samson* (1893, Los Angeles County Museum); *The Dead Christ Mourned* (1895, Grenoble Museum of Art). His landscapes were both romantic and tragic in feeling.

In 1903, Rouault became curator of the Musée Gustave-Moreau, and a new period in his painting style, lasting until 1914, became apparent. During this period he concentrated almost exclusively on watercolour and gouache on paper, with prostitutes, clowns and Italian actors as subjects. These works were lighter in colour and texture, already showing the beginnings of Rouault's later style of composing with a few large shapes heavily outlined in black, eg *Fallen Eve* (1905, Paris MAMVP), *Prostitute* (1906, Copenhagen, Ny Carlsberg Glyptotek), *Aunt Sallies* (1907, London Tate), *Clown* (1908, Harvard, Busch-Reisinger Museum). In 1905 he exhibited his pictures of clowns in the same gallery as the Fauves at the Salon d'Automne. His style, with its blacks and dark blues, and forceful drawing, drew nothing but scornful comment from the public, but in certain female figures, he attained truly dramatic greatness, eg *Au Miroir* (1906, Paris MNAM). At this time he began to paint judges and court scenes, a subject to which he returned throughout his life, eg *Man of Justice* (1913, Paris MAMVP), *Three Judges* (c 1937, London Tate), as well as poor people, peasants and workers, eg *The Fugitives* (1911, Zurich, Kunsthaus). In 1913 Vollard bought the entire contents of his studio. After 1914 the artist devoted much of his activity to engraving, producing a series of illustrations for Vollard; these are often very large, heavily outlined and contain a profound pathos, predominantly religious in symbolism.

After 1918 Rouault returned to oil painting, and dealt almost exclusively with religious subjects. He became friendly with the Catholic philosopher Maritain, under whose influence his own religious faith took on an increasingly intransigent and austere character. While the message of his work became increasingly sombre, his palette became brighter and more varied, and his impasto richer, as in *Christ Mocked* (1932, New York MMA). In 1929 he designed the sets and costumes for Diaghilev's ballet, *Le Fils Prodigue*. He produced (1930–9) large paintings on his favourite themes, clowns, judges, and religious subjects: *The Old King* (1937, Pittsburgh, Carnegie Institute); *The Dwarf* (1937, Chicago Art Inst.); *The Flight into Egypt* (1938, Paris MAMVP). In all these, he used a heavy outlining technique reminiscent of stained glass. Rouault also painted several still lifes and figure studies, full of psychological penetration, eg *The Apprentice* (c 1925, Paris MNAM), which in fact was a self-portrait, containing the luminosity and emotional poignancy of the self-portraits of Rembrandt. The Museum of Modern Art, New York, staged exhibitions of his engraved work (1938) and paintings (1945). In 1945 he also received a commission for stained glass designs for the Church of Our Lady at Assy. He was a most scrupulous artist, constantly retouching his paintings, which often took years to finish. His *Passion* (Paris MNAM), for example, began as a symphony of greens and yellows, but ended with reds and blues predominating. Rouault's palette underwent (1948–52) further transformations and he began to use bright greens, reds and yellows and a still richer impasto so that his paintings began to resemble Byzantine mosaics.

Rouault was truculent, defiant and solitary, hated publicity and detested

Georges Rouault: Christ on the Cross *(stained-glass window, 1945, Church of Our Lady at Assy); ph. Marc Vaux.*

modern morality. He made a veritable cult of craftsmanship, his great source of joy. Rouault's moral and humanitarian feeling gives much strength and beauty to his work, in which medieval spirituality, romantic passion, and modern Expressionism are so potently blended.

ROUSSEAU, Henri ('Le Douanier') (1844–1910), French painter. He was a low-grade official in the Paris customs until 1893. As an amateur painter he received a licence to copy paintings in the national museums. In 1886 he exhibited at the Salon des Indépendants, where he was introduced by Signac. The Indépendants had no jury, and Rousseau's work appeared there almost every year so that his notoriety was initially due to that Salon. At the turn of the century he was playing in the Orchestre de l'Amicale du V Arrondissement, and made a living teaching painting and music. In 1899, he painted portraits of many of the shopkeepers who were his neighbours, taking their measurements with a ruler. The first of his many exotic subjects was the *Scout Attacked by a Tiger*, shown at the Salon des Indépendants in 1904. In 1905 he exhibited in the Fauve room at the Salon d'Automne, where he was represented by the large *The Hungry Lion* (private collection). He met Apollinaire and Robert Delaunay, who became his friend, and whose mother commissioned *The Snake Charmer* (1907, Paris Jeu de Paume). In December of the same year he was sent to prison over a false cheque which he had been given by a confidence trickster. In order to gain his freedom, he showed the authorities the paintings of which he was so proud; and was thereupon liberated as unfit to plead.

His first biographer, Wilhelm Uhde, became interested in him in 1911, as did several artists, although in some cases they did not take him very seriously. In 1908 Picasso held a famous banquet in Rousseau's honour in his studio in Bateau-Lavoir. In his own studio, Rousseau used to give musical evenings 'for the entire family', where he would play melodies of his own composition. His *Muse Inspiring the Poet* (Basle, Kunstmuseum), representing Apollinaire and Marie Laurençin, was shown (1909) at the Salon des Indépendants.

Rousseau's life remains enigmatic in many respects, because he lived for so long in obscurity, and because he seems not to have been the ingenuous, simple soul he is often made out to be. His very personal style was thus a deliberate creation, and though it reveals a **Naive** sensibility, it was technically extremely sophisticated.

Rousseau's work can be divided into several categories. There are the portraits, still lifes and scenes from everyday life, *eg Portrait of Filette* (1893, Philadelphia MA), *The Wedding* (1905, Paris Orangerie), *The Football Players* (1908, New York Guggenheim), *Flowers* (1910, London Tate). In these works, the figures are presented frontally, with rather stiff expressions. The compositions are pyramidal, the drawing gauche but very exact, and the colours have the solid and harmonious brilliance one expects from primitive painting. A second series comprises Parisian landscapes, the quays of the Seine and surburban streets, peopled with little figures walking or fishing and a profoundly poetic, idyllic atmosphere, *eg Walk in the Forest* (1886, Zurich, Kunsthaus), *Saw Mill near Paris* (1893–5, Chicago Art Inst.), *The Toll-House* (c 1900, London, Courtauld Galleries), *Spring in the Vallée de la Bièvre* (1908, New York Metropolitan). In these, the stylization of the trees so as to resemble embroidery, the cotton-wool clouds, the delicate rendering of surfaces and light confer a mysterious atmosphere on these glimpses of *Paradise Lost*. A third category comprises patriotic paintings which contain allegories based on the painter's republican convictions. This symbolic intention is seen at its most developed stage in the near-fantastic works such as *War* (1894, Paris, Jeu de Paume) and *The Dream* (1910, New York MMA). Such themes were highly fashionable at this time, and Rousseau breathed new life and poetry into what were, frequently, the hackneyed subjects of 'official' painting. But the best-known of all Rousseau's works are the group of exotic paintings, developed on a large scale towards the end of his life, which brought him commissions and a measure of success, *eg* the disturbingly evocative *Sleeping Gypsy* (1897, New York MMA), and the series of jungle scenes: *Virgin Forest* (1907, Basle, Kunstmuseum); *The Snake Charmer* (1907, Paris, Jeu de Paume); *Tiger Attacking a Buffalo* (1908, Cleveland MA). It is

Henri Rousseau: La Guerre *(1894, Paris, Jeu de Paume); ph. Giraudon.*

certain that Rousseau's inspiration for these pictures was not his pretended visit to Mexico, but pictures in magazines, and his memories of visits to the Paris Jardin des Plantes. But the fantastically stylized treatment of vegetation and his direct apprehension of the animal kingdom gave a new meaning to the work 'exotic'. He himself said that he was terrified by the wild beasts he painted. Not all these paintings, admittedly, are as vivid or as carefully painted as those mentioned above. Rousseau's technique was characterized by its formal clarity, which stood with Gauguin's in opposition to the formal diffuseness of the Impressionists and by the subtlety of the clear and delicately modulated colours, reminding one of the primitives of the Italian *quattrocento*. His influence on modern painting has been considerable, particularly on the Surrealists, and although he was not the founder of a school, a number of so-called Naive painters owe much to him.

ROUSSEL, Ker Xavier (1867–1944), French painter. A friend of Vuillard at the Lycée Condorcet, he later became his brother-in-law and went with him to the Académie Julian. He met Bonnard and joined the **Nabis** under whose influence he lightened his palette. Roussel began to paint portraits and landscapes in an open, direct manner, *eg The Road* (1905, Paris MNAM). He then turned his attention to mythological subjects in the tradition of Delacroix, Watteau, Fragonard and Rubens, but placed his figures in landscapes which had an Impressionist freshness. The southern climate had a visible influence on Roussel's style: his palette became luminous and serene, as in *The Cortège of Bacchus* (1908, Paris MNAM). He undertook several large decorative projects, of which the frescoes *Spring* and *Autumn*, executed (1918) for the Kunstmuseum, Winterthur, are the most typical.

ROY, Pierre (1880–1950), French painter. An exponent of **Surrealism** from 1920 until his death, Roy was strongly influenced by De Chirico and in consequence, all his paintings had a strong sense of perspective and a pregnant silence. His Surrealism was thus close to that of Magritte; he operated either by placing unexpected objects in realistic and familiar settings, as in *Danger on the Stair* (1927, New York MMA) which shows a poisonous snake sliding around the stair corner on an apartment house landing, or else by combining familiar articles with an out-of-scale landscape, as in *Day in the Country* (1931, Paris MNAM) in which a château is framed by huge wine glasses.

RUSSELL, Morgan (1886–1953), American painter. After studying in New York with Robert Henri, he moved to Paris in 1906, where he met Matisse and also Macdonald-Wright, with whom he founded **Synchromism** in 1912. He exhibited at this time in Paris and Munich and at the Armory Show in New York. In 1919 he returned to representational painting, but continued to live in France until 1946. Russell's style was rather more angular than Macdonald-Wright's and, though both were interested in colour-rhythm, it was for Russell a structural rather than a lyrical concept.

RUSSOLO, Luigi (1885–1947), Italian painter and musician. Of all the founder members of **Futurism**, he was probably the most schematic: paintings such as *The Revolt* (1911, Hague, Gemeentemuseum) and *Houses + Light + Sky* (1912, Basle Kunstmuseum) link the various elements of the picture in a solid, girder-like framework precluding the sense of movement and flux suggested by the work of his colleagues. He was very fond of music and in his painting *Music* (1911, London Tate, Estorick Loan) he represented a common chord in a rather obvious way as rising from the keyboard to generate an abstract colour pattern over the rest of the canvas. After World War I he gave up painting except for a few representational works, though he continued to evolve a series of sound-producing machines or 'Intonarumori', roughly equivalent to the modern use of the tape-recorder for 'musique concrète'.

RYSSELBERGHE, Theo van (1862–1926), Belgian painter. During a stay in Paris he was overwhelmed by Seurat's *Grande Jatte*. He became a friend of the artist, and adopted **Neo-Impressionism**; his originality lay in its application to portraiture, *eg Octave Maus* (1885) and *Madame Charles Maus* (1890), both in the Brussels MBA. Van Rysselberghe played an important role in the renewal of pictorial and decorative art in Belgium. On his return to Paris in 1898, he frequented the company of the Symbolists. One of his most important paintings, *La Lecture* (1903, Ghent Museum) has considerable documentary value, as it groups together some of the most important literary figures of the period including Gide, Fénéon, Maeterlinck, and Verhaeren, who is reading his poems. Subsequently, van Rysselberghe lived in the south of France, where he painted in a vigorous style influenced by **Fauvism**, *eg Emile Verhaeren* (1915, Brussels MBA).

S

SALONS. It is in France that the tradition of exhibiting in salons, or large regular exhibitions in which a number of artists are represented by a few paintings each, is best established. The name derives from the Salon Carré at the Louvre, where the painters of the Académie Royale exhibited their works from the beginning of the 18th century, and the official salons have always been the showplace of Academic art where the successful would be favoured by official purchases and commissions. This restrictive system had many enemies among avant-garde artists and it was pressure from them that led to the foundation in 1863 of the splendid non-recurring 'Salon des Refusés' for the rejected artists, among them Manet and Whistler. The first important breakaway movement was the juryless *SALON DES INDEPENDANTS*, founded in 1884, at which the Neo-Impressionists were first made welcome, and where Rousseau exhibited regularly. The *SALON D'AUTOMNE*, founded in 1903 by Bonnard, Marquet and Matisse, launched **Fauvism**, and gave regular retrospectives of Post-Impressionist masters such as Gauguin and Cézanne. The more recent *SALON DE MAI* and *SALON DES REALITES NOUVELLES* cater for avant-garde art, the latter specifically for abstract work.

Outside France, equivalents of the Salons do exist, generally in the regular exhibitions organized by official bodies, such as the British Royal Academy, or by local or regional art groups. Much good work does appear in these, but in general they tend to be conservative. Internationally, the equivalent of the Salons are the great Biennales at which artists exhibit by invitation, particularly those at Venice and São

Paulo, and the *Documenta* at Cassel. Otherwise, to see a representative selection of the best of current work, one must rely on the large travelling exhibitions organized by many commercial and other organizations.

SANTOMASO, Giuseppe (1907–   ), Italian painter. He was educated in Venice, where he now teaches at the Academy of Fine Arts. Briefly influenced by van Gogh, after a trip to Amsterdam and Paris in 1937, he began to paint in a near-abstract style influenced by Braque and Matisse. Santomaso was a co-founder of the 'Fronte Nuovo delle Arti' in 1947, attempting to create an Italian art which would not be bound by narrow traditionalism or nationalism. His works of this period are remarkable for their brilliance of colour and combination of quasi-representational Cubist forms and calligraphic marks, *eg L'Ora delle Cicale* (1953, Rio de Janeiro MAM). Towards 1960 he began to explore the textures and colours of paint independently of represented form, at first with a restricted palette, as in *Terra di Castiglia* (1960, Buffalo AG), then later with glowing chromatic effects, *eg Il Muro del Ricordo* (1964, Venice GAM). These paintings place him firmly in the **Abstract Expressionism** school, though belonging to that European tradition (see **Tapiès**) which revels in the solidity of paint substance rather than its use merely as a colouring medium. Santomaso's most recent works are studies in one or two colours only, a large subtly varied expanse of pigment being activated by one or more fine lines of contrasting paint piped onto the surface.

SARGENT, John Singer (1856–1925), American painter, resident in England. He studied art in Rome, Florence and Paris. He made London his permanent base in 1885, exhibiting regularly at the Royal Academy and becoming an Academician in 1897: nonetheless he still retained his American citizenship. Sargent was a very successful portrait painter and commanded high prices throughout the Western world; his pictures tend to be dull in pose and appearance, like a darkened version of some of the less inventive Whistler poses, but he did have an uncanny eye for character. His other works are more interesting however. He met Monet several times in France and was considerably influenced by **Impressionism** in his landscapes and genre-pieces, *eg Claude Monet Painting* (1888, London Tate). In his imaginative subjects, however, he could not shake off the decorative tradition inherited from the Pre-Raphaelites: this is particularly true of *Carnation, Lily, Lily, Rose* (1885, London Tate), but is also seen in his decorations for the Boston Library (1890–1916), the Boston Museum of Fine Arts (1916–21) and even in his great war picture *Gassed* (1919, London, Imperial War Museum).

SARTHOU, Maurice (1911–   ), French painter. A student at the art school in Montpellier, he began sending pictures to the Salon de Mai in 1949, winning the Critics' Prize in 1955. His painting is highly coloured and is basically figurative, but in recent works the representational elements have taken second place to the vigorous abstract design of bold patterns, *eg Bulls in the Camargue* (1961, Geneva, Musée d'Art); *Bird Cage* (1960, Princeton Univ.). In his landscapes, the formal elements have been still further reduced and the paintings approach a free Abstract Expressionism with soft blobs of glowing colour.

SAURA, Antonio (1930–   ), Spanish painter. After a long illness in 1947, he began to paint in a style influenced by Matta, specializing in dream landscapes filled with strange vegetable forms. Gradually he developed by way of experiments with Tachism, in the manner of Wols (see Schulze), to a full **Abstract Expressionism** from about 1954 onwards. However, he is closer to the manner of the **Cobra group** and de Kooning than to the purely abstract Americans. Almost all his works have a figurative content on which he pins the violent handling. The *Crucifixion* theme recurs frequently, as does the female figure. The principal interest in his work, however, is the richness of his colour as in *Imaginary Portrait (Goya)* (1966, London Tate).

SAVIN, Maurice (1894–   ), French painter. A student at the Ecole des Arts Décoratifs, he was a regular exhibitor at the Salon d'Automne after 1922. In 1933 he took up ceramics, and after 1941 he composed important tapestry designs for the Gobelins workshop. His painting style evolved from a naturalistic realism which featured strong contrasts of light, *eg Nu au Rideau* (1929, Epinal Museum), *Marie* (1933, Valence MBA), to one of increasing freedom. His paintings are in a rather monotonous ochre palette and feature large heavy-limbed nudes. His tapestries have been more successful as the drawing is more firm and the subject-matter more varied.

SCHAMBERG, Morton (1882–1918), American painter. He studied at the Chase School, New York, and began painting in an Impressionist style. In 1914 he began to paint near-abstract works, influenced by Cubism and particularly by Synchromism, *eg Landscape* (*c* 1916, Philadelphia MA). In 1916 he came under the influence of Duchamp, and was one of the first to follow him in painting imaginary machinery, as in *Machine* (1916, Yale Univ. AG), and in exhibiting Dadaistic ready-mades, much as the plumbing U-bend entitled *God* (1918, Philadelphia MA). He earned his living as a photographer.

SCHIELE, Egon (1890–1918), Austrian painter. He produced Expressionist paintings which have only gradually been recognized. Unfortunately, there remains insufficient material in public collections to testify to its great variety. Schiele studied (1906–9) in Vienna, where he met Kokoschka, and the dominant painter in Vienna at the time, **Gustav Klimt**. Klimt's flat, bejewelled style with its expressive contours was a decisive influence on Schiele and most of his student works continued this tradition. However, in 1910 he suddenly found his own style in a series of portraits, very possibly influenced by Kokoschka, *eg The Rainer Boy* (1910, Vienna, Oesterreichische Galerie). There was still the flat presentation and patterning of surfaces, but he manipulated the patterns formed by the sitter's clothes into a van Gogh-like swirl of tormented lines, sweeping the limbs of the sitter into the same rhythm. This element of pattern never left his work, but he used it for many different ends. In some works, such as *Agony* (1912, Munich NG), it was almost Cubist in framework, linking one figure to another and intensifying the feeling binding them together. In his views of towns, *eg Wachau* (1914, New York Guggenheim), it had a

more formal function, yet enhanced Schiele's power to invest even a place with tragic personality. There are some remarkable studies of *Winter Trees* (1910–12, all private collections) in which the few bare branches shoot across the heavy paint of the sky in jagged lines making them in effect some of the first pictures to explore the textures and contrasts of pigment.

Schiele also developed Klimt's type of figure outline; so far from it being the necessary result of compression into two dimensions, it was for Schiele an end in itself and he would take it to extremes of expressive distortion in his numerous figure drawings and paintings. These works, nearly all nudes or half-nudes, with their emphasis on the skinny, bony and uncouth aspects of the body and their preoccupation with the sexual organs are often criticized as being Expressionist for the sake of sensation only. All his best works, however, convey a great sense of life as a marvellous, undeserved gift, precisely because the body is so ugly, *eg Lovers* (1917, Vienna, Osterreichische Galerie). Towards the end of his life, Schiele produced a few works suggesting a move towards a new, more painterly, direction, as in *Paris von Gütersloh* (1918, Minneapolis Art Inst.).

SCHLEMMER, Oskar (1888–1943), German painter. At first influenced by Cézanne and the Cubists, he entered the **Bauhaus** in 1920 as head of the departments of sculpture and theatre design, taught at Breslau (1929), and at Berlin (1932). During the same period he created several ballets which were entirely conceived by him and in which he also danced. The designs for these were revolutionary in their attempt to conceal the human figure behind abstract solids such as cones and cylinders (*cf* the painting *Dancer*, 1922, Munich NG). This interest in regularizing the human form was carried through all his paintings, characterized by perfectly proportioned figures, from which every trace of individuality and awareness had been withdrawn. They are arranged like human skittles in abstract patterns in space, but possess considerable power, as in *Group of 14 in Imaginary Architecture* (1930, Cologne, Wallraff-Richartz-Museum). His later works, however, were rather more naturalistic, *eg Bauhaus Staircase* (1932, New York MMA).

SCHMIDT-ROTTLUFF, Karl (1884–   ), German painter. A student at the Dresden Technical School, he became the youngest founder member of **Die Brücke** in 1905. His landscapes at this time were arranged so that large areas of bright colour contrasted in a fairly close resemblance to the motif, *eg Hotel in Dangast* (1910, Berlin, 20th C Gallery), *Lofthus* (1911, Hamburg, Kunsthalle). He also painted religious and other figure paintings in which the influence of Negro sculpture is apparent, rather as in the work of his friend Nolde, but creating a sterner expression, as in *Pharisees* (1912, New York MMA), *Two Women* (1912, London Tate). These qualities are particularly strong in the large number of woodcuts which he executed throughout his life, and their bold simplification and harsh contrasts of black and white do succeed in giving the Christian mysteries the naked force of primitive myth. They also show the influence of Cubism after about 1914, but Schmidt-Rottluff merely used Cubist stylization to sharpen his **Expressionism**, he never adopted it as a coherent system, *eg Evening by the Sea* (1919, Detroit Art Inst.). In 1931, he joined the staff of the Prussian Academy in Berlin, but was dismissed in 1941 and forbidden to paint. His later style returned more subtly to his earliest manner, *ie* with fewer Cubist distortions.

SCHNEIDER, Gérard (1896–   ), Swiss painter, of the School of Paris. He was a pupil of Cormon at the Ecole des Beaux-Arts and worked in Switzerland until his return to Paris in 1924. He gradually developed an abstract style close to **Gesture Painting** which he adopted definitively in 1944. His paintings are dominated by a few large strokes of strong colour, combined with a lot of black, *eg Painting 67C* (1957, Phoenix AM); *Painting 98D* (1960, Zurich, Kunsthaus). His style has affinities with that of Soulages.

SCHOFFER, Nicolas (1912–   ), French sculptor, born in Hungary. He went to Paris in 1937 and began as a painter. He became interested in the theories of Constructivism and turned to **Kinetic** sculpture, inventing 'spatio-dynamism' in 1948. His sculptures consist of constructions of vertical and horizontal metal bars and rectangular plates, often on a huge scale, defining spaces by moving coloured elements. The movements are programmed by complex cybernetic systems. In 1957 he added light projected through coloured filters and revolving perforated discs, and also electronic sound scores commissioned from composers such as Henri Pousseur and Pierre Henri. One of his first 'luminodynamic' works, as he calls them, *Lux I* (1957) is in the MNAM in Paris. His ideas have been demonstrated on a large scale in several spectacles involving the illumination of whole buildings, notably in New York Central Station (1957) and at the Palace of Congresses, Liège (1961). He has also collaborated with theatrical artists, notably with Maurice Béjart and his ballet.

SCHULZE, Alfred Otto Wolfgang (**'Wols'**) (1913–51), German painter. Schulze studied music and then photography until his friendship with **Moholy-Nagy** led to an interest in abstract art. He went to Paris in 1932, and produced several watercolours, while making his living at photography. He was employed as a photographer at the Salon de l'Elégance during the 1937 exhibition; his photographs were a success and were exhibited under his pseudonym. After World War II he went to paint in the south of France. He returned to Paris, and met Sartre and Simone de Beauvoir, who supported him until his early death. His work was both a forerunner of Abstract Expressionism and its apotheosis. It reveals, in a form of Action Painting, the artist's creative energy like an electric charge discharging itself in a shower of sparks. Both his drawings and paintings consist of a conglomeration of lines on a thick scrambled background, grouped into feverish masses, and always conjuring up some sign of primitive power, *eg Composition* (1947, New York MMA).

SCHWITTERS, Kurt (1887–1948), German painter and sculptor. After training at the Dresden Academy, he had his first exhibition at Der Sturm Gallery (1918). In 1920 Schwitters took up collage of a type which he called 'Merz'. The word 'Merz' arose accidently by the cutting-up of a piece of paper with the word 'Kommerz' printed on it, but Schwitters seized upon it as typifying his endeavours to create a new art from the rubbish of commerce: used bus tickets, wrapping papers, advertisements, buttons, matchsticks, *etc.* His pictures transcend their origins and become marvellous multi-coloured patterns of abstract shapes, *eg Merz: Santa Claus* (1922, New York MMA), *Opened by Customs* (*c* 1938, London Tate). Schwitters carried this principle into the other arts. In his home in Hanover, he created a *Merzbau*, a grotto built of bric-a-brac, including objects associated with his friends (a pair of Moholy-Nagy's socks, Sophie Täuber-Arp's brassière). From 1923 he edited the *Merz* magazine and contributed poems, which he used to recite in public, often consisting only of repeated letter-sounds or, as in the case of his 'Ursonate', a wordless symphony of noises. He earned his living by painting Academic portraits. Because of his habit of setting a portrait of Hitler, up to ridicule **Dada**-fashion, at his recitals, he had to flee Germany in 1937, going first to Norway and then to England, where he remained until his death.

SCILTIAN, Gregorio (1900–   ), Italian painter, born in Armenia. A remarkable example of a modern painter working in the style of the 17th century artists, Sciltian went in 1923 to Italy to study their works, notably those of Caravaggio. His style is minutely realistic and involves the copying of the smallest detail although the pictures themselves are often large, *eg Nude* (1928, Brussels MBA), *Books* (1949, Nîmes MBA). His poses have often been very original and he has shown considerable imagination in giving his subjects modern settings, as in *Susanna* (1939, private collection), seen as a theatre star visited unexpectedly in her dressing room by two elderly men with bouquets.

SCOTT, Tim (1937–   ), English sculptor. He studied as an architect while attending Caro's class at the St. Martin's School of Art in 1955. He was also influenced by Brancusi as is seen in sculptures such as *Agrippa* (1964, London Tate). Most of his works of the early 1960s show inventive, and often Surrealist, combinations of fibreglass and glass. In the later 1960s he began to make open structures of welded steel tubing, set off against solid units or against coloured flat plates, as in *Birds in Airas IV* (1969, London Tate) and other sculptures.

SCOTT, William (1913–   ), British painter. He went (1931) to the Royal Academy School, London, after three years at the Belfast College of Art. Between 1937 and 1939 he was in France, notably at Pont-Aven, and unfortunately much of his early work was lost there at the outbreak of World War II. After the War, Scott took up painting again in a highly simplified figurative style influenced by Bonnard and Cézanne, *eg Flowers and a Jug* (1946, Birmingham City AG), *Mackerel on a Plate* (1951–2, London Tate). He also did a few figure paintings inspired by Corot in order to clarify ideas about the reduction of a composition to its essentials, as in *A Memory of Corot* (1946, Toledo, Ohio, MA). In the late 1940s, too, he did the first of the kitchen-table still lifes, comprising pots and pans and simple utensils, *eg Frying-pan and Eggs* (1949, Sydney AG). At first these were realistic, but challenged to paint a large canvas for the Festival of Britain (1951), he simplified the compositions greatly and eliminated perspective, *vide Still Life* (1951, Buffalo, Knox Foundation). From there (especially after a visit to the U.S. in 1953 when he met leaders of **Abstract Expressionism**) the objects were reduced to abstract circles and squares of paint on a vibrantly-textured ground, *eg Yellow and Black Composition* (1953, New York, Guggenheim) based on a coffee-pot motif; *Blue Still Life* (1959, Leeds City AG). Something similar can be seen in his treatment of landscape and figure subjects, *eg Nude, Red Background* (1957, Ottawa NG). However, Scott is not a doctrinaire abstractionist, and in many even of his recent works he has returned to clear figurative references. All his works are distinguished by amplitude of design, by an informal, often centrifugal composition, by rich handling and glowing colour-schemes, showing a true colourist's power even with 'dull' colours such as ochre, khaki and blue-grey, and by an ability to distil beauty and harmony from the simplest things, reflecting his debt to Bonnard.

SECESSION, group originally founded (1892) in Berlin by a number of artists who split with the 'Verein Berliner Künstler' in order to hold exhibitions on their own. The cause of the split was a row over an exhibition devoted to Edvard Munch, but the Secession group, headed by **Max**

Liebermann, Max Slevogt and **Lovis Corinth**, was in fact more interested in propagating a type of Impressionism. A parallel Secession was set up in Munich and in 1897 **Gustav Klimt** founded in Vienna the most important Secession group. In these later two, the Impressionist-influenced naturalism of the Berlin painters was combined with the influence of the Jugendstil and the literary Symbolist aim, in what might be called a 'secessionist style'. This was characterized by painting in a flat, highly coloured monumental style, but tending to idealize rather than to draw material from life. The Vienna Secession was a focus for artists from many countries, two of the most important contributors being Charles Rennie Mackintosh of Scotland and Jan Toorop of Belgium.

SECTION D'OR, the name of a group which first exhibited at the Galerie La Boétie, Paris, in 1912. Its founder was **Jacques Villon** and the members included Marcel Duchamp, Gris, Picabia, Lhote, Herbin, Metzinger, Marcoussis, Gleizes, La Fresnaye and de Segonzac. Léger and Delaunay were also briefly associated with the group, and indeed it was from this milieu that Delaunay developed his **Orphism**, starting from a similar view of Cubism. The aesthetics of the group could be defined as an attempt to reconcile the art of Cézanne (and the Cubists' development of it) with the colour of the Fauves. It wished to bring colour back into Cubist painting, while retaining its formal organization. Indeed this organization became something to be studied for its own sake, unlike the approach of, say, Picasso whose shapes (at least in the analytical stage of Cubism) were derived more intuitively from the motif itself. This approach was indicated by the name of the group, meaning 'Golden Section' and referring to semi-mystical canons of proportion already explored by the **Nabis**. On the whole, comparatively little major work was produced within the group's orbit, but it pointed the way to a particularly clear and neat synthesis of Cubist and realistic elements to which other artists have since returned, but whose best exponent was Villon himself.

SEDGLEY, Peter (1930–), English painter. He is an exponent of Op Art,

working particularly with colour images, eg *Yellow Attenuation* (1965, London Tate). Many of his works use target shapes similar to Noland, except that they have a blurred focus and are hypnotic in effect. He has recently turned to Kinetic Art, eg *Colourcycle 3* (1970, London Tate).

SEGAL, George (1924–), American sculptor. He studied at New York University and Rutgers University under Hans Hofmann. He began as a painter of religious and allegorical subjects, but became interested in Pop Art and especially in **Happenings** and **Environments** through meeting Oldenburg and Allan Kaprow in the late 1950s. In 1961 he produced a 'ready made sculpture . . . as a kind of **Dada** joke' a life-sized figure of a man seated at a real dining table, cast in plaster and cheesecloth from the live model. He found this technique so interesting that he continued to elaborate upon it, placing his figures in very carefully chosen surroundings: an illuminated cinema sign for *Cinema* (1963, Buffalo AG); an apartment house doorway for *Girl in Doorway* (1965, New York, Whitney Museum); and a reconstructed kosher butcher's shop in *The Butcher Shop* (1965, Toronto AG). Although Segal's art is frequently witty, it is closer to the poetic realism of Hopper than to Pop itself. Like Hopper, he is sensitive to the pathos, loneliness and vulnerability of people in the modern world, while respecting their individual dignity. So well are the settings chosen that a whole milieu can be summoned up by little more than a bench and a table, evoking a powerful depth of feeling on the rough, white, featureless plaster figure, who, though anonymous, projects a sympathy for aspects of life too often considered trivial.

SEGAL, Simon (1898–), French painter, born in Russia. An engineering student, he left Russia in 1918 to go to Paris. A self-taught artist, his painting is figurative, making use of radical simplifications rather like children's art. Animals or figures are presented frontally with no attempt at space and landscapes are split into their simplest, highly coloured, elements, eg *Peasant Woman* (1948, Beauvais MBA), *Horses by the Sea* (1950, Cherbourg MBA). He became a French citizen in 1949.

SEGALL, Lasar (1891–1957), Brazilian painter, born in Lithuania. A student in Berlin and Dresden, he exhibited (1911–23) at the Berlin Secession and participated in the German Expressionist movement. He was a friend of Grosz and of Dix, and many of his drawings of poor people and Jews resembled theirs. His paintings, however, were less detailed but used a monumental and restrained form of Cubism to express themes of great poignancy, *eg Eternal Wanderers* (1918, Dresden, Schloss Pillnitz); *Indigents' Interior* (1920, São Paulo Modern Art Museum). In 1923 he settled in Brazil and painted exotic scenes influenced by Klee in his Blaue Reiter period. After 1936, however, in reaction against the Nazi ascendancy, he returned to his earlier themes and produced a series of monumental pictures on the horrors of war and of Jewish persecution which proved to be his masterpieces, *eg Exodus* (1947, New York, Jewish Museum).

SERUSIER, Paul (1863–1927), French painter. He studied at the Académie Julian, where, with Bonnard, Denis, Ranson and several others, he founded the **Nabis**. In 1888 he exhibited a very traditional canvas, *Atelier de Tisserand Breton*, at the Salon. In the same year he met Gauguin at **Pont-Aven** and, under his direction, painted on the back of a cigar box the famous *Paysage du Bois d'Amour*. This he proudly brought back to the Nabis as the 'Talisman', upon which they were to base their style. The synthetic composition and flat areas of pure colour showed the way to a simpler, more symbolic painting style, as in *Roots of Pont-Aven* (1889, London Tate). Sérusier held an authoritative position within the group. His reunions (1897, 1899) with a former pupil, Verkade, then a monk in the monastery at Beuron, led to his publication (*Esthétique de Beuron*, 1905) of Verkade's ideas on the golden mean. He was to use them extensively while working on the decorations of the baptistery of Châteauneuf-du-Faou. In 1908 he became a professor at the Académie Ranson and wrote the *ABC of Painting* (1921).

SEURAT, Georges (1859–91), French painter. Seurat's work was of great importance to modern art for he was among the great innovators of the 19th century, and the most completely Classical in his approach. Almost every painting in his relatively small oeuvre has a perfection of draughtsmanship and composition, unique in his time and comparable only with such masters as Poussin and Piero della Francesca in the history of art as a whole. He was intensely interested in developing new techniques and studying the new discoveries in the law of optics. Seurat entered the Ecole des Beaux-Arts, Paris, in 1878 and during the next few years executed over 400 drawings. Unlike many other avant-garde artists, he did not rebel against Academic teaching and these drawings included studies of casts of antique sculptures, studies of the nude and studies after the great masters, especially Poussin, Ingres and the Renaissance artists. Seurat was also influenced by Couture and Puvis de Chavannes, learning much from the frieze-like poised compositions of the latter. He also made numerous sketches of everyday life, using black chalk on rough paper in such a way as to break up the forms into little spots of light, going back to the true conception of chiaroscuro modelling. Many of these sketches were of country scenes, with peasants working in very simple landscapes, and in these he was strongly influenced by Millet, both in technique and in the power of the simple understatement of the subject. Towards 1882 he began to paint little sketches of these subjects in a broad **Impressionism** technique, with big broken brushstrokes. The way in which the composition was simplified and tightened up, and his manner of reducing the space in the picture began to show a new mind at work, *eg Ville d'Avray* (1882, Liverpool, Walker AG), *Peasant with a Hoe* (c 1883, New York, Guggenheim), *Peasant Seated* (1882, Glasgow, Kelvingrove).

Meanwhile, he had been studying the colour theories of Chevreul and Ogden Rood, and was beginning to experiment with **Divisionism**. This involved the systematic division of his colours into separate touches of pure hues, selected for their interaction upon one another and for their ability to represent the complex balance of local or reflected colour and light or shadow, which makes up the colour seen in any natural situation. In 1884, Seurat showed at the inaugural Salon des Indépendants his first undoubted masterpiece, the large *Une Baignade,*

Asnières (London NG). This picture united a perfect grasp of the qualities sought by the Impressionists (a marvellous rendering of the sunlight, the limpid atmosphere, and the harmony of colour) with qualities they had never dreamed of, a perfectly controlled balance of figures both nude and clothed and a composition uniting all the parts into a frieze-like whole. It was both Classical in its approach and yet unmistakably modern and realistic: the subject was a group of *petit-bourgeois* having an afternoon out by the Seine; even the factories in the background were not glossed over but brought into the total scheme. Seurat did not however employ the Divisionist techniques systematically in this picture, although he touched it up and added varied spots of colour in 1887. The first full appearance of this technique was in the great *Un dimanche d'été à l'île de la Grande Jatte* (1884–6, Chicago Art Inst.), which he exhibited at the last Impressionist exhibition (1886). This, too, was the result of numerous sketches in which one can see Seurat perfecting the empty setting and then filling it with figures, each group of which was the subject of separate studies.

In the last five years of his life Seurat found himself the object of a cult but was reluctant to explain himself; his principal apologists were the critic Félix Fénéon and his disciple Signac. He painted a number of landscapes developing the formal constructions of the earlier paintings to new heights, *eg Courbevoie Bridge* (1886–7, London, Courtauld Galleries). Among the most remarkable of these were the seascapes done in Honfleur (1886) and at Gravelines (1890): the pattern of masts and quays was set off in eternal repose against the pure light reflected off the water, *eg The Mouth of the Seine at Evening, Honfleur* (1886, New York MMA), *The Canal at Gravelines* (1890, Indianapolis, Herron Museum). Meanwhile, he continued to apply the Divisionist technique to figure pictures of increasing complexity, as though setting himself a series of problems. In *Les Poseuses* (1886–8, Merion, Penn., Barnes Foundation) he posed three nude models beside his own *Grande Jatte*, as if deliberately challenging the traditional Academic subject. This was immediately repeated in a smaller version, probably in order to study the effect of the size of the picture in relation to the size of the individual paint spots. In *La Parade* (1887–8, New York Metropolitan) he attempted a circus subject. This was treated as a frieze composition but in his last works he seems to have been determined to break new ground by portraying lively movement, as in *Le Chahut* (1890, Otterloo RKM), the unfinished *Le Cirque* (1890–1, Paris, Jeu de Paume). Seurat's immediate imitators in **Neo-Impressionism** were mediocre and sterile in achievement; his lasting importance lies in the example he set in distilling a timeless essence from contemporary subjects.

SEVERINI, Gino (1883–1966), Italian painter. He met Boccioni, the theoretician of **Futurism** in 1901, and went to Paris in 1906, where he was particularly impressed by Divisionism. In 1910 he signed the Futurist manifesto and brought about the meeting of the Parisian Cubists (Picasso, Braque and Gris) with the Italian Futurists. He organized the Futurist exhibition with Fénéon in Paris. Severini later employed a Classical technique, explaining his development in *From Cubism to Classicism* (1921). In 1922 he executed important mural decorations for the Montegufoni Castle near Florence, and numerous mosaics. He decorated several churches in Switzerland. He won the Prize for Painting at the Venice Biennale in 1950. His style was more radically Cubist than that of the other Futurists, though he always combined it with a Divisionist technique, as in *The Boulevard* (1910, London Tate, Estorick Loan). He was interested in dance subjects and in capturing the quality of music in his pictures, sometimes by using printed signs and symbols, *eg Bal Tabarin* (1912, New York MMA). He also painted everyday scenes, *eg Suburban Train Arriving in Paris* (1915, London Tate), but he was less capable in this than Boccioni.

SHAHN, Ben (1898–1969), American painter born in Lithuania. His father, a Jewish carpenter, emigrated to the United States in 1906. Shahn studied painting in New York but worked at first principally as a lithographer and then travelled extensively in Europe and North Africa (1927–9). His first major paintings, a series of portrayals of the murderers *Sacco and Vanzetti* (*eg* 1931, New York MMA) were realistic and politically engaged works with an incisive drawing style similar to that of Grosz. Indeed Shahn was one of the chief American realists (see **Realism**) and, in his interest in the life of the poorer people and his use of advertisements, photographs and other ephemera as subject-matter, he was a precursor of Pop Art, *eg Handball* (1939, New York MMA). He executed a number of murals, first as an assistant to Diego Rivera at the Rockefeller Center, then on his own, *eg* Bronx Post Office (1938), Washington Social Security Building (1940). During World War II, his work assumed an atmosphere of oblique horror conveyed by disturbing elements in ordinary landscapes, as in *The Red Stairway* (1944, St. Louis AM), *Pacific Landscape* (1945, New York MMA). In his later pictures he abandoned realism and adopted a style close to Synthetic **Cubism**, though with considerable emphasis on drawing in a hard line, like barbed wire. These later works have an aura of myth and are disturbingly compelling, *eg Epoch* (1950, Philadelphia MA), *Parable* (1958, Utica Art Inst.).

SHEELER, Charles (1883–1965), American painter and photographer. A student at both the Philadelphia School of Industrial Art and the Pensylvania Academy of Fine Arts, he came into contact with the principal avant-garde art movements during extensive travels in Europe (1904–9). He was particularly influenced by Cubism, especially after the **Armory Show** of 1913, at which he exhibited the very Cézannesque *Chrysanthemums* (1912, New York, Whitney Museum). In 1912 he began to take photographs of buildings and machinery and this activity continued alongside his painting for the rest of his career. He was constantly searching for man-made forms which would have the formal interest of a Cubist picture (factory machinery, chimney stacks, grain silos, boarding and shuttering, *etc*), and he chose his viewpoints in order to bring out the formal relationships. His paintings after 1917 had the same approach; they were realistic yet reduced to a regular pattern on the picture-plane, *eg Barn Abstraction* (1918, Philadelphia MA). His friendship with Duchamp probably also stimulated his use of machinery in pictures such as *Rolling Power* (1939, Northampton, Mass.,

Smith College) a close-up of the wheels and pistons of a railway locomotive. Had they no representational aspects these pictures would have been in the main line of Cubism, but their interest lies in their ability to assimilate an enormous quantity of realistic detail in an abstract design. The name 'Cubo-Realism' is often given to this style.

SHINN, Everett (1876–1953), American painter. One of the members of the **Ash Can School**, he specialized in theatre subjects like those of Degas, although his oil paintings are marred by their dark tone and heavy detail, *eg Revue* (1908, New York, Whitney Museum). However, on a trip to Paris in 1901 he produced several sensitive pastels in an Impressionist style, *eg Early Morning, Paris* (1901, Chicago Art Inst.).

SICKERT, Walter (1860–1942), English painter, born in Munich. His father was a painter of Danish descent, but the family moved to England in 1868. Sickert began to study painting at the Slade School in 1881, and also under **Whistler**, whose closest disciple he was to become. He first went to Paris in 1883, and there met Degas. He went abroad frequently, particularly to Dieppe, where he lived from 1899 to 1905, and to Venice between 1895 and 1904.

Although Sickert was an innovator only in an English context and his style remained considerably different from that of his Continental contemporaries, he was of great importance in introducing French ideas into English art, organizing the 'London Impressionists' exhibition of 1889 and founding (1911) the **Camden Town Group**. His early style was closely modelled on Whistler, especially in his pictures of shop-fronts and in his portraits, *eg The Laundry Shop, Dieppe* (1885–6, Leeds City AG), *Self Portrait* (1887, Sydney AG). He painted a number of theatre and music-hall scenes which owe something to Degas, while placing greater emphasis on the audiences, *eg La Gaîté Montparnasse* (1895, New York MMA). Until well after 1900 his landscapes and town views, though freely handled in an Impressionist manner, were sombre in colour, but rich glowing effects could be obtained, as in *Façade of St. Mark's* (1896, London Tate) and *Le Grand Duquesne, Dieppe* (1900, Melbourne NG). A few of the later Venetian views have a lighter and more sparkling palette, *eg Rio di San Paolo, Venice* (1903, Toledo, Ohio, MA). In his pictures from 1905 to about 1915, Sickert primarily painted scenes of Camden Town, and this was the most realistic period of his work, *eg Off to the Pub* (1912, London Tate). Towards the end of this period the influence of the Fauves began to reach England and Sickert's later works became lighter in colour, *eg Lansdown Crescent, Bath* (1916–18, Fredericton, Beaverbrook Art Gallery) while a few had a French brilliance, *eg Victor Lecour* (1924, Manchester City AG).

SIGNAC, Paul (1863–1935), French painter. He was able to devote himself to painting at an early age. Inspired by a Monet exhibition in 1880, he decided to concentrate on landscapes, and painted at first in the Impressionist style, *eg Windmills at Montmartre* (1884, Paris, Musée Carnavalet). He was one of the founders of the Salon des Indépendants in 1884. In the same year he met Seurat with whom he worked closely in the creation of **Neo-Impressionism**, the style he used for the rest of his life. After Seurat's death in 1891, he continued to lead the group. As theoretician, he wrote *D'Eugène Delacroix au Néo-Impressionisme* (1899). In 1892 he discovered the little Provençal port of Saint-Tropez, which was then completely unspoiled, and attracted many painters to it. He visited Collioure and Port-en-Bessin, Holland, Italy and Istanbul, in a succession of small yachts, and brought back innumerable watercolours, from which he painted large and more elaborate oils in his studio. In 1908 he became President of the Société des Artistes Indépendants, and encouraged many young artists, including Matisse.

Signac's early works were relatively simple, containing something of Seurat's formal composition with repeated verticals set against a long horizon, *eg La Route, Pontoise* (1886, Leeds City AG), *Quai de Clichy* (1887, Baltimore MA). He also attempted a few figure compositions recalling the hieratic quality of Seurat's work but they were darker and lacked his balance, *eg Le Petit Déjeuner* (1887, Otterloo, RKM). Later his colours became brighter, and

wider in range than those Seurat had used, some of which (a recurrent violet, for example) were used non-naturalistically. At the same time the brush strokes became broader and the designs, particularly those involving masts and sails, more complex and closer to a Baroque style, as in *Venice* (1905, Toledo, Ohio, MA), *Marseille* (1905, New York MMA). Signac gave musical subtitles to many of his works, indicating qualities such as 'rhythm' and 'tempo' which he must have had in mind. His watercolours, more lyrical and less systematized than his oil paintings, are among his finest works, but are rarely seen in museums.

SINGIER, Gustave (1909–   ), French painter, born in Belgium. He went to Paris in 1919, studied at the Ecole Boulle, and worked as a furniture designer. A self-taught painter, he made his début at the Salon des Indépendants in 1936, and helped found the Salon de Mai (1945). His style, at first a rather highly coloured descendant of Orphism, became more or less abstract after 1946. He employs a delicate and supple line, accentuating shapes which may have some faint figurative reference, against a glowing, harmonized, coloured background, *eg Collioure, Collines* (1956, Hamburg, Kunsthalle), *Provence I* (1957, London Tate).

SINTENIS, Renée (1888–   ), German sculptor. A student at Art School in Stuttgart, then in Berlin, she was elected to the Prussian Academy in 1929, from which she was expelled by the Nazis. She joined the staff of the Berlin Academy in 1947. Her work mainly comprises small-scale animal sculptures remarkable for their lively surface modelling, and for the way in which they capture movement. She has also produced numerous portraits and self-portraits (*eg* 1931, London Tate).

SIQUEIROS, David Alfaro (1898–   ), Mexican painter. After meeting Diego Rivera in Paris, he formed with him the idea of 'an art at once heroic and monumental after the example of the great pre-Hispanic traditions of America'. On his return to Mexico, he painted his first mural, *The Elements* (1922), for the National Preparatory School of Mexico. After fighting in the Spanish Civil War, he painted several vast compositions, *eg Death to the In-*

vader (in Chile), *Allegory of Racial Equality* (in Cuba) and many frescoes in Mexico itself. Siqueiros' painting was influenced by Expressionism and Surrealism, but its inspiration has been essentially racial and proletarian, yet idealistic.

SIRONI, Mario (1885–1961), Italian painter. A student at Art School in Rome, he met Severini and Boccioni, taking part in **Futurism**: (*Self-Portrait*, 1913, Milan GAM). He was also much influenced by Léger. In 1923 he was a co-founder of the Novecento group which later developed a style of Fascist realism, but he personally developed a style influenced by Pittura Metafisica. His later works tended to be sombre in colour and composed like low reliefs *eg Five Figures* (1938, London Tate).

SLOAN, John (1871–1951), American painter. He went to New York in 1904 and became a leading member of the group later known as the **Ash Can School**. Sloan's paintings were much influenced by Manet, but he had a fine eye for good-humoured realist detail, *eg Hairdresser's Window* (1907, Hartford, Wadsworth Atheneum). Occasionally he also showed a sensitive feeling for atmosphere, *eg The Wake of The Ferry* (1907, Washington Phillips Collection). He executed some cutting political cartoons, but in general his paintings became more facile in the 1920s. His last works show the influence of Renoir, but have a curious 'grained' technique: *Nude and Nine Apples* (1937, New York, Whitney Museum).

SLUYTERS, Jan (1881–1957), Dutch painter. A student at the Art School in Amsterdam, he won the Prix de Rome in 1904 and went to France and Italy. He was most influenced by Toulouse-Lautrec, *eg Two Women Dancing* (1906, Amsterdam, Sluyters Collection) and by the Fauves, *eg Self Portrait* (1924, Amsterdam, Stedelijk M). His most interesting canvases were executed in the village of Staphorst, *eg The Peasants of Staphorst* (1917, Amsterdam Stedelijk M). They are linear, realistic and expressionistic, with dark contrasted colours.

SMET, Gustav de (1877–1943), Belgian painter. He studied at the Academy of Ghent. He was a co-founder of the second

school of **Laethem-Saint-Martin**. He fled to Holland in 1914, and there was influenced by Le Fauconnier. He subsequently settled in the Vallée de la Lys. His painting had Expressionist tendencies and showed traces of Cubist influence, deliberately unsophisticated, *eg Snowy Night* (1918, The Hague, Gemeentemuseum), *Beatrice* (1923, Brussels MBA).

SMITH, David (1906–65), American sculptor. As a metal worker in a car factory, he learned techniques he was later to use in his sculpture. For many years he studied and practised painting part time. Initially, he worked in an Impressionist style, but in 1928 he moved to New York, met John Graham and Stuart Davis and was influenced by Cubism. In 1931 Smith began to attach various objects to his paintings and in the same year took up sculpture proper, working in welded steel. In 1934 he gained the use of an iron works forge and other equipment and in 1940 built a similarly equipped studio at his house. He was a close friend of artists such as Helen Frankenthaler, Motherwell and Noland who developed a style of Post-Painterly Abstraction which in many respects paralleled Smith's work. He has had a great influence on many post-War sculptors, especially on Caro and his pupils.

David Smith's sculpture is extraordinarily varied although it is almost all based on forged and welded steel. The principal influences on his work were the Cubist sculptors such as Gargallo, Chillida and Picasso himself, and nearly all his works bear a relationship to Synthetic **Cubism** in their open, even quirky form. Nevertheless, Smith's inspiration generally came from specific visual ideas: *Hudson River Landscape* (1951, New York, Whitney Museum). Many of his earlier works were influenced by Giacometti, and show Surrealist juxtapositions of apparently representational symbols, for example the egg/womb forms in *Royal Incubator* (1949). In 1962 Smith spent a month at the Spoleto Festival in Italy, producing the 26 sculptures of his Voltri scenes which juxtapose sheets and bars of metal with various mechanical objects *eg Voltri XIII* (1962, Berkeley, Univ. of California). These sculptures are important in that they show that monumental sculpture can also teasingly invite participation in a Dada way. Smith's last works tended to be rather more formal, often conceived with a single principal viewpoint, like pictures. The series of *Circles* begun about 1960 introduces the use of paint, sometimes applied in subtle combinations of browns and ochres, sometimes in bold primary colours. The *Cubi* series comes close to a Constructivist aesthetic; each work balances a tightly organized group of rectangular metal boxes at shoulder height on a steel column thus giving each composition a charge of potential energy vis à vis the spectator, *eg Cubi XIX* (1959, London Tate).

SMITH, Jack (1928–   ), English painter. He studied at the Sheffield College of Art and after the War went to St. Martin's School of Art and the Royal College in London. His first works after leaving college in 1953 were realist in theme, painted in a stark style, *eg Mother Bathing Child* (1953, London Tate). In 1956 he won first prize in the John Moores Liverpool Exhibition with *Creation and Crucifixion* (1956, Liverpool, Walker AG). This is ostensibly a domestic interior, but Smith sees in the shirts in various parts of the picture images of death and rebirth. After this he became more interested in exploring effects of light on water and on glass, an Impressionist concern, but treated by Smith in a manner approaching abstraction, *eg Bottles II* (1959, Sydney, AG). His work of the 1960s is completely abstract, as in *Black, White and Grey Movement, No 2* (1962, London Tate).

SMITH, Matthew Arnold Bracy (1879–1959), English painter. He entered the Manchester School of Art to study design and went to the Slade School in 1905. He lived in France intermittently from 1908 until 1940, staying first in Pont-Aven and later in Paris. He attended the art school run for a time by Matisse who was the greatest influence on his work, releasing his natural gift for exuberant colour. He was thus the outstanding English successor to the Fauves. His earlier works are simple and taut in construction, *eg Lilies* (1913, Leeds City AG) with its van Gogh-like blue background and rather Japanese pattern, or *Nude, Fitzroy Street* (1916, London Tate) in which the green-and-gold nude owes much to Matisse, but the daring attempt to define space by the green bars converging on the red background was his own. In *Cornish Church* (1920, London Tate), Smith attempted a Matisse-type open window composition, and achieved an original perspective and a particularly rich colour chord. In his later nudes, *eg Reclining Nude* (1924, Leicester AG), and flower pieces, *eg White Roses and Pears* (1930, Bradford AG), Smith became far more painterly and his rigid compositions became more Baroque, even Rubensian, in treatment. He was knighted in 1954.

SMITH, Richard (1931–   ), English painter. His development has been extraordinarily fast: in 1957 he was a student at the Royal College of Art in London, in 1967 he won the Grand Prize at the São Paulo Bienal. He is a remarkable painter, not only in that he combines some of the best features of English and American painting (and in fact divides his time between the two countries), but also in that he is one of the very few abstract artists to react to the modern world of **Pop Art** entirely in terms of pure painting. His earlier work was influenced by **Sam Francis** (*Salem*, 1958, Bristol AG), but his style began to change between 1959 and 1961, when he was living in New York on a Harkness Fellowship. He gradually added his responses to advertising billboards, wide-screen cinema and packaging of consumer goods to the range of visual experience which could be explored in abstract, and always painterly, terms. For example the *trompe l'oeil* effects of perspective used in advertising became the subject of many paintings, *eg Vista* (1963, London Tate). The more recent paintings use irregular shaped canvases and even three-dimensional structures, again based on display hoardings, to create works in which the spatial relationships implied in paint are played off against 'real' space, *eg Quartet* (1964, Minneapolis, Walker Art Center).

SMITH, Tony (1912–   ), American sculptor and former architect. His earlier sculptures are massive and simple; *Black Box* (1962, New York MMA), for example, is merely a metal cube on a large scale. In these works he is related to Minimal Art. His works, which are executed first in wood and later in metal, have been getting more varied and frequently have an architectural effect on the beholder: *Arch* (1968–70,

Sonebeek Park, Belgium). Recently his work has become less symmetrical.

SMITHSON, Robert (1938–), American sculptor. See **Minimal Art**.

SNELSON, Kenneth (1927–), American sculptor. While studying at Black Mountain College in 1948–9, he developed the idea of 'tensegrity', that is to say the building of non-rigid sculptures held in position solely by the balance of tensions. In his *Needle Tower* (1968, Otterloo, Kröller-Müller Museum) for example, a 28 metre high tower is entirely composed of bars of tubular aluminium, the top end of each supporting by a wire the bottom end of the one above. Since the form of his works is so visibly the result of simple principles, Snelson's work virtually epitomizes the sculpture of **Constructivism**.

SOFFICI, Ardegno (1879–1964), Italian painter. After training at the Florence Academy, he lived in Paris until 1907. Although basically a realistic painter, towards the end of his stay there he adopted a stark style with hard black lines, a muted reflection of Fauvism. He also adopted some Futurist techniques after 1912. By 1920, however, he had settled down to a finely-balanced basically Impressionist landscape style, which he continued with increasing emphasis on atmosphere at the expense of form, *eg Casa Colonica* (1920, São Paulo Modern Art Museum).

SONDERBORG, (1923–), German painter, originally K. R. Hoffmann. He attended the Landeskunstschule in Hamburg, from 1947–9. He lived in Hamburg until 1958, when he moved to Paris, visiting New York in 1960–1. His inspiration was the dockland of Hamburg, though it is treated almost non-figuratively in an Abstract Expressionist technique, *eg Nautical* (1953, Cologne, Wallraff-Richartz-Museum). These works are very open in form, but they quickly become more heavily worked, and covered by frenzied scratchings through the paint as in *Hamburg 18.7.1955* (Hamburg, Kunsthalle). Sonderborg's more recent paintings are much stronger in form though they continue to make use of the techniques of scraping, scratching and squeezing the paint, *eg Paris, Villa Santos Dumont* (1961, New York, Guggenheim).

SOTO, Jesus-Rafael (1923–), Venezuelan painter. He worked as a sign-painter until being awarded a scholarship to the Caracas School of Fine Arts in 1942. From 1947–50 he was Director of the Art School at Maracaibo. In 1950 he went to Paris, where he earned his living as a guitarist. His first paintings were geometrical in character, but in 1954 he began to experiment with the effects of painting patterns on superimposed perspex sheets, which seem to move as the observer changes his viewpoint: he calls these works *Vibrations*. In 1962 he began to use suspended solid objects against a patterned background, and rich hallucinatory colour as in *Relationships of Contrasting Elements* (1965, London Tate); *Courbes Immaterielles-Vert* (1966, Providence, Rhode Island, School of Design). He has designed large murals in a similar style for the University of Caracas and for the Venice Biennale of 1966. He is one of the chief exponents of **Op Art**.

SOULAGES, Pierre (1919–), French painter. A self-taught painter, he began in a Romantic style influenced by van Gogh. When he was discharged from the army in 1946, he settled in Paris and became a leading French exponent of **Abstract Expressionism**. He won prizes at the International Exhibitions at São Paulo (1953) and Tokyo (1957). His canvases explore on a very large scale a type of Gesture Painting with bold slashes of dark paint. The dark tonality and the sheer size of the brushmarks give his work a primitive quality, *eg 23 May 1953* (London Tate).

SOUTINE, Chaïm (1894–1943), French painter, born in Lithuania. The tenth child in a poor Jewish family, he ran away to Minsk, attended classes at the art school (where he met Kikoïne and Krémègne), and earned a living as an apprentice photographer. When he arrived in Paris in 1911 he rushed to the Louvre to see the paintings by Rembrandt, who remained an influence on his work. His first canvases were sombre still lifes, some of which Modigliani's dealer Zborowski tried to sell. Zborowski sent Soutine to Céret to paint in 1919. He stayed there for several years, travelling to Cagnes and painting a series of convulsive works which he later tried to destroy. In 1923, he met Paul Guillaume,

Chaïm Soutine: The Pastry Cook *(1922–3, private collection); ph. Giraudon.*

who bought his *Pastry Cook* (Paris, Orangerie), and also Dr. Barnes of Philadelphia who bought other works. In 1924 he worked at Cagnes, developing a more stable, open style. Returning (1925) to Paris, he settled in the Rue du Saint-Gothard, where he painted his famous pictures of flayed ox carcasses modelled on Rembrandt, having acquired a carcass which he would sprinkle with fresh blood from time to time. He led a lonely, unsettled and Bohemian life, spending 1930–5 at the Château de Lèves near Chartres. When war came, Soutine, in danger because of his Jewish nationality, took refuge in the Touraine district, but died of a perforated ulcer.

Soutine learned about composition from Cézanne and about colour from van Gogh; he remained essentially an individualist and aloof from contemporary fashions in that his paintings express nothing so much as his own troubled mind. However, he is classifiable in **Expressionism**. He always worked in bursts of feverish inspiration. His palette was darkest in his early paintings, but he began to add brighter colours after his stay at Céret. His interest in colour contrast was a permanent feature of his style. The Céret pictures show a mass of conflicting, impenetrable planes and are the most violent of his output, *eg Landscape at Céret* (1920, Harvard, Fogg Museum); *Landscape at Céret* (1920–1, London Tate). In the period of the Cagnes landscapes (*c* 1924) he developed a style in which the elements in the picture, though distorted, could be organized into a coherent space that one could 'walk through', *eg The Road up the Hill* (1924, London Tate). In the still lifes and portraits which occupied him throughout the 1920s he brought the simple motif (*eg* a side of beef, a dead fowl or a human figure) forward and, instead of making it take its place in a three-dimensional space, built around it an area of tormented paint which carried the force of the expression, *eg Carcass of Beef* (1925, Buffalo AG). This was particularly the case with the paintings of cooks or page-boys whose uniforms flared out against the background and contrasted with the hopeless faces and pitiable bodies, as in *Page-boy at Maxim's* (1927, Paris MNAM). The last works were fresher and more open than anything before, *eg Return from School* (*c* 1939, Washington, Phillips Collection).

SPENCER, Niles (1893–1952), American painter. A student at the Rhode Island School of Design and then at the Art Students' League in New York, under Bellows and Henri, he settled in New York in 1916, subsequently making several trips to France and to Italy. His subject was the urban scene, treated with a strong sense of pattern and precision of form. His large coloured planes were far more simplified and less detailed than those of Cubo-Realists such as Sheeler, while his sense of place and atmosphere distinguished him from Purism; but he had much in common with both tendencies. He was also able to suggest quite complex spaces without disrupting the surface pattern of his pictures, *eg City Walls* (1921, New York MMA); *Erie Underpass* (1949, New York, Metropolitan Museum).

SPENCER, Stanley (1891–1959), English painter. Although standing aloof both from the principal movements of his time, and from conventional Academicism, Spencer nonetheless was a well-grounded student, winning the Composition Prize (1912) at the Slade School. He was particularly interested in the primitive Italians Giotto, Masaccio and Fra Angelico. This influence manifested itself in the style of his work at the time, *eg The Nativity* (1912, London Univ. College), and filled him with a desire to rework the subjects and their forms in modern terms. He served in Macedonia (1915–18) and his picture of the experience, *The Dressing Station* (1919, London, Imperial War Museum), already conveyed the characteristic feeling that an event was not only local and actual but an allegory for something basic in mankind. This he portrayed in realistic detail but frozen by the use of sharp light and shadow and with a strong element of pattern, as if imposing a Cubist superstructure on the action. The use of allegory, essential to all religious painting, was developed in a number of works setting the Bible stories in his native village, Cookham: *Christ Carrying the Cross* (1920, London Tate); *The Betrayal* (1922, Belfast, Ulster Museum); *Resurrection Cookham* (1923–7, London Tate). Perhaps the greatest of these works is the *Resurrection* (1928), painted as a war memorial in the Oratory of All Souls, Burghclere, in which soldiers rise from their graves, embracing their white crosses while gradually becoming aware that they too have partaken of the Crucifixion and Resurrection of Christ. In his later years, Spencer reduced the overt religious content of his pictures, painting instead well-observed genre pieces to express the idea that there is something religious in *all* everyday action, *eg The Marriage at Cana* (1952–3, Fredericton, Beaverbrook AG). He was knighted in 1959.

STAEL, Nicolas de (1914–55), French painter, born in Russia. He fled with his parents to Poland in 1919. He was educated in Brussels, first at the Jesuit College and later at the Academy of Fine Arts. He travelled much in the 1930s, painting all the time, but little of his work survived. He settled in Nice and later in Paris. He met Braque, Kandinsky and many members of the School of Paris. He exhibited at the Biennales of São Paulo (1953) and Venice (1954). In March 1955 he committed suicide. Although he shared with the other Russian artists of the School of Paris a liking for strong colour and thick impasto, there was not really an Expressionist streak in de Staël's make-up. His painting was in the French tradition, stemming from both **Impressionism** and **Fauvism**, coupled with an original grasp of abstract composition.

De Staël's earlier work was realistic in a rather sombre style. In 1940 he began painting abstracts, using dark colours and covering the canvas with long bars of thick paint applied with the brush, *eg Marathon* (1948, London Tate). By 1950 these bars were becoming shorter, the paint thicker, the colour brighter and he used a knife rather than a brush. The pictures of the years 1952–3, which many consider his greatest, can be considered figuratively, but only just, for the heavy blocks of impasto always establish an independent existence for themselves. In some landscapes, *eg Parc de Sceaux* (1952, Washington, Phillips Collection), the colours are close to nature, but in others, particularly the beach scenes such as *Figure by the Sea* (1952, Dusseldorf, Schloss Jägerhof), he used brilliant reds, oranges and violets. He also painted figure compositions, a series of *Footballers* (1952), and of *Musicians* (1953, *eg* Washington, Phillips Collection), in which the lively action of the figures contrasted even more strongly with de Staël's elemental

technique. At this stage he applied areas of colour with a knife over quite different colour. This seeped through and appeared round the edges adding a new dimension of richness and depth. In 1954 he began to modify this style considerably and returned to a much more realistic manner

STAHLY, François (1911–), Swiss sculptor. In Paris, he was taught by Malfray at the Académie Ranson and took part in various Salons. He won a gold medal at the Milan Triennale in 1954. He specializes in large-scale work for architectural commissions: *Signal* (1955, on the motorway at Orly); stained-glass reliefs for the church of Baccarat (1956); *Fountain* (1962, Seattle Civic Center). Although all his sculptures are highly finished, he has a predilection for natural forms, *eg* the smooth stones lapped by the water in *Fountain* (1959) at Asnières. For his wood sculpture, he has frequently started from tree roots, polishing, but hardly altering the shape, *eg Le Combat d'Oiseaux* (1960, Park of Louveciennes).

STAMOS, Theodoros (1922–), American painter. The son of Greek immigrants, he won a scholarship to the American Artists' School, New York, at the age of 14 and had his first exhibition at 22. Stamos' first paintings were not representational but were nonetheless based on small marine plant and animal forms, and influenced by Oriental painting. Soon, influenced by Dove, he abandoned figurative elements and produced taut compositions of block-like shapes executed in near-monochrome, *eg Sounds from the Rock* (1946, New York MMA). Since then he has been gradually heightening his colour and developing the forms on his canvas to reveal a great spaciousness. In the 'Field' paintings of 1957–8, patches of loosely brushed but brilliant colour emerge from behind a cloud of paint, white or coloured, in a manner similar to Gottlieb. In 1959 he simplified still further, producing works which were just a single band of colour across the canvas on a background of another, *eg Ahab for R.J.H.* (1959, San Francisco MA). Although reminiscent of Rothko they use heavy impasto and emphasize the strong aggressive aspect of **Abstract Expressionism**, rather than the suggestive one.

STANKIEWICZ, Richard (1922–), American sculptor. He went to Paris but soon returned to study painting with Hofmann. He turned to sculpture, however, and has become known as a creator of **Assemblages** of scrap metal. Formally, his style owes much to David Smith; but in his use of miscellaneous fragments from the junk yard he is more akin to Neo-Dadaists such as Tinguely. However, the witty humanity of his works is not at all nihilistic, *eg Kabuki Dancer* (1955, New York, Whitney Museum).

STEELE, Jeffrey (1931–), Welsh painter. He specializes in repeated pattern, often in black and white, having an illusory effect on the perception: *Gespentische Gestalt* (1961, Liverpool AG). See **Op Art**.

STEER, Philip Wilson (1860–1942), English painter. He studied at Gloucester School of Art, then at the Académie Julian and the Ecole des Beaux-Arts in Paris. He also taught from 1893 to 1930 at the Slade School. His paintings belong to the English Impressionist movement, influenced by Whistler and by French **Impressionism**. His early landscapes and figure paintings are notable for sensitive draughtsmanship, simplified palette and lyrical use of colour, *eg The Beach of Walberswick* (1890, London Tate). Towards the end of his life he painted sentimental genre pieces and erotic fantasies, *eg Sleep* (*c* 1900, London Tate), *The End of the Chapter* (1911, Bradford AG).

STELLA, Frank (1936–), American painter. After studying at Phillips Academy and Princeton University, he had his first exhibition in 1960. Originally influenced by the *Flags* of Jasper Johns, he began painting striped canvases, first in a painterly style, and after 1960 in **Hard-edge** patterns. In this period, he avoided the lyricism of other stripe painters such as Noland, by using metallic and harsh commercial colours, and by combining his stripes in patterns that contain disturbing contradictions, *eg Hyena Stomp* (1962, London Tate). These paintings are intended to be taken as objects in themselves, an approach encouraged by the use of thick or irregularly-shaped supports; this idea has also been influential in **Minimal Art**. In 1964 he began a series of works, with 'Moroccan'

titles, using bright fluorescent paints and achieving the teasing effects of Op Art, *eg Fez* (1964, Buffalo AG). These colours persisted in a later series of 'irregular polygons', unusually shaped canvases, in which the stripe motif is no longer important, somewhat similar to the work of Ellsworth Kelly: *Effingham I* (1967, Eindhoven Museum). Since 1967 he has increasingly used circles as compositional shapes, accompanied by more lyrical colour.

STELLA, Joseph (1877–1946), American painter, born in Italy. After studying medicine in Italy, he began to paint, and upon emigrating to the U.S. in 1902 studied at the New York School of Art. He became enthralled by the American industrial scene, the subject of his best paintings. In a visit to Italy and France (1909–11) he met the Futurists and on his return to New York exhibited at the **Armory Show**. He continued to produce works viewing America very appropriately through Futurist eyes (specifically influenced by Severini) *eg Battle of Lights* (1913, Yale Univ. AG), the polyptych, *New York Interpreted* (1922, Newark Museum). Around 1920 he executed a number of collages rather in the manner of Schwitters, with an extraordinary feeling for abstract texture.

STIJL, De, the title of a Dutch periodical founded (1917) by Mondrian and van Doesburg for the propagation of the ideas of **Neo-Plasticism**. The name was sometimes used to refer to the contributing artists as a group, which included the painter Bart van der Leck, the sculptor Vantongerloo and the architects J. J. P. Oud, Gerrit Rietveld, Jan Wils and Van't Hoff. Many other architects later joined the movement, as did the painters Domela and Vordemberge-Gildewart. Van Doesburg initiated **Elementarism** in 1926 as a variant of Neo-Plasticism, causing a break with Mondrian. The importance of the movement lies as much in the work of the architects and designers connected with it as in that of the artists with the exception of Mondrian. For in the buildings of Oud, the furniture of Rietveld, or the typography of the magazine itself, the ideas of Neo-Plasticism were given more general application. This led to a new aesthetic of totally functional design, based on regular shapes, in which colour was used as an adjunct to form, but from which ornament, as such, was rigorously excluded. These ideas made a decisive contribution to the aesthetic of the **Bauhaus**, thus asserting a lasting influence on design.

STILL, Clifford (1904–), American painter. He taught at the California School of Fine Arts and settled in New York in 1950. Still's painting is Abstract Expressionist, but is concerned neither with Action Painting nor with the suggestiveness of Rothko. His large canvases are completely covered with a thick layer of heavy impasto of one dominant colour, forming a wall through which burst patches of other colours contrasting in line and brilliance. They suggest powerful forces at play underneath the visible paint layer, *eg Painting, 1951* (New York MMA). He was one of the first to paint on a huge scale as a matter of principle.

STROUD, Peter (1921–), English painter. He was one of the exhibitors in the 'Situation' shows held between 1960 and 1963 which launched Post-Painterly Abstraction in Britain. His very austere art, which perhaps owes something to Newman, employs large fields of colour articulated by thin, straight, relief ridges of a second colour, *eg Six Thin Reds* (1960, London Tate).

STURM, Der, see **Galleries**.

SUPREMATISM, abstract movement founded by **Malevich** in 1913. Malevich defined suprematism as 'the supremacy of pure emotion in art'; in fact it was the first abstract movement to start from scratch with non-figurative ideas, aiming, in Malevich's words, 'to liberate art from the ballast of the representational world'. Suprematism was then the foundation of the Constructivist aesthetic. Malevich's first works consisted of squares on a plain ground; he later began to introduce other elements and to use colour. Rodchenko, Lissitzky, Moholy-Nagy and Pougny also took part in the movement, and brought its ideas to the Bauhaus.

SURREALISM, the last of the great revolutionary aesthetic movements of the first half of the 20th century. Surrealism embraces philosophy, poetry and other fields of human activity as well as the visual arts. Its origin officially dates from 1924, when **André Breton**, chief organizer and theoretician of the movement, published his Surrealist Manifesto. He defined it thus: 'A psychic automatism through which can be expressed . . . in whatever manner, the true working of the mind.' The first Surrealists, Eluard, Aragon, Soupault, Arp, Man Ray and Miró, were Dadaists who had broken with Tzara in 1922. While retaining the Dadaist spirit of revolt against the social and moral order, they wished to draw positive conclusions from it; they wanted to remake the world and society. Their cult of the dream, instinct and spiritual exile, and the interest they took in masters of the past whose subject-matter or style was most fantastic, facilitate their classification as very late Romantics.

Picabia's ballet *Relâche* (1924, a joke title, as·this is the word put up on French theatres when they are closed for holidays), was one of the earliest Surrealist works. The first Surrealist exhibition (1925) included works by Max Ernst, Arp, Man Ray, Miró, Picasso (only temporarily a Surrealist) and **De Chirico**, their great predecessor. Also in 1925, Breton began to direct the review *La Révolution Surréaliste*. In 1926 a Surrealist gallery, in which **Marcel Duchamp** exhibited, was opened. The ranks of the group were increased when Magritte, and then **Dali**, joined them. Breton's Second Surrealist Manifesto (1929) excluded a considerable number of his friends from the movement and he declared (with Aragon and Eluard) his Communist sympathies in *Le Surréalisme au Service de la Révolution*. Dali and Buñuel made two films, *Le Chien Andalou* and *L'Age d'Or*, which had considerable impact. New members joining the group included Giacometti, Brauner and Paalen. By 1935 the movement had won an international audience. But the breach with the Communists in the movement became wider: Aragon was the first to withdraw, Eluard following in 1938. A retrospective exhibition, from which André Breton dissociated himself, was held in Paris in 1964.

Surrealism has numbered among its adherents several important and influential persons, such as Max Ernst, Arp and Masson, who used extremely varied techniques, combining painting, sculpture and collage in the most diverse manner, frequently in an attempt to shock or scandalize. There are two main tendencies to be distinguished: first, the direct expression of mental processes and, second, painting which will stimulate and analyze mental processes through symbols, roughly corresponding to abstract and figurative approaches respectively. Abstract Surrealism depends very much on unconscious, chance procedures such as the Automatic Writing of Masson and others, the free collages of Arp, the elaborate experiments of Duchamp. Action painting to a certain extent is another expression of this. Figurative Surrealism depends on illusionistic painting to convince the viewer of the reality of a world which does not follow the ordinary rules of logic. The forms represented need not be real ones, and in the work of Tanguy they clearly are not, while Brauner returns to a deliberately primitive world. But the most powerful painters of this group have been those capable of representing familiar things so vividly that one has to accept the unfamiliar, or is affected by the strange combinations of objects. The haunted world of De Chirico has an uncanny effect precisely because it is so close to reality. The work of Delvaux often has a similar power. Magritte's paintings are more fantastic, turning physical laws upside down, but always presenting a very clear, and disturbing, intellectual paradox. Dali is both the most gifted of these painters in a technical sense and the one whose distortions are the most extraordinary; for many he is the supreme exponent of Surrealism.

SUTHERLAND, Graham (1903–   ), English painter. After studying at Goldsmith's College School of Art from 1920–5, he began to work as an etcher and engraver, much in the tradition of William Blake and Samuel Palmer, and taught engraving at Chelsea School of Art. In 1935, inspired by a visit to Pembrokeshire, he decided to devote himself to painting. Sutherland's landscapes were at first influenced by Turner and Paul Nash, but he was preoccupied with finding a means of containing the landscape within the borders of the canvas rather than have it extending beyond the frame on all sides. This led him to develop his characteristic curving forms and tilted perspective as in *Landscape with Turning Roads* (1936, Ottawa NG) and to a type of painting in

which all the forms wrap round the centre of the picture and enclose it, *eg Entrance to a Lane* (1939, London Tate).

As an Official War Artist in 1941–4, he painted studies of bomb devastation and scenes of work in factories and mines. Commissioned to paint a *Crucifixion* for St. Matthew's Church, Northampton (completed 1946; study London Tate), Sutherland became interested in the forms of thorns, thistles and gnarled trees, *eg Horned Forms* (1944, New York MMA). This interest, which has lasted to the present day, was also influenced by Henry Moore's study of natural forms. In a similar way, Sutherland uses these shapes applied to human figures, in a semi-abstract, emotive style. Most of his later work features abstract forms built up in this way, out of thorn-shapes (*Thorn Cross*, Berlin, 20th C Gallery), shell-shapes (*Two Standing Forms against a Palisade*, 1949, Vancouver AG) and, increasingly, machinery (*Hanging Form over Water*, 1960, Southampton AG); (*The Scales*, 1961–2, London Tate). His post-War work also shows the effects of his long friendship with **Francis Bacon**. This can be seen in a new type of composition in receding planes, *eg Path through Plantation* (1951, Fredericton, Beaverbrook AG) and in the ambiguous character of some of Sutherland's figures, *eg Head* (1951, Ottawa NG). Between 1954 and 1957 Sutherland was working on the tapestry *Christ in Glory in the Tetramorph* which occupies the entire east wall of Coventry Cathedral; the flattened space and compartmentalized composition which he employed is reflected in many of his later works such as *Dark Entrance* (1959, Washington, Phillips Collection). Sutherland is an exceptional portrait painter, with a sharp eye for revealing detail, *eg Somerset Maugham* (1949, London Tate).

SUTTON, Philip (1928–   ), English painter. He studied at the Slade School from 1949–53 and then went to France on a French state scholarship. He won prizes at the John Moores Liverpool Exhibitions of 1957 and 1963. He has always been drawn to French painting, and in his earlier landscapes he uses patches of light bright colour to beautiful effect in a manner derived from **Impressionism**, but more sophisticated in hue, *eg Landscape* (1956, Leeds City AG). The other great influence on his work is that of Matisse, which shows particularly in his figure paintings of 1961–3. In 1963 he visited the Fiji Islands for a year and returned with pictures even more brilliant in colour, but considerably firmer in design.

SYMBOLISM. Although primarily a literary movement of the late 19th century, the doctrine of Symbolism had a profound effect on music, drama and the visual arts. Objects were considered almost entirely as symbols to arouse associations, which could be further expounded by combining with other symbols in a manner which is perhaps not logical in the everyday world, but which provides co-ordinates, as it were, for a map to define the inner world. These juxtapositions are most clearly seen in the work of **Redon**, whose painting is the most typical of symbolist art. The movement was started by Jean Moréas, author of a Symbolist Manifesto (1886), who founded a review *Le Symboliste*. The principal figures however, were the poets Mallarmé and Verlaine, the composer Debussy, the playwrights Maeterlinck and Claudel, and the painters Redon, Puvis de Chavannes and Moreau. The greatest influences acknowledged by these artists were Baudelaire, Rossetti and Poe in literature, Warner in music, and Delacroix and the English Pre-Raphaelites in painting. The work of Gauguin was much admired and he, in turn, was influenced by Symbolist ideas. The mystical ideas of the movement had a close influence on Toorop, Bernard and Hodler (and thus on the painters associated with the Vienna Secession) and they were continued in a guise by the Nabis, and contributed ultimately to Surrealism.

SYNCHROMISM, movement, considered an American variant of **Orphism**, making similar use of flat, Cubist-influenced patterns of regular shapes, but placing even more importance on colour and its use in creating apparent spatial relationships. The movement was launched (1912) by two acquaintances of Delaunay, **Morgan Russell** and **Stanton Macdonald-Wright**. They exhibited in Munich, Paris and at the Armory Show, New York. By 1918 both the leaders had reverted to figurative art but the example set by the movement in the United States was not to be forgotten.

Macdonald-Wright's *Oriental Synchromy in Blue-Green* (1918), one of the movement's major monuments, is in the Whitney Museum, New York.

T

TACHISM, term signifying the application of patches ('taches') of colour, interesting in themselves, quite apart from the motif, if any, represented. Historically, the word has had several meanings. It was used in the 19th century to refer to the 'Macchaiuoli', an Italian realist group; it was also a pejorative term for the Divisionists. It has recently been favourably revived, particularly in France, to describe the work of a number of painters, including Bazaine, Dubuffet, de Staël, Poliakoff, Wols, Fautrier, Hartung and Soulages, whose styles are usefully discussed under **Abstract Expressionism** and **Gesture Painting**.

TAKIS (1925–   ), Greek sculptor. He made his first sculpture in 1946. From 1954–8 he lived in London when he made his 'Signals': tiny modelled forms on the end of long vibrating rods so that they move in relationship to each other when set in motion, *eg Signal 'Insect-Animal of Space'* (1956, London Tate). In 1959, living in Paris, Takis produced his first *Telemagnetic Sculpture* in which suspended magnets and metal objects react to pulses of current through an electromagnet. This invention has placed him at the forefront of the **Kinetic Art** movement.

TAMAYO, Rufino (1899–   ), Mexican painter. After studying at the Academy of Mexico City, he executed (1933) murals in the Conservatory of Music there, in a monumental style strongly influenced by Orozco. In 1943 he painted another fresco in the Art Library of Smith College, Northampton, Mass. In 1950 he went to Europe, where he exhibited at the Venice Biennale; he has since lived mainly in Paris. Tamayo's art is firmly rooted in Mexican folklore but is sharpened and stylized under the distant influence of Cubism, *eg Women of Tehuantepec* (1938, Buffalo AG). This became stronger in the 1940s. *eg The Lovers* (1943, San Francisco MA), but it was the influence of the inter-

Rufino Tamayo: Homme chantant *(1950, Paris MNAM); ph. Giraudon.*

War style of **Picasso** which has been greatest, *eg Animals* (1941, New York MMA), or the animals in Picasso's *Guernica*. Towards the end of World War II his subjects became less literal and more Surrealistic in feeling, as in *Dancers over the Sea* (1945, Cincinnati AM), *Women Reaching for the Moon* (1946, Cleveland MA).

TANGUY, Yves (1900–55), American painter, born in France. He served as a merchant seaman until he was drafted into the army in 1920. There, he met Jacques Prévert and with him became interested in **Surrealism**. But it was the sight of a De Chirico picture in 1923 which made him become a full-time painter. He quickly became one of the leading members of the Surrealist movement, showing at all their exhibitions. He left for the United States in 1939, settling eventually in Woodbury, Connecticut, where he lived and worked on an isolated farm. He became an American citizen in 1948. Tanguy's early work was deliberately Naive in style, often attempting to capture some of the disturbing spatial qualities of De Chirico's work. In 1926 he began a number of sparser works suspend-

ing strange forms in a bleak crepuscular landscape. Despite their titles they are completely non-figurative and thus differ from the works of Dali, many of which have a similar setting, *eg Mama, Papa is Wounded!* (1927, New York MMA). Starting, roughly, from Tanguy's arrival in the U.S., the pictures became harder, more definite and the forms larger; although they seemed rock-hard they had curious similarities with plant or bone forms, as in *The Five Strangers* (1941, Hartford, Wadsworth Atheneum), *The Rapidity of Sleep* (1945, Chicago Art Inst.), *The Transparent Ones* (1951, London Tate). At the end of his life, Tanguy painted large-scale pictures, the 'objects' practically taking over the setting, *eg Multiplication of Arcs* (1954, New York MMA).

TAPIES, Antonio (1923–), Spanish painter. A law student, he began to paint in 1946 without any formal training. He received the Lissone Prize (1956) and the Carnegie Award (1958). His work is Abstract Expressionist and derives particularly from **Dubuffet** in being largely concerned with the texture of the paint surface. Tapiès mixes his paint with sand and glue and spreads it on in thick uniform masses, subsequently moulding it (by hand or with the imprint of common objects), scratching it, or using it as the base for further collage. The inspiration for this is often the texture of old walls, blistered paintwork, *etc*. Unlike Dubuffet, Tapiès uses no shock tactics; his works, simple as they are, are formally composed and have an inherent poise, *eg Painting* (1966, London, Institute of Contemporary Arts). Also, although many of his works are in near-monochrome, as in *Grey and Green Painting* (1957, London Tate), he occasionally uses rich colour to great effect, *eg Garnet Velvet* (1963, Montreal, Museum of Contemporary Arts).

TATLIN, Vladimir (1885–1953), Russian sculptor. He studied at the Moscow Academy under Larionov, painting comparatively conventional works. In 1912 he visited Paris as a singer with a folksong group and visited Picasso. Cubism gave him the idea of making relief constructions of glass, metal and wood, which were completely abstract as early as 1913. These were shown at the famous 'Tramway W' exhibition in Moscow. In 1915 he began to suspend these constructions in space, thus passing from painting to sculpture. In 1919 he became a Professor at the Moscow Academy and began to work on his huge *Monument of the Third International*, a spiralling steel tower containing rotating abstract constructions. Tatlin's work can be said to have formed the root of **Constructivism**, although this did not become an international force until after Gabo and Pevsner had joined it in 1917.

TAUBER-ARP, Sophie (1889–1943), Swiss painter. A student at the School of Applied Art, Hamburg, she later taught (1916–20) at the School of Applied Art in Zurich. She took part in the Dada movement, but this had little influence on her work. In 1915 she met **Hans Arp** and married him in 1921. She collaborated with him on several works and joined the Cercle et Carré (1930) and Abstraction-Création (1931) groups. Her work is mostly in the media of gouache, collage and relief. Though resembling that of her husband, her style is always precise and controlled without the lyricism of much of his work. The precision of her forms relates her art to Constructivism and to Neo-Plasticism, though the full impact is often weakened by a certain decorative quality, *eg Rectangular Relief* (1936, New York MMA).

TCHELITCHEW, Pavel (1898–1953), American painter, born in Russia. After studying in Kiev, he went in 1921 to Berlin, where he worked as a stage designer. He moved to Paris in 1923 and began to paint portraits, *eg Mrs R. A. Gorer* (1930, London Tate), and genre pieces influenced by the 'blue period' of Picasso. He settled in the United States in 1934. About 1940 he began to develop a psychic, Surrealist style in which figures are seen as in a vision, interlaced with flowers, roots and veins, one form merging into another, as in *Hide-and-Seek* (1940–2, New York MMA). In his last years, Tchelitchew developed this mystical vision into an abstract style, similar to that of Tobey.

TELEMAQUE, Herve (1937–   ), Haitian painter. Having studied in New York at the Art Students' League from 1957–60, he settled in Paris. His style is related to Pop Art in his use of representations of everyday objects, cartoon figures and stencilled lettering. He uses hard outlines and loose, half-finished colouring-in. The overall quality of his pictures, however, is closer to Surrealism, for the various forms scattered apparently at random over a plain ground do not have any logical coherence, but nevertheless seem to link up in a language half understood.

TERECHKOVITCH, Constantin (1902–   ), French painter, born in Russia. He was trained at the Moscow Academy, but settled in Paris in 1920. He met Bonnard who was to become a constant adviser. His earlier works were close to Bonnard's style but less penetrating and lighter in colour and handling. The influence of the Fauves, especially Matisse, was a lasting feature in his work, *eg Portrait au Chapeau* (1927, Paris, Petit Palais), *Petite Fille au Lit* (1944, Paris MNAM). His more recent works tend to be altogether lighter, using brilliant colour and a broken touch, like scattered flower petals, applied to subjects such as horse races and rather sentimental portraits and figure-studies, *eg Young Girl* (Philadelphia MA).

THIEBAUD, Wayne (1920–   ), American painter. He worked as a designer and advertising artist until joining Sacramento State College in 1951. He is a realistic artist concentrating on a range of subject matter associated with Pop Art, *eg Pie Counter* (1963, New York, Whitney Museum). His style is distinguished by the use of pale colours on a white ground, negating normal perspective.

TILSON, Joe (1928–   ), English artist. Before his National Service he worked for three years as a carpenter, which partly accounts for the frequent use of wood in his works. He studied at the St. Martin's School of Art and at the Royal College of Art (1952–5) where he won a prize allowing him to work in Rome for two years. He won a John Moores prize in 1957, a Gulbenkian award in 1963, and a prize at the San Marino Biennale of 1963; he exhibited at the Venice Biennale, and at the Milan Triennale in 1964. His work has been classed as Pop Art since much of his material is influenced by popular sources, but he is far closer to **Jasper Johns**, though working in the Constructivist medium of wood rather than painting, *eg*

Wood Relief No. 17 (1961, London Tate). Around 1963 he made a series of reliefs illustrating simple words, sometimes in a witty manner, sometimes using the cut-out letters as the basis of an abstract composition as in *Spiral Box* (1963, Rotterdam, Boymans Museum). In 1965 he became interested in the *Ziggurat* theme (a pyramid composed of rows of blocks) which he treated in increasingly inventive ways, using mirrors to add depth to the reliefs, *eg Reflector Column Ziglical I* (1965, London, Victoria and Albert M). He has also branched out into a wider variety of media to tackle straight 'Pop' subjects, *eg Rainbow Grill* (1965, London, Victoria and Albert M), an enormous silk-screened cardboard relief of a presentation book of matches.

TINGUELY, Jean (1925–   ), Swiss sculptor. After attending the Basle School of Fine Arts he produced abstract paintings and constructions, including some 'edible sculptures' in grass. He moved to Paris in 1952 and began to develop his 'Meta-mechanisms'. These are types of **Kinetic** sculpture, usually of great complexity, in which wheels turn, gears enmesh, antennae shake and flap, all for purely aesthetic purposes. His machines even emit sounds and smells. In 1960, he staged a Happening in the Museum of Modern Art, New York, during which his huge machine *Homage to New York* sawed itself up and set itself on fire while simultaneously writing poetry on a paper roll and accompanying itself on piano and drums. **Marcel Duchamp**, a major influence on Tinguely, was in the audience and characterized the event with the onomatopoeic pun: 'Si la scie scie la scie et si la scie qui scie la scie est la scie que scie la scie c'est un suicide mécanique.' The intentional inconsequentiality of most of Tinguely's machines make him a late exponent of Dada.

TOBEY, Mark (1890–   ), American painter. A self-taught artist, he travelled a good deal, painting first of all fashion drawings and then society portraits, which earned him considerable fame. In 1918 he was converted to the Bahai faith, which encouraged his mysticism. He taught from 1922 to 1925 at the Cornish School of Art, Seattle, and was painter in residence at Dartington Hall School, Devon (1931–8).

During these years he became increasingly interested in the arts of the east, visiting Japan in 1934 and spending some months in a Zen monastery, studying calligraphy. With his picture *Broadway* (1936, New York Metropolitan), in which the neon lights and the car-lamps form an independent pattern on the picture surface more important than the perspective of the street behind, he initiated the style known as 'white writing'. From then on his paintings have been exclusively calligraphic and progressively less figurative (although Tobey always works from detailed drawings of nature), until in a picture like *New York Tablet* (1946, Utica Art Inst.) there was merely a network of fine white marks on a monochrome ground. More recently Tobey has been using more colour and has been experimenting with forms more free than his usual rectangle covered with close writing, *eg Northwest Drift* (1958, London Tate). Tobey is often compared with that other great Abstract Expressionist **Jackson Pollock**, but he developed his calligraphic style earlier than Pollock and never entered the Abstract Expressionist movement. Beside Pollock's scale and brashness, Tobey is restrained, meditative and essentially introspective.

TOMLIN, Bradley Walker (1899–1953), American painter. He was successful initially as a painter in a rather Cézannesque style, as could be seen as late as 1932 in his *Self Portrait* (New York, Whitney Museum). He moved (1921) to New York and visited Europe in 1923 and 1926, each time for a year, spent mostly in Paris. Tomlin worked in a Cubist style at this time, *eg The Goblet* (1940, Washington, Phillips Collection), though this became softer in the early 1940s under the influence of Gottlieb. He retained an overall compartmented structure, though combining a wider variety of pictorial ideas, treated in a more painterly fashion, tending to summarize them in pictographs rather than in representational terms, *eg Arrangement* (*c* 1944, Urbana, Ill., Krannert Museum). From there it was a short step to the non-representational **Abstract Expressionism** of his last period in which the whole canvas becomes a field for broad stubby calligraphic symbols and hieroglyphics, still roughly arranged in a grid pattern and painted in muted colours, eg *Number 9, in praise of Gertrude Stein* (1950, New York MMA).

TOOROP, Jan (1858–1928), Dutch painter, born in Java. After studying at the Art Schools of Amsterdam and Brussels he came into contact with the main streams of French art and painted both in the Divisionist style, *eg Seduction* (1886, Otterloo RKM), and in the manner of Gauguin, *eg Motherhood* (1890, Otterloo RKM). In 1890 he met the poet Maeterlinck and was converted to **Symbolism**. His pictures in this vein developed the Gauguinesque style, exaggerating its linear features and creating large areas of pure pattern in the manner of Art Nouveau, as in *The Three Bridges* (1894, Otterloo RKM). He also did a number of striking posters. This style was one of the contributing forces in the Vienna Secession. In 1905 he was converted to Catholicism and produced a number of religious works in which the traditions of the early Dutch and Flemish painters were stylized in Expressionist compositions slightly influenced by Cubism, *eg Deposition* (1918, Oosterbeek Church).

TORRES-GARCIA, Joaquin (1874–1949), Uruguayan painter. At the age of seventeen he went to Barcelona where he painted frescoes in the Palace of the Deputation. He lived (1924–32) in Paris, where he became a member of the Cercle et Carré group. On his return to Montevideo he became an important influence as a defender of avant-garde art, and received many commissions. Apart from a few works, his painting was then totally abstract, with figurative elements in an angular style influenced by Cubism and by Klee, *eg Railway* (1946, Buenos Aires, Museo de Arte Moderno).

TOULOUSE-LAUTREC, Henri de (1864–1901), French painter and lithographer. Despite his death at the age of 37, he was to gain fame before his contemporaries Bonnard and Vuillard. However, the full influence of his highly personal art was not felt until the 20th century, notably in Expressionism and the earlier work of Picasso.

Toulouse-Lautrec's earliest works, preserved in the museum at Albi, were conventional. In 1882 he went to Paris and enrolled at Bonnat's studio; when the latter decried his drawing as 'atrocious' he went to study with Cormon, meeting Emile Bernard and **van Gogh**, who was to remain his lifelong friend. A frequenter of Montmartre cafés and dance halls, he came to admire the singer Aristide Bruant. He illustrated his songs and decorated the walls of his cabaret with dance scenes, including pictures of La Goulue. At this time he was still working in a realist style, as in *Gueule de Bois* (1889, Harvard, Fogg Museum) posed by Suzanne Valadon. In a series of portraits of women painted in the nearby gardens of Père Forest he gradually lightened his palette under the influence of **Impressionism**; unlike the Impressionists, he distorted and simplified forms to increase their expressiveness, *eg A la Rue* (1891, Boston MFA). It is interesting to compare his *Moulin de la Galette* (1889, Chicago Art Inst.) with that of Renoir.

In 1891 the director of the Moulin-Rouge, Zidler, commissioned a poster from him. This made Toulouse-Lautrec's name; from then on the artist produced over 500 lithographs, many of which were designed as posters. Probably the simplification (almost caricaturing) of draughtsmanship, restriction of colour and novel conception of space which he developed as an idiom of the poster medium also had its effect on his oils. He continued to paint Montmartre scenes and figures, less and less naturalistically, but with a realism characterizing the essential qualities of the subject with subtle exaggeration. He painted a group of habitués of the *Moulin Rouge* (1892, Chicago Art Inst.) which included himself, and telling portraits of the dancers: *Jane Avril leaving the Moulin Rouge* (1892, Hartford, Wadsworth Atheneum), *Jane Avril putting on her Gloves* (1892, London, Courtauld Galleries), *Yvette Guilbert* (1894, Albi Museum) and *La Goulue* (1892, Toledo, Ohio, MA). He also decorated a canvas fair booth for La Goulue (since reconstructed and preserved in the Jeu de Paume, Paris). Toulouse-Lautrec was also interested in the theatre and the circus, *eg Au Cirque Fernando* (c 1888, Chicago Art Inst.), *La Clownesse Cha-u-kao* (1895, Paris, Jeu de Paume). His particular interest was in brothel subjects, particularly penetrating studies of the women during their leisure, *eg Femmes de Maison* (1894, Paris, Jeu de Paume), *Les Deux Amies* (1894, London

Tate), *Au Salon* (1895, Albi Museum). He had no wish to create scandal in such works, and his interest was certainly not prurient. He was more concerned with understanding the psychology of these women: the brothel series was in some ways akin to Degas' studies of dancers, also off-duty, but with considerably more human interest. To find unposed subjects he would go, like Daumier, to the Law Courts and even into the hospitals, *eg Dr Péan performing a Tracheotomy* (1891, Chicago Art Inst.). He used to return from time to time to his family's estate near Albi, overcome with work and heavy drinking. In 1898 his health declined sharply; he had to undergo a cure for alcoholism, becoming paralyzed before his death.

Toulouse-Lautrec's painting was only loosely related to Impressionism, despite the great admiration he had for Degas. Perhaps more important were the non-Impressionist aspects of Degas to be found in his work: the unusual viewpoint, the composition based on **Japanese prints**, the interest in the unexpected but expressive pose. They also shared the quality of always commencing from close and detailed observation, but Toulouse-Lautrec was always prepared to depart from what the eye could see, grossly simplifying whole areas of the composition to concentrate on the essential expression which interested him, *eg* the almost caricature-like line of five 'stuffed shirts' in the background of *Au Nouveau-Cirque: Les Cinq Plastrons* (1891, Philadelphia MA). This was particularly the case in his posters, in which much was omitted, and trivial details could be blown up to perform an essential compositional function (*eg* the double-bass framing *Jane Avril*), and in which the lettering combined with the drawing in a novel way, *eg Reine de Joie*. These qualities were responsible for the peculiar balance of realism with abstract design in Toulouse-Lautrec's work, an attribute which has made him a powerful influence on numerous 20th century artists attempting a similar balance.

TUCKER, William (1935–   ), English sculptor. After graduating from Oxford he went in 1959 to the St. Martin's School of Art where he studied under Caro. Although all his sculpture is in coloured materials and is of medium scale, standing on the floor, Tucker's work is very varied since he works in series, each series having a different theme. One of his recurrent preoccupations is with slight differences in height, whether obtained by a metal sheet curling gently off the floor as in *Orpheus II* (1965, London Tate), or by a group of pieces piled so as to overlap slightly as in *Memphis* (1966, London Tate).

TURNBULL, William (1922–   ), Scottish painter and sculptor. Having studied at the Slade School he visited Paris for two years before settling in London in 1950. His painting is related to that of American Chromatic Abstractionists such as Newman and Rothko, and usually involves barely modulated fields of intense colour, *eg No. 2* (1962, London Tate). His earlier sculpture was completely different, making use of wood, stone and plaster in a crude but forceful way, retaining strong links with the past, *eg Horse* (1954, London Tate). In 1962 he began to work in steel and to paint his sculptures, which are often Minimal units, brightly coloured, which can articulate their environment in much the same way as the stripes on a Newman painting articulate the painted field, *eg Parallèls* (1967, London Tate).

TURNER, Joseph Mallord William (1775–1851), English painter. A painter outside his time, particularly in his later works, he has inevitably been considered the forerunner of many modern movements, from Impressionism to Abstract Expressionism. In fact, the details of his influence are difficult to trace. His prodigious career falls roughly into three parts. He started as a topographical painter, watercolourist and engraver, and although his compositions grew in skill, showing increasing painterly qualities, most of his works up to about 1819 were closely linked with the scene he was representing. After his first trip to Italy (1819), he began to explore the glowing lighting effects found in Claude's work, characterized by large areas of detail disappearing into a flood of light and colour, and leaning towards the general rather than the particular. Towards 1840, form disappeared completely as an articulating force in Turner's pictures, although odd incrustations of detail could be seen through the painting of light and atmosphere which were the real subjects of his pictures, *eg The Snow Storm* (1842), *Rain, Steam and Speed* (1842), both in London NG. Turner developed this technique first in the watercolour medium; his oil-painting style changed as he began to treat oil paint in washes like watercolour. His sketches, scarcely concerned with detail, combined these free washes with thick paint applied with the knife and were more remarkable still, but were not shown publicly in his lifetime.

In the 1890s Turner's influence began to gain: Signac and Henri Delacroix turned to his example when developing the more highly coloured phase of Neo-Impressionism (in contrast to Seurat); Matisse was encouraged by Moreau to see the Turners in London; and Signac discussed Turner at length in his *D'Eugène Delacroix au Néo-Impressionisme* (1899). This enrolment of Turner among the great theoreticians of colour was not groundless, because colour theory was a known interest of his, which he celebrated in his two pictures entitled *Light and Colour* (*Geothe's Theory*) (1843, London Tate). Finally, with the greater accessibility of Turner's sketches, many modern artists see him as an early Abstract Expressionist.

TWORKOV, Jack (1900–   ), American painter, born in Poland. After emigrating to the U.S. with his parents in 1913, he studied (1920–6) at Columbia University, the National Academy of Design and the Art Students' League. Tworkov worked on the Treasury Arts Project and on the WPA Arts Project. His post-War work has been Abstract Expressionist and he has aimed at being particularly free from preconceived intentions or the trappings of a style, even his own. Nevertheless, one can say that his paintings, which seem to explore the conflict between form and formlessness, consist typically of an underpainting with some sort of regular grid structure, partially obliterated by numerous large strokes of monochrome paint, as in *Duo I* (1956, New York, Whitney Museum).

TYTGAT, Edgar (1879–1957), Belgian painter. His artistic training was acquired in his father's lithographic studio and later at the Brussels Academy. Tytgat produced a number of Expressionist paintings, but his work was mostly in wood-cut. In 1953 he won the Grand Prix of Menton.

U

UTRILLO, Maurice (1883–1955), French painter. He was born in Montmartre, the illegitimate son of the painter **Suzanne Valadon**. In 1891 he was adopted by Miguel Utrillo y Molins, a Spanish painter whom he had never seen. At college he acquired habits of truancy and of drinking. After many scandals, he was sent to an alcoholic institution (1900), where a doctor advised his mother to encourage him to paint as a distraction. From 1902, he painted Montmartre and the Paris suburbs in a sombre and weighty manner. After 1907 he began to lighten his palette, and about 1910 started to use the whites which led to the nickname 'white period' (1908–15). The dealer Libaude made an arrangement with him in 1909 to buy his work for a small regular allowance and through him he met many critics and connoisseurs. In the same year he began to exhibit at the Salon d'Automne and the Salon des Indépendants. Nonetheless, he had little contact with other painters and his days were divided between the café and the cabaret (he painted neither of these subjects). In 1912 and 1916 he spent two months in an asylum as a result of severe attacks of delirium tremens.

It is difficult to classify Utrillo's painting. He has been placed with the Naive painters on the basis of the minuteness of his drawing, his unsophisticated composition, and his little figures from everyday life. But although Utrillo was virtually self-taught (apart from his mother, who gave him occasional advice, he only really associated with the painter Quizet, a solitary like himself), these qualities only appeared in his later, highly-coloured work. In the earlier years, he painted exclusively from the motif (he did postcards much later) and subjected it to an extremely rigorous (if instinctive) sense of design. He can also be considered as a late Impressionist, especially influenced by Sisley and by Pissarro's early style. He completely ignored the developments of Divisionism, or even of Monet's later works, rejecting many of its theories, particularly in his earlier works, in which he used a restricted palette and a solid touch. His subjects were scenes of Montmartre, the Paris suburbs and a few churches and other buildings in the country.

Q

To these he applied an individual concept of space, making use of novel effects of perspective and arranging the volumes of buildings in a composition as ordered as those of the Cubists. He could also achieve a rare poignancy in the textures of the leprous walls of poor houses, in the hallucinatory repetition of black windows, and in the loneliness of deserted streets and pavements. In his early years he could produce striking effects from the perspective of the boulevards, *eg La Porte Saint-Martin* (1909, London Tate), from the nobility of churches rising up amid low houses, as in *L'Eglise Saint-Séverin* (Washington NG), from winter trees standing like sentinels in a deserted square, in *La Place du Tertre* (*c* 1911, London Tate), even from the spritual bankruptcy of the suburbs, in *House in the Suburbs* (Bern, Kunstmuseum). The 'white period' is represented above all by views of Montmartre, *eg Montmartre* (1912, London Tate) and of churches. With the onset of his coloured manner (after *c* 1915) his painting became more conscious in its virtuosity, filled with little coloured details, picturesque figures seen from behind, and set all against a vivid blue sky. Particularly in his suburban scenes, this detail, equivalent to the rustic decoration on the *petit-bourgeois* bungalows which he often painted, has a profoundly depressing quality. Nonetheless, in his finest works, Utrillo, unstable in himself, achieved a balanced and lasting portraiture of the city making him a contemporary Canaletto or a Guardi. Most of his canvases were signed 'Maurice Utrillo V.', the last initial standing for his mother's name.

V

VALADON, Susanne (1867–1938), French painter. A painter's model at sixteen, she posed for the most important artists. Toulouse-Lautrec introduced her to Degas, who, normally sparing with his praise, complimented her on 'those excellent drawings of yours, so solid, so melting, and so malicious'; he even bought some of them, and gave her advice. In 1906 she gave up drawing in order to paint, after encouraging the early painting career of her illegitimate son **Maurice Utrillo**,

Suzanne Valadon: Portrait of her son, Maurice Utrillo *(1921, private collection); ph. 'Aux écoutes'.*

who, contrary to popular opinion, was little influenced by her. She was self-taught, her style being slightly influenced by the **Nabis** group. Her subjects ranged from portraits and nude studies to landscapes and still lifes, showing a vigorous sense of outline and colour. Her essential quality remained directness, the confident frontality of her portrayal of human beings, whom she painted in natural poses in brightly coloured domestic settings. Valadon was the only artist to give such a convincing portrayal of the unimportant small citizen of her time.

VALLOTTON, Féiix (1865–1925), French painter, born in Switzerland. He went to Paris in 1882, where he enrolled at the Académie Julian. In 1885 he exhibited his *Portrait of an Old Man* (Zurich Kunsthaus), at the Salon where it attracted little attention. He made his living as a journalist and restorer. He first exhibited at the Salon des Indépendants in 1893, and published a series of lithographs called *Immortels, Presents et Futurs* in the same year. He took part in the **Nabis** exhibitions. Vallotton was a man of singular and somewhat uneven talent. His illustrations provide a trenchant commentary on the *fin-de-siècle* period; he delighted in the vigorous interplay of blacks and whites. The early paintings were full of realism combined with Nabi stylization and composition; they reveal a remarkable sense of lighting and great tonal richness, *eg La Troisième Galerie au Châtelet* (1895, Paris MNAM), *La Partie de Poker* (1902, Paris MNAM). In the following period, he returned to a sterile Academicism on a large scale, sometimes creating a curious effect because of the naturalness of some of the figures, as in *Baigneuses* (1922, Winterthur Kunstmuseum). In several of his stylized, deliberately **Naive** landscapes, he could reveal both invention and freshness, *eg Route à Saint-Paul* (1922, London Tate).

VALMIER, Georges (1885–1937), French painter. A student at the Ecole des Beaux-Arts in 1905, he early began to work on his own and exhibited at the Salon d'Automne in 1911, becoming a follower of **Cubism**. He designed sets for the Futurist plays of Marinetti, joined (1932) the **Abstraction-Création** group, and in 1937 executed three large panels for the Exposition Universelle in Paris. He was also passionately fond of music and gave his paintings musical titles, *eg Fugue, Scherzo, Improvisation* (1919–23, New York Guggenheim). He took Cubism very far in the direction of abstraction, and his work is notable for its delicate tonality and extremely high finish.

VALORI PLASTICI, the title of a magazine founded in 1918 by Mario Broglio and published in Rome. In the opening numbers were articles by De Chirico and Carrà putting forward the ideals of **Pittura Metafisica**. However, the aesthetics of Valori Plastici, while retaining this Classical bias, gradually developed a realist tendency against the excesses of contemporary French and German art, and advocated a national purity in painting.

VALTAT, Louis (1869–1952), French painter. He entered Gustave Moreau's studio at the Ecole des Beaux-Arts before studying with Jules Dupré at the Académie Julian. He was a regular exhibitor at the Salon des Indépendants from 1889. While staying at Collioure, he met Maillol (1894). In 1903 he sent canvases which clearly anticipated **Fauvism** to the Salon, and a seascape of his exhibited in 1905 provoked an outcry. He retired to the Chevreuse valley and lost his sight in 1948. His prolific and varied style was remarkable for its sureness of touch and broad, tumultuous brushstrokes. The use of areas of pure colour in his *Nu dans un Jardin* (1894) clearly anticipated the Fauves.

VANTONGERLOO, Georges (1886–), Belgian sculptor. A student at the Art School in Antwerp, he moved during World War I to the Netherlands, where he became a prominent member of the **De Stijl** group. An early exponent of abstract sculpture, *eg Spherical Construction* (1917, New York MMA) he continued a rigid adherence to the De Stijl aesthetic. All his sculptures are based on mathematical formulae, *eg Construction* $y = 2x3$— $13.5x2+21x$ (1935, Basle Kunstmuseum). In 1927 he settled in Paris and was a leader (1931–7) of the **Abstraction-Création** group. In 1938 he abandoned the right angle as the dominant motif of his work, and produced a series of swirling wire sculptures also expressing mathematical functions. Vantongerloo had considerable influence on Max Bill and on American sculpture.

VASARELY, Victor de (1908–), Hungarian painter of the School of Paris. At the Bauhaus in Budapest, he was taught by **Moholy-Nagy**. In 1930 he settled in Paris, where he produced a large body of graphic work in the fields of decoration and advertising. He turned to painting in 1944, while continuing to produce tapestry designs, lithographs, and silk-screen work. He had major retrospectives in Paris in 1963 and in Kassel in 1964. His style is related to **Constructivism** in its severe abstraction and its restrained vocabulary of shape and colour. His earlier work, based on the shapes of pebbles or crystals or the pattern of cracked tiles, was simple and lyrical. More recently he has been studying Kinetic effects in painting, not through actual mechanical movement, but in geometrical grids or patterns painted on a deep relief surface which give the impression of movement. He is thus one of the chief pioneers of **Op Art**, as in *0519 Banya* (1964, London Tate). Many of these works are in black and white, though his colour, when he uses it, is always bright and uncompromising. He works particularly effectively on the monumental scale and in 1954 executed *Archetectonic Integration* and other murals for the University of Caracas.

VAUGHAN, Keith (1912–), English painter. He did not have a formal training but entered the art department of an advertising agency as a trainee. Many of his early paintings and gouaches are studies of landscape or country labourers influenced by **Graham Sutherland**, who encouraged him at the time. Gradually he developed his characteristic stylizations in which landscape and figures are expressed with relatively few broad slabs of paint in rich colours with much dark blue and ochre-browns, *eg Figure Undressing* (1950, Leeds City AG); *Demolished Houses* (1953, London Tate). An exhibition of **de Staël** in London in 1953 opened his eyes to the possibility of making his work more abstract without losing contact with nature, *eg Landscape, Berkshire* (1957, Huddersfield City AG). His more recent work is generally based on a figure or landscape motif, but he has written that he partially erases the picture each time the image becomes too positive and threatens to destroy the movement of the picture, *eg Bather* (1961, London Tate).

VEDOVA, Emilio (1919–), Italian painter. He is self-taught though Cubism and Expressionism were early influences on him. He developed a type of **Abstract Expressionism** using black and white and patches of primary, colour as in *Crucifixion* (1953, Rome GAM).

VELDE, Bram van (1895–), Dutch painter. After working as a house painter, he began to paint in an Expressionist, naturalistic style, especially during the years 1922–4, when he was at Worpswede, *eg The Sower* (1923, Amsterdam Stedelijk M). He went to Paris in 1924 and began to paint in a lighter style, influenced by Matisse and then by Cubism. His more recent work has been non-figurative, characterized by areas of limpid colour bounded by flowing lines.

VELDE, Geer van (1898–), Dutch painter of the School of Paris. The brother of Bram van Velde, he went to Paris in 1925. He held his first exhibition at the age of forty and won the Menton Prize in 1952. His non-figurative style is characterized by calmly flowing lines and delicately refined colour harmonies.

VELDE, Henri Clemens van de (1863–1957), Belgian painter, decorator and architect. At first attracted to painting, he worked in Carolus-Duran's studio in Paris. He returned (1887) to Belgium and took part in the founding of the Art Indépendant group and the Société des Vingt. His painting style was based on that of **van Gogh**, but he carried the latter's swirling lines into rhythms that dominated the whole canvas with finger-print lines, *eg Garden at Kalmthout* (1891, Munich NG). These curvilinear rhythms also dominated his decorative work, important as an example of **Art Nouveau**. In 1890 he devoted himself almost exclusively to the applied arts and founded the avant-garde review *Van Nu en Strak* ('Of Now and By-and-by'). He decorated the Galerie L'Art Nouveau in Paris, and founded a studio for the ornamental and industrial arts, teaching from his own designs. At the end of the century, he concentrated on architecture, working in Germany (1899–1917). He designed the Werkbund Theatre, Cologne (1914) and the Kröller-Müller museum at Otterloo (1931–54).

VENARD, Claude (1913–), French painter. Self-taught, he has travelled a great deal and was a member of the Forces Nouvelles group. He has exhibited at the most important Salons. His early style was representational, as in *Portrait dans un Intérieur* (1943, Paris MNAM), but has developed a more accented style with vivid and rather crude colours conveying a feeling of dynamic energy, *eg Still Life* (1957, London Tate).

VERDILHAN, Louis Mathieu (1875–1928), French painter. While working as a house-painter, he began (1900) to exhibit in Paris. He specialized in harbour scenes, particularly of Marseilles, using a style related to that of Marquet with simple broad outlines and areas of transparent colour, Fauve-influenced but more limpid and poised, *eg The Port of Marseilles* (Paris Petit Palais).

VIEIRA DA SILVA, Maria Eléna (1908–), Portuguese painter of the School of Paris. Arriving in Paris at the age of twenty, she studied sculpture with Bourdelle and Despiau, and painting with Friesz and Léger. From 1936 to 1937 she worked in Lisbon painting expressive views in a partially realistic geometrical style. She then stayed in Brazil (1940–7), where she held exhibitions of her work, of which the most important was in Rio de Janeiro (1942). In 1953 she received a prize at the São Paulo Bieñal; and in 1958 at the Carnegie International, Pittsburgh. Vieira da Silva's art is concerned with spatial values, both in her panoramic landscapes and in her interior studies. The former, perhaps owing something to the cityscapes of **Mark Tobey**, rely on a fine mesh of verticals and horizontals, with receding diagonals often indicating depth, *eg Paris* (1951, London Tate). In the interiors, especially the series of *Libraries*, the figurative elements are often clearer and the spatial construction more definite, as in *Grey Room* (1950, London Tate).

VIGELAND, Adolf Gustav (1869–1943), Norwegian sculptor. Extremely poor as a young man he made wood carvings and read the Bible, Homer and Dante. He went to Paris in 1892 and was welcomed by Rodin in his studio. On his return to Norway, he earned a living carving Gothic-style statues, and also produced several monuments. He then conceived the monumental groups in the Frogner Park, Oslo, to which he devoted forty years of his life. The theme of this work, obviously related to **Expressionism**, is the life struggle from birth to death, shown sometimes with repulsive naturalism, sometimes symbolically, sometimes with touching pathos. Nude men, women and children, gesticulating and grouped in fantastic clusters, frame the steps, line the bridge parapets, swarm up the enormous fountain, and disappear into labyrinths. *The Monolith*, the centre piece of the group, is an obelisk 100 feet high, formed of 100 interlaced and superimposed figures, an invention without precedent since Viking sculpture. The individual figure studies are somewhat Academic, but the groups as a whole were conceived on a scale comparable only to the *Portes d'Enfer* of Rodin.

VILLON, Jacques (1875–1963), French painter, originally Gaston Duchamp. The grandson of the Rouen painter and engraver Emile Nicolle, he was the brother of the sculptor Raymond Duchamp-Villon and of the painters Marcel Duchamp and Suzanne Duchamp. He went to Paris in 1894 and took as a pseudonym the name of his favourite poet. He studied under Cormon at the Académie des Beaux-Arts and became known for his humorous drawings in weekly journals. In the early period, his style owed something to **Toulouse-Lautrec**, whom he used to meet every evening at the Moulin Rouge. He began to concentrate more exclusively on painting in 1906. In 1910 he came into the orbit of Cubism, but soon began to paint in his own version of the style, more simply constructed and stronger in colour, *eg Portrait of Raymond Duchamp-Villon* (1911, Paris MNAM). He founded the **Section d'Or** group and organized its 1912 exhibition. In 1913 he sent nine paintings to the **Armory Show** in New York, all of which were sold, and his greatest successes after World War I took place in the U.S., where he stayed in 1930. His painting at this time was broader in style, though still figurative, *eg The Philosopher* (1930, New York, Brooklyn Museum). He continued to paint in a style incorporating figurative indications, but dividing the canvas into crisply contrasted colour areas in cool harmony, as in *Clos Normand* (1953, St. Louis AM). He won the Carnegie Prize in 1950 and the painting prize at the 1956 Venice Biennale. In the same year he was commissioned to design five stained-glass windows for Metz Cathedral. Villon's work is remarkable for its intellectual and formal qualities. His colour is always precisely controlled and his line, often assuming a completely separate life from the background, very carefully placed. His painting is a synthesis of **Cubism**, abstract formal schemes and representational elements. See illus. p. 246.

VITULLO, Sésostris (1899–1953), Argentinian sculptor. He went to Paris in 1925 where he studied with Rodin and Bourdelle: the latter's influence is clearly visible in his *Monument to Martin Fierrot*

Jacques Villon: Portrait of the sculptor Duchamp-Villon *(1911, Paris MNAM); ph. Giraudon.*

(1940–5) and in the exuberant *Luxury* (1946). He moved gradually towards an unadorned style with sharply separated planes, using many different materials. His sculptures, whether comparatively re-strained like *Rio Plata* (1942, Amsterdam Stedelijk M) in pink granite, active like *The Idiot* (1951) representing a prancing horse carved in rosewood, or simply massive like the *Monument to José de San-Martin* (1952), invariably contain the energy and rude strength which allowed Vitullo to evoke his country.

VIVIN, Louis (1861–1936), French painter. During his childhood, he painted views of his own village. He worked for the Post Office until his retirement at the age of 61. Wilhelm Uhde (see **Naive Art**) began to promote his work. Vivin's painting never ceased to be minutely descriptive, but it became increasingly simplified, mono-chromatic and schematic. He painted urban landscapes with flattened perspectives, the windows and the stones of the houses forming a grid-like pattern. The Cubists found in his work an instinctive solution to some of their problems, such as simul-taneous perspective, a method of denoting three dimensions, and the division of the surface into geometrical elements.

VLAMINCK, Maurice de (1876–1958),

French painter. While earning a living playing in a band and writing articles for anarchist journals, he met **Derain** in 1900, with whom he shared a rented studio at Chatou. He continued to earn money playing his violin at café concerts and wrote licentious novels. A visit to a **van Gogh** exhibition was a revelation to him; on leaving it, he said: 'I love van Gogh more than my own father.' Derain introduced him to Matisse, who encouraged him to exhibit in 1905 in the gallery of the artists of **Fauvism**, at the Salon d'Automne. In the following year Vollard bought all his work. During this period he was frequenting the Bateau-Lavoir and Picasso's circle in Mont-martre, and he soon renounced the excesses of Fauvism to follow the teaching of **Cézanne**. He said: 'I suffered from my inability to strike harder, to arrive at maximum intensity in my painting.' He produced a series of canvases (1908–14) which were well constructed and had a sense of depth. Although the scene was rendered somewhat geometrically, Vlaminck violently repudiated **Cubism**, distrusting its intellectualism. He never ceased to champion instinct in painting, affirming that 'each generation must start again

Maurice de Vlaminck: Bougival *(1911, Paris, Petit Palais); ph. Giraudon.*

from the beginning' in art. He declared himself an enemy of culture and boasted that he had never set foot in the Louvre. He was among the first to take an interest in Negro carvings. In 1925 he bought a large farm at Rueil-la-Gadelière where he installed himself with his wife and five daughters to lead a quiet country life. His art at this time returned to a raw, direct variety of realism. He painted snow-covered landscapes, murky skies, houses with vivid white walls covered with multi-coloured posters, strident green vegetation, and roads disappearing into the distance.

Above all else, Vlaminck's art was the expression of a forceful and highly self-aware individual. He said: 'You don't do *a* painting, you do *your* painting. If you are a painter just look into yourself for what it is that attracts you.' At the beginning of the century he used dark colours and a heavy impasto energetically applied with large brushstrokes, *eg The Kitchen* (1904, Paris MNAM). His palette brightened later, and he painted areas of strong self-colour divided by bold blue lines, as in *Houses at Chatou* (1905, Chicago Art Inst.). He then adopted a style notable for its restless, whirling brushstrokes and fulminating colours dancing in every direction, *eg Locks at Bougival* (1906, Ottawa NG). In his so-called Cézannesque period he achieved a balance between natural objects and atmospheric skies, *eg The River* (1910, Washington NG). Vlaminck's final manner was immediately effective with its strong perspectives and lowering, unusual lighting, although he repeated the formula rather too often, *eg Street Scene* (*c* 1930, Aberdeen AG).

VOLLARD, Ambroise (1865–1939), French picture dealer and publisher. He established his own business in 1893. He organized in his gallery in the Rue Lafitte the first important exhibition ever held of Cézanne's work (1895) which attracted crowds of people. Thenceforth his gallery became the artistic centre of Paris: important exhibitions of Rodin, Pissarro, Renoir, Degas and Bonnard were held. He gave Picasso his first exhibition (1901), Matisse (1904). He bought all Derain's available works (1905), and all of Vlaminck's (1906). He met Rouault in 1907 and took him into his household. His portrait was painted by famous contemporary artists.

VOLTI Antoniucci (1915–), French sculptor, born in Italy. After studying at the Ecole des Beaux-Arts, Nice, he went (1932) to Paris, where he studied under Jean Boucher at the Ecole des Beaux-Arts. He began working in stone, and then turned to clay modelling either for purposes of baking or casting in bronze. His main theme has been the female nude, which he treats with a vigorous sensuality; his repertoire of poses is wide and includes a number of works in which the figure is compressed into a ball (*eg* 1952, Valenciennes MBA). His style is not unlike that of Maillol.

VORTICISM, movement founded in 1914 by **Wyndham Lewis** and the poet Ezra Pound; its doctrines were set out in a Manifesto and in the periodical *Blast*. It can best be described as a form of English **Futurism** and was inaugurated as a riposte to a bogus manifesto which the Futurist leader, Marinetti, claimed had been signed by a number of English artists. Vorticism was closer to being an abstract movement than Futurism, however, and was more directly influenced by **Cubism**. Among the signatories were Gaudier-Brzeska, William Roberts and Edward Wadsworth; David Bomberg and C. R. W. Nevinson were also closely associated with the group.

VUILLARD, Edouard (1868–1940), French painter and illustrator. He studied at the Lycée Condorcet where he had three friends who were later to play an important part in his life: his future brother-in-law, **Roussel**, and Maurice Denis and Lugné-Poe. Vuillard first thought of entering the army, but Roussel and Lugné-Poe encouraged his interest in painting. Vuillard failed in his first attempt to enter the Ecole des Beaux-Arts, which he considered a terrifying place; instead he attended the Académie Julian for two years. In 1889 he had a charcoal drawing hung at the Salon des Artistes Français, but after having work refused in 1890 he stopped sending to official salons and only exhibited at the Salon des Indépendants and some small galleries. He was influenced by Toulouse-Lautrec, Gauguin, by **Japanese prints** and by what he could see of Chardin and Rembrandt. At the Académie Julian he met Bonnard, Sérusier and the other **Nabis**,

Edouard Vuillard: Portrait de Lugné-Poe
(c *1891*).

but, not convinced by their theories, he pursued a personal course; Symbolism did not hold any attraction for him. He continued to paint intimate interiors (he jokingly called himself an 'intimiste'), looking for no other subjects than those contained in his mother's flat, where he lived until her death in 1929. He exhibited (1891–4) at Le Barc de Boutteville and was introduced to the *Revue Blanche*, a journal run by the Natanson brothers, on whose premises he also exhibited. Lugné-Poe, by then director of the Théâtre Libre, attracted him to the theatre and he designed programmes and sets. At about the same time, Vuillard was active in the field of decorative art, designing screens, furniture, windows, tapestries, ceramics and books. His original sense of composition, restrained refined use of colour and inventive use of line brought him rapid renown. Vollard and the Bernheim brothers regularly staged exhibitions of his work (1903–14); he was one of the founders of the Salon d'Automne (1903), sending paintings there until 1911. He did not exhibit after 1914 and lived a quiet life in his studios, especially in the Rue de Vintimille, where he finished a series of magnificent landscapes from his window. He travelled to Holland (1913), Spain (1930), and after 1924 stayed for long periods with his friends at Vaucresson and the Château des Clayes. A large retrospective exhibition of his works was held in Paris at the Musée des Arts Décoratifs in 1938. In the same

year he became a member of the Institut. After 1900 he carried out several large mural commissions: his *Le Petit Café* and *Le Malade Imaginaire*, for the Comédie des Champs-Elysées are especially noteworthy. In 1938 and 1939 he completed the only two commissions he ever received from the government: *La Comédie*, for the Théâtre de Chaillot, and *Peace Protecting the Muses* for the League of Nations, Geneva.

Vuillard's painting shows gradual and scrupulous development towards perfection. His early works were still lifes, delicately coloured and conventionally handled, and indeed the genre never lost its fascination for him. He continued throughout his career to invent subtleties and refinements of colour and light, and to establish ingenious harmonies between materials, flowers and solid objects. Towards 1890 a revolution took place in his style, and Vuillard began to practise an art of extremely bold elimination and understatement, eg *Au Lit* (1891, Paris MNAM). But he quickly renounced this manner (which some regard as his best) and returned to delicate harmonies of tonally-related colours, and to his former realistic inspiration. He produced a large number of interior studies showing his mother in her modest living room or at table, eg *Le Prétendant* (1893, Northampton, Mass., Smith College), *La Veuve en Visite* (1899, Toronto AG). Into such paintings, with their subtle lighting and deep feeling, Vuillard put the best of himself and it was here that he was comparable to the masters he most venerated, Chardin and Rembrandt. The same qualities are to be found in those compositions which depict contemporaries enveloped in bourgeois interiors, such as *La Soupe d'Annette* (1900, St. Tropez Museum), *Roussel and Annette* (c 1904, Buffalo AG), *Girl in an Interior* (1910–15, London Tate). Each of these canvases evokes perfectly a whole society by capturing and giving permanent expression to its domestic aspect, in a manner recalling the Dutch interior painting.

Vuillard was always interested in detail and texture. The fact that several of his relations had been textile designers may explain his concern for the textures of wallpaper, upholstery and dresses as well as of flowers, trees and the patterns made by light on the ground. His numerous still lifes are largely interesting for the balance of texture, as in *The Mantelpiece* (1905, London NG). In even the simplest interiors the rhythm of patterns (often around a single dominating texture) forms a counterpoint to the actual representation of objects, *eg La Robe a Ramages* (1891, São Paulo Modern Art Museum). But it is in the landscapes, *eg Red Roof* (1900, London Tate), and the larger compositions that the details of the world Vuillard summoned up come together in a symphony of terrible richness. It may seem that in some of the society portraits executed after World War I, Vuillard was forced and uninspired, but his energy continued to manifest itself until the very end of his life. No one who has seen the series of paintings of artists at work (Paris, Petit Palais) which he executed (1925–37) can doubt that. Roussel, in an intensely nostalgic painting, is shown standing before a large window at dusk. The painting of Pierre Bonnard, who stands in front of the canvas, shows all the pride and anxiety of the artist, while that of Maillol at Marly, who is shown working at a large white statue, possesses an incomparable nobility. In these works Vuillard united realism, psychological profundity and sheer plastic beauty with such authority that it is hard not to consider him as one of the complete modern painters.

W

WADSWORTH, Edward Alexander (1889–1949), English painter. A student at the Slade School, he later exhibited abstract works with the Vorticists, *eg Abstract Composition* (1915, London Tate). In 1920 he published a collection of drawings of the Black Country, in which the landscape was inconspicuously given a Post-Cubist stylization, as in *Granite* (1919, London Tate). He also produced woodcuts and a collection of naval engravings (*c* 1925–6). In his later painting, mostly in tempera, he concentrated on sea subjects painted in a style similar to American Cubo-Realism, *eg Signals* (1942, London Tate). They are extremely exact and vividly coloured, the various objects always being arranged as components of a taut formal composition and possessing many qualities of abstract art without sacrificing realism.

WALCH, Charles (1898–1948), French painter. He painted principally genre scenes. Relying on simple outlines in drawing, he used very bright colours and lively compositions. His earlier work strongly recalls Chagall, *eg The Innocent* (1934, Grenoble Museum of Art), *July* (1938, Paris MNAM). In his last few years he adopted a more angular, Cubist-inspired style, as in *Le Ballet des Flammes* (1945, Paris MNAM).

WALKOWITZ, Abraham (1880–1965), American painter of Russian birth. Having emigrated to America as a child he studied in New York and then at the Académie Julian in Paris, and made several extended stays in Europe between 1906 and 1931. Although he had painted abstract works as early as 1910, Walkowitz first developed a kind of primitive figuration, influenced by children's drawings and by Gauguin. He exhibited with Stieglitz in 1912 (see **Galleries**) and at the **Armory Show** in 1913. After that he faded into obscurity although he was producing most original abstract work based upon the rhythms of criss-crossing lines, looking forward to Tobey, *eg New York* (1917, New York Whitney Museum).

WALLIS, Alfred (1855–1942), English painter. Probably the best-known and most influential English **Naive** painter, he did not begin to paint until about his 70th year, after he had settled in St. Ives following a lifetime at sea. Almost all his pictures were done on old scraps of boxes or cardboard with crude brushes and coarse ship's paint. They generally show marine or local subjects taken from memory, *eg Voyage to Labrador* (London Tate) and the complicated *Cornish Port* (New York MMA). His work was discovered in 1928 by **Ben Nicholson** and **Christopher Wood** and some of it was shown in London exhibitions. His simple means of presentation, particularly the blue-grey-brown colour scheme, was a great influence on these painters.

WARHOL, Andy (1930–   ), American artist. One of the most extreme practitioners of **Pop Art**, he has deliberately excluded himself from his works, delegating much of his work to assistants. Using silk-screen photographic techniques, he often repeats the same image again and again, both in different works and as a multiple image on the one canvas. The most famous example of this is the *Campbell's Soup Can*, which first appeared in the early 1960s, printed in natural colours square in the middle of the canvas. Later Warhol multiplied the image so that the slight differences between each printing challenged the visual response to the patterns accidentally created, *eg 100 Soup Cans* (1962, Buffalo AG). More recently he has used unnatural, 'Fauve', colours, as in *Campbell's Soup* (1965, New York MMA). Warhol has also used photographs of popular heroes, *eg Elvis I & II* (1964, Toronto AG) and reproductions of Old Masters for the same treatment, *eg Mona Lisa* (1963, New York Metropolitan Museum). A number of other works use news photographs, such as car accidents, and although these are presented without comment, they do have considerable impact; *Saturday Disaster* (1964, Waltham, Mass., Rose AM). Since the mid-1960s, he has moved further in the direction of **Minimal Art**, his displays consisting of nothing but large-scale Brillo cartons, or floating helium-filled silver pillows, entitled *Clouds*.

WAROQUIER, Henry de (1881–), French painter, engraver and sculptor. He began by studying architecture, natural history and classical mythology, teaching himself how to paint. Waroquier's painting before 1914 was derived from **Cubism**, although its decorative rhythms, inspired by Far Eastern art, were original. As a landscapist, he has painted views of Brittany, and also of Italy, *eg Santa Maria della Salute* (1913, Paris MNAM), the latter remarkable for their sense of psychological atmosphere. A journey to Spain added a troubled, tragic dimension to his style. His canvases of 1917, his so-called 'white' period, are pervaded by a feeling of catastrophe. Between 1917 and 1932 he painted imaginary landscapes, and then concentrated on the study of the human figure, characterized by a hieratic quality reminiscent of Byzantine art, and expressions of great pathos. He also sculpted heads on a monumental scale after 1930, giving them symbolical titles, *eg La Verbe* (1934, Paris MNAM).

WATTS, Robert (1923–), American sculptor. He attended Columbia University and the Art Students' League. After 1948,

he worked as a mechanical engineer until he started teaching (1952) engineering and art at Rutgers University. He is one of the few artists who has achieved the marriage of art and technology. As a **Pop** artist, one of Watts' best known sculptures is his *B L T Sandwich* (1966), of painted wax in solid Plexiglass.

WEBER, Max (1881–1961), American painter, born in Russia. Settling in Brooklyn with his family in 1891, he studied at the Pratt Institute. In 1905, Weber went to Paris where he remained for three years, studying first at the Académie Julian and later with Matisse. His earlier works were in the **Fauvism** tradition and showed scenes from city life drawn in an incisive style similar to Picasso's 'blue period'. His development as well roughly paralleled Picasso's in his interest in African sculpture, *eg Figure Study* (1911, Buffalo AG), **Cubism** and **Collage** although Weber, like Delaunay and the Futurists, preferred to apply Cubism to urban scenes, and to employ a richer colour range *eg Chinese Restaurant* (1915, New York Whitney Museum). Although he was one of the few artists in America in the World War I period with a real grasp of the principles of Cubism, Weber was little understood, and, after about 1925, returned to a more naturalistic style similar to Cézanne, as in *Zinnias* (1927, Newark Museum). His last works recreate scenes from his Jewish upbringing in a graphic though painterly style with the cartoonist's power of capturing expression, *eg At the Mill* (1939, Newark Museum).

WESSELMANN, Tom (1931–), American painter. After studying cartoon drawing for a year in Cincinnati, he transferred to the Cooper Union School, New York. His earliest debt was to de Kooning, but in 1961 he began to develop his own **Pop** style with the *Great American Nude* series, of which there are now nearly a hundred paintings. Each of these treats the female nude in a flat cut-out style, often without modelling or features except for the lips, nipples and hair, and painted in a restricted colour range reminiscent of **Matisse**. When he combines the nude with magazine and advertisement collage, the effect is satirical. In more ambitious work, he places the nude in an interior environment framed by real objects such as a door, radiator, carpet, coat hanging on a peg and telephone: the contrast of humanity and pathos of the real world and the possibilities it offers (the telephone rings, but is never answered) with the imagined world of stereotyped always-available sex. In the works since 1965, Wesselmann has concentrated on details of the figure, treating it formally, as part of a seascape theme. He has also executed Pop still lifes.

WHISTLER, James Abbott McNeill (1834–1903), American painter and engraver. An important innovator in his own right, he also played a significant role as one of the links between painting in France and England in the latter half of the 19th century. He arrived in Paris in 1854 and stayed there until 1863, the year in which his *Symphony in White No. 1: the White Girl* (1862, Washington NG) scored a *succès de scandale* at the Salon des Refusés. Whistler was a friend of most of the artists and many of the writers of the time. He was one of the first to take an interest in **Japanese prints**, not only for their exotic qualities, as in *Rose and Silver: 'La Princesse du Pays de la Porcelaine'* (1864, Washington Freer Gallery), but also for their compositional schemes in parallel planes, making much use of horizontals and verticals. His portraits were probably an influence on Degas, *eg At the Piano* (1858, Cincinnati AM). Although he did not go so far as the French painter, all his later works convey, by the simplest compositional means, a great psychological atmosphere, *eg Arrangement in Grey and Black No. 1: The Artist's Mother* (1873, Paris Louvre), *Harmony in Grey and Green: Miss Cicely Alexander* (1872–4, London Tate), *Arrangement in Grey and Black No. 2: Thomas Carlyle* (1872–3, Glasgow Kelvingrove). Probably his greatest importance, in France but even more so in England, was his refusal to regard art on anything but a pure aesthetic basis ('art for art's sake'). The musical primary titles of his works emphasized it.

Whistler never followed Impressionism, but in some of his finest landscapes his concern for abstract qualities led him to a gradual dissolution of the figurative elements, *eg Harmony in Blue and Silver: Trouville* (1865, Boston Gardner Museum), *Nocturne in Blue and Gold: Old Battersea*

Bridge (1872–5, London Tate), *Nocturne in Black and Gold: the Falling Rocket* (1874, Detroit Inst. of Art). This last picture led to the famous attack by Ruskin; the succeeding lawsuit effectively destroyed Whistler's career, although he was awarded damages of a farthing. He considerably influenced Sickert and the **Camden Town** group. Whistler was also an original decorator: the Peacock Room (1876–7), now in the Freer Gallery, Washington, was his best achievement. The Freer Gallery and Glasgow University have particularly fine collections of his work.

WHITELEY, Brett (1939–), Australian painter. He studied art at night school while working in an advertising agency. In 1960, after a year in Italy, where he was particularly impressed by Piero della Francesca, he settled in London. At the time he was painting large abstract paintings with recurrent cuspid shapes that alluded ambiguously to landscape and erotic themes, *eg Untitled Red Painting* (1960, London Tate). He won an International Prize at the Paris Biennale of 1961. In 1963 he began a series of 'Bathroom' pictures, all starting from the theme of the nude but locked into a pattern of swirling forms on the canvas surface in a manner recalling Bacon, *eg Woman in a Bath II* (1963, London Tate). His recent work is influenced by **Rauschenberg** and involves collage of photographs. The addition of three-dimensional objects and deliberate contrasts between clear figuration and abstract painting is more explicit than Rauschenberg's, however, and includes some powerful treatments of the themes of war and famine, made all the more horrible by the introduction of erotic imagery.

WILSON, Robert ('Scottie') (1889–), Scottish painter. After running away from home and serving in the army, Wilson went to Canada (*c* 1930). Coming upon a pen one day with a very heavy nib he began to draw, colouring his work with crayons. Unlike most Naive artists, he does not attempt to portray the real world at all but draws fantastic animals, plants and other shapes from his imagination, *eg The Tree of Life* (1958, London Tate). This has given him considerable appeal in the **Surrealism** circles and he has had several exhibitions, both with the Surrealists and by himself.

His designs have been used both for tapestry and ceramics.

WITKIN, Isaac (1936–), South African sculptor. On arriving in England in 1957 he studied at the St. Martin's School under Caro and then worked until 1964 as assistant to Henry Moore. Most of his sculptures are in fibreglass and oppose sections of great solidity with sections enclosing a hollow space, *eg Alter Ego* (1963, London Tate). He has also a fine sense of colour (since 1965 he has spent much of his time teaching at Bennington College, Vermont, where he would also have met Noland). His recent work, *eg Baaebec* (1968, London Tate), is more austere and shows **David Smith**'s influence.

WLERICK, Robert (1882–1944), French sculptor. Enthusiastically encouraged by Rodin, Wlérick was a realist and exploited the muscular rhythms and living surface of the human body without searching for naturalism or Expressionism, *eg Buste de Femme* (1923, Paris MNAM), *Condorcet Monument* (Ribemont). His style was balanced, calm and robust, and his treatment of pose and face expressive.

WOLS, see **Schulze, Alfred Otto Wolfgang**.

WOOD, Christopher (1901–30), English painter known as Kit Wood. He spent most of his short adult life travelling; he studied at the Académie Julian, Paris (1921), and thereafter moved between Italy, Provence, Brittany, London and Cornwall. He became friends with **Picasso**, whose influence is seen in the heavy rounded forms of his figure painting, but who probably also influenced his manner of rearranging the planes in a picture, and the calligraphic shorthand with which he summarized detail. He was also a close friend of **Ben Nicholson**, exhibited with him, and was with him in St. Ives in 1928 when they discovered **Alfred Wallis'** work: his directness of presentation, summary drawing technique, rough surfaces and colour scheme were all reflected in Wood's last paintings, done between 1929 and 1930 in Brittany. However, they were used with great sophistication, conveying a real liking for the little, windswept fishing villages

that were his subjects, as in *Boat in Harbour, Brittany* (1929, London Tate), *Drying Nets, Treboul Harbour* (1930, Toledo, Ohio, MA).

WOOD, Grant (1891–1942), American painter. A 'Regionalist' (see **Realism**) painting the people and the countryside of his native Iowa, he worked in deliberate reaction against the excessive European influence on American painting following the **Armory Show**. Wood studied art part-time in Minneapolis and Chicago, but it was not until he returned to Cedar Rapids, where he taught in a school, that he really developed a personal style. He visited Europe four times between 1920 and 1928, but was most interested in the intense realism applied to genre subjects of German and Flemish painting of the 15th and 16th centuries. Wood's own pictures, painted with something of their meticulous technique, included broad, rolling Midwest landscapes, *eg Stone City* (1930, Omaha AM) and most perceptive evocations of country life, *eg American Gothic* (1930, Chicago Art Inst.). Of this picture he said: 'I imagined people with their faces stretched out long to go with this American Gothic house'; but the picture was more than a joke, it was the evocation of an entire way of life.

WOTRUBA, Fritz (1907–), Austrian sculptor. He studied engraving, and then sculpture with Anton Hanak. His first exhibitions were held in Essen and Zurich (1931). After the Anschluss, he emigrated to Switzerland, returning to Vienna in 1945, where he became a member of the Academy. His first sculptures were rigorously Classical, and, while in Switzerland, his style was even more severe, even archaic. He subsequently achieved a more architectural and Expressionist style, sculpting the human figure in great blocks of stone which were left rough, *eg Seated Figure* (1949, Vienna Osterreichische Galerie). Since about 1950, he has begun to dress the stone and to model it in a more subtle, disjointed way, as in *Large Reclining Form* (1951, Vienna Osterreichische Galerie). He has also used bronze, *eg Standing Figure* (1949–50, London Tate). His *Torso* in bronze (1955) is simply four cylinders ingeniously welded together. He has said: 'The human body has always been my first concern; and it is as present at the end of my work as it is at the beginning.'

WOUTERS, Rik (1882–1916), Belgian painter and sculptor. At the age of twelve he learned to carve wood, later receiving formal training at the Academies of Malines and Brussels. Although he continued to sculpt until 1913, he had begun painting in 1908, in a style influenced by **Ensor**. He went to Paris in 1912. Although his career as a painter was extremely short and its early interruption tragic, Wouters' art is of the greatest value. Despite using the bright colour of the Fauves, his pictures were altogether more solid in composition and handling, which was no doubt the influence of **Cézanne**, *eg Portrait of his Wife* (1912, Paris MNAM), *Humour Sombre* (1915, Brussels MBA). He was particularly good at capturing the atmosphere of interior subjects, scenes from everyday family life, as in *Woman Sewing* (1912, Antwerp Museum), *Sick Woman with White Shawl* (1915, Antwerp MBA); in this he was most akin to Bonnard, but possessed less formal sense, despite a greater human sympathy. His most moving work was his last self-portrait called *Rik with the Eye-patch* (1915, private collection), in which the painter stands tragically, dressed in light blue against the background of a red curtain. Wouters' sculpture is dynamically naturalistic, rather like that of Degas, but with a Flemish fullness and independence. One of his best-known works, *Mad Virgin* (1912, Antwerp MBA) was inspired by the dancer Isadora Duncan. In his other sculptures, often modelled for by his wife, *eg In the Sun* (1909, Brussels MBA), *Domestic Cares* (1913, Antwerp MBA), the power of the modelling and the natural humanity of the poses have a simple and imposing strength.

WPA Federal Arts Project. In 1935, under the chairmanship of President Franklin D. Roosevelt, the American Works Progress Administration set up a nationwide project to commission art of all kinds, especially murals for public buildings. The Project was wide in scope and enlightened, although almost all the work it produced was figurative. Almost every promising artist in his 20s or 30s at the time was involved, and it thus became the occasion for an extensive cross-fertilization between artists. American **Abstract Expressionism** grew up largely among artists who, like Pollock, de Kooning and Rothko, had met on the WPA Project. From about 1939 the WPA gradually turned the direction of the Project towards specifically military purposes, and by 1945 it had faded out as an important force.

WYETH, Andrew Newell (1917–   ), American painter. Trained entirely by his father, a professional illustrator, Wyeth gained his characteristic grasp of anatomy and modelling and meticulous technical ability. His painting, like that of **Grant Wood**, to whom he may be compared, is entirely devoted to scenes of his immediate neighbourhood. Most if it has been in tempera, a medium allowing extremely fine detail; however he has offset the effect of this by broadly spacious compositions so that his paintings show both the scale and the intimate texture of America. *Christina's World* (1948, New York MMA) is a fine example of this and it also shows, in the portrait of the cripple in the foreground, Wyeth's ability to put himself completely into the soul of his sitters. His watercolours, in contrast to his temperas, are remarkably lively and free, *eg The Coot Hunter* (1941, Chicago Art Inst.).

WYNTER, Bryan (1915–   ), English painter. Having studied at the Slade School from 1938–40 he settled near St. Ives in 1945. He established his reputation with landscapes executed in gouache, rather romantic in subject but showing Cubist influence in their structure. In 1955 he stopped painting. Then experiments with hallucinogenic drugs and the influence of American **Abstract Expressionism** (and especially of Mark Tobey, seen in a London Exhibition in 1956) started him off in a new non-figurative direction in which the canvas is covered with a maze of **Calligraphic** signs, as in *Seed-time* (1958–9, London Tate). The strokes are broader than Tobey's and generate a sense of the movement of water, plants and earth rather than of air and light; in their interplay of colours they develop a great sense of space behind the canvas which one can gradually explore. He has recently become interested in **Kinetic Art**: *Imoos VI* (1965, London Tate).

Y

YEATS, Jack Butler (1871–1957), Irish painter, born in London. The son of the Irish portraitist John Butler Yeats and younger brother of the poet W. B. Yeats, he spent his boyhood in Sligo. His subject-matter was the ever-changing colours and refracting light of the Irish countryside, as well as the work and pastimes of the Irish people. He studied at the Westminster School of Art, and began working as an illustrator and watercolourist. Many of these early watercolours reflect something of **Degas**, **Toulouse-Lautrec** and the **Nabis**, but have glowing colour effects that belong exclusively to the aquarelle medium, though these influences continued into his early oils, as in *A Lift in the Long Car* (1914, Leeds City AG). In 1905 he began painting regularly in oils and in 1913 sent five works to the **Armory Show**. In about 1925 he suddenly developed a far freer style, using heavy impasto, slashing strokes and much richer colours. This continued throughout his life, *eg The Two Travellers* (1942, London Tate), though in the late works the impasto, by then in primary colours only, had almost submerged representational form, *eg Grief* (1951, Dublin NG). Yeats was a master of Expressionist landscape in much the same vein as **Kokoschka**, who was an ardent admirer of his work in his last years.

YOUNGERMAN, Jack (1926–), American painter. He attended the Universities of North Carolina and Missouri and then after World War II, studied at the Ecole des Beaux-Arts in Paris, where he became interested in **Constructivism**. Returning to New York in the 1950s, he developed a clear hard-edge style which was not geometric, however, but used lyrical abstract forms of great power. Many of his pictures have been concerned with grouping forms around an empty centre, and his recent work places mere touches of colour around a circular field, as if they joined up around the back of the painting.

YVARAL, Jean-Pierre (1934–), French painter. The son of Vasarely, he has changed his name for convenience. With **Le Parc** he founded the Groupe de Récherche d'Art Visuel in Paris in 1959, and he is concerned with the borders between Op Art and Kinetic. Many of his works, like those of Agam, use three-dimensional surfaces to alter the abstract colour patterns as the observer moves round: *Optical Acceleration* (1963, London Tate).

Z

ZACK, Léon (1892–), Russian painter of the School of Paris. He began to paint at the age of thirteen and was exhibiting in Russia by 1907. He settled in Paris in 1923 after spending a year in Italy. Until 1940 Zack's style featured violent effects of lighting and was filled with anguish. Since then it has become completely abstract, showing the influence of **Poliakoff** and **de Stäel**, but always with a restricted colour range, at first pale and mystical, latterly more sombre, *eg Painting* (1959, London Tate). He has tended since 1950 to concentrate on religious art.

ZADKINE, Ossip (1890–1967), French sculptor, born in Russia. He went in 1905 to Britain to stay with the family of his Scottish mother, and attended classes at art schools in Sunderland and London. Zadkine arrived in Paris in 1909, studied at the Ecole des Beaux-Arts, and associated with the Cubists, whose style he was one of the first (with **Lipchitz**) to introduce to sculpture, *eg Woman with Fan* (1920, Paris MNAM). In the 1920s he abandoned the total re-organization of parts, implicit in Cubism, and produced some monumental works, stylized but lyrical, *eg Venus* (1923, London Tate), *Discobolus* (1928, Philadelphia MA), *Musicians* (1924, Aberdeen AG and Miami MMA), *The Concert* (1928, Bristol AG). Some works of this period, such as *Girl with Bird* (1926, Worcester, Mass., AM), indicate the direction that his art was to take by reversing normal sculptural techniques: hollow taking the place of relief, sharp edges and incised lines replacing conventional modelling, *eg Diana* (1934, Manchester City AG), *Statue for a Garden* (1936, Bordeaux MBA). This style was particularly suitable for depicting features and he used it for portraits. After 1940, in his concern to alleviate the massiveness of his sculpture, he opened

Ossip Zadkine: Tête d'homme; *ph. Marc Vaux.*

out his sculptures, arranging the forms in a loose lattice-work, lending them an extraordinary feeling of animation, as in *Phoenix* (1944, Amsterdam Stedelijk M), *The Messenger* (1955, Antwerp Middelheim Museum) and a number of statues of musicians and artists in which (like *Concert*, 1928) the bodies are interpenetrated by the paraphernalia of their profession: *Orpheus* (1956, Antwerp, Middelheim Museum). His most expressive masterpiece is the immense monumental statue *The Destroyed City* (1954), erected in Rotterdam to commemorate the destruction of the town during World War II. This gigantic figure of a man in flight with his limbs spread out, twisted round to utter a cry of despair, his arms raised to heaven, is among the dramatic modern works.

Zadkine was indebted to the **School of Paris** for the plastic qualities of his style, although his differed completely in so many ways from Western tradition. A distant affinity with the humble pre-Christian statuary of his country is discernable in Zadkine's work. He avoided the dryness which is often a pitfall of pure abstraction. His sculpture is full of human feeling, underlined by a very acute decorative and poetic sensibility.

ZAO WOU-KI (1920–   ), Chinese painter of the School of Paris. A student at the Hangchow School of Art, where he became (1941) Professor of Drawing, he went to Paris in 1948, and in 1955 was awarded a prize at the Carnegie Institute. His painting was figurative at first, and somewhat mannered. Gradually he has developed an abstract, **Calligraphic** style which is more transparent and fluorescent, but does not lack subtlety, *eg Before the Storm* (1955, London Tate).

ZULOAGA Y ZABALETA, Ignacio (1870–1945), Spanish painter. Settling in Paris (1889), he quickly became a well-established society painter. He remained aloof from the currents of modern art, painting portraits, landscapes, *eg View of the Escorial* (1905, London Tate), and scenes of Spanish life in the tradition of Velazquez and Goya, as in *The Dwarf Dona Mercedes* (1899, Paris MNAM), *Open-air Meal* (1900, Berlin NG). Though these influences must have been conscious, Zuloaga's best work is undeniably vital. His portaits are very fine, *eg Oscar Browning* (1900, Cambridge University), and if in the later ones he was overbound by the dictates of fashion he had the ability of his predecessors to turn these requirements to advantage.

ZWARC, Marek (1892–1958), Polish sculptor. He settled in Paris in 1909 and exhibited at the 1913 Salon d'Automne. After World War I he devoted himself to painting, and then to sculpture, mainly in metal (especially copper). He executed several low reliefs on Biblical subjects, later returning to free-standing sculpture, both in stone and bronze. After his return to Paris in 1945, his art attained stability; he chiefly used wood, as in *Resistance* (1949, London Institut Français), *Auschwitz* (1953, Tel-Aviv Museum). Zwarc's sculpture is naturalistic, but simplified in form; the simple masses have something of the character of folk art.